PETE CULLER ON
WOODEN BOATS

PETE CULLER ON WOODEN BOATS

The Master Craftsman's Collected Teachings on Boat Design, Building, Repair, and Use

Compiled by John Burke

 INTERNATIONAL MARINE / McGRAW-HILL
CAMDEN, MAINE ■ NEW YORK ■ CHICAGO ■ SAN FRANCISCO
LISBON ■ LONDON ■ MADRID ■ MEXICO CITY ■ MILAN ■ NEW DELHI
SAN JUAN ■ SEOUL ■ SINGAPORE ■ SYDNEY ■ TORONTO

10 9 8 7 6 5 4 3 2 1 CCW CCW 0 9 8 7

Library of Congress Cataloging-in-Publication Data
     Pete Culler on wooden boats : the master craftsman's collected teachings on boat
design, building, repair, and use / compiled by John Burke.
          p.   cm.
     Includes bibliographical references and index.
     ISBN 978-0-07-148979-9 (softcover : alk. paper)
   1. Culler, R. D.   2. Boatbuilding.   3. Boats and boating.   I. Burke, John,
1948-
     VM321.P375   2007
     623.8'184—dc22   2007031770

ISBN 978-0-07-148979-9
MHID 0-07-148979-7

Questions regarding the content of this book should be addressed to
International Marine
P.O. Box 220
Camden, ME 04843
www.internationalmarine.com

Questions regarding the ordering of this book should be addressed to
The McGraw-Hill Companies
Customer Service Department
P.O. Box 547
Blacklick, OH 43004
Retail customers: 1-800-262-4729
Bookstores: 1-800-722-4726

All photos and line drawings by Pete Culler unless otherwise noted.

Books: *Skiffs and Schooners* was first published in 1974 by International Marine; *Boats, Oars, and Rowing* was first published in 1978 by International Marine.

Articles: "Old Ways Work" first appeared in *Mariner's Catalog* Vol. 1, 1973, pp. 96–102; "Boatbuilding . . . Used to Be" first appeared in *Mariner's Catalog* Vol. 2, 1974, pp. 58–63; "On Rowing and Boats" first appeared in *Mariner's Catalog* Vol. 2, 1974, p. 177; "Sand Dolly" first appeared in *Mariner's Catalog* Vol. 3, 1975, p. 26; "Wheelbarrow Boat" first appeared in *Mariner's Catalog* Vol. 3, 1975, p. 27; "What Makes Classics Real" first appeared in *Mariner's Catalog* Vol. 3, 1975, pp. 52–59; "Fish Oil, Sour Milk, and Stale Beer" first appeared in *Mariner's Catalog* Vol. 3, 1975, p. 69; "The Mallets Cried, Hollered, Bellowed, and Chirped" first appeared in *Mariner's Catalog* Vol. 4, 1976, pp. 41–45; "Natural Knees" first appeared in *Mariner's Catalog* Vol. 4, 1976, pp. 61–62; "Motorboats for the Masses" first appeared in *Mariner's Catalog* Vol. 5, 1977, pp. 64–67; "Tarred Rigging and Stropped Blocks" first appeared in *Mariner's Catalog* Vol. 5, 1977, pp. 140–143.

Design Commentaries are taken from *Pete Culler's Boats*, John Burke, ed., Camden, ME: International Marine, 1984.

CONTENTS

FOREWORD

Mystic Seaport Museum is delighted that the best of Robert D. "Pete" Culler's writings on small craft are being reprinted, and salutes both John Burke and International Marine for making it possible.

Sharing the same goals and values, Pete Culler and Mystic Seaport were partners in the best sense of the word. Both valued the heritage of traditional small boats and recognized how much these traditional craft could teach those with the willingness to learn.

Along with that of his friend and patron Waldo Howland, Pete's connections with Mystic Seaport began in the late 1960s. At the time, Waldo owned and ran the Concordia Company boatyard in Padanaram, Massachusetts, famous for its high standards, its Concordia yawls, and its Beetle Cats; Pete served there as a naval architect and occasionally as a boatbuilder when he wasn't working for himself. Both men were concerned about the condition of the Museum's ships and boats because the Museum had been following a practice of boom or bust: restoration for display followed by neglect and decay. Pete and Waldo joined a few others who shared their concern. Eventually a change in philosophy took place at the Museum, with the result that the Trustees established a Ships Committee to oversee the Museum's fleet; Pete and Waldo were invited to join this important new body. Flowing from the Ships Committee were several signal changes in the Museum's policies. Maynard Bray was hired to help design and build a proper shipyard that could handle the Museum's ships and boats in-house. Skilled staff were hired, and, perhaps of more importance, a program of ongoing, day-to-day

maintenance was established. Pete's advice and counsel were central to the practice of what came to be known as "the Mystic way," an approach to the preservation of traditional watercraft that became admired and imitated the world over.

Those of us fortunate enough to start out in the Museum's Shipyard during the 1970s looked forward to Ships Committee meetings because they meant a visit from Pete. Not a man to tolerate meetings lightly, Pete would slip away from those formal exchanges in order to tour the Shipyard. We'd spot him from afar by his gait; by his clothing, which never varied much; and especially by his head covering, which in summer was a swordfisherman's long-billed cap and, in winter, a black and white checked woolen lumberman's hat. Pete's experience in shipyards made him respectfully sensitive about inserting his advice, but if someone asked him a question, Pete answered straight from the shoulder. We paid attention to what Pete said because we knew he had "done it." We knew he had spent his life as a seaman, a charter boat captain, a boatbuilder, and a designer. He had the experience we needed.

When we workers in the Shipyard couldn't talk with Pete himself, we often turned to *Skiffs and Schooners* and *Boats, Oars, and Rowing* for answers to our questions. In many cases, the information we were seeking simply didn't exist elsewhere. Pete was one of the leading figures in what came to be known as the "wooden boat revival," the embrace of wooden boatbuilding by amateurs during the late 60s and 70s. He was one of a diminishing number of traditional boatbuilders who was willing to share his knowledge without reservation and who was able to articulate what others might know but might express less clearly.

Pete had few equals at this. One of them, John Gardner, said in a review of *Skiffs and Schooners*, after praising its content, "And, the man can write!" Pete's books helped to fill the vacuum of knowledge that occurred after World War II when fiberglass replaced wood in the pleasure boat market, causing those who would have taken up traditional wooden boatbuilding, and thus preserved its skills, to look for other work. With his books so long out of print, amateur builders and designers have had few reliable resources available for this information. Their re-publication in this volume provides a valuable service to builders worldwide, and to the continued preservation of traditional wooden boat skills.

In 1970, the Coast Guard considered imposing restrictions on the use of traditional small craft, policies that simply didn't make sense to those who used these small boats. Pete was in the forefront of putting together a lobbying effort that defeated these restrictions. Out of this effort came the Traditional Small Craft Association, still extant nationwide, and the Small Craft Workshop (now named for John Gardner), which still takes place on the first weekend in June. Pete Culler and Waldo Howland collaborated to design and build the "Good Little Skiff," bringing the original skiff to the first Workshop. The Good Little Skiff has been reproduced hundreds of times and given great joy to many families. In season, a Good Little Skiff is available to row or sail at the Museum's Boat House livery. *Dixie Belle*, the skiff Pete built for Waldo's post-retirement use in Florida, is part of the Museum's historic Watercraft Collection and can be seen by appointment. Close inspection of the latter boat is an education in itself because *Dixie Belle* represents the highest development of Pete's and

Waldo's thoughts about skiff design and use. As long as his health allowed, Pete continued to attend the Small Craft Workshops. He would frequently bring with him either *Butternut*, his Henry Rushton-style double-paddle canoe, or *Otter*, his "clipper bateau." It was always a treat to see Pete expertly handle these boats as he went down the Mystic River on the Sunday morning of the Workshop weekend, followed by his half dozen close friends from Cape Cod, affectionately known as the "Hyannis Mafia." Both *Butternut* and *Otter*, plus *Punch, Quitsa Pilot, Svarmisk*, and a few other of Pete's boats are additional Culler craft that may also be seen (by appointment) at the Museum.

When Pete died in 1978, his widow, Toni, graciously offered the Museum the pick of whatever it wanted from Pete's shop. Some of us wanted to uproot the entire shop and reestablish it at the Museum, but this was not practical. Instead, the shop was photo-documented and a few unique tools were selected. Pete's close friend, George Kelly, oversaw the sale of Pete's plans on Toni's behalf. Upon George's and Toni's deaths, the plans passed to Mystic Seaport. Recently, John Burke has given the Museum Culler's preliminary drawings for some of his boats; these drawings offer a glimpse of Culler's thought processes leading up to the final designs.

In keeping with its mission of preserving traditional maritime knowledge and skills, Mystic Seaport offers the boat plans of R. D. Culler for sale through its Daniel S. Gregory Ships Plans Library. For a list of more than 100 available plans, see page 372.

Peter T. Vermilya
J. Revell Carr Associate Curator of Small Craft
Mystic Seaport Museum, Inc.

INTRODUCTION

Captain R.D. "Pete" Culler (1909–1978) was a sailor, boatman, boatbuilder, Master Shipwright, skipper, and designer of wholesome craft. Anyone who has glimpsed his boats rowing, sailing, or motoring upon the water would also agree that he was an artist as well.

My introduction to Pete Culler and his life's work was as a young boy—I was fortunate to grow up across the street from the Culler boatshop and home in Hyannis, Massachusetts. In those early years, access to the shop was via an interior ladder and trap door. As a young boy I used to play in the Cullers' yard. During one of those playtimes I found the barn door open, and, being very young and curious, I began to explore. I was halfway up the ladder when Mrs. Culler pounced on me like a cat. "Don't you go up there," she scolded. "Don't you ever go up there. That's the Captain's shop!" I was promptly led away by the scruff of the neck and the door was refastened. Well, it took me another 20 years, but I finally got inside Captain Pete's shop.

It was a wonderful place. For a young aspiring boatbuilder it was an answer to questions, and Pete was always generous with his time and knowledge; during our time together I learned a lot. After his death, Pete's widow, Toni, asked me to compile a catalog of his designs and *Pete Culler's Boats* was the result.

The pillars of Culler's design philosophy were simplicity, economy, and ease of use. This design foundation was based on considerable experience, starting in 1929 with his building of a replica of Joshua Slocum's yawl *Spray* while apprenticing at the Alonzo Conley Shipyard in Oxford, Maryland. (The tale of this experience is wonderfully told in

"Building the *Spray*" from *Skiffs and Schooners*; see page 12.) Culler's education continued through years of skippering and chartering and exposure to countless difficulties of sea and shore during the 1930s. The principles forged and lessons learned during these hard years were soon put to use building wooden boats for the war effort and subsequently delivering these vessels for the Army Transport Service. Much of Culler's hard-won experience and knowledge building and transporting these boats might have remained hidden from a wider audience were it not for an unfortunate occurrence in the decade after the war.

Culler sold his beloved *Spray* in 1951 because a larger vessel was needed to successfully adapt his charter business to passenger needs. He chose a schooner of good size and model (it was an Alden design) and named her *Rigadoon*, and continued operating his business from Hyannis, Massachusetts. He was content with the vessel and his charter business was making money with an expanding, but select, client base. Life was good. Then the two hurricanes of 1954 hit. The first, on August 31, did all the damage. Culler had sought refuge in Menemsha Harbor and tied up to Dutcher Dock on Martha's Vineyard, Massachusetts, but nevertheless *Rigadoon* was a total loss. The following September 11 storm only worsened her condition. Culler would have to find another way to make a living.

Shortly after their marriage in 1938 Toni (Antoinette Oakert) Culler had encouraged Pete to write down the informative, instructive, and engaging stories that she heard him yarn together for the paying guests in cabin and cockpit during their many cruises aboard *Spray* up and down the east

(© Mystic Seaport, Richard White Collection, Mystic, CT)

coast. As a Smith College graduate, Toni knew a good story. Pete, however, was not receptive. He didn't feel writing was worth his time and effort. So Toni wrote down one of his stories and sent the manuscript to *Rudder* magazine ("*Spray* is Our Home," April 1940). *Rudder* promptly accepted the story and sent a check. Once Culler saw the amount paid everything changed and he never again hesitated to share his voice with the greater public. As you read Pete's writings in this volume you will surely thank Toni Culler for her persistence.

Writing became a joy to Pete and he worked diligently at improving, but initially his style was not universally accepted and he realized that more than writing was needed to keep his family afloat. He tried many things, including house building and furniture repair, and these pursuits helped in the short term. Boat design held the greatest attraction, even though in the early 1950s it held the least promise. It was a leap of faith for both Pete and Toni

when he decided to concentrate on boat design, both large and small. Once the choice was made neither looked back nor questioned Pete's chosen course. Over 100 designs later, and with many successful boats built and sailing, this was the genesis of Pete's design legacy. All of Culler's designs now reside at Mystic Seaport Museum (see page 372).

Culler's design career slowly gained traction and many of his early efforts were small craft. From his early days Pete was always "doodling" with design. He sketched a concept first and then fleshed it out with more refined drawings as his ideas evolved. Culler used any media at hand. As the current caretaker of much of Pete's "stuff," I have found these conceptual musings on outdated charts, on the margins of calendars, magazines, and even cigar boxes, as well as more traditional media. In this way much of the body of his work was already completed. But Culler needed clients who would pay him to formalize those design ideas. Up until the mid-1950s

Culler's compensated work included designs for sampans, skiffs, outboards (both flat and v-bottom), and a fortuitous collaboration with Murray Peterson, a well-known designer of traditional vessels.

After the loss of *Rigadoon* in 1954 Pete was hired by a wealthy yachtsman as a racing skipper, and over several seasons the crew won their share of hardware. Eventually, pouring money and effort into the temporary possession of a tiny cup became tedious to the racer-owner, who then shifted his attention and commissioned a cruising schooner to be designed by Murray Peterson and built by Paul Luke of East Boothbay, Maine. The task of designing the schooner's tender was given to Culler. Pete had a great deal of fun doing this, and the opportunity to exchange ideas and opinions with the well-regarded Peterson on the origin and evolution of traditional vessels helped Culler refine and solidify his own views on the subject. This little boat was the first of many to utilize a familiar Culler model for tenders to larger craft. (See "Wherry Yawl for a Schooner," page 343.) These conclusions would bear fruit as the 1950s were coming to a close.

Back in the 1940s during their winter chartering seasons Pete and Toni had homeported *Spray* at Dooley's Boatyard in Ft. Lauderdale, Florida. One winter a fellow showed up to assist a friend in completing a boat. This was Waldo Howland, and a friendship quickly formed between Waldo, Pete, and Toni, one that was cemented over the years during gunkhole gatherings and visits to Padanaram, a part of South Dartmouth, Massachusetts, where Waldo's boatyard, Concordia Company, was located. Pete and Waldo were of like mind when it came to wooden boats generally and traditional vessels in particular, so it was natural for Waldo to confer with Pete when he had a small boat to build and dreams of a larger one to be designed, built, and owned. The small boat was the 15'9" v-bottom beach boat *Java*, designed and built by Culler in his Hyannis shop in the 1950s. The larger vessel would be the

52' schooner *Integrity* that was designed and built by Culler and crew during the years 1960–62 on the Smith Neck grounds of Concordia Company, adjacent to the Beetle catboat shop.

For Culler this opportunity to design and be Master Shipwright on a vessel the size and tonnage of *Integrity* was what he had prepared his whole life for. He did the "hull" of it, as it is said—from design, to building, and eventually sailing as captain for the first years. (See "Yawlboat for *Integrity*," page 347.) It was a marvelous experience and it did not go unnoticed. After this project was completed in 1962 the pace of Culler's design career accelerated, and for the next six years his drafting table was filled with large traditional sailing craft, including an 82' schooner for Henry Sears, the 60' schooner *Gallant Lady*, the 45' schooner *Joseph W. Russell,* the 40' *Gallant*, and the 36' *Old Glory*, to name a few. During the same period, he also drew the 17' Concordia sloopboat, outboard boats, steamers, and a variety of small skiffs, sampans, and yawl boats. Many of these were built and proved successful. During the sixties Culler's ideas were being acclaimed in the marketplace and he was in demand.

Prior to this resurgence the fifties had been a decade of decline for the majority of wooden boat building. Most boat and yacht builders rushed to fabricate their products with the "other" material, and those who stubbornly held onto the trade began to feel mighty lonely. But with the activity at the Concordia Co. boatyard and at isolated pockets elsewhere, there began a change of perception, and it started with amateur boatbuilders, both young and old. These folks wanted a boat that fit their needs and reflected their own requirements, something other than what was offered by the mass marketers of fiberglass boats.

These enthusiasts discovered that one way to acquire a unique craft was to build it themselves with wood. These aspirants discovered a growing voice of traditional-craft and wooden-boat proponents. Howard Chapelle was one such voice, an historian who had gathered the rich and divergent currents of maritime history, picking up the themes from Martin C. Erismann in the 1930s and weaving them into a coherent whole. Thank God for Howard Chapelle! Beginning in 1930 with *The Baltimore Clipper: Its Origin and Development* (published by the Marine Research Society of Salem, Massachusetts) and continuing in 1936 with *American Sailing Craft* and *American Small Sailing Craft* in 1951 (both published by W. W. Norton), it culminated in 1960 with the publication of *The National Watercraft Collection.* Chapelle, who also served as curator of Transportation with the Smithsonian Institution, greatly influenced the use of traditional boat types for today's pleasure boating.

John Gardner maintained a long correspondence during the fifties and sixties in the *Maine Coast Fisherman* (later *National Fisherman*) with Pete Culler and small boat enthusiasts everywhere. Gardner's "retirement" to Mystic Seaport Museum in 1969, after a long boat-building career, led to the establishment in 1970 of the Small Craft Workshop, an annual gathering at Mystic Seaport whose mission was to promote a wider understanding of historic boats. At the initial Workshop the Traditional Small Craft Association was formed to preserve historic craft; Pete Culler and John Gardner were founding members, among others. Culler was also a member of the Ships and Small Craft Committees at Mystic Seaport Museum. Gardner's efforts both before and during his tenure at Mystic Seaport Museum met with great success. However, there was one figure who appeared to embody everything this new and emerging movement was seeking—one man who was doing it, had always been doing it, and could write about doing it in a way that fulfilled the expectations of his audience. This man was Pete Culler.

From 1967 until a heart attack slowed him in 1976, Culler built an average of four small boats a year in his Hyannis shop. All boats were under 20 feet, traditional construction by a lone worker, and each boat, except two, a unique Culler design. Even those that were from the same design differed in styling and detail. The bulk of Culler's design work, both large and small, was produced during this decade as well. This was prodigious effort by one man. All the while, Culler wrote about his projects and ideas in various publications, including *Maine Coast Fisherman, National Fisherman, Small Boat Journal, Ash Breeze, Tell-Tale Compass, The Mariner's Catalog,* and *WoodenBoat.* This output prompted Roger Taylor, then publisher of International Marine, to ask Culler to write a book. *Skiffs and Schooners* (1974) was the result. Culler's book editor Peter Spectre came up with the title and it fits, as the book (reprinted here) was a compilation of all you needed to know to get salt-soaked, wind-blown, and wood-dust-encrusted. This book hit the sweet spot and, along with the founding of *WoodenBoat* magazine, reestablished the wooden boat movement. Wood as a boat-building material and the traditions and culture of wooden boats have been expanding ever since.

Just prior to Culler's 1976 heart attack, Spectre had asked him for a follow-up book to *Skiffs and Schooners*, a book addressing rowing and rowboats in greater detail. While Culler was in the hospital recuperating, he wrote in longhand with a pencil—his trusty Underwood typewriter was at home—the second book reprinted in this volume, *Boats, Oars, and Rowing.* The little book became deservedly popular.

In choosing the various designs, commentaries, and articles for this volume I have been guided by what I have found inspirational in Culler's work in the hope that you will be similarly moved to look further and discover the steadfast relevance of Culler's approach for today's traditional boatbuilders. In addition to his charming and conversational style, Culler included much historic information and instructional advice.

Culler advocated the traditional approach—to him this was the simple, economical, and readily available path. Read his writings and study his plans and you will find out how. In the essay "Natural Knees" (see page 319) Culler describes how to find and shape the crooks that are used in classic craft. In "Tarred Rigging and Stropped Blocks" (see page 331) you are instructed on the construction of the traditional bits of gear necessary for sailing craft. In other essays Culler shares the dos and don'ts of sailmaking, how to carve a stemhead, bend an oak frame, as well as choose the colors and types of paint to finish your boat.

Culler's designs call for wooden construction. Wood as a boatbuilding material is perhaps more readily available in more choices today than it has ever been. In these writings Culler strongly advocates for accessible materials and techniques—this "use-what-is-at-hand" philosophy and instructional nature of the writings was a key consideration in deciding what to include herein. None of this is new, but since Culler's methods are still in use by builders of traditional craft, they have stood the test of time and are presented here for you to absorb and enjoy.

For anyone searching for accessible, affordable, common-sensible, and rewarding boating, here is a mother lode of information to guide you, because one man felt strongly enough about it to put it down on paper. I have been grateful to Culler—once you read what is here you will be, too.

John Burke, 2007
Arrowsic Island, Maine

PETE CULLER ON
WOODEN BOATS

(Jim Brown)

SKIFFS AND SCHOONERS

PREFACE

There have been so many books on boats and boatbuilding—and good ones too—by experts and some near experts that it may seem almost ostentatious for a person to write another. However, being of an age whence I can look back on a good many years at just plain messing around with boats and on the experience acquired thereby—you can never get enough experience at anything—I feel the urge to put down some things connected with boats and their building. None of it is new; most of it is half forgotten; all of it can be useful. Best of all, most of it is very simple.

Realizing that boats, like whiskey, are all good, I make no attempt nor have any intention of making adamant statements of how things should be done, or of preaching dogma until it sounds almost like truth. I put down things our forefathers knew and acquired the hard way, things we have been exposed to, often the very same hard way. One learns by his mistakes. If I have produced anything, however small, of further use to the World of Boats, it will make my efforts worthwhile. All whiskey has its place.

R. D. Culler
Hyannis, Massachusetts

EXPERIENCE
STARTS WHEN
YOU BEGIN

My early exposure to boats involved expeditions that we glorified with the name "cruises." I would pick a buddy with like inclinations and we would prepare for the trip with care. Once our big skiff was ready, we'd Head Out.

We took long rows with some assistance from sail to likely beaches or surf-barred slough entrances, all deserted. We became rather good at surf work. Usually these voyages were just after the winter gales, so there was much plunder to pick up on the beaches. When the bacon and pancakes ran out and the craft had such a load that it was hard to launch her off, we made for the home port. On these trips it was not the feet suffering near the end, but the hands and back! I think our greed was part of it; we just couldn't pass up another steamer deck chair, or a couple more lobster buoys, and that part of an old net was very necessary to have. An over-loaded skiff of good size, built of Oregon pine, made the last mile sort of desperate. Fees, permits for fires or for anything else were unheard of, and on land or sea we never saw another soul, except for an occasional steam schooner far offshore. I wonder if such goings on are possible anywhere now?

While we no doubt caused worry at home, I cannot recall ever being in real danger or experiencing any sort of near disaster. We knew nothing of drugs except that they were something connected with Orientals. Booze was for grown-ups. In many ways we were quite grown up, though by some of today's standards we were just babes. We did know a lot about tobacco; all our tutors smoked pipes or chewed. These men took time for boys who were boat crazy; looking back on it, I think they remembered how it was when they were boys.

There was Pop Cannon, master shipwright retired, who took a small job now and then. Eighty, frail-looking, and blue-eyed, he could turn out much more work in a day than many younger men. He knew considerable about ballasting and trim, rake of masts, and the tuning of a vessel. There was Nick, the loner cod fisherman with his handsome power dory. He was a squat, swart, powerhouse of a man. From him, we learned "the marks" for Eleven Mile Reef, and the art of mackerel trolling. There was Jeemy, the Italian seacook, who, true to type, was full of bombast, and noise, and sea lore. There was Mario, of the pretty little seiner; he knew much about reading the weather. And above all,

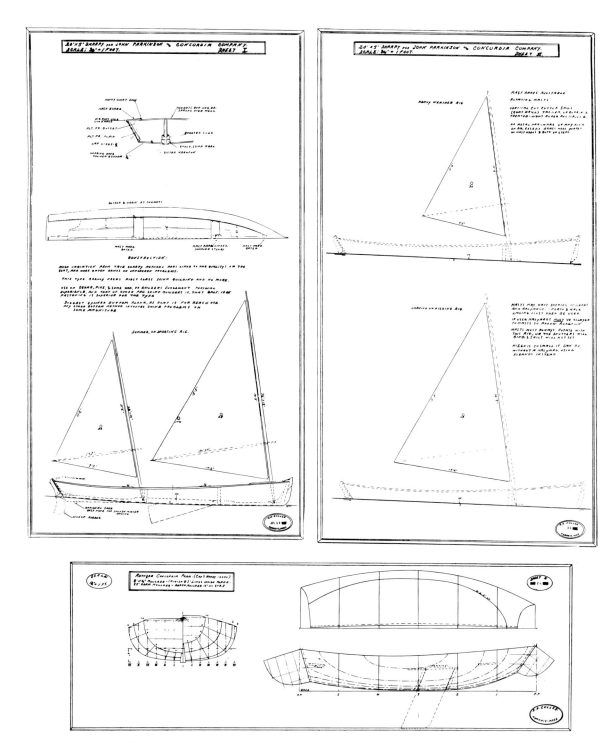

(TOP, LEFT AND RIGHT) *The 20' v-bottom sharpie for John Parkinson was originally drawn by Capt. Pete for his own use. It shows three different sail combinations for varying conditions. This ability to mix and match rig elements according to the forces of wind and sea is an ongoing theme with the small boat designs of Pete Culler. The reader perusing the text and studying the photographs, boat plans, and artwork in this volume will quickly realize that this approach is grounded in the wisdom and experience of an everyday sailor. This 20' sharpie would be very fast under sail or oars.* (BOTTOM) *This Concordia pram is a revision of the model supplied with every Concordia yawl. The design was a collaboration between Pete and Capt. Hardy, a Deer Isle, Maine, man and skipper of the Howland family Concordia yawl* Java. *They both felt this was an improvement on the original.* (© Mystic Seaport, Ships Plans Collection, Mystic, CT)

there was Captain George, large, paunchy, and gruff. He was a thorough seaman and superb boat handler, under oars or sail. His disgust with "farmers" and "backwoodsmen" around boats was something to behold. I think he kept an eye on us at all times, though he was not obvious about it. If we pulled off a difficult bit of boat handling in nasty conditions, Cap would grunt and say as how "it was a mite airish." If we bungled, even slightly, we were Hair-Brained Yazzoos, whatever they are.

Becoming accepted as boatmen with some surf experience, one summer my schoolmate and I turned pro. We crewed on a fine motor craft that was chartered to "take scientific fellers about." We felt quite some stuff, for this was offshore work at times, and there was much surf work and ferrying of gear and scientific finds. We launched off with many a load of bones, some of them human. We were always wet, tired much of the time, and occasionally somewhat seasick. Oh, it was a fine life! The vessel was nearly new, had a handsome Frisco Standard engine, and a master who was all seaman and a stickler for neatness. In idle moments, we soogeed white paint; the hooker seemed to have miles of it.

Seamanship was thrown at us in chunks, for where we worked was the real thing, no mill pond. There were some desperate times, for we went into desperate places with the weather turning bad to pick up men who had been there weeks with their grub running low. They and their collection had to be boated off. We learned of embayment and of having to clear out in the wee hours of the wildest night, working on the jumping foredeck and securing great anchors as we went, for there was no time to lose; the whole place was a mass of white. We were pooped once, and we broached another time and nearly lost a man. Near the end of our season, we were pounding along in a fierce nor'wester, ship and all a smother of white. We had strict orders; no one on deck. So we young crew are in our "quarters,"

the forecastle, same as two walnuts in a rolling tin can. Sleep is impossible, so we puff a pipe, talk a bit, and make an occasional trip through the engine room, where the never-failing Frisco is thumping away (I think she turned 275), to tend the stove and have a mug. It was pretty heady in that engine room, but we felt tough and salty. I suppose to some extent we were.

Later I became the lone paid hand on a nice sailing craft whose design was based on that of a small fishing boat. That was quite a berth. I was also the engineer, for she had a one-jug Bridgeport of monumental stubbornness. Without knowing really why, I could make her go.

This boat needed her wire rigging replaced, which, as yet, I was not up to, though I was much interested in marlinespike seamanship. The services of Captain Barrie were obtained. This handsome Scot was then 85, a huge man with a white trimmed beard that made him look very like King George V of England. He started his sea career at the age of nine in collier brigs. He had learned his seamanship under men who had sailed with Nelson. This at first seems improbable, but it was the mid-1920's, and 1805 was not so far away! Rigging wire did wonderful things under his powerful hands, and, of course, I learned much of brigs. The full-rigged collier brig was a handy craft to use in narrow, congested waters. She was short and dumpy, and her square rig made it possible to back, haul, and box about in the tightest places. Under the command of such men as this, I'm sure it was so. Captain Barrie was a good carpenter and sailmaker too, and knew all about overlapping jibs, which were not around on yachts in those days. He called them "tow fores'ls." His own vessel at this time, a partially decked sloop, seemed to give him great pleasure. Though plumb in the ends and with a single stick, she somehow had the smack of a brig! He made his own oilskins; they had no buttons, but instead, wood toggles and loops, and they were waterproofed with a fearsome mixture of pine tar, beeswax, kerosene, tallow, linseed oil, and I don't know what-all else. Boarding the street car (yes, they were around then) after a wet day of it, these oilskins made the car smell like a brig's forecastle.

Yes, it was wonderful to have such teachers, and they seemed to enjoy telling how to do it right. I think this kind of teaching has not changed much. Nelson's time is further away. Those men I mention are gone; a later set of old timers is around—

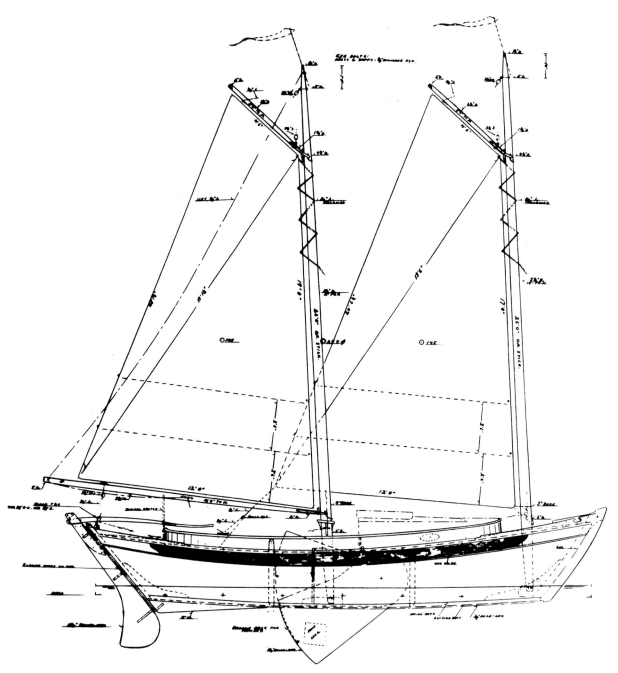

The 25' flat-bottom cowhorn dory is a pocket cruiser with space for two pipe berths and a small woodstove. Although this design uses the dory hull, it is reminiscent in style and rig of the Block Island boats of yesteryear. Pete felt that since this design would "violate all yachting standards" his expectation was that it would be a very pleasant little craft to own. The photo of Trudi *on page 10 is a built example of this boat.*
(© Mystic Seaport, Ships Plans Collection, Mystic, CT)

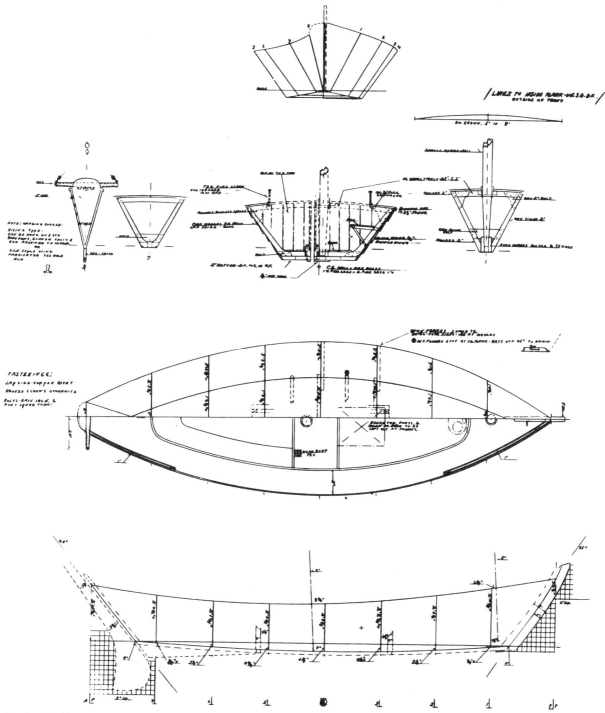

Details of Trudi. (© Mystic Seaport, Ships Plans Collection, Mystic, CT)

some call 'em old fools—men who have learned from men who learned from Nelson's men. I find for the most part that they are a friendly lot, willing to talk and teach. They all agree that the Sea has not changed, only the way of going on it, and that in very small vessels and boats, the way has changed the least.

My Old Man I think had hope for me in the ministry. Higher learning was available, but it did not appeal to me. So he said if I was so wrapped up

Jim Brown's 25' cowhorn dory Trudi *enjoying a day sail off Newport, Rhode Island, shortly after launching.* (Jim Brown)

in boats as to make boating a career, I had better learn it inside out and stick with it. As a medical man, he felt that to be good around boats, you should have a thorough grounding in their anatomy. He could draw anatomy, human or animal, and see it, feel it, sense it. In his day, he was much sought after as a diagnostician. He felt boats were to be

approached in about the same way as medicine, and he was right. I spent many happy, often tiring, wet and dirty years exposed to boats in yards, machine shops, sail lofts, and foundries, along with plenty of sailing. It was certainly no way to get rich, except in varied experiences, which are often the greatest riches of all.

10

When I passed 50, I thought it time to see if I had any designing ability. The mechanics of it are not much different than what I'd done in mould lofts time and again, laying down, taking up, and converting into craft of some sort. In fact I had found long ago that some designers had little knowledge about deadwoods, and rabbets, and fairing in to heavy timber; they left that to the builder, who as a rule took it as a matter of course and used his judgement. I found I had a feel for form within the limit of those types of craft in which I was really interested. After all, I had scrubbed and painted many a bottom when I was "copper paint man." To learn any trade, you used to start at the bottom! Many of these boats were fine designs, often by unknowns. Having gone over them first with a broom, then scraper, and often more brooming, and finally paint, was a good way to get a feel of their shape. Some were worth more study, and sometimes I came back after supper and looked at the vessel's lines some more. She might be a classic, living on borrowed time, barely supported by a dying trade. She might never come to haul up again.

With a building background, I saw no point at all in drawing lines to outside of plank, as is now the only way. Why draw some line that has to be altered, sometimes with error? The old way was to draw to inside of plank and back rabbet, which is what the builder was interested in and still is. Some folks say drawing to inside of plank fouls up displacement calculations. There is a readily available formula for this if you like such things, or there is the old builder's rule, once much used and quite simple. If you figure displacement by both methods, you find that they agree closely.

You may wonder why I give all this background about my doings with boats, much of it probably not very interesting, and most of it, by certain standards, outdated. That's the point; this is like it was and like it can be for the man who is going to do it himself, and by this I mean Do It.

That's what it's all about: Any man who wants to can produce a good boat. It takes some study, some practice, and, of course, experience. The experience starts coming the minute you begin, and not one jot before. I sometimes hear the wail, "I have no experience." Start. Start anything, and experience comes. Some say building a boat is one of man's nobler efforts. Maybe so; it's a lot of fun, anyway. As one of my builder friends says, "It's only a boat; go ahead and build it." If the first effort is a bit lumpy, so what? There will be another much less lumpy later on.

BUILDING
THE *SPRAY*

Looking back forty-three years to the building of a wooden vessel, in what was then considered a somewhat backward part of the country, and then comparing it to one built in the early 1960s in a highly industrialized area, is most interesting. I was a learner on the first vessel and head shipwright on the later one. I'm struck by the very little difference between the two jobs. Both vessels were built outdoors, which, I think, has some advantages. There were some things available to work with in the later craft that were unheard of when the early one took shape, such as a heated shop for a mill and workroom. In practice these "advantages," if they can be called so, were of little use. Some were discarded, some were used mostly just because they were there and are now the custom. The heated shop was a total flop until the heat ducts were blocked off. Men can't do real work in what is now considered the proper temperature in a modern shop.

The early vessel was a reproduction of Captain Joshua Slocum's *Spray*, and, as she's been discussed, hashed over, and fought over for years, I won't go into the reasons for choosing the model. There was money available for the project, about

what a half-way-decent daysailer now costs. Some study was given to locations for building, timber, and men skilled in constructing such a craft and in shipbuilding in general. Around 1929, there were many skilled yards on the East Coast; however, a part of the country where the economics were suited to the type of craft was very important. The model was not a type suited to or needing the skills of such as Lawley or Nevins.

The Eastern Shore of Chesapeake Bay was chosen, and Oxford, Maryland, a very small village devoted to the oyster trade, was picked. After all, the old *Spray* was considered by some folks to be "only an old oyster boat," so what better set-up? The community at the time was said, by those who knew, to be very much like small New England coastal villages in about 1870. There were great changes just around the corner, however, and in a very few short years all was different. Progress caught up, and, to my way of thinking, the place was spoiled forever.

The master builder, Alonzo R. Conley, was a man of much skill and long experience. He had several large vessels to his credit, both in design and building. He was willing to take me on as a learning apprentice; what I produced I saved on the vessel. Let it be said

Pete Culler was a great admirer of Joshua Slocum. From modest beginnings, Slocum rose to the top of his profession as a Master Mariner and endured many hardships at sea including mutiny, shipwreck, the Krakatoa eruption and, most difficult of all, the death of his beloved wife. Finding himself in 1895 on the beach without a vessel, he rebuilt an old oyster sloop in Fairhaven, Massachusetts, and called the 37' yawl Spray. *Over the following three years he sailed it around the world and wrote a book about his adventures, the classic* Sailing Alone Around the World. *Of all of Capt. Slocum's literary gems, I feel this one is the best: "to a young man contemplating a voyage, I would say go."*

required on the oyster fleet and freighters, most of these still being sailing vessels, though some were cargo power craft. There would be slack periods on my vessel on this account, when I would go it alone when and where I was able. Payment was to be so much a month; sometimes I was ahead, sometimes behind, but for the most part it ran pretty even, and no one was hurt.

There was plenty of good timber. This was white oak country, and hard pine was available in baulks from "the city." White cedar came in by boat, and in those days yards stocked ahead. Hardware

Alonzo R. Conley, the Master Builder at the yard in Oxford, Maryland, where Pete's replica of the Spray *was built in 1929. Pete signed on as an apprentice during the* Spray*'s construction, learning the boatbuilding trade and significantly reducing his costs for the boat. Pete considered Mr. Conley a fine teacher.* (The Mariners' Museum, Newport News, Virginia)

he was a fine teacher. Though of small formal education, this man had a vast working knowledge of his trade and was quite familiar with many of the older written works on the subject; he promptly lent me some classic books on shipbuilding.

The business arrangement was simple, and one which I still find good for a builder who really knows his stuff and a client who is honest about his own finances. The arrangement was this: The builder thought the vessel "would not cost over so much." He was right; she was a little less. The work on her was not to interfere with the seasonal work

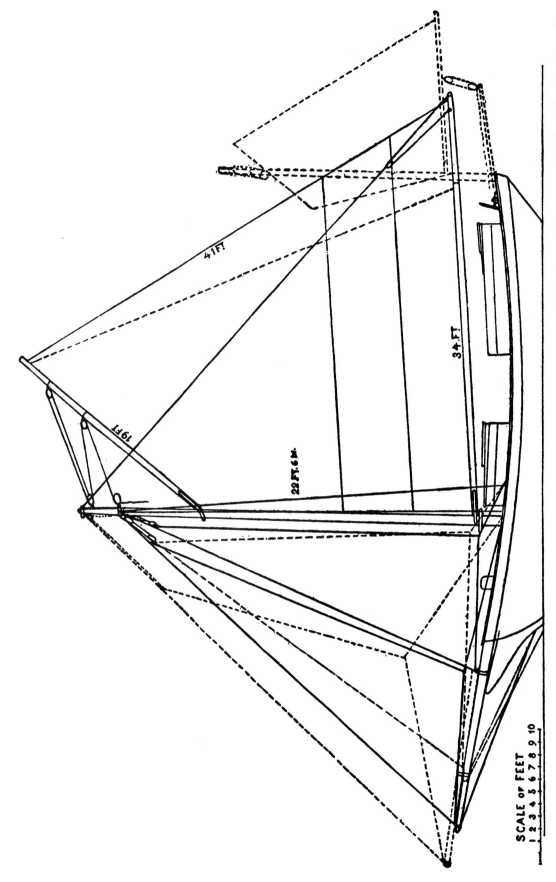

The Spray's sail plan, taken from Joshua Slocum's book Sailing Alone Around the World. The solid lines show how she was rigged when she started the voyage, and the dotted lines show the modifications Slocum made during the cruise to make the rig easier to handle.

SCALE OF FEET
1 2 3 4 5 6 7 8 9 10

41 FT

34 FT

19 FT

22 FT. 6 IN.

was no problem, or sails either, as there were both shipsmith and sailmaker right next door.

The yard layout was about what was customary then. There was sloping land to a creek and anchorage, with several big shade trees and plenty of room, two railways, and space to set up three or more new vessels. The main building was a stark old post-and-rail affair, framed with local gum wood so hard with age it would refuse a nail, sheathed with vertical boards, battened, and covered with a ternplate roof. The building was the traditional ochre color. One small corner was the office and storeroom and had wonderful smells. The other end was the mill, which had a shipsaw and planer only, these being the total machinery and both very old. The rest of the lower floor was devoted to work benches, toolboxes, and space to work timber or build a motor yawlboat. Large sliding doors were in many places in the building, so there was always a clear shot for getting big timber to the machines.

There was a loft upstairs for laying down and a small room off it for oakum and for storing the large jeer blocks (each filling a wheelbarrow) and fall used to rig the big sheer legs on the end of the dock. (A wooden, walk-around capstan was near the sheers.) At the other end of the loft was a home-built wood lathe of large capacity, driven by a tiny hopper engine that was quite short-tempered on a cold morning.

Outside, the yard had a cluttered and messy look by some standards, for there was much work going on. There would be time enough to clean up when things were slack. Winters were cold, and there was much need of firewood. Much good ship timber was about, piled everywhere, and carefully "stuck." There were timber wheels, peaveys, and many clamps, some of them huge, and, of course, "planking jacks." The railways were driven by locally-made, single-cylinder, hit-and-miss, gas engines, cooled by toted creek water kept in pickle barrels. These engines were rated at 5 h.p. each.

There was the outhouse, which hung over the end of a bulkhead at a rakish angle. It was fearsomely cold or hot inside it, depending on the season, but it never needed maintenance. There was no electricity at all in the yard, though the owner's house next door and most of the village had it, made locally, as was the custom then. Hand-held power tools were unknown. Water for drinking came from the icehouse next door, where it ran in a fine cool stream. Each workman went for his own water with a "can," which was really a half-gallon mason jar of the bootleg era.

How, many folks ask now, can you build a vessel with such a crude setup? You can, and they did, and, sad to say, the man-hours per ton of vessel then were less, sometimes very much less, than they are now. Lest you might think the work was crude, let me say it was just the opposite. The yard was known for the fair hulls, fine planking, and excellence of fastening on the craft it turned out. There seemed to be no great effort to accomplish this; all hands just knew how.

Everyone walked to work, for the village was small, few people owned autos, and all was geared to the yards and oyster trade. You worked at what the place offered, or left for greener fields. Few left. There were few amusements; we didn't need any, for the country store was the men's social place. For yarns of hard sailings, great feats of hunting, gossip, lies, and all sorts of exciting things, you went to the store evenings. The layout was just like the pictures of a real country store. The smoke got pretty thick (many of the men smoked black Five Brothers) and things got pretty deep, but we all wore boots!

Looking back on it, knowing there were what would now be considered great discomforts, it was still a good way to live, maybe because we did not know any better. To hear "Captain Harry" get going and take the floor for a full evening (being baited now and then to keep it hot) was a far better show than any purveyors of the boob tube can put on now!

Grub was hearty; oysters in many forms were commonplace at table, cooked by experts. Nowadays, oysters cost a fortune, and the cooks louse 'em up. A breakfast of biscuits, or "corn cake and aigs" with fried fatback was fit to do hard work on. The dinner bucket carried solid food too. There were no thermos bottles; coffee was brought in an ordinary bottle and cuddled close to the office stove in winter so it was just right at noon. Sometimes it almost froze on the way to work. In summer, and it can be frightfully hot on the Bay, the kindly engineer in charge of the nearby icehouse made ice tea or coffee commonplace. You could even have it frozen if you wanted. Working hours were longer than they are now, based on available daylight. There were no rules for workmen, no regulations, except what the Master made. This was the pre-Roosevelt era, and the yard was fairly isolated from city ways. There was no insurance of any kind, no guards on the belts, no fire equipment. It was probably not much different from, say, a farm a hundred years ago. Everyone knew his work, and accidents or mishaps of any kind were most rare.

A yard must have a crew of workmen; this crew was small and was supplemented at times of much work by some old timers from what had once been a very active shipbuilding area further down the Bay. These fellows came for a specific job, saw it through, and departed, to return later on for some other project. They were highly skilled, experienced in large work, and could pretty much run any job without supervision. The boss of this little yard was shown considerable deference by these seasoned old timers, though he was younger than they, for he had once been a designer and builder in the Big Time, and these men had been under him. He had something they lacked.

The regular crew was, as they always are, varied in looks, build, and personality. The common trait was that they knew their work and very much knew that the Master Shipwright knew his. There was Hamilton, a leathery, sparse man of excellent ability in all phases of his trade, besides being an accomplished rigger. Edward, who was black, though his head was quite white, was no doubt much older than he looked. Caulker and fastener extraordinary, he lent magic to a pin maul with his hands. Isaac, short, round, and strong, though his legs were giving out, had a Santa Claus face without the whiskers. He could dub and hew accurately with the dispatch of a machine, and from the most impossible positions. In his retirement years, he kindly sold me one of his fine adzes for one dollar. I've used it for years, and still do occasionally. The bell-like ring that is its trademark is still with it! Tom was addicted to bad whiskey; it was an unwritten rule that he was not to show up when in bad shape. To make up for his tardiness, he would turn out at one o'clock in the morning, if necessary, to man the railway to haul some leaking craft that was about to go down. Going overboard in the total darkness of a winter night to find out what was ailing a sticking poppet bothered him not at all. Wedges, clamps, jacks, and all sorts of heavy work were his specialty. Tom was not very robust looking, probably couldn't see out of one eye, and was racked by demon rum, but none of these ailments seemed to cramp his style any.

Edgar, somewhat younger than the others, was the foreman. He kept time for all and rang the old, dismal, cracked bell for starting work and knocking off. He generally kept the run of the others' work and did most of the spiling and laying off, once a job was started. Edgar maintained the mill and engines, for which he had a great knack. He set and filed the miles of bandsaw blades. He did most of the interior joiner-work, including fine, paneled doors. There was no small machinery for joinerwork; it was all done by hand, rapidly, and in good style. Edgar owned a Stanley 55 plane, "a joiner shop in itself," if you get behind it and push! Besides all this, he was a sawyer, and a wizard at it.

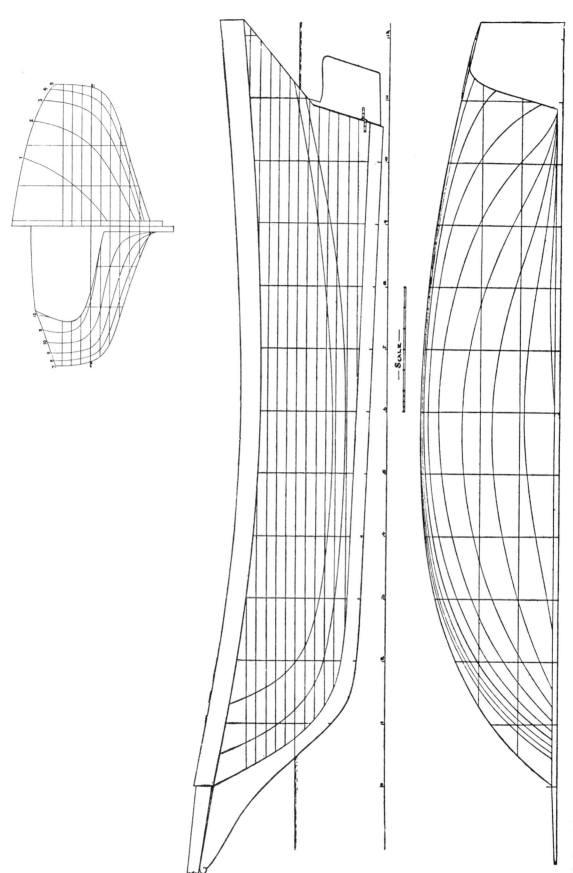

—Scale—

The Spray's lines as presented by Slocum in his book. Pete obtained the plans that he used to build his copy of the Spray from Capt. Slocum's son Victor.

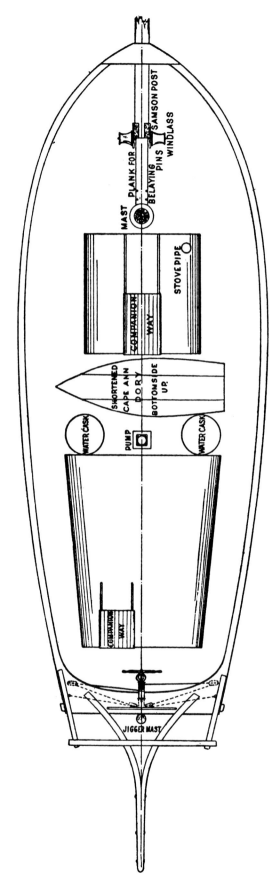

The Spray's deck plan as shown in Sailing Alone Around the World. Pete's Spray had a single cabin trunk, an improvement suggested by Capt. Slocum if the vessel was to be used for chartering. Pete also incorporated Bay-style davits for storing the tender, and added a topsail to the mainmast. Many consider Pete's copy of the Spray to be the best of all of those that followed the original.

So money was passed, and I was put to work in the loft with a broom. Then I was introduced to the fine points of lofting, many of which seem not to be found in books. I flattened the points of hundreds of thin wire nails. Though the floor was old and dark, it was treated with respect. The flattened points left little or no holes and had other advantages. Much work was done with chalk, and I learned you can work quite accurately to chalk lines, once shown how. I also learned what "fair" is, a thing many of the highly skilled can still argue about. A master can show you just what a very slight adjustment can do for a line that seems good already. I learned about lifting the bevels, for my vessel was to be a sawn-frame craft. I had never seen a bevel-lifting instrument; no shipbuilding books I've seen show such a thing. The Master had built it. I've since built one and have had it for a good many years. I learned mould making; the whole backbone and all the frames had moulds, for this was all gone about as if she were a big four-master. This is, in the end, the fastest, most accurate way to build a sawn-frame vessel.

Nailed on one wall, looking down on all this was the profile and sail plan of a fine four-masted schooner, the past work of my designer-builder-teacher. She had made some maritime history as "The Ship The Sea Couldn't Kill." Her sails and all spars and rigging were made from this plan; it was drawn in pencil on common matchboarding. Men of these skills got right at the heart of the matter without the frills of offices, tidy draftsmen, and much paperwork, and they never failed to be artistic in their work.

There was plenty of stock on hand for framing. During the lofting, a most battered truck came with the keel, stem, and deadwood stock from a back-woods mill by some swamp. All mill trucks were battered, but this one was special. The mill owner unfolds from the cab, an elderly Mennonite in the garb of his sect. Immediate haggling follows between shipwright and mill owner, as, though both are good churchmen, neither trusts the other's lumber tally. Some Eastern Sho' white oak won't float when green, and, while the haggle proceeds, a huge giant, unshorn since birth, unloads this great pile in short order, single-handed, with a peavey and a simple (so it seems) twist of the wrist. He's an astonishing fellow. He thinks maybe he's thirty-six years old. His boss says he has eighteen children. It's rumored that he lives in a true serfdom under this small lumber baron.

This timber is soon converted. There is much screeching from the ancient bandsaw and bellowing from the engine. Both are quite up to it and labor not at all. There is considerable adz work, rabbet cutting, drifting, and then setting up. The mysteries of setting to drag and plumbing up were fully explained, doing it in a wind, too! The ground where the backbone was set up was traditional to these yards, a hard-packed, unknown depth of adz and axe chips from 125 years of building by various men on the same site. The old railways had seen all kinds of power. First a horse walk-around, then steam, now gasoline engines.

It was soon time to frame up, and getting cold. The oyster season was well started and all the craft were on the beds. Framing is an all-hands job. The Master moulded. Much flitch was spread around for his easy access. The timber wheels were much in use. As he moulded, the work was taken to the saw. Four-inch white oak flitch is heavy.

To this day I very much enjoy the sawing of frame for a vessel. Usually there is a cold wind sweeping across the huge saw table. There is the heady smell of new-sawn oak, the rumble of rollers as the flitch is jockeyed into position to start the cut. There is the idling saw, veteran of a billion cuts, and the loafing engine, sounding sort of slack in the rod. The saw is rolled down to the proper starting bevel, the motions from the sawyer's hand guiding the crew in lining her up, and the roller

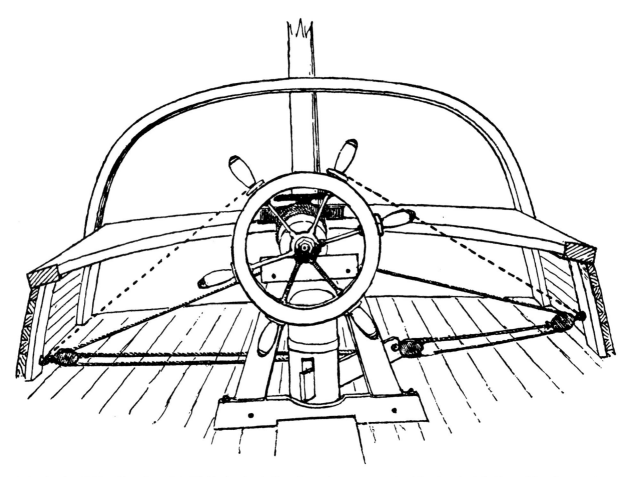

A drawing from Sailing Alone Around the World, *showing the* Spray's *steering arrangement and the strongback that braced the mizzen mast.*

crank is then rigged. And the cut starts, hesitantly at first, then, as she's lined up, the big saw cuts in earnest, and the machinery and crew settle into stride. With gentle motions occasionally from the sawyer's hand, the saw gradually lays back more and more as the bevel increases. There is much sawdust in the eyes, as it's windy, and an occasional spark from the saw guides. It's through, the tempo of the machine slacks off again, the bevel man stands her up and she rumbles back to get the other side.

If it's a cant frame with rapidly changing shape and bevel, things can become quite tense. The bevel man can only just keep up with the changes and cranks the wheel for all he's worth. Usually the sharpest curve is at one end, when the crew is carrying most of the weight of the timber. The sawyer's signals become somewhat rapid, the old saw is almost lying on its back, a stream of sparks strikes from the blade, she whines and yammers, there is a hysterical shriek from the drive belt with much slapping, and the old engine thumps manfully. Then she's through, right on the line. There's little dubbing to do with this kind of work.

Yes, it gets in the blood, and though modern ship saws have improved slightly, with their heavy, solid lower wheels to act as a flywheel and their swage-tooth blades, driven by five vee belts connected to quiet electric motors that need no water or gas toted by hand for them, there is little other change. New-sawn oak smells the same, and the saw blade has the same screech. I am glad to have heard the fine slap of the big, totally-exposed, flat belts and the bark of a steam mill exhaust when the engine's governor said "go to work," and to have seen the drunken rocking of the big upright gas engines when they were Laying Into It. Wooden shipbuilding sounds and smells good!

Framing up took just a week; this sounds fantastic to many folks who have not experienced such things. Men who knew their trade, rugged though very simple equipment just suited to such work, and a vessel of only 15 tons made this possible. The fact that she was framed much heavier than usual for a craft of her length made no difference; the same motions had to be gone through. The main reason for the heavy framing was that the vessel is of a naturally weak shape and maybe overly stiff, so it seemed well to build some of the ballast into her. Much subsequent use proved this approach.

There was a coaster waiting her fate anchored off the yard. Old and worn with work, she was a sad sight, with drooping stern and other signs of a hard life. It was suddenly decided to rebuild her, as at this time there was a local economic reason to rebuild old vessels, some being converted to power.

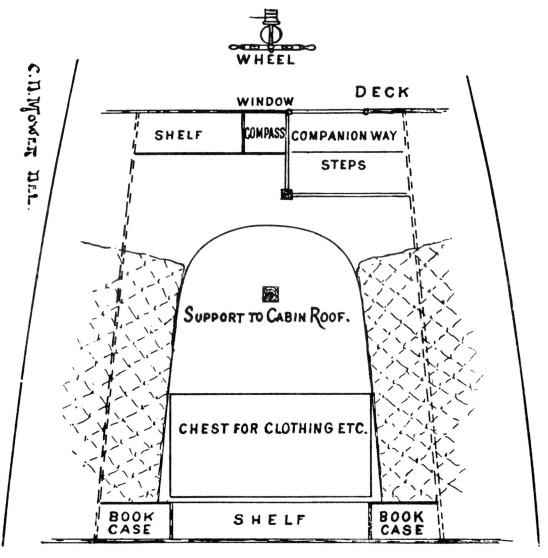

The plan of the original Spray's *cabin. Owing to the different deck arrangement of Pete's* Spray, *his cabin plan was different.*

It later turned out that this was the last big effort at this sort of thing on the Bay.

As the schooner job was urgent, it was decided to let the *Spray* frame set for the winter, and "find and set" itself, to be horned and trued again when work started on her later. I still think this is a good practice; it was once common in first-class house-building too. "Lets the snow work the sap out."

I was put to work on deck beams, beams for the cabin trunk, parts for hatches, and spars, all under the Master's direction. Prefab was well understood here. I went alone, mostly in the old drafty loft, the ternplate roof rattling dismally to winter Nor'westers that turned the river "feather white."

Meanwhile, the schooner was hauled on the big railway and prepared for her major operation. This in itself was quite a project, salted with much knowhow.

Her ends were knocked out, and most of her top-work taken off to the waterline. Old bottoms usually are in good shape, except for the ends. Her deck was cut loose from her sides with her masts still in her. She was all jacked, shored, and stayed to dead-men buried in the yard, of which there was many, some dating back to the beginning. I had an excellent view of all of this from the loft, for the vessel was right below me, with her headstays secured to the head of the railway. I began to realize I was witnessing The Big Time, a master shipwright at his best. The battered mill truck and giant were frequent visitors with huge piles of oak. The stem liner, otherwise known as an apron piece, arrived. It was a noble chunk, 18" × 24" × 20 feet. Isaac, the axe wizard, was put on it, and some of the days were so cold it's a wonder his axe stood it.

A drawing by Thomas Fogarty from Sailing Alone Around the World. *The caption was, "It'll crawl!" Slocum had plenty of spectators as he rebuilt the* Spray, *and the gent with the heavy basket evidently disapproved of Slocum's caulking technique.*

The old timers from Down the Bay showed up, all of 'em, and boarded locally in the village during the working week. Captain Bill, framer-planker-ceiler extraordinary, was sort of chief, under the Master. His hands were so big that cotton work gloves covered only a little more than half of them. John, aged 74, who "could lay off work for 25 head of men and do a full day's work besides," could and did! His brother, 72 and hunch-backed, had a 42-inch handle in his maul and could do anything with it. No one else could do a thing with the tool. It was just too long. Pap, who was supposed to be 84, was so shrunken and withered it was said he had a brick in each pocket to keep from blowing away, yet he was right in it with the rest. There were a couple of younger men making up, with the yard steadies, quite a crew.

The mill roared, and the old building creaked with its efforts, as all the strain was transmitted to the frame through the big overhead line shaft. I heard the ring of pin mauls, the chunking of adz and axe, and the constant rumble of rollers moving heavy stuff. Then a sick cruiser showed up, and this job was taken on. One of the younger men from Down the Bay was put to "opening her up." The Master stopped by daily to check my lone progress, and he seemed satisfied. One day he said, "Harly needs help on the cruiser." Would I give him a hand? I was part of the crew the rest of the winter, and the cruiser turned out well after we gave her a new stem and replanked her topwork. Harly knew considerable about yacht planking.

By early spring the schooner was about finished. Soon she was launched. She had the yard's handsome, springy sheer and was every inch a smart coaster. Her new master had been by her all winter. A thorough seaman and somewhat of a dude (always wore a store suit), he was a stickler for doing it right, and she was properly rigged and fitted out in record time. One day she sailed, in half a gale. She made a short board across the creek, went about with much volleying from the new canvas, and then she was standing down river, leaving "a wake as wide as the State Road."

The *Spray*'s hull in frame was worked on as the oyster fleet's spring repairs allowed, and, as it got warm, planking and ceiling started in earnest. A steam box was, of course, used, as hard pine is stiff, and the curves were full. Right here I learned about ceiling run and planking run too, things which seem to be overlooked in books and seem to have been forgotten. Later on, in the World War II years, this fact began immediately to show up. In that era, I suddenly found myself as Boss Planker "with twenty-nine head of men under me," a most successful one, they said, and I lay it all to the teaching of those who really knew.

Soon beams were going into the *Spray*, and waterways, decks, and the trunk were started. When she was about together on top, it was time to think of getting her tight so work could go on below in bad weather, for fall storms were not far away. It was time to caulk her hull, too. Edward, the caulker, got a couple of his crew from the old days from Down the Bay, and they went at it. This was quite a show in itself. Caulking was a trade of its own and took much learning. Morning starts were slow and hesitant, especially if it was a bit chilly. Then the tempo would increase slightly, the magic black hands feeding the cotton and oakum like machines. There would come a moan from somewhere under her, an answering hum, and shortly a hymn would start, lightly at first, in time with the mallets. Each mallet had a voice of its own. The tempo would increase, with much punctuation from the mallets. The crab pickers next door would pick up the hymn, and soon there would be a real old rouser going. At some mystic signal from the boss mallet, all would stop; at a cry from it another would start, a real old foot-stomper this time! By then, the sun would be beating down, happy looks were on the shiny black faces, and the real fun would start. Suddenly all mallets would stop but one, he would solo with much art and many flourishes, and then the chorus would come in again, until some other would do his solo. This went on all day until she was caulked; no wonder it did not take long.

I asked Edward how it was in the days of the big vessels. His face lighted up. "When 'e done the *White*, had a thick oak bottom, first-class seams, and twenty head of men under her. Man, that were Music!" He was referring to the fourmaster, the *Purnell T. White*. My vessel was, of course, tight, and stayed so. Fifteen years later she was "set back" for the first time. Ancient Ed was still around, though others did the job. I had consulted him about it, and he thought, "it was about time."

Deck details were worked on as the weather allowed, and, as it was getting cool, the stove was set up below. On bad days, we built the cabin around it. Simple though attractive, it was a vessel's cabin. Then there was much bunging and painting outside, with much effort on the seams, which were all rodded back. She sat at the edge of a bulkhead near the sheers. A big November tide was needed, as otherwise there was quite a drop and not much water ordinarily.

The line of the launching just cleared the old backhouse. It was a true shipways launching, on grease, as that was the custom, even for very small vessels. Ways were built, and she had the customary trial packing. Then, as the day approached, tallow was heated, the ways greased, stops rigged, and the whole thing repacked. Launching day was cold and raw with little wind. The tide came well, as there was a gale in the offing. The bulkhead was cut down in way of the keel passage in case the ways settled; no one wanted any toe-stubbing. There was no check line, as the creek was wide, the vessel small, and what wind there was would drift her back to the dock.

This was an honest saw-off launching. The wedges were driven to raise her, the keel blocks were knocked out, and she bore on the sliding ways. The dogs were tripped, the tide lapped the bulkhead, and the order was given to start the big cross-cuts, just sharpened for this occasion. Halfway through came an order to stop; the Master measured each side. Then he said, "Cut her off," and they did. She sat. Edward dropped his end of the saw, faced the vessel, and salaamed mightily, speaking in some strange lingo. A rumble went through the whole structure and she started, slowly at first, then with a rapid increase, a Splash, and much popping up of spewed blocks. A blue cloud appeared at the end of the ways; the tallow had smoked, so it was a proper launching. She was warped in to the dock, the pump was tried, and she was well made fast, for there was wind coming. The cabin stove felt fine, for we had been "keeping fire" now for several days. Tomorrow was Thanksgiving, and to hell with the mess of battered ways for this week. Those that used it had something to take home and warm up with, for all hands were chilled through. Even a small launching can be an exhausting business. The vessel was checked as to water late that night, and next morning the pump was frozen. What matter? She did not need it.

The rest was routine: masting, rigging, trials, and many years of sailing in good weather and bad, many ups and downs. Her construction never let her down. I had her a long time, and she has not had very many owners since. Rumor has it she's still afloat at 43 and is for sale at many, many times her first cost. At 23, when I parted with her, she was quite sound. Now, I don't know. Like many of us getting along, she might well "have considerable dote." I leave the *Spray* at that.

I've mentioned before doing it like it was, with simple, honest materials and good workmanship. I think the *Spray* is a monument to this approach, yet in those days this kind of shipbuilding was the common thing. A vessel twenty years old was considered quite young. All it took was oak, hard pine,

THOMAS FOGARTY.

Another Fogarty drawing from Slocum's book showing the Spray being passed by the U.S. battleship Oregon, on her way from Puget Sound round Cape Horn to help the Navy fight the Spanish in the Caribbean in 1898.

Capt. Pete and his wife Toni aboard the Oxford Spray, *as Pete's copy is known, heading down Chesapeake Bay. Until their marriage, Pete would charter* Spray *in the Chesapeake area in the spring and fall, and Newport, Rhode Island, during the summer. He would then work at a Chesapeake area shipyard over the winter. With Toni aboard to double the crew, operations expanded to year-round cruising that included Florida, the Bahamas, and the Caribbean.*

some cedar, and some galvanized iron. If she had been built in some other place, maybe other materials would have been used and done just as well. So many things get lost and forgotten; I spend much of my time now trying to pass it on, by talking, writing, designing, and by what I'm able to build, all in very fond memory of those cud-chewing masters

of it. There was never a sour face, never a rush, never a false move; the trade was almost a religion with them.

Having become accepted and somewhat adept, I worked off and on between sailing with this same yard for some time, and at other smaller yards in the village. The Master wanted to retire; his boys were not interested in the yard, as is often the case. Finally, the place went to new owners; the old crew drifted off to nearby yards, and some passed on.

The new owners had to start from scratch and appointed a capable local man as manager. A job turned up and I was asked to come back, as I knew the set-up. I suddenly found I was a sawyer; I then realized I knew how. I raised an 80-foot vessel and put on a new shoe, with one other man. Nothing to it; I found I knew just how to do that, too. The railway downhaul broke. I had helped place the big sheave at the outer end some time back, so I "knew how it was" down in nine feet of water. I found myself shinning down a long pike pole in April water with a messenger line to fish through the monster iron block. I got her through, and I didn't like it one bit. Shades of Old Tom. No wonder he was addicted to Rotgut! I guess I had become a shipyard man. So it went, here and there, trying to make a vessel pay summers, for there was something called a Depression around.

I got work in yards down South, not much, for there was not much. Some Nut started a War. This always calls for vessels. Someone heard I could loft. Right quick I was down on my knees lofting the first of a big Government contract under the eye of a past acquaintance. One thing and another, I did it all. I became known as a hot number with an adz, Isaac's adz. I got pretty good at boring alleyways, some big. Big chunks of timber and seemingly impossible shapes fell to me, because I had been trained by men who thought in this medium. After

Often the Spray *would travel to southern cruising grounds with other live-aboard sailors. Here, she is heading south in the Intracoastal Waterway under power, in company with Jim Emmet's schooner* Heart's Desire. (Jim Emmet)

The Oxford Spray *off Ft. Lauderdale, Florida, with sheets just started and a nice bow wave.* (George Yater)

all, some of my teachers had been log canoe builders, or their fathers had. The art of working "chunks" was still around on the Bay.

A planking louse-up developed, and the whole problem was dumped on me. I found myself a planker boss with quite a crew, maybe by default, because no one there had worked with a master of it. I had. The old fellow was gone now, but I think he looked to my efforts, for I often turned to his teachings when things were sticky. I must say that they almost always were right.

Many years later I found myself master shipwright building a sailing vessel in New England,

the schooner *Integrity*. I "done the hull of it," as they say, from design on. It was just like of old, the sounds, the sights, the smells, no sour faces, and a happy gleam, though nobody chewed. There was electricity and a warm toilet. The caulkers were the same, only with mystic rites in Portagee, and much taking of snuff. She was "humming tight." I felt the Old Master's presence strongly. I spoke of it to others.

The vessel had some happy years, made a long, successful voyage, was later acquired by lubbers who ruined her, but "The Sea Couldn't Kill Her."

The Master was there all right!

BOATBUILDING

Being still active with boats, I'm constantly exposed to much discussion about them, and one of the main topics is cost. Current prices in any age seem to have little to do with it; the point is, boats always were expensive. To make the first hollowed-out log took much time and labor that could not be devoted to hunting and fishing. Good things are expensive, and some of us think boats are very good things.

Possibly because boats are supposed to be so very good, we have, over many years, come to the idea they must be made in as difficult and expensive a way as possible. Certainly this was not the original approach, especially in working craft. Good enough to do the job and do it well was what was required. And pride of workmanship was involved to make the boat look as fine as one's resources and her intended use allowed.

Many folks now seem to be trying to think along these lines again. At least there is renewed interest in simple, and thus often traditional, craft. It is said Man has been building boats for 5,000 years, maybe longer. Certainly something has been learned about it in that length of time. Some think this should be pushed aside, for there are all sorts of breakthroughs, new wonder materials, and even newer thinking—all still very young compared to the past development of boats. The new methods of boatbuilding, however, are mostly very much out of reach to the ordinary fellow.

Having worked with everything from cheap skiffs, up through yachts plain and fancy, and Uncle Sam's best in wood, I have long ago come to the conclusion that the traditional craft is by far the most economical and useful in the end, and the most pleasing to the eye. I feel the same way about traditional construction methods, especially if the boat is built by the home builder or the small shop that cannot and should not spend too much money tooling up for just one craft. Many builders get befuddled by "production thinking" in setting up to build a rather simple wooden boat, possibly because they hope orders will come in for many. This rarely happens, and if by chance it does, you simply go on building the same thing, improving where you can, and taking care not to repeat any previous mistakes.

I doubt if there has been much improvement in the design and building of rowing craft since ancient times. Obviously, moving boats by manual labor over the years led to the development of models most suited to that form of propulsion. In connection with the present revival of pleasure rowing, we can do well to study the smart craft of the past. This also applies to traditional sailing craft; the very recent improvements are largely in the availability of better materials: ballast, rope, wire, and sail cloth. Simplicity of rig and ease of repair were always sought after in craft of the past. Those intended for speed could sail, for, in some trades at least, to lose the race was to hang!

All this background makes traditional craft most appealing, the more so when you consider how very practical they are, each for her own special use. Needless to say, you should use some judgment in which craft to select. This involves not a little study of the waters she will sail and her intended use, as well as how the type chosen suits available materials. This last applies to small craft or large, and is of much more importance in a boat of some size. Chasing for non-existent stock is most frustrating.

Assuming you have chosen a boat, and are about to build her, either yourself at home or professionally at a yard, once a start is made, you should get on with the job. Many backyard builders figure a long project, even up to five or more years. Some pros start a job and then put it aside for a long period to work at something that brings in ready cash. In both cases, troubles begin. You learn the hard way. Very little timber is really thoroughly dry. A long layoff, and checks develop. The shed or shelter starts to leak unnoticed. A shore or two drops out. Mice or chickens move in. Space is limited, so the half-finished hull becomes a storehouse for all sorts of junk.

One fellow knocked off for a year, just when his planking was ready to bung. The result was the bung holes shrank and became somewhat egg-shaped. He had to give up bungs and go to putty. Another was ten years at it, and then died, and by that time some of his work was starting to rot! Better he had attempted a small sailing skiff and had her done in time to use. You hear occasionally of very large craft

built by one man. Many more are started but not finished. You must consider that most of your time can be spent rigging mechanical aids and shifting staging, rather than on actual construction. If this goes on too long, your spirit can weaken.

A fellow can be overcome by equipment that is too expensive and by too much "tooling up." Having a lot of stuff to work with sounds nice, but it takes money, often better used elsewhere; it takes up

A flat-bottom skiff being bottom and side planked in Pete Culler's shop. The boat is the 18'6" Good Little Skiff Dixie Belle *built for Waldo Howland. The flat, cross-planked bottom is clearly seen prior to the skeg and bottom shoe being fastened. Later, the centerboard box will be bolted to the skeg and bottom shoe. In the foreground, the stem is left long so it can be used to jam and hold the bottom shoe/skeg member while it is fastened.*

space, which is often at a premium; and above all it takes maintenance. You can have too much of a good thing. Most traditional craft were built with the simplest equipment, for they are of fairly simple construction as a rule. The usual way was to build outdoors with no shelter at all, or at most a "shade," as they say in the tropics. Nowadays, in certain climates, more shelter is needed, though not as much as many suppose, especially if the building of the craft is a one-shot thing. In the Northeast, many think a fully heated shop is the only possible way, and by heated they mean like our living room. While heat is a must for fiberglass or large amounts of gluing, it's all wrong for the construction of traditional wooden boats. Building a small wooden boat in the modern heated cellar brings on all sorts of troubles. Better a shed of some sort and a drum stove to burn the scrap.

One of my friends built a 36-foot boat in a two-car garage. His method was this: One bay for lumber and tools, the other for the bow half of the boat. The stern half was outdoors, protected by a tarp when needed. He prefabbed parts and pieces during the winter in the cellar, where most of his very modest power equipment was, along with a good workbench. He set her up in very early spring, pushed along during the summer, working forward on bad days and aft on good ones. She was fairly well closed in by fall. He had a stove in the cabin so he could work below during the tough months. Before launching, he had a dry run with his rig to be sure all was right; this also checked out his gin pole setup for getting his masts in and out. He launched in early spring and was sailing the same day, as his preparations were so thorough he did not have to wait for her "to make up," or sit up and

The 18'6" Good Little Skiff Dixie Belle *being finished with seats and sternsheets. The centerboard cap is next and then paint and varnish.*

pump during the night. She had been swelled carefully with a hose.

The idea is you can make do in many ways with proper planning. Heavy, warm clothes and boots are far cheaper than a heated building. And speaking again of heat in a proper boatshop in winter, I find 40 to 60 degrees the most you want, the lesser for active work with tools, the greater for paint and varnish. Big glue jobs require at least 70 degrees to be successful; if you can't raise that much in winter, wait till spring! You can take a lot of cold when out of the wind, dressed for it, and, say, working out a stem or keel. Oh yes! I've seen it 130 degrees in a Southern boatshop in summer, working on deck, under a roof, and with big floodlights. Some modern shops are kept so hot—about as hot as the attached office—that one soon feels in a stupor. Meanwhile, those "upstairs" rack their brains as to why "production" is falling off and the heating bills are rising. They also wonder why they have so much checked timber and warping.

Turning to floors, or what the craft will be set up on, a stout wood floor is best of all. You can nail to it, lag, cleat, cut holes in it if the need arises, and it's easy on the building crew. If it's a light wooden floor, it's still pretty good, as you can usually block and shore it here and there and get by. Thousands upon thousands of craft have been built on the ground; it's pretty good, be it rocky, muddy, sandy, or just plain along the shore or in your back yard. Tools stand dropping on the ground better than a wooden floor. If it pitches this way and that, so what? That's what a level and plumb are for. You are often stuck with a cement floor. If so, you put up with it and build on a grid. If the builder does not already know it, he will soon find that cement is very hard on the legs and feet. There is nothing to nail to, and if a hand or power tool falls, often that's it for the tool. A lot of things seem to get jarred and fall off in boatbuilding. Falls by workmen are not unknown, and a cement floor seems to be a bad place to take a

spill. To set up a new professional boatshop with a cement floor shows a total lack of understanding of wooden boatbuilding, the trade in general, and the welfare of the working crew and equipment. The day comes when a long keel bolt must be got out, or a long stock rudder unshipped. The instigators of the cement floor then see their sins; they have to hire a jackhammer! Later the holes are covered with wooden hatches; they are learning.

There is quite a lot in choosing just what time of year to start a craft, depending on her type, the available working time, location, and what stock you can get and when. A home builder doing a small craft in the North usually works in winter, assuming he has some kind of shelter. A yard, large or small, usually prefers winter, too, and it's apt to be the slackest time. Though many give it no thought now, there is much advantage in using fall-cut timber, usually for the keel and the bigger timbers. In the fall the ground is mostly dry, and timber can be got out of the woods relatively easily. Sap is down, so many think the timber more healthy and less liable to decay, and there is less blue stain in the sapwood, especially in pine. In some places, timber is cut in late fall and winter and trucked out as soon as roads are usable in early summer. While many books on the subject and many elaborately written specifications call for "thoroughly dry stock," in practice dry stock is generally not available for big timber, or for much other timber for that matter. No builder is going to store much big timber for long periods. He has no real idea of the sizes he will need in the future, or even if he will have a boat to build. This all more or less applies to the home builder too, especially for the heavy parts. The fact that most craft are built of green or semi green timber in the keels, deadwoods, and so forth and that they seem to last speaks well for what the book says is shoddy practice. Personally, I've seen much good timber, including spar timber, that was left over from some job go bad before there was any use for it. It's in the way, is pushed aside, the covering blows off, and soon sun and water do their work. Some may be resawed later into smaller stuff, but most seems to end up as sleepers and props for some new project. If you must build outdoors, and with possibly no more than a tarp to cover some of the work, there is much advantage in laying your stock in the fall, sticking it carefully, and at least covering the top of the lumber and painting the ends. It will dry considerably by the time it's needed.

You have to have a place to lay down, and if space is limited, this can be done "by halves," or even quarters, or, as one well-known Southern builder, now retired, always did, by the half-size method, which is suited to some craft. With a sheltered place to make moulds and other parts, you bring the job well along the first winter. Come early spring, set her up and push along during the good months. Even if the craft is only a modest cabin type, it takes plenty of pushing. The idea is to "get her shut in" by fall, and most of the outside stuff done, then set up the stove, even if only temporarily, and do the inside work when the weather is unfit for anything else.

I've seen a very nice lobster boat more or less prefabbed in a cellar during a Maine winter. As soon as the ground was bare, she was set up outside. In a few days, she stood in frame. Shortly, she was planked, and, so it seemed, as soon as the weather was good, she was at work. Obviously, this was the result of good planning and a skilled man.

To the man who has never done it before, a boatbuilding project looks big and difficult. The more you think about it the worse it seems, when actually the hardest part is making the start. Once you start, one thing follows another in the natural order of boatbuilding, none being really much of a chore. It's just thinking of the whole pile of steps at once that makes the job seem so much of a mountain.

The proper choice of a craft suited to your abilities plus care in planning and careful lofting get a boat off to a good start. Even pros have been known to take on a craft that was too much for their setup. And as to lofting, some get carried away and do more than is really needed. "Loft everything but the galley sink." Some designs require much lofting and some do not. In either case, do a thorough job, for it always pays off later.

Lofting on paper is very unsatisfactory, especially if the craft is of some size and the job protracted. Paper does not wear well, and is much affected by changes in humidity. It's surprising how a long length of paper will come and go. For a very small craft that can be laid down and moulds made in a day or two, you can get by using paper. I've found white pine, and in some cases fir, battens the best, made from near the edge of a plank. Oak and cedar battens just don't seem to stay fair long. Sometimes a hard pine one will work well. I might mention that I seldom nail through a batten in lofting, always alongside. Besides being better for the life of the batten, you avoid the slight swell around the nail, if it's a very light batten. As is often the case, the batten is not long enough, so you have to overlap a second batten, one inside, and the other outside the line. The side nailing helps the overlapping situation and makes all lie fair. You partially remove one batten at the lap, mark the line, replace the batten and remove the other, continuing the marking of the line. All experienced loftsmen know this, but the beginner has to learn it from others. For short quick curves, such as body lines, you sometimes try many methods, and break some battens too, in many cases resorting to a bandsaw blade in the end. While building a boat, you should be on the lookout for rippings that will make good battens for the going job or a future boat.

Having tried several colors for a loft floor and worked on several brand new unpainted ones (very good) and many much-worn dark ones, I think very light, dull gray paint the best. Colored pencils and marking pens are handy, especially if there are many lines. These things, not being intended for such work, wear fast, but are worth it. Clinch box nails, when they can be had, are most handy lofting nails. Some of these come blued, which is no matter. They can be used for fastening light moulds and in setting battens, as the points are flat and thin. They also stay put in taking up lines by the string-of-nails method, that is they don't roll and have thin heads. If clinch box nails are not available, you can use pot nails, lath nails, or something similar.

Many people may be unfamiliar with picking up lines with nails, though it seems that most older builders use the method. Probably, while it's not as old as boats, it's at least as old as manufactured nails. Here's how it works: A piece of mould stock, plywood, or thin plank sufficient to cover the area to be raised is laid over the spot. If more than one piece is needed, it's fitted to the first. Three or more nails are driven against the stock, so it can't shift two ways; the other two ways don't matter, as in placing the stock, one simply crowds it to the nails. When this is set, remove the mould stock. Then place the small picking-up nails, heads on the lofted line, shanks at right angles to it, an inch or more apart. The less curve in the line, the farther apart the nails. All you want is an accurate enough spotting

The 10'6" yawlboat designed for Stephen Forbes set up in Capt. Pete's shop. The boat has been lined off with battens for lapstrake planking on the far side, with the near side showing only the sheer batten. This boat is similar in model to the 10'6" wherry yawlboat also shown in this chapter. The principal difference between the two is the keel construction. Pete Culler's practice was to line off his boats for plank the same way, whether they were flat, round, or v-bottom. The batten was the same width as the lap and the same thickness as the plank, and he would mark the molds on both the top and bottom of the batten. This assisted in keeping the plank, lap, and widths from getting confused while planking up the hull.

from the nail heads so a batten can be set in the spots they make. When all the area to be moulded is covered with nails, not forgetting such things as sheer height and other needed marks, lower the mould stock almost to the floor, crowd it to the positioning nails, and, taking care not to shift it, lower it right to the floor and kneel on it. Then step over all of the mould stock to press the nail heads into it. Some also tap along the approximate line with a hammer. Then the whole thing is lifted, turned over, and, if small enough, taken to the bench, otherwise laid on the floor. Many of the nails will stick to the mould stock, especially if it's soft, less so to plywood, and no matter; what you want is the marks from the nails. These are battened off in the usual way, marked, and the mould carefully sawed out. With practice and a clean-running bandsaw, you can "split the line" and that's it, or cut slightly wide and

bring to the line with a light plane. You then place the mould in position on the floor, and find it fits the lines perfectly.

From the loftman's standpoint, this one's at least, it's better to work from lines to inside of plank. One seldom finds lines produced this way now. Many think they know how to allow for plank thickness and really don't. Even some books on lofting fail really to go into this matter. It's not quite the way it would seem. The usual method of striking arcs of plank thickness in from the body plan station lines, or using a gauge block of the plank thickness, doesn't quite give the true picture except near the middle of the craft, though in a very sharp, thin-planked boat, the error is small. Picture a very fullbowed, thick-planked craft, say with the sheer plank cutting a bow station at about 40 degrees. Imagine cutting this plank through vertically with

The 40' schooner Gallant, *designed by Pete for Richard Tilghman and built at Concordia Co., Padanaram, Massachusetts, in 1965. The vessel is based on the pilot schooners that were common in Virginia waters many years ago.*

a saw, at right angles to the keel. The face of the cut, "square with the keel," is much wider than the thickness of the actual plank. Or, take it another way: A standard 2 × 4 is 1⅝ inches thick; cut it vertically at 40 degrees and measure the face. You will see right off that considerable error can develop in a buxom craft with a thick skin. A bevel board can be made, based on the proposed plank thickness of the craft, which will show the amount to allow for the amount of bevel.

A heavily raked, curved stern is apt to be the pons asinorum of lofting for many. A close study of the shape and often a doubling up on some lines make it work out. Many naval architects do this doubling up as a matter of course. Certain traditional craft seem always to have had curvature, or "radius," in the stern, and to look the part must be built that way. I doubt, however, if the radius stern has any practical value, only looks. Many sterns that are flat across are quite handsome if otherwise properly shaped, and flatness allows building by flitching up, or using thick stock edge-bolted, plus a nailing frame. Assuming the topwork is kept tight, and the joints are good, I feel this method of construction is possibly less subject to decay than a radius stern that must be made up of many smaller pieces. No doubt many builders won't agree, and I do not wholly condemn the radius stern; sometimes it's worth the trouble. One sometimes sees a rather ugly radius stern; in this case, I think it's a total waste of time and material.

Some round-bilge designs show a minimum of diagonal lines, often not enough. Small matter; you can always strike in more, especially down near the rabbet. This is where things tend not to work out if the craft has much reverse curve and widely spaced lines. This adding of lines sometimes is a help in other than diagonals, say in the ends if the craft is of quick shape. These additions don't always have to go the length of the vessel. You usually have few problems near the middle of a craft. I personally

have a great liking for plenty of diagonal lines properly placed. They tend very much to the run of the planking lines in round-bilge boats, which helps very much in lining off for the plank. You can usually tell from the placing of the diagonals on a plan if the designer has a good working knowledge of planking.

In most craft, especially those of classic model with deep heel and sharp forefoot, you should line out your garboard quite wide in the ends. The object is to gain fast there so as to keep the hook out of the hood ends of following planks. One often hears it said, "plank should follow the waterline as nearly as possible," and that some sort of master-width batten should be used to figure the strake widths at all stations. Possibly this works on a craft with a cigar-shaped hull. This method will probably be accompanied, however, by much edge setting of plank, or fitting the plank by bending it edgeways, "to save stock." Nothing I know of can cause more bother, trouble, fight, and waste of stock than this method, the more so the more shapely the craft. I strongly suggest that when in doubt about lining off for plank, you batten off the whole craft in advance if she's small, so you can see the errors in advance and can make corrections. In larger craft, placing the ribbands along the diagonal lines will give about the same effect. The builder can see his planking run, only in larger panels, and make any small correction as he goes, by sections. In very stout, large, sawn-frame vessels, the harping bands of very stout timber are placed the same way, as nearly as possible along the diagonals, for the same reason. Approached as suggested, planking done this way is by far the easiest, least wasteful of stock, most pleasing to the eye, and best for the boat. In large craft with narrow strakes and with rather long lengths of plank, some edge setting can be done, but the less the better.

Modest errors in lining off seldom show once a carvel-planked craft is joined off and seams are filled and painted, except possibly to the critical eye looking for such things. However, in light, lapstrake craft, the line of the plank can be a most important matter if the boat is to look well. For these craft, I feel it pays to line off completely with battens of about the same width as the laps. Do one side only, of course. Take plenty of time and look from all angles, not always easy in a crowded shop. Make corrections a strake at a time; adjusting one usually calls for tinkering with another. Finally it Looks Right and that's it. And never—I said never—attempt to plank a lapstrake hull by edge setting!

Most of the "outmoded" methods of the past still work, science to the contrary. Consider, for example, the half model. If you have doubts as to the looks of your craft, you should construct one. Among other things, you will find it an excellent medium on which to practice lining off plank, with the aid of a light batten and pins. After all, many a steel vessel has been built with the aid of a "plating model." While the use of models is frowned on, even laughed at today by some at least, it's well to point out that many of the craft seen now would have been better in many ways if there had been a model used somewhere in their development. Some of the quickie steel jobs around could have well used a plating model. This last is also an aid if you are considering some design in plywood that was not originally intended for it. A little fooling around with cardboard panels will soon show what's what.

Without going into the details of half model making, since they have been well covered by able writers of experience (L. Francis Herreshoff and Howard Chapelle both cover it well, and their works are readily available), it's well to mention that much additional information can be had from a half model with quite reasonable accuracy. Displacement can be worked out rather closely by several methods, all based on the same principle. Various centers can be arrived at. You can see what the craft will look like afloat, using the lifts above the

L.W.L. only, and you can appreciate what the fish will see. Besides, a half model is often the only way to get across to a builder unfamiliar with the type just what the craft really looks like, what problems lie ahead, and, above all, if the stern is extremely shapely, just what this is to look like.

If expensive towing tank tests using models are of use to the big-time designer and builder, and they no doubt are, then the use of the cheap half model can be of much help to the small professional builder and backyard shipyard. You don't expect way-out answers from a block of wood, no matter how nicely made, but rather practical guides useful in building ordinary craft.

While it may seem very much the backwoods way, I seldom start a craft without a half model, even a skiff, unless the boat is only a slight variation of some previous design. In larger craft, somewhere along in working up the design, a half model is built, often more than one, or the first one altered. Yes, the model can show you the error of your ways. Besides, it's a fine thing to have around for all the experts to pick apart. After all is done, and this sometimes runs into months and even years, and whether or not the finished craft is a success, the model makes a fine shop decoration, and reminds you of your errors; if any. Usually there are some.

Some amateurs and small boatshop owners like to tinker with design, and that's just fine; excellent craft often come from their efforts. Sometimes, however, a fellow gets a passion for design, learns on his own, or is taught all the very up-to-date approaches, and is good at math so loves all sorts of calculations, but unfortunately has not had the interest or time to learn about boats from a practical standpoint. Any design he turns out lacks something; it's hard to say just what, but one might say it lacks Boat Sense. This fellow is also apt to be a pain in the neck to some builder.

Some years back one of these chaps came to me to learn the real workings of a boatshop. We started from scratch and built him a beach boat. He "worked" along with the builder, and I think he got a lot out of it; we both did, though my neck hurt! Being a whiz at math and the use of the slipstick, he was at first appalled at what seemed slapdash methods of the small shop. We started with picking the lumber and other stock. The fact that cedar is full of pin knots was the first surprise. You so often read about "perfectly clear, dry stock in long lengths" in boat specs. My own experience has been that it's nice reading, but the stock seldom exists. After loading the truck, taking the lumber to mill and unloading, jacking it through the ear-splitting old planer (which, by the way, had no shavings blower; she just spewed to the atmosphere), loading again, transporting to shop and sticking, the budding shipwright allowed as how it was a bit of hard work, and dusty too.

After a terrific battle with the lofting, done by methods more enlightened than others use, a warped grid, and miles of erasing and all the other pitfalls

of the know-it-all greenie (the craft, by the way, was a flat-bottomed thing), he finally allowed it was not all in the book. "Taking up" by Noah's method was viewed with extreme doubt; then it all fit exactly. This was a shock in itself. There was an attempt at calculating (by the book) the coming performance of the craft. As no one seemed to know what the prismatic co-efficient of a rowing-sailing beach boat should be, this effort fell on its face. As to balance, it depends on where you put your big butt!

By now we were into drilling properly, tight seams, and all the other routine, along with a couple of cut fingers and other mishaps, such as having to draw a botched fastening, or raise a Nova Scotia Dimple (no offense, it's just a boatbuilder's term) with spit or hot water. Oh yes, he learned to build the shop fire, sweep, and sharpen tools. Some days the shop temperature never got above 35 degrees, but we were too busy and interested to care.

The end result was a nice craft with an ancient background, so therefore successful in spite of a

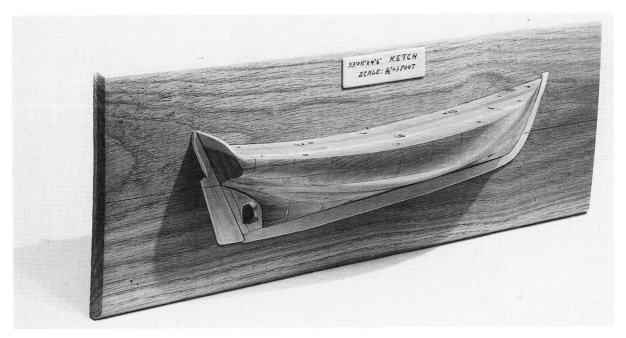

This 33' ketch was designed for Robin Laggeman by Pete. Pete invariably started his designs with the carving of a half-hull as it was easy for him to work out any potential problems with the designs' form with this method. When the client completed the building and finishing of the vessel, Pete would then present the mounted and finished half-hull to the owner.

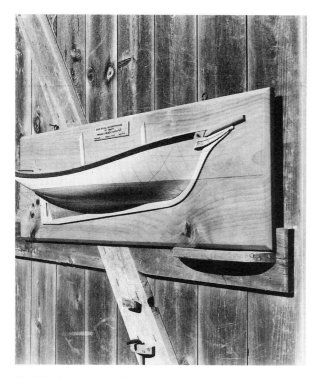

The 82' schooner designed for Henry Sears was based on the fast fruit runners of the Caribbean. This design would be a fast sailor and a handsome hull. This vessel was all set to be built right after the 52' schooner Integrity, *but Waldo Howland decided it was too large for the capabilities of Concordia Co. and to my knowledge the design has never been built. The lines appear on pages 138–139.*

little science. We both enjoyed it and learned a lot about each other, and I hope something about the art of building small craft. It seems in these little boats we are no more advanced than the old-timers were, and possibly have gone backwards. How far this art of building goes when applied to larger vessels is a moot point. Suffice to say, regardless of your formal training, to design a good schooner you must know something about schooners. Exposure to boats and vessels of your liking is no doubt the best way to train for the future design and building of them.

Many builders of the past, and present too for that matter, have had little or no formal training in the science of it or in higher math. Yet these same men turn out routine work that would seem to require the highest order of calculation. While formal training is no doubt of much advantage, if you can't get it, you pick up the knowledge from some master, who in turn learned it the same way. There is nothing like being exposed to a master shipwright or boatbuilder for long periods. A man learns many things about the trade not covered in writings, and like most other worthwhile pursuits, considerable study is required to fill out his knowledge. Home builders as a rule cannot get much of this exposure to trained men; however, with study, a real will to do it, and all the contact they can get with pros, they are soon on the way. Many amateurs have turned pro, and one is often much impressed with the craft turned out by home builders who really have desire.

Some may think professional builders don't care to discuss the workings of their trade. My experience has been the opposite; they love to gab endlessly about the subject they love, once they are sure of genuine interest. The rare exceptions are those who don't know their trade, and this seems to apply in any trade, the kind who will tell nothing in case the other may use it and get ahead of him. One thing about it, you can't take it with you, so if you have something on the ball, pass it on, so another can create a good boat.

MATERIALS

You may decide to build a certain size and type of craft, a boat well suited to her use, and of course one which you can afford. In choosing a boat to build, it's well to consider what stock and materials are reasonably available. There is no point at all in planning a craft for which you can't get material, or for which you can get material only under great difficulty. Maybe worse yet, it doesn't make sense to plan a boat that will require stuff you are unable to work with readily, due to lack of equipment or skill in the particular material.

We hear about a lot of wonderful new materials; no doubt they are great when used in the right places. Many of them are as yet unsuited to ease of working in a small shop. Some require controlled conditions; others may require out-of-reach equipment. Many folks think wood is now outdated; the fact is, it's the easiest medium for the small-time builder to work in, and is still the most economically practical for one-of-a-kind boats. Besides, it's available.

This last statement may be doubted by many people now, as they know of just three woods: teak, for trimming out fiberglass boats, and, as L. Francis Herreshoff said, two others, one red, and one not. From the beginning, boats were built with what was available. Ships finally made great voyages, and it became possible to import timber. For the most part now, we use wood that comes from many places. Some lumber mills make a point of milling for the marine trade. And it's often quite surprising what you can turn up at a really first-class lumber yard, geared only to shore building trades, and what these yards can get for a boatbuilder.

Many books on boatbuilding go very much into the pros and cons of various woods, where to use each in a hull, and their lasting qualities, which is fine. They fail to point out, however, that many very simple craft can be built with very simple materials, and in most cases be better off for it. A little open boat, constructed with reasonable care, and by nature having plenty of ventilation, does not have to be built of priceless and rare woods supposed to last forever. No wood does anyhow, or anything else for that matter, except possibly granite. This, by the way, makes excellent ballast for some types of craft. It's cheap where it's available, it's non-magnetic, it won't rust, and when the craft is done for, assuming she dies on the beach, you can build a stone wall with it.

Log canoes the world around have been built of local woods. Uncounted numbers of bateaux, dories, scows, skiffs, and other craft have been built of local stuff and continue to be. It's true that transportation is now so readily available, it can be cheaper sometimes to build from "imported" stuff.

Many prejudices, largely unfounded, have grown up about timber that isn't local. It's often said that timber from local sources lasts best in its own area; possibly it does to some extent. However, when you consider the huge number of powerline poles used in the East, nearly all of which seem to come from the West, and the large amount of really good piling which seems also to come from away, both used in situations where lasting really matters, the theory of "local woods only" loses a lot of its meaning. To "the Westward," Maine gray oak is often looked on as inferior, yet uncounted numbers of ships and boats have used it in the past, as well as the present, and made the state famous. The same with West Coast stock; many consider it inferior, yet Oregon pine and a famous Western spruce have been masting, decking, and planking Eastern vessels for a long time.

Capt. Pete draws a crowd demonstrating the use of natural knees as the ideal material for quarter knees, breasthooks, and thwart supports. The 18' round-bilge fast gig Quitsa Pilot *alongside is a testament to the structural use of natural knees in small craft.* (Ben Fuller)

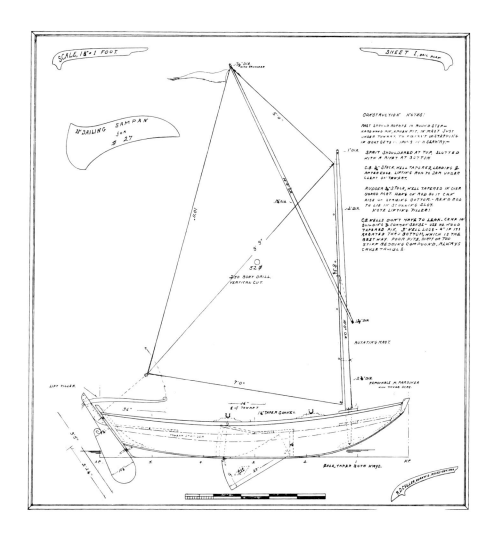

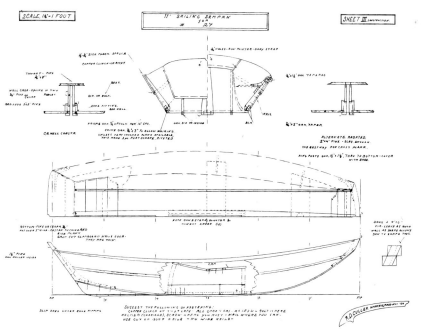

Pete liked this 11' sampan design so much for its intended uses of rowing, sailing, and serving as a tender to larger craft that no fewer than seven were built at his Hyannis shop. (© Mystic Seaport, Ships Plans Collection, Mystic, CT)

The just-for-rowing 11' sampan clearly showing the cross bottom planking and the interior construction. Pine would be used for the bow, stern, risers, and seats; white oak for the frames, chines, and stern and bow seat supports; and cedar for side and bottom planking. This was based largely upon what is available in the northeast U.S. Your locale may have different species traditionally used for boatbuilding stock, but if you keep in mind lightness with strength and durability, plus good holding for fastenings, you should do fine with what is available locally.

A government, or other outfit supported by taxpayers, can well build without regard to cost, and a few of the very wealthy indulge their fancy for what they think or have been told is the best. Others, not being able to do so, must use what is available. Probably more craft have gone to pot from lack of care than from lack of the finest lumber. Care of boats and craft is really much misunderstood nowadays. Many are killed by too much swaddling and covering up. Tight upperworks and plenty of ventilation, plus keeping a clean ship, are the first lines of defense. Decay likes dirt and foul air, along with a bit of a drip of fresh water. Other maintenance chores help some: making sure broken places in paint or varnish are attended to; drain holes if any, kept open; metal work attended to; and so on, but they alone cannot replace The Big Three: dryness, air, and cleanliness.

The first fastenings were no doubt lashings of some kind; then came pegs and pins of wood, which developed into the treenail and dowel. There were also devised joints that held themselves together with little aid. All these methods are still in use in many parts of the world. We hear much of Monel, bronze, and stainless steel, and just how bad galvanized fastenings are. Personally, I think it's all good in its place, but when you price much of it in today's economy, you are apt to do some thinking.

A fellow must consider what he can afford, and the type of craft he proposes to build. Buying Monel and bronze in thousand-pound lots for a big boat makes the cost mount rapidly. On the other hand, a light lapstrake boat, canoe, or other small craft of rather sophisticated construction is most suited to bronze and copper no matter the cost, for the amount used by the pound will be small. Fastenings on these craft may have to be set flush and therefore will be subject to striking with sandpaper, which is not healthy for galvanizing. All fastenings eventually corrode or become somewhat porous; the smaller they are, the sooner they lose strength. Even in light craft, it's often advisable to use galvanized iron bolts where strain is great, as very small bronze bolts are very weak. This was the practice in many past craft.

The mixing of fastenings as suggested above, has not, in my experience, done any harm in small craft. On the other hand, as soon as some electrical stuff is installed, over and above a flashlight, there is a chance of electrical leaks developing, which hasten the failure of mixed metals, or unmixed ones

A just-for-rowing version of the 11' sampan shown in the previous photo, but with no centerboard trunk or mast partners.

for that matter. Many will doubt the above state-ment, yet many of the fine craft of the past—strange to us nowadays—had mixing of metals, yet they lasted. Some are still around, notably the clipper *Cutty Sark*, and the whaler *Charles W. Morgan*. On studying these craft and their construction, one finds he has a lot more to learn. They had no man-made electric currents aboard until fairly recent times. I wonder if this is the real answer. We are now sup-posed to know a great deal about such things, yet every once in a while some situation turns up that seems to refute the theories.

A stout-built craft, large or small, suited to a lot of nailing, bolting, and drifting, does quite well with galvanized iron fastenings, in fact may be stronger for them. The fastenings are big, so they go a long time without much weakening. You often hear the argument that yes, it was once so when real iron was used, but now it's all steel. Except in rare and special cases, I think little real wrought iron was used after Bessemer got his method of steel making going, and certainly not in the lifetime of most of those vessels still around.

The stock drift bolts, carriage and machine bolts, and boat nails and spikes seem to be of just the same make-up now as in my youth. You used to, and still do, run into occasional poor galvanizing, poor threads, and other lesser defects, just as you can find in more costly fastenings. A batch of poor threads or shallow and out-of-center slots is not uncommon in bronze screws. Usually returning the batch and a little fuss with the supplier straightens things out. Machines get out of whack and inspec-tion misses mistakes sometimes.

Galvanized steel screws have problems of their own. First, they must be tough, and most really are. This means fairly hard steel and one that is rather subject to rust. The galvanizing is easily damaged in driving, partly because it's difficult to get really clean slots and very sharp threads in making the screws. The larger the screws, the better they seem to be. For any size of fastening, the quality of the galvanizing should be watched. Galvanized screws can be set up far tighter than bronze ones without breaking. Naturally, they are much used in fasten-ing down galvanized iron fittings. Though there is

The 10'6" wherry yawlboat under sail. This little boat incorporated many different woods in its construction. (This is discussed on pages 343–346.)
The idea is that with these classic little boats, the amount of material required is relatively small, and the different woods can be used to their
best advantage in the various parts and pieces. (Bart Hauthaway)

some doubt as to their being long-lasting in certain parts of hull construction, there are many examples around which have lasted, so here again the theories don't always work. I have noticed galvanized fastenings last quite well in properly fitted deck joiner work. In very small sizes, galvanized screws are troublesome; anything below a 1-inch #8 I don't care for.

Every size screw should have a driver bit that fits it, both in width and thickness. In practice, this is never quite so, and much unnecessary slot damage is done. Often, the pilot hole is not quite right.

I much favor starting any screw slightly with a hammer before driving, so it takes the line-up of the pilot hole. This saves much jumping off and damage by the bit in starting the drive. This hammer starting is of course commonplace, yet it's often neglected too.

The choice of fastenings depends as much on the type of craft as the size of the pocketbook. The fact that certain types of fastenings may not be available in any area or place has not hindered boatbuilding very much; one can always make do with what is on hand and still produce a good boat. Good

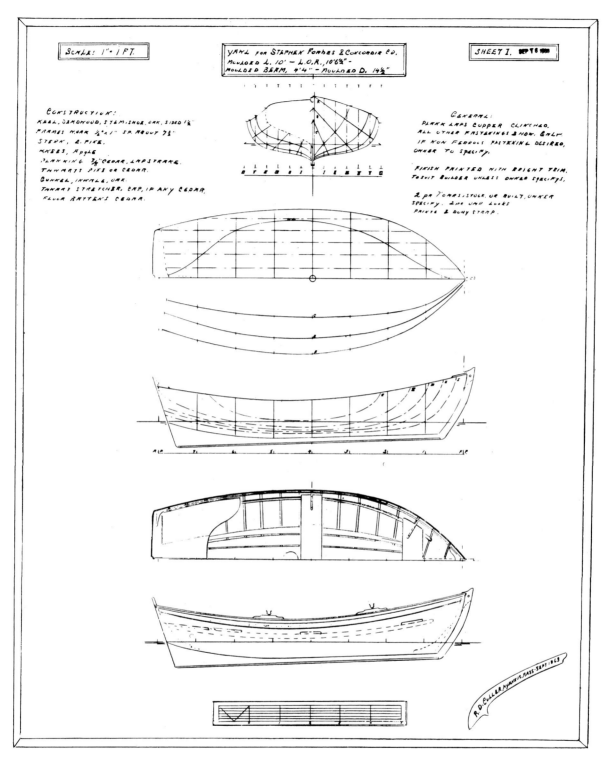

This 10'6" yawlboat was designed and built for Stephen Forbes of Nashawena Island, Massachusetts. Nashawena is one of the Elizabeth Islands, which stretch between Buzzards Bay and Vineyard Sound. The topography of Nashawena is such that there is much pasture land ending at high steep sand cliffs, which slide down to a narrow beach. A large flock of sheep is kept on the island and left to roam freely. It seems that in their grazing near the sand cliffs, the sheep have a tendency to lose their footing and slide down to the beach. Or so the story goes. The yawlboat was designed to rescue the sheep and bring them to higher ground. Because of this, the boat has come to be known as the "sheep boat."

Aside from the skeg keel, the sheep boat is nearly identical to the 10'6" wherry yawl on pages 343–346. Capt. Pete had a special affinity for little yawls like these and the 12'6" v-bottom yawl for Integrity (on pages 347–351) because of their competency to perform the jobs for which they were designed. A photo of the sheep boat being planked up appears on page 35. (© Mystic Seaport, Ships Plans Collection, Mystic, CT) workmanship, using what is available, is really the backbone of successful building, rather than setting some unreachable standard and not really achieving it.

Once in a while someone decides to build a boat "regardless of cost." In doing so, many things are lost sight of, and it's been my experience that the craft so produced are seldom successful, as they tend to be very complicated, which in itself makes a bothersome craft to use and maintain. A sound design well suited to its use, and I stress the word *use*, as simple as possible within the limits of its type, always tends to be a good craft, often with a long life, perils of the sea excepted. Such a boat is usually loved and therefore gets care. She is apt to be easy to use, so gets lots of it; a well-used boat tends to last. Like people, boats get doughy and flabby just lying around. A neglected boat will most certainly fall apart, even though she may be built of the very finest material.

TOOLS

Doing things with boats takes, besides money, tools and equipment, but not nearly as much, if you start small, as it might seem. Much is made of good tools for obvious reasons, yet to rush out and load up on many tools, without knowing just what is useful and what is not, can be quite wasteful. In this era of power tools, these are felt to be very necessary. Some are; some are not; some are very specialized. One can say the same of hand tools, I suppose. Boatbuilding tools are considered very specialized too, and to some extent they are, though many not readily bought can be made, for they are simple for the most part.

Starting with some suggestions on hand tools, I say a good broom is the first thing. A new apprentice was always started on a broom; once he learned to sweep properly he was promoted, usually to a scrub broom under a bottom. An orderly and clean shop is a workable place and is safer for men and far less of a fire hazard than a messy, dirty shop. By their nature, boat shops are considerable fire hazards. Yes, a good broom can save a lot; use it often, and always the afternoon of the last day of the working week. Weekends often bring visitors, or the

naval architect and his client; a tidy shop speaks well for the builder. Large professional shops using many men must have almost continuous sweeping, and the practiced sweeper does much more than that. He collects uncounted pounds of dropped fastenings, spots trouble in a junction box, and generally knows what's going on. He also has a "gosh box" somewhere, with all the lost pencils, rules, bevels, and other small tools he finds. If something's missing from a man's pockets, a visit to the sweeper will usually turn it up.

As very small children, we take to pounding, and if we like to make things, continue to do so the rest of our lives, which brings up hammers. In my experience at least, the ordinary carpenter's claw hammer has been standard with boatbuilders. For many years I owned just one, bought from a now-extinct mail-order house for 65 cents. It was known as a "second best," which then meant not highly finished. By the price you will know it was bought a long time ago; it's still working and has the original handle. They built well in those days. When I owned just one hammer, I could keep track of it. Now owning six, some of them specialized, I often can't find any; you can have too much of a good thing.

Often, the claw hammer is too light for bolt driving, general thumping, setting wedges, and such, yet the shipwright's pin maul is too much. Most men acquire something stout of the sort that goes by various pet names in various places. Such a tool might be called Thumping Hammer, Tunker, Belaboring Iron, or, as I remember one of strange shape and undetermined original use, Old Thumphead. These tunkers seem to be of no set model, just what's around; I've seen large ball peens, stone masons' hammers, blacksmiths', retired heavy bolt-sets, and other oddballs in use. A peen hammer of some kind is handy for upsetting bolts. A pin maul is not necessary for the small craft builder.

Hand saws, like hammers, have nothing special about them for boat work. A good saw, taken care of, will last until it's literally filed away, and any saw is only as good as its filing and settings. Besides the

standard length of 26 inches, shorter saws are handy for boat work, say 24 and 22 inches. Many of the saws made today don't feel the way they used to; the steel seems different. I have seen and used a recent English saw, which was excellent, and I think came from a well-known tool supply house near Boston. I was much impressed; the price might be impressive too. Few men now file their own saws, yet if one is doing much work, he should learn this skill. And as the saw is the first cutting tool we discuss, it might be said here that all cutting tools must be kept sharp, which means you must learn how. Some wise ones have said: after you learn to sweep, next comes learning to sharpen. I stress this, and will say more about it as we go.

I don't care for a very hard saw. Steel that is tough but soft, so it will file with a good burr (like a scraper) by far cuts the best. Saws made in the

Tools for boatbuilding used in Pete Culler's shop. All of these tools (except the rulers on the facing page) were made by Pete for his own use. Pictured are bevels of various sizes, carving tools, wooden planes, and clamps—one with a unique cam for tightening easily when used alone, as Pete usually worked.

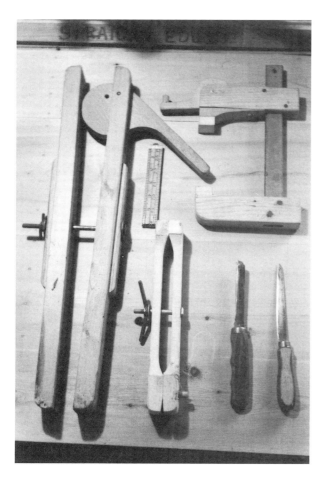

past and those still hand-filed usually have a slight downward curve or belly along the teeth fore and aft. New saws seldom do, for the automatic filing machine does not get along with this curve; besides, we are now told this curve is not needed. A good saw has plenty of "gauge," or thickness at the teeth and thinness to the back. It is also tapered some from handle to tip. You don't need many saws; an 8-point, standard length; a 10, which can be shorter; a compass saw; and the usual hacksaw for metal. A hand rip-saw is now seldom needed. If you get the Tool Bug, more will show up. Being a collecting nut, I must have a dozen or more, but the ones I mention get nearly all the use, with the exception of a fine-tooth panel saw or a backsaw for bench work sometimes. As a fellow's interest and skill develop, he will find some favorites and one or two old types that do a certain thing well.

Good chisels are hard to buy over the counter now, though they are still made. Any hardware man who has his customers' interests at heart has, or can get, the industrial tool catalogues; some are still

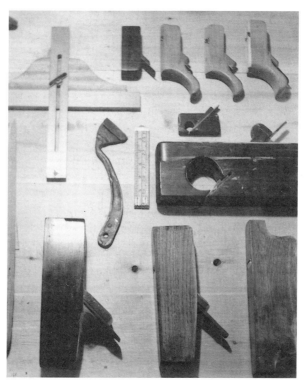

issued in the United States, and they extend the selection a store can offer. The "tang" chisel and gouge (I include the gouge here, for it's a kind of chisel) must be used for their intended purpose: pushing or paring by hand, or very occasional light tapping. Any cutting that is at all heavy requires the socket type, which comes in butt (short), firmer, and framing, or sometimes called mortise, patterns. I still prefer wooden handles; when one plays out, another can be made. I have not used many plastic handles, and those I have used seemed to bounce back, which is no good. There may be some good ones. Good steel is naturally the important thing, along with nice shape; you acquire an eye for this after awhile. A man does not need many chisels to do a lot of work: $\frac{1}{4}$, $\frac{1}{2}$, $1\frac{1}{4}$, and 2-inch firmer pattern chisels would be a fine assortment. Later you will acquire more. At times butts are handy, and some old semi-retired one with excellent steel will be fitted with a long push handle for paring. For much mortising, such as door making, the chisel must be the exact width of the mortise. A full collection of every kind of wood chisel is quite a pile, and you won't use most of them.

Gouges are worse. I don't know that I've seen all there is here: inside and outside bevels and dozens of radii. Start with a couple and build as needed. If you come across a wide, say 2-inch, very shallow-radius, inside-bevel gouge, grab it. You will always find use for it; in some sticky place other things don't work, but this tool probably will. And grinding can change a bevel; if you come on two alike, one can be changed.

There is that monster, the "slick," common to the old timers and much sought after now by coming boatbuilders, pro or amateur. Slicks can still be had new, but the price knocks a big chunk off one of those bills with U. S. Grant on it, so there is much searching for the old. Once in awhile someone I know finds one, which produces more excitement than finding an old Strad. The slick is a nice tool to

have, but you can get along without it. In my early days of ship carpentry, the slick was part of a pair of tools. The slick was a chisel about 3 inches wide with a length in proportion; in the pair, the larger tool, about 4 inches wide, was called a "slice." I know of one that was at least 5 inches wide, a huge tool with a standard, D-type shovel handle, offset and all, which made a lot of sense. Its original use was the shaping of very wide, long plank suited to building an oystering skiff of about 26 feet, in place of using the rip saw. I'm told a full set of slicks and slices was as follows, and I've seen only one supposedly full set: the lesser slick; the big slice; a Beavertail, which was a lesser slice ground to considerable radius though flat in section; and one lesser slick with a very slight gouge-like radius. For light boat work, a large, heavy, framing chisel, well ground back and with a long push handle, makes a good substitute for slicks and slices. I base this last statement on having both a slick and a slice and finding the big slice mostly too hearty for light boat work.

Planes, of course, you can't do without, though a big collection is not needed. Wooden planes are now much sought after. There has been some good advice on making your own in the *National Fisherman* and other earlier publications. Most chronic boatbuilders eventually make some. Good iron planes work just fine, but I prefer wooden ones for outboard joining. With the exception of many specialized planes, mostly small, I own just two: a smooth plane and a big jointer that is very old as iron planes go. Except rarely, I use only these few planes: the skew block, iron, smooth plane; occasionally the iron jointer; and various wooden ones with radius bottoms. One exception is spar work, where more of the wooden planes are used. A rabbet plane is needed, either wooden or iron. You can get along quite well at first—years in fact—without a great collection of planes; they seem to come with time.

Most anyone seems to be able to use a plane right off without ever having done it before, though practice develops the skill to a high degree. Using the plane at all angles in all positions is common to boat work and has little in common with bench planing. Some pointers to the new man may help him toward good and easy planing: I, for one, grind my irons to more bevel than some folks do; how much depends on the type of plane and what the steel will stand. I whet often, and always finish up on a leather; this is good practice on any cutting edge for wood. I set the cap iron no more than $\frac{1}{16}$th inch from the cutting edge. I make sure that the bed, either wood or iron, which the bit rests on, is clean and free of gum. For some work a very slight radius to the cutting edge is good; considerable radius will help if the plane is used as a "scrub," to hog off stock roughly.

Probably considered in the plane family are spokeshaves, sometimes just called shaves. They seem to come flat, round, or hollow, and once in awhile have some special shape. There are various patterns of shaves, some with fancy adjustments. I've found that if a new one does not seem to act quite right, rounding the back edge of the sole will usually pep things up.

Sometimes a tool not originally intended for boat work will turn out to be just the thing. A box scraper has found its place with me, and with some others who have seen it work and borrowed it. Its body is somewhat like a shave, only somewhat wider fore and aft, with a slight radius athwartships. The single handle is made for two-hand use and is on trunnions so it can be pushed or pulled. Its original use was for planing the marks off packing boxes for reuse. It cuts, rather than scrapes as its name implies. I find nothing handier for joining off the planking of staved, vee-bottom boats, especially in the forefoot and way aft in any tuck, which other tools reach only with difficulty. In other words, it's happy on an inside compound curve. This tool

works equally well across or with the grain. While not a tool that gives a high finish, it does quite well enough for following up with a Jitterbug sander. I highly recommend this tool to any boatbuilder.

I find that I now use hand-turned boring tools very little. Though there are times when nothing does quite as well, power has put hand drills into the background. I've never owned a first-class bit brace, just several old wrecks, each of different pattern. I keep them loaded with various screwdriver bits, which is now about the only way they are used, except sometimes for turning a reamer. A hand drill and an old breast drill are kept handy for the occasional odd hole, when it's not worth the trouble to rig the power drill. I do find small drills, and at times bigger ones, hard to come by in longer-than-usual lengths. Using various sizes of drill rod, and sometimes steel knitting needles for small stuff, drills can, with a bit of practice, be extended by brazing. I think ability in brazing is very valuable to cultivate; it makes you independent when it comes to long bits. I mention again that drills and bits, like other cutting tools, should be kept sharp.

We seem now to have all sorts of measuring devices. I was brought up on the two-foot-four folding rule, large steel tape, and "rule staffs," which are simply accurately cut pieces of wood of definite lengths. In some localities, builders seem to favor the three-foot wooden folding rule. Except in lofting, I seldom use the zigzag rule. The pocket steel tape, unknown or at least uncommon when I started, has eliminated some other measuring tools. The chalk line, plumb bob, and level have their places in boat work; in fact many—nay, most—of the usual hand tools do, and those made just for boat work are few.

The house carpenter's "bevel square" is a hateful thing for boat work. The body is way too thick, and the thumbscrew is always in the way, for most boat bevels are compound (they have to be taken two ways), and the above-mentioned parts "fetch up," so it's hard to get an accurate bevel. The ship-wright's bevel is thin of body and thin of blade. It works by friction, usually that of a rivet. Sometimes there is a blade at each end, like a penknife, so that two bevels can be picked up at once. It's not usually available store-bought, but is easily made. Give it a wooden or metal body, the thinner the better, and a metal blade. Some very big ones are all wood. The making is entirely up to a fellow's artistic ability, what stock he has, and what his experience dictates. I use several, from 2 inches to 2 feet long. This last is handy for lofting and setting transoms. A 6-inch bevel is the right size for much work. One trick to making a bevel is to be sure that the body sides and blade sides are parallel; otherwise an outside read-ing will not be the same inside. Also, the pivot ends must be an arc, and the rivet hole must be centered to it. Many simple tools such as this, just suited to boatbuilding, can be made, and many always were. As a person's skill develops and the need arises, many tools will just come naturally. Talk with oth-ers in the trade will turn up some snazzy ideas. I think each man tends to work out his own stuff, though it may be based very much on what others have worked out in the past.

Besides bevels, there are other tools particularly associated with boatbuilding and shipwrights. Some are of little or no use to the builder of small boats. Returning to pounding, the pin maul is needed when bolts and other fastenings are big enough. I find this tool of little use in boats under 30 feet long, and then only for setting a shore or wedge occasion-ally. And, if a maul is needed on a bigger craft, I find for most of today's work that it should be on the light side, say $4\frac{1}{2}$ pounds.

The lip adz is a kind of badge of the ship carpen-ter, and though power tools have replaced it in many operations, it's still the only tool for certain work. Contrary to first appearances, the adz is not at all a difficult tool to learn to use. Having trained a num-ber of men in its use, I find they "catch on" in an hour or so, though the first day sees little improve-ment in ability. The second day starts differently right off, and there is considerable confidence. On the third day, much useful work is produced, though the effort is tiring. After a week or ten days, the user becomes quite hardened and relaxed, and that's it; you have a useful dubber. Conditioning a brand-new adz takes some work and know-how; there is usually much filing, mostly on the back of the blade, and the lips need attention. The bevel of the cutting edge nearly always needs alteration. Hanging the adz, or fitting the handle, is most important. Often the stock handle, if any, is a bit too long. Sometimes a handle has to bc made, usually borrowing some old-timer's pattern. Some like 'em thick, others thin, and with more or less crook. Even the experts argue about these points, and the actual hanging, or pitch of the bit, is even more controversial. The angle is adjusted by a wedge in the head, or eye. Being a $\frac{3}{4}$-inch man myself, I go at it this way: Assuming I'm satisfied with the handle and its length, I put it in the eye. Taking a measure with a tape from eye to handle end, I sweep the tape from eye to cutting edge, keep-ing the tape fixed at the handle end. There should be $\frac{3}{4}$ of an inch less measure from the cutting edge than from the eye, the bit hanging down toward the handle. Some like $\frac{5}{8}$ inch, some as much as $\frac{7}{8}$ inch. I've known some pros who used only $\frac{1}{2}$ inch. Though I'm not just sure, I think a man's build, the particular shape of the adz head, the length of handle preferred, and maybe some unknown things, all have bearing on a happy "hang." It's said a new adz improves with use; the steel gets better with repeated blows—at least some of us think so—and much tin-kering with the cutting edge finally gets it "right." A small, one-hand adz is useful in tight places. A Portagee adz is liked by many, with its strange wooden handle. Or an old-time cooper's adz does well, and a little searching often turns one up. There is also the hollow, or sternpost, adz, sometimes called the canoe adz.

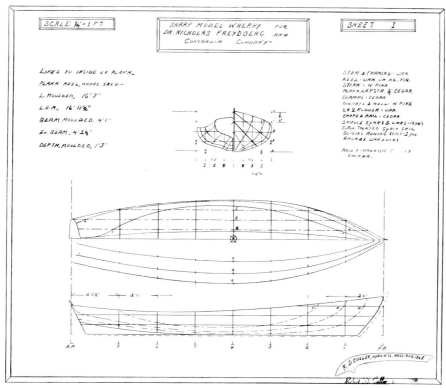

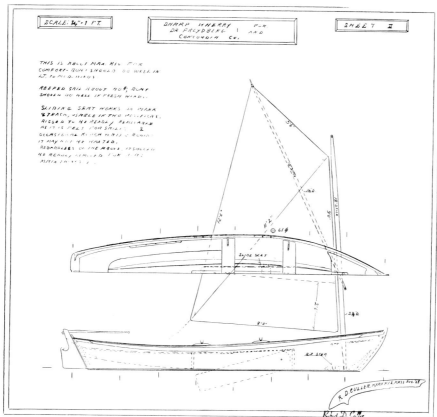

Pete designed and built the 17' sharp wherry in his Hyannis shop for his friend and patron Dr. Nicholas Freydberg. Later, Pete built a copy for John West of North Haven, Maine, which was eventually donated for use as a tender on the S/V Westward. Pete liked this design so much that when the boat became available he bought it back from the Westward group and fitted it with a larger spritsail and lugsail. He found that this design was a very good rowboat and an excellent sailer that would exceed six knots on a beam reach. (© Mystic Seaport, Ships Plans Collection, Mystic, CT)

55

The ship carpenter's broad axe is now seldom seen in use, for, like so many of these tools, the power tools have replaced it. It's handy for some work though, or when some heavy machine is not available.

Long augers are now generally on the electrician or bell hanger's pattern, though for ease of boring and accurate holes, the barefoot ship auger (with no starting worm) is by far the best. This last can now be had with shanks suited to power drive. There never seem to be enough bits and augers around of all the different lengths, types, and sizes required. As mentioned, if a man will learn to splice long shanks onto bits, he can be very independent, and save much cash outlay. Also, he suddenly seems to have a lot of friends interested in borrowing. The man in the village who has all the long augers is often sought out!

There are never enough C clamps; own all you can if you are doing any serious boatbuilding. I find for most uses the kind with a sliding upper part, sometimes known as the German pattern, is just fine. A large collection of clamps for all purposes costs quite a lot, but you can readily make some of the special ones for limited use. An example would be lapstrake clamps, either operating by wedge or wooden cam, or by bolts and wing nuts. These usually can't be bought in any case. Most boatbuilding books show some version of them. Wood and metal sliding C clamps can be bought, but they are not difficult to make. They work by cam action and so have limited take-up and therefore limited use. The cabinet or Jorgensen clamp I find to be of little use in boat work, though it's nice to have some around when you run out of C clamps. Bar clamps are needed at times; the kind that fits onto a pipe is not expensive and has the advantage that it can be used on various lengths of pipe. I keep some very short lengths of pipe around, so that when struck with the usual sudden shortage of C clamps, bar clamps can pinch hit. A shot of chain and some wedges are most

handy at times for big work, and, along with this chain, an ordinary trucker's load binder can do a lot of useful work on big timbers. The shipwright's tools for big craft were fairly few, and many were based on using wedges, shores, iron dogs, wrain staves, loggers, and other simple gear.

I have played down large numbers of hand tools as necessary to boatbuilding. The right tools, and good ones, kept sharp, are all that is needed. If you like to collect tools and enjoy restoring and occasionally using them, that is to me a separate thing. I do this myself. I have some for which few people know the use, and one I don't know what to do with myself. Doing many kinds of work, I may use a few of these oddballs more than some collectors.

I've mentioned power tools taking over the functions of many of the old shipwright's and boatbuilder's tools. Much is made of power tools, and advertising keeps them in the forefront. Some folks think they can't possibly build a kit pram without a lot of power tools. Certainly a few power tools have taken the pure drudgery out of many phases of boatbuilding. For all of this, it seems to take just as long as it ever did to build a boat, often even more time, for boats are becoming more complicated. Your back seems to ache just as much as in the past. It used to be said that a man who dubbed with the adz and hewed with the axe all his life as a specialized trade, and many did, "was all broken up" at an early age, usually something past 70. Things are easier now. Hand-held power tools are the thing these days, and I find that, as with straight hand tools, there need not be many, if they are the right ones, big enough for the job, and of good quality—meaning industrial grade, which makes them expensive.

Except in cutting large, thin sheets of stuff, I find little use for the hand jig, or saber saw. That's just one man's opinion; most builders won't agree. However many electric drills you intend to own, have one big enough so that the smaller ones won't have to attempt work that is too much for them.

There is a lot to be said for variable speed drills for some work. Boat work generally does not require drills that turn very fast. Assuming it's in good shape, any electric tool that tends to overheat is either being overworked, or the local voltage is too low, or the extension cord, if any, is too light.

The hand electric saw has radically changed the getting out of planking as I used to know it, and has changed some other operations too. After the plank was spiled and laid off on the stock, it was lugged to the bandsaw and cut out, and then lugged to the bench for jointing. On thick work, the bevels were done on the saw too, for it was a tilthead, or ship saw. Nowadays, much of getting out the plank is done right where the stock lies, with the electric saw, and often the jointing is by power too, of which more later. A good electric saw can be accurate if well built and if the operator is practiced. The saw can be moved from place to place and save much jacking about of heavy stock. I consider it a most useful tool, especially for the lone workman. Getting stock of any size through a bandsaw by yourself, even with good rollers, is a tiresome business, with possibly more risk than with the use of the electric saw. The big reciprocating hand electric saws have uses, mostly for alterations in craft already built. I've found little or no use for them in new work.

The electric hand plane, or industrial jointer, is a wonderful tool that is little known to amateurs, though familiar to pros. I'm not impressed by brand names usually, but for electric hand planes, I think Skil is the best. This tool costs big money but it is worth it to any man building a boat bigger than a small, open craft. While not exactly a finishing tool, it can be worked pretty fine with practice. When it comes to the really hard planing, hogging down, and rough fairing, this tool does it all in minutes without fuss and puts the adz into the background. With a second set of knives ground to radius, the electric hand plane makes short work of backing out plank. It's easy to keep sharp using the jigs supplied with it and cares little for direction of grain or tough knots. It is even more impressive for spar making, having upset many of the time-honored methods. For most spars of fewer than 6 inches, it does the whole job without the use of other tools, except in the final finishing. Even with bigger sticks, this tool still can do most of the work. It sizes big timber, too big sometimes to pass through a stationary machine, and seems to do all the things that were at one time just plain hard work. I've outboard joined the wale strakes of a 30-ton schooner with an electric hand plane, to the point where they were ready for sanding. The tool is heavy and should be; using it vertically, about a half day is enough.

A word of warning: all power tools obviously can be dangerous. The electric hand plane is heavy, and it tends to coast after the switch is off. You tend to want to set it down quickly; have a block of wood handy to set the nose on to keep the still-moving blades from digging into something. Using it vertically, you tend to drop it down to arm's length to rest, knives still turning though the power is off for the moment. This operation has snagged many a pants leg, or worse. Once this danger is understood, I don't think the hand plane is any more risky than other power tools. Most people realize, for example, that the electric saw has kickback possibilities and that its protective guards sometimes hang up. Or, you can "hang" an electric drill and get terribly wound up. Clamps can fly off under repeated thumping somewhere in the boat. In other words, any risks should be studied and guarded against. Don't hurry.

Sanding machines are plentiful now, as is good paper to go with them. These tools seem well understood. In the day of "flint paper," we did not do so much sanding, relying on sharp planes and scrapers. For small boats, a Jitterbug sander does fine, though as boat size increases, a belt job comes in handy. Disks I seldom use except for metal work, such as hogging down stem bands, rudder fittings, and so forth.

There are of course many other specialized hand power tools, but I find those mentioned are the only ones really needed. If you build one small boat only occasionally, the lower priced power tools will do for awhile, but I think in the end the very best should be bought. Own one or two really good power tools instead of many junky ones. Even the best sometimes gives out, for fairly small motors are doing pretty big work. I never try to stall a tool; slack up and let her turn, for she is fan cooled. Sharp tools cut freely. I suggest anyone owning power tools for the first time learns the art of keeping them sharp. A dull power tool fights back and is a high risk; besides, you become independent of that shop up the street that is not open on Saturdays! These tools like a little pampering at times. Switches get balky, cords fray, and plugs get bent. Look after them. A bit of wax, tallow, or such on the base makes her push steadily. A gummy blade or knife is always unhappy. If you do any building at all, there will come a time when you will nick a cord, or, as has happened, cut it right off! Most of these tools take a tumble or two sometime in their lives; it's not good for them, so try to guard against falls. I notice more and more that the hired help in professional shops doesn't have much regard for nice machines. Lunch time, quittin' time, pay day. Some say it's The Times. The better the mechanic, the more respect he has for tools.

The principle of economy also applies to the bigger, fixed-position tools; you can get power-tool happy and have too many with too much money tied up in them, and you may find that only a few are worthwhile. First you must consider the size of your power line into the shop. It's a nice idea to own a big, powerful wood-working machine, but can your line take it? Perhaps it is worth running in bigger voltage—sometimes it is, depending on many things. I find that when using 110 volts you are limited to about $\frac{1}{2}$-h.p. motors, which, for many small shops and home builders, is the usual thing. More

can be done with 220 volts, and probably somewhat cheaper. It's fine to have a really big production planer, say 6 inches by 30 inches, but you'll find it will require a motor of such size as to require 440 volts. Sometimes what you think is a bargain is a big but old machine with a high cost of moving to your site. It probably will require more power than your line can handle, and, if it's a jointer or planer, it may be an old "square header," which is outlawed insurance-wise in any shops hiring men and is no good for the loner.

It's sometimes said that the table saw is the basic machine for wood working; maybe so for a cabinet shop, but definitely not for boat work. It has its place in cabin joinery and some straight ripping, but after building a boat or two, you will find the table saw does not get as much use as you thought it would, assuming you have the boatbuilder's friend, the bandsaw. I say own a table saw if you can, but not at the expense of more useful tools. I have no particular choice on these saws—tilt blade, tilt table, micro adjusting fence, and what not. They all work quite well enough for boatbuilding if they are stout and if the controls work with reasonable ease.

The bandsaw you can't do without; it will do more than any other machine: rip, crosscut at all angles, and dozens of other things. Its ability to butt cut and back out is constantly used. I suggest owning as large a machine as you think your power can handle, and of the best industrial grade. Put money into your bandsaw, even if you must do without other machines. A home builder can do much work with a 12-inch machine; 14 inches is better, and 16- to 20-inch saws can face up to pretty big work if used with care. These machines all have the tilt table for bevels, which can be unhandy for some big beveling. Only big yards can support the true ship saw, which has the tilting head with the table remaining level, so heavy work does not tend to slide off.

Though it will probably be of no real interest to those building small or moderate sized craft, it's nice to know how these big ship saws work. They are usually 48 inches in the wheels and massive in construction, for wood-working machines need to be rigid. The head usually tilts to 45 degrees, operated by a curved rack and pinion, and the table is slotted to allow the blade to clear as the head tilts. The heavy stock sits on pairs of rollers, at each end of the table and farther away to take the weight along the timber's length. The table rollers can be fitted with hand cranks to take the strain off the sawyer and provide a steady feed. All the rollers are "traverse," that is, they can slew sideways in making a turn or curved cut and pivot the stock at the blade. They also allow the stock to move sideways as the bevel changes. The point is, these saws cut changing bevels, the usual thing in a sawn-frame vessel, as a matter of course. There is another model, in which both wheels swing so that the saw blade pivots around the cutting point. This rig usually tilts 45 degrees both ways, so the stock does not have to be reversed. This is the Rolls Royce of ship saws. The mechanism that keeps the drive belts following the wheels as they move is wonderful to behold.

Now let's come back down out of the clouds to more practical saws for small shops. Good maintenance, sharp blades, and occasional cleaning make any well-built bandsaw give good service. For the amount of work a bandsaw does, it takes modest power, partly because it is a fairly slow-speed machine. As with all power tools, the use of a bandsaw is attended with some risk, though for the amount it's used—more than any other machine in the shop—there seem to be few accidents, and these mostly from cutting oddball stock. When cutting off round stock, or anything that can twist or roll, vee or similar blocks should support the stock. When cutting a short piece with overhang, such as cutting the side bevel on a wooden cleat, the overhang should be supported, usually by inserting the chunk that was cut out. Take your time and use common

sense. If you have much odd work, it will pay to make a supporting jig. I've never yet seen a bandsaw blade break and do any harm. Way back, we used to work big ship saws entirely unguarded. There were no insurance inspectors as there was no insurance. An old-time sawyer explained it this way: The instant the blade breaks, it ceases to turn; it can lash, but not cut. He said he "had one wrapped around his neck many a time." He also had a thumb missing. The way these machines are shielded now, I see no risk at all, unless the operator makes a mistake.

In my area at least, tools of any kind are sought after, power tools in particular. Yet by keeping an ear to the ground and looking about, you may be able to pick up a nice machine secondhand, perhaps when some fellow retires or goes out of business. Personally, I prefer some of the older machines, made before die casting of "pot metal," steel stampings, and other lightweight stuff became prevalent. I've never yet seen any reason to build a stationary wood-working machine light, except to sell it cheap. My present bandsaw is a monument to cast iron, is at least forty years old, and shows no wear. It seems capable of going on forever. I wondered about the motor. Not knowing much about electric motors but suspecting some things, I consulted a motor electrician. He put it thus: It's a matter of heat and cost. A motor of a certain horsepower can be made of most any size and be designed to run at several speeds. In practice, there are motors designed for intermittent use, light duty, standard performance, and continuous heavy duty. The windings for these motors vary for the use. For a motor of a given horsepower to last well, it should be big (which means expensive) and should be designed for its use. Then it will run cool. After tutoring, which I still don't fully understand, I have been using, as much as possible, repulsion induction motors that are large for their power. The starting voltage is low, they do much work without heating, and they need very little

Pete taking in the scene aboard his 17' sharp wherry Seaman's Friend. *On this day he had been using the lugsail, which can be seen furled and lying in the bow. This particular boat was built for John West; today it is owned by Joe Youcha of Alexandria, Virginia, who teaches boatbuilding to inner-city youth.*

get along with a small jointer, but of course you always wish it were bigger. Large yards often have a whopper with 16-inch knives and an 8- or 9-foot table. A 6-inch jointer will do in most cases, or even a 4-incher, though this last is a bit small. This is a dangerous machine and should be treated as such. When dull, it's doubly dangerous. Here again, if you have a choice, take a heavily built machine. I've known men who worked for years with this tool without realizing it can rabbet to a limited degree. The jointer can also be very handy for some joiner work, in some cases more so than the table saw.

A shaper is even more dangerous, and I think most builders of small craft can get along quite well without it. Except for odd stuff and curved work, I think a moulding head on a table saw is far safer than a shaper and keeps an often idle machine in more employment. I seem to favor the very heavy flywheel-like moulding head.

Every boatbuilder wants a planer, even the backyarder. Alas, this is an expensive machine and takes much power. The more heavily built, the better, for this tool takes considerable strain. Unless you are well heeled and have plenty of room and power, forget the planer. Some professional builders with small shops find it cheaper to farm out the heavy dressing and make do with a small, hand-fed machine for occasional light stock, or else use a hand plane. Of course this is not a happy and independent situation. A really big planer that is capable of producing requires a sawdust blower, ducts, and a big bin, or else you spend much time shoveling away mounds of shavings. If a fellow has the voltage, space, and money, the little 12-inch finishing planer will do a wonderful job, though it's still best to have the mill do the rough dressing. Most mills are equipped for this. I think those who have not actually worked around planers of all sizes may not realize just how big a machine is needed to work heavy stock with any degree of rapidity.

service, even in what's naturally a dusty business. I think many folks now consider these motors old-fashioned, with their heavy copper starting commutators and their fully-wound armatures. Maybe so, but it seems to me my adviser is right. If anybody has a heavy, old "R. I." he wants to get rid of, let me know; I have a fine 3400 high-speed job that always has sawdust indigestion.

I find a power jointer more useful than a table saw; at least I seem to use it much more. You can

Working a small machine on rough-sawn stock, often with overly thick spots produced by a small saw mill, can be a very tedious business. You make pass after pass, each making a light cut, for that's all the rig will take, and there is much jacking around of stock. Besides, the small feed rolls cannot cope with the heavy stuff. It's better to have the work done at a mill and save a little machine for its intended use, finish work.

There is another angle here: assuming you can find a buy on a small planer but your power line won't take it, you can run the planer, and it only, with a gasoline engine, saving up enough dressing work to make it worthwhile to fire up the engine. This can be a bothersome chore in winter when the machine has been idle for awhile. Here, a big air-cooled engine might be best, with no water problems and necessity for draining in cold weather. Even so, any gas engine that has been asleep awhile in winter can be fussy to start. A gas engine seems to take about twice as much rated power as an electric motor to run the same machine. A governor is needed on a gas engine; it must turn at close to its rated speed; overload it and it stalls.

A wood-turning lathe is handy at times for belaying pins, stanchions, bull's eyes, and so forth, but you can well do without it. Building a wood lathe is not a difficult thing if it's found one is needed; the few metal parts are not difficult to come by, and the rest is made of timber. The wood-working lathe is a nonprecision machine, unlike the metal lathe. Nowadays, the idea of making such a tool might dismay many people, yet in the past many yards had lathes built without benefit of machine supply houses. In fact, many a small lathe was built at sea in whalers and other ships, some in the pursuit of hobbies. One old-time sea captain, who later gained fame as a single-hander, built his own bandsaw at sea and later took it ashore and used it in the building of a small steamer, if the reports about this are correct.

There are several other wood-working machines, mostly specialized, or suited to big mills, or in some cases, to very big yards. They are of no use to the kind of boatbuilding we discuss here. I say again, have no more than earn their keep, and have good ones if possible. They all take maintenance, power to run, and must, for your own good and theirs, be kept sharp. A dull tool of any kind has no place in boat work. Good fits, reasonable speed in getting things done, and safety, all dictate sharp tools.

In this age of the motorization of everything, including toothbrushes, we tend to lose sight of some of the basics. Boatbuilding tools should not be motorized gadgets. If a power tool will save a lot of time, by all means use it. Hand tools certainly still have their place. What is needed is a basic assortment of high-quality hand and power tools. Really good tools always have high resale value.

Perhaps the most basic principle of acquiring and using tools is simply not to expect a tool to do a job it was never intended for. When you rationalize this principle away in a moment of haste, you generally regret it. As one of my longtime friends in boating has pointed out many times, "A lightweight, high-speed steam roller just can't do the job!"

FLAT BOTTOMS

I have mentioned choosing a type of boat appropriate to the intended use several times, and also the importance of working within your abilities. Hence, we start with the simplest form, the flat-bottomed craft. Many people do not understand flat ones and condemn them. Probably the aversion to them comes from their looks; they can be just plain ugly, but need not be so. Flat-bottomed boats have been with us for a long time; there must be good reasons for the durability of the type.

It's been said by others that a flat-bottomed skiff is easy to build but hard to design. This seems to be mostly because in the process of designing one, there are only three important lines to work with, which severely limits what a designer can do. Over the years and through the efforts of many seamen and builders, certain limits and rules have been worked out. They are not very scientific, but they work. If these rules are not violated too much in seeking the impossible, a good workable craft results, and she will be good looking, too, for her kind.

Howard Chapelle's book, *American Small Sailing Craft*, spells out in detail what makes a good flat-bottomed boat. I cannot hope to improve on his

pointers, but to try to drive home the worth of the flat-bottomed boat, and how she should be shaped, will repeat in my own way what the experts of the past have worked out by trial and error.

Whether for rowing, or sailing, or power, the flat-bottomed skiff should not be too wide. She can, under most circumstances in fact, be rather long and slim. The freeboard should be rather low, by today's standards. A wide, high craft becomes unmanageable except in the lightest weather. She must not sit deep in the water when not loaded. The idea, now popular, that "a boat must be high, wide, and deep, so she will be safe" is particularly bad in flat-bottomed craft. It's her shape that makes a boat able, not the height of her sides or vast initial stability. Some flare to the sides is always good; for certain uses, very great flare makes sense. I have heard many excuses for not using good flare in recent years, and the fact that one of the ways of getting an able and good looking design is by the use of flare makes these excuses hard to understand. A boat without flare is like a ship painter's pontoon, and about as handy underway. If the advantages of flare are pointed out, the reply may be, "Plenty of power will take care of things," which it does not.

Most of the bad design in flat-bottomed boats seems to stem from trying to get too much out of a simple, and in many ways limited, boat: usually headroom and capacity on a short length. It now seems the accepted fact that a short boat is a cheap boat, rather than the real truth that displacement, complicated construction and fittings, and much power to drive an ill-shaped hull, whether by oars, sail, or motor, are the big cost makers. Some pros do boats of bad design against their better judgment; they may need the work, and the client is adamant. I've done it myself, and always say never again. A handsome craft is often relatively easy to build, and her shape is apt to make her quite durable.

Over the years, the method of building flat-bottomed boats has become more or less standardized, with local variations to suit exact types and available materials. Lately, there have been attempts to change the methods, often to suit new materials. Yet most troubles with recent craft have been caused by not building them the way they used to be built, probably through not understanding why it was done that way. Flat-bottomed craft don't take kindly to Gilding the Lily. Honest, careful workmanship in the tradition of these boats is all that's required, along with a good design. Beyond this, you simply run into complications for no good reason.

The cross-planked bottom is now frowned on as being crude, as much from misunderstanding of just how it works and how it is built as anything else. If a cross-planked bottom is properly done, you never have chine troubles with it, as there is little 'thwartship pressure to force off the chines. Moreover, its swelling, being mostly fore and aft, is a help in preventing a boat's natural tendency to hog. Of two flat-bottomed craft of about the same model, one cross-planked and the other fore-and-aft planked with bottom framing, the cross-planked boat is apt to be the stiffer hull. Possibly the bottom bucking the hogging tendency has a lot to do with it.

A pretty young lass rowing the 13'6" Good Little Skiff Waterwings. (John Burke)

She is less cluttered in the bottom too, and she is lighter, for there are no frames. While fore-and-aft bottom plank is standard in dories and works well, it's been my observation that a very wide bottom planked by this method often pushes open at the chine, be it the dory style with the bottom landing inside the side plank, or the skiff style with the bottom lapping the sides. A dory's bottom, particularly on a Swampscott dory, is a rather small part of her whole structure, which minimizes any disadvantage of fore-and-aft planking.

Cross plank is laid in three ways. There is ordinary "tight-lay" with no caulking, and with wicking or marline on the side plank, clear of the chine, for the bottom plank to land on; I prefer marline of a good grade and even lay. There is totally caulked bottom and chines, using outgauge as for any caulked plank; this method may be best if the craft is hauled out of the water much. And there is the splined bottom for special use, say for a boat that is mostly on shore and is afloat only for short periods. This last, though not much used, is quite easy to make using the standard power table saw. A bottom can be built somewhat lighter using splines.

In some places and with certain stock, the tight-lay bottom is not always driven up to show a tight joint, but some opening is left for swelling. Some woods swell very much. Usually, in leaving this swelling space, some sort of gauge is used. One old way was to use the thin, brass blade of a ship carpenter's bevel. The back of a thin hand saw, without taper, was also much used. Nowadays, a thin piece of sheet metal, without bumps or wrinkles, works just fine. How much do you allow for each kind of wood? I really don't know. Assuming the wood is reasonably dry, Maryland loblolly pine seems to take kindly to the thin saw back. Local cedar I set right up, and so far, as long as the planks are less than six inches wide, have never had a bottom coper; that is, bulge the plank and leak at the chine. Our local cedar is soft and compresses a lot. Southern

cedar is harder and slower to "make up." Cypress, which we don't see much of now, swells a lot and shrinks accordingly. At one time, lots of skiffs were built of cypress; it's very durable, even though it takes up a lot of water. At the end of the season, some of the old boats were very "sobbed" and were a chore to haul up, though if of good model the extra weight affected their rowing very little. Whether using the tight-lay, caulked, or splined method, it's essential that the plank edges be joined true, without humps or hollows, otherwise the bottom often won't make up tight. This is no chore with a properly set power joiner and not much more so with a hand jointer plane. On a caulked seam, either tool will make the outgauge also.

Flat-bottomed boats should always use a chine timber; oak is best if it can be had, though other wood that holds fastenings and bends reasonably well will do. Sometimes it must do; you build with what is available. Usually these bottoms are nailed. This is really the place for boatnails, though ring nails can be used, and bronze at that, if you want to pay for it. There's really no point in bronze, as skiffs, some of very large size, have been boatnailed and lasted for years and years. The fastenings should, of course, be bored for, and on a tight-lay bottom should be raked, so as to jam one plank against the next. If the boat has a good flare, which rakes the nails yet another way, her bottom cannot be taken off without destroying it. With a hardwood keel plank, nicely tapered of course, and possibly with a couple of parallel, tapered skids, this construction makes a very tough bottom. The skids, as well as the keel plank, should be hardwood, either screwed from inside out, or clinched if you see fit. Skids or chafing strips should *never* be bent around the bottom of the chine, as is so often seen. Put on that way, they make a great oblong hoop in the water, and cause the craft to be very dull, under oars, sail, or power. Usually flat-bottomed craft have some sort of skeg to help directional stability.

In rare cases, two parallel skegs are used, and once in awhile a lesser bow skeg or foregripe is added.

Most flat-bottomed boats are built with rather heavy side planks, set on edge and caulked, unless one wide plank is available. A pair of wide skiff planks, cut out near the center of a big pine or cypress tree wide enough so each will make a complete side, is seldom seen today. My own preference, unless the boat is some sort of heavy work scow, is to use rather light plank, say $1/2$-inch for a 16-foot boat, and lap the planks, using two, three, or sometimes more planks if the craft is large. I think lapped sides are strong, light, and good looking in a nice model boat. You can use the full lap, dory lap, or some variation, though I prefer the full lap. This requires clinching, and dory nails can be used if available. For the small amount of metal required, I prefer to use copper cut nails. I see little point in using copper rivets, as clinched cut nails seem, from much experience with them, to do just as well in these boats and are simpler for one man to handle. Lapstrake planking is now much misunderstood. Many think lapping is a waste of time in flatty-type boats. I think it makes a superior and lasting skiff.

Along this line, it's now thought that flat-bottomed boats are best built of plywood. I'm sure a good one can be built, but most of the plywood skiffs you see are rather limber even when new, and tend to have chine troubles. The "engineering" is often poor, even though the material and fits may be fine. The point is that plywood requires far more framing to produce a good boat than most people suppose. The lavish use of glue and bedding compounds cannot overcome the lack of framing for long. I notice that so many of these craft bell and pant in the bottom, and often to some extent in the sides. Many transoms flex also, especially with an outboard motor, and most plywood skiffs seem to be built for outboards. Rudders and even centerboards are seen that flex like cardboard. Such plywood skiffs needlessly give the flat-bottomed boat a bad name.

For many uses, nothing does quite so well as the flat bottom, cost and ease of building aside. Handiness on the beach, ease of hauling up with plank and rollers, even with considerable size and weight, and shoal draft often overshadow other needs. With proper design, a flat-bottomed skiff can row extremely well, not quite as well as more complicated models, but outstandingly compared to most rowing craft accepted nowadays. For best results, you want a rather long, narrow bottom, and otherwise fine lines, and not unduly heavy construction. I mention weight again, for you should keep in mind that the type is heavier than, say, a round-bottomed craft of similar capacity. In designing for good pulling under oars, some care and planning is necessary. Use poor oars of the wrong length, and the boat already has a strike against her.

These skiffs can be very good sailers too; they are usually useful boats. If you design for it, a very fast boat is possible. Most flat-bottomed craft, however, are not good drifters in very light airs, though some are better than others. A Swampscott dory, properly rigged, largely overcomes this weakness; probably the round sides and very narrow bottom help. This lack of ability in very light airs has been one of the reasons for designing away from the true flat bottom by using some deadrise or an arc bottom, of which more later.

A true flatty can be designed that both rows and sails well, but trying to design for rowing, sailing, *and* power with good results all around just does not seem to work out. The run is apt to be too flat for good rowing or sailing, or not flat enough for good results under power. The flat-bottomed boat that is designed for power, however, takes very kindly to both inboard and outboard motors, within certain limits. Properly shaped, these flatties can be very fast, especially with outboard motors, and, let's face it, if really fast they can hammer and pound fearfully. Yet for sheltered waters and with some common sense in handling, they can be most satisfactory.

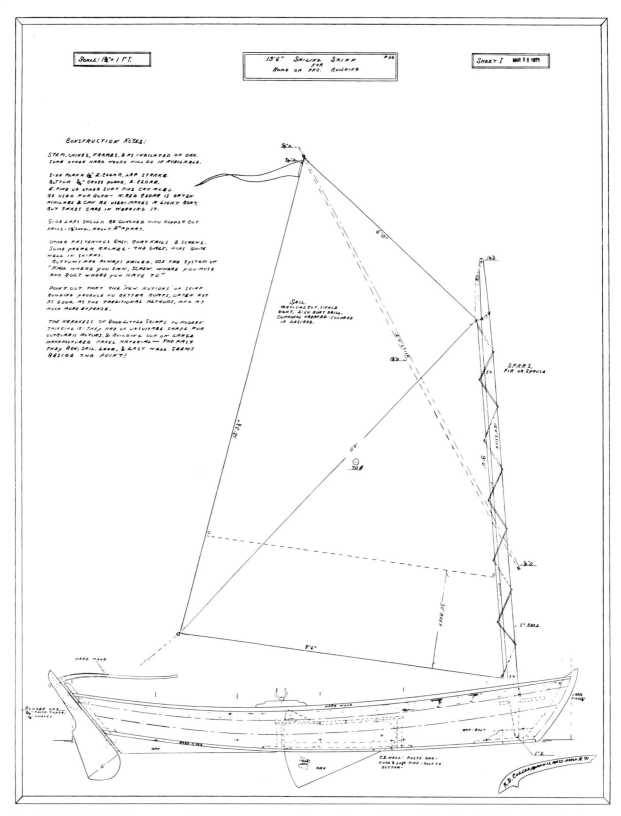

The 13'6" Good Little Skiff was a concept begun as an attempt to supply a need for a useful, accessible, and good-looking skiff for "messing about" on the water. The boat has been built countless times and is a successful design. (© Mystic Seaport, Ships Plans Collection, Mystic, CT)

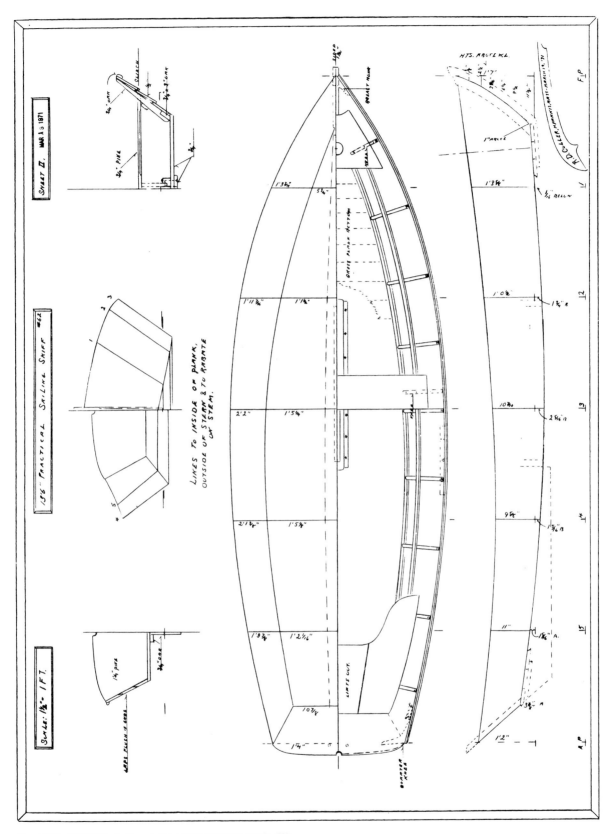

Good Little Skiff (© Mystic Seaport, Ships Plans Collection, Mystic, CT)

While the care and maintenance of flat-bottomed boats is simple and most of it needs no dwelling on, there are some points that seem to have been forgotten. The inside bottom of flatty skiffs is usually painted, and I doubt that the paint does much good. The bottom gets lots of wear and tear with people tramping on sand and shells, so the paint does not last, looks messy, and has a tendency to scale off. It's better for the wood to treat it with boiled oil and turps, with a bit of pine tar added. The mixture drives into dry wood; it's all the better if it's put on hot. If put on a new boat, this stuff can, with proper application, fully penetrate the bottom. It turns dark in time but never looks really messy and is easy to keep. Once the bottom is thoroughly soaked, an annual treatment is very easy and cheap.

This oil treatment, once standard in the bottoms of log canoes and open bateaux on the Chesapeake, helps very much in slowing the shrinking to which these cross-plank bottoms are prone when hauled out for long periods. This drying out, largely preventable, has been the cause of much condemnation of this kind of construction. Of course, there are some folks looking for the totally maintenance-free boat. Such things are said to be around, and my observations of them have been: You acquire one, run it to death, and get another, meanwhile putting up with a production craft that fills the bill somewhat but is intended to suit all people and all places and all conditions, and so suits none really well. And for some reason, few such craft can be called very good-looking. If this is what boating means to many people, so be it, but they are missing out on much that makes just messing around in boats worthwhile.

The annual drying out is not nearly as bad as it seems and can, as said, be prevented to a great extent. Some woods tend to dry out more than others, but with a little help, swell tight again quite readily. Often a new owner will spoil his bottom right off the second season; he has an uncontrollable

urge to stuff the dried-out seams full of something. He does not stop to think that if it was once tight, it will swell up again, which it does against his stuffing, often forcing the plank off. By now he's fussing at the builder, who explains it all again and usually points out, "Now you have learned it the hard way."

Assuming laying a skiff up for the winter, she goes in a barn, shed, or garage—never in a heated cellar or any heated building. If the building has a dirt floor, so much the better. Block up the boat or set her on horses, never upside down except when bottom work is going on. Be sure the craft is clean, having been well washed inside and out with fresh water and a strong soogy and then well rinsed. She will dry off very nicely once the salt is removed. A dust cover can be put over her, especially if birds use the shed too. Sometime in the middle of winter, a charge of oil and turps can be applied to the bottom inside, put on very hot with lots of turps, as it will be going on chilly wood. Assuming the bottom outside is clean, a brushing, sanding, or both, if needed, and a thin coat of copper paint at this time are also good. Come spring, you will find there has been little or no drying out, that is, if you fit out fairly early. If you wait till the March winds have had their go, there will be some drying out, but nothing some water won't cure after she's all painted. If you store outdoors, still keep her upright and use a tight tarp with ridgepole and stay pieces, and with ventilated ends. March winds get in more work on a boat stored outside, so the winter treatment, weather allowing, is a big help.

As to swelling up a craft that needs it, remember that warm water swells wood much faster than does cold water. Water at near freezing temperature has little swelling ability. Most of us now have hoses, though lugging some water, if done right, is not much of a chore. Old clean rags, sacks, canvas, or just plain worn-out long-johns should be spread on the bottom to help the water work and keep it in the ends. Don't expect to hurry it. There can be a not

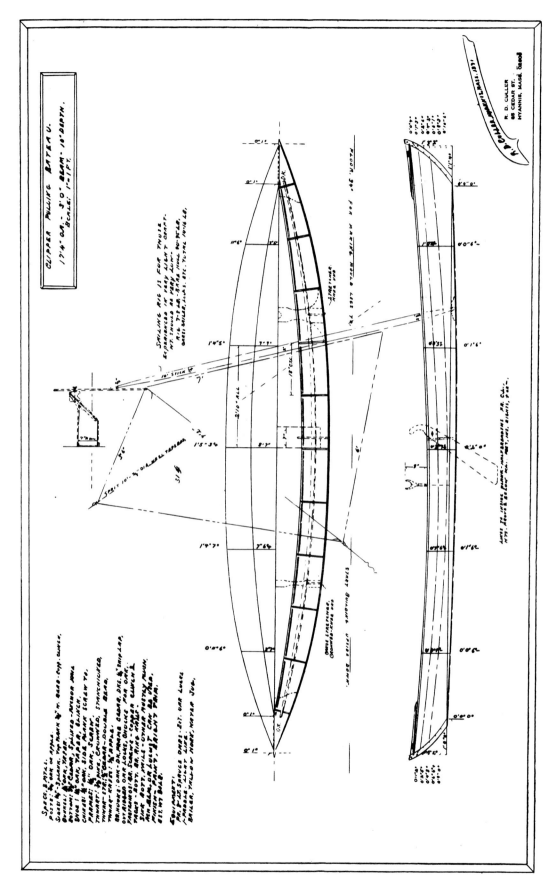

Pete Culler had been pondering the rowing qualities of the bateau when in 1971 he took his first week's vacation in memory and built the 17' Otter. She is a simple, yet elegantly refined craft that moves through the water with a slipperiness that does her namesake proud. The boat is about as close as you can get to a racing shell with a traditional design. She was designed to be used with Pete's "sand dolly," and a photo of them together can be found on page 291. (© Mystic Seaport, Ships Plans Collection, Mystic, CT)

Pete designed and built this 18'8" Swampscott dory for Capt. Charles Sayle. The design grew from discussions between the two men on dories, including Pete's dory Dancing Feather *and the dories that Capt. Sayle remembered from the 1920s, when he served aboard fishing schooners out of Gloucester, Massachusetts. This photo was taken on Nantucket, where Pete often called while chartering* Spray, *and where a visit to Capt. Charley and his wife Mickey was always on the agenda.* (John Burke)

uncommon disaster; some guy does all the above, turns the hose on full as it seems the water runs right through her, then rushes off to work. Some woods have a way of going along for a spell and then taking up rather quickly. The day turns warm, the sun beats down, and about three p.m., she takes up considerably. The blasting hose fills her right up, breaks the horses down, and the craft tumbles, often hurting herself with maybe a ton of water in her.

Another way some folks swell a boat is to put her in and let the sea do it, which in some ways is fine. If she's in shoal water and takes the bottom at low tide, chances are she'll fill with both water and sand. Then she "comes together" on a mess in her seams. Three or four seasons of this, and she refuses to make up. She needs a new bottom; the seams are sand-hollowed. Seams full of sand eventually wear

hollow due to the slight working of the craft, to a point where they will never be tight. If the boat is re-bottomed, the builder will end up with about a half a bushel of sand on his shop floor. Some people avoid the sand problems by anchoring the skiff in deep water and letting her fill right up, certainly a better practice, but with some drawbacks. If the boat is in an exposed location, she could wash the sternsheets or foredeck out from the constant surging of considerable weight of water. And with the present-day dirty harbors in many places, the boat can be plastered with gunk and oil inside and out. The proper way is certainly the easy way in the end.

My method for my Swampscott dory, based on her location and method of storing, is geared to cooperating with Nature as much as possible. Though the craft is small, she stores outdoors under

The flat-bottomed 24' Sharptown barge pictured on the beach in Hyannis, Massachusetts, was originally designed by Robert M. Steward and was revised by Culler for his friend and neighbor Dick White (pictured next to the boat) to row, sail, and power with an outboard.

a proper cover. I start work as soon in March as that month allows. Roll the cover partly back to go at it, cold fingers, drippy nose, and all, covering again each night, or sooner, rather hastily for sudden falling weather to protect the work completed. This is no different from doing the bigger craft in boat-yards. I get it done eventually, usually about the end of the month. Comes a day to pull the cover off for good and do the rails; by then it's April. The Swampscott has dried out very little, and tomorrow it rains. The plug is put in partially and Nature does the rest. Finally a good spell, she's launched and moored, for all is ready, and, being tight, she often goes for a sail the same day. Her season is long, about seven months, as the Cape Cod fall is pro-tracted. Her bottom is copper-painted at least once in mid-season, sometimes twice, depending on how "weedy" the summer is. The dory is a smart sailer and I like to keep her so. I notice that as the season advances, she sails faster and faster compared to many craft; near the end of it, she's extremely fast. It pays to keep a clean bottom.

The above maintenance points pretty much apply to other than flat-bottomed cross-planked craft, and now we can discuss some of these others and why they may be of more advantage to own, for some uses and some places, than the true flatty.

FILE BOTTOMS

File bottoms were probably so named because they looked somewhat like a cant-saw file in bottom section; later they were called vee-bottomed boats or, on the Chesapeake, "deadrises." Deadrise is the rise of floor in craft, so the "deadrises" had some, as opposed to the flat-bottomed boat, which had none. Just how and why the vee-bottom developed seems quite apparent, and there were two different approaches. One was an effort to simplify round-bottomed construction and utilize materials not well suited to it. The other was an attempt to improve the usefulness and ability of true flat-bottomed craft.

The significant changes from a flat-bottomed boat to a file bottom are: an increase in displacement when needed, sometimes a better run when heavily loaded, slightly more depth of hull, and a somewhat stronger craft if she must be large. It has often been said that the use of deadrise is to eliminate pounding in a head sea. With proper design and intelligent handling and sailing, in my experience at least, this terrible pounding in either type is far less than some folks think, and often non-existent in ordinary weather. All craft, large or small and of various types and shapes, find at times a sea and

wind condition in which they are unhappy. I have been quite comfortable sailing along well at sea in a modestly small cruising craft while a large steamer nearby was rolling most dismally; conditions of the moment did not fit her. A sudden let-up in wind with some sea running does cause pounding in many shoal craft of angular construction; they are sitting upright instead of at a nice sailing angle. Nearly any sailing craft is not at her best in such conditions, though some are better than others.

There was a period in yachting when racing rules, speed at any cost in summer weather, and just wanting to follow the style of the moment caused the development of a type, round-bottomed to be sure, that was a fierce pounder. Some of these boats had such flattish sections that their design shortened the life of many a hull. In some ways we seem to be going back to this style again in both sail and power. This same thinking has done some strange things to the vee-bottomed boat, which, like the flatty, has had a long and skilled development as a working craft. Rough and ready "rules" have long been worked out, which, if followed, tend to produce a good boat. Much departure from these traditional craft, and the design begins to get out of hand. The notion that if a little helps, a lot will do much more is often tried here. Give her a lot of deadrise so you can get headroom, stow ballast low and make her able, and reduce pounding. What actually happens is the development of a short, deep run and a pot belly. Such craft are usually dull sailers and not attractive to the knowing eye. Often moulded frames with reverse curve are used aft to improve the run; there is full fore-and-aft planking and even curved sides and other complications. Then the whole principle of the vee-bottom is lost, and you have a difficult craft to build—often more so than a true round-bottom. The "secret" of the file bottom is: Don't use too much deadrise amidships.

The deep-vee powerboat was considered quite a breakthrough, and I suppose it is for some uses. One thing for sure, it's a type that needs a lot of power. I note, now that the first flush is off, a trend back to shallow vee for some conditions. All types have their drawbacks.

The file bottom is considered a good boat for the home builder, as well as for the small professional shop trying to meet competition, because it's "easy to build"; it can be rather easy if the above-mentioned complications are left out. Except in high-performance planing power craft, these complications offer no real return for the work and cost involved, and even in very fast motor craft, that little extra gained is seldom needed.

The simple approach to building a file bottom is only a modest variation from flat-bottomed skiff construction in that you can use the well-tried, cross-plank, "herringbone" bottom. This is very strong, tough, and easy to repair. The only real trick in building it is—as in all boat carpentry—to get good fits, well fastened. It's often pointed out that the slight washboard effect on these bottoms slows a boat down. My own experience in rowing and sailing these craft is that if it does, it's not noticeable. Some folks think that the herringbone pattern is a benefit in a fast craft that planes—"lets her

break out of it and get on top." One can argue the point; my own feeling on it, based on designing and building this type, is that the cross-planking does help.

With the herringbone bottom construction, a stout keel is a must, along with a couple of sister keelsons, for there is no bottom framing unless the craft is of some size. On larger boats, two or more strongbacks are used; they are not true frames, as they rest on the keelsons, chines, and, of course, on the main keel, being well bolted to all. This method is well described in good books on boatbuilding, and clearly illustrated. In small beach boats of this construction, I place the sister keelsons outside on the bottom to act as chafing strips, bilge keel, and additional lateral resistance. Properly placed the same way on fast planing motor craft, they act as skis, and I find add much to the boat's performance. On sailing craft or non-planing motorboats, I place them in the usual inside position. In either case, they should be very well fastened.

In general, these craft, like the true flat-bottomed skiff, take only common sense and common care in their upkeep. Kept clean, well painted, properly stored and ventilated, they have a long life, even with much use, and seem to go on as long as any other type of construction, often outlasting more complicated hulls. However, I do notice one exception. Very fast planing boats—and this seems to apply to all types of construction—are often driven without mercy. Such driving shortens a boat's life, and I sometimes think might shorten the operator's life too—possibly suddenly.

For the home builder, the traditional deadrise boat built the way she originally was, and of a design suited to her mode of propulsion, is a most satisfactory and economical craft. Rather than say, "It's easy to build," I will say it's "undifficult," if there is such a word. Nothing really good is totally easy. Many amateurs, and some pros, want to build in plywood, but they don't consider the model.

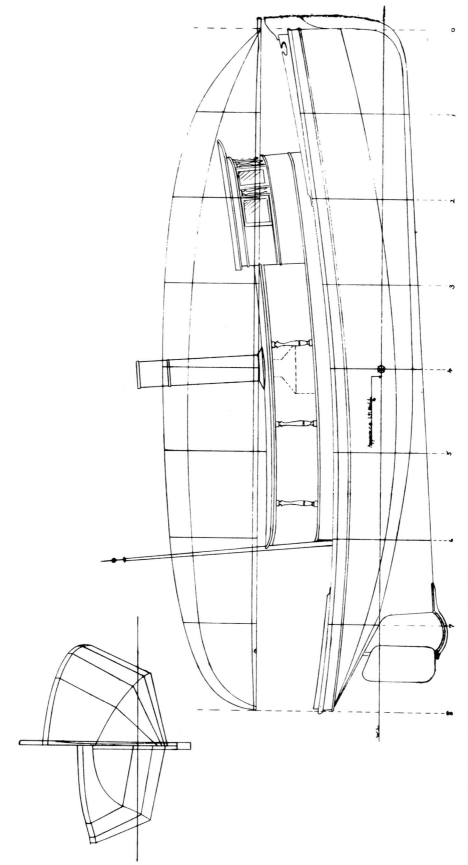

The v-bottom hull can be applied to a variety of types, and Pete Culler was a master in its application, from big to small. Row, sail, or outboard or steam power, he felt this style of hull could be used successfully with all forms of propulsion. This pretty little steamer design by Pete is a good example of the v-hull's (and the designer's) versatility. (© Mystic Seaport, Ships Plans Collection, Mystic, CT)

Once they do it, they become educated. Plywood can make a good vee-bottomed boat, but *she must be designed for it.* In other words, she must not have what are compound curves for the plywood. Some folks still think they can bend this stuff both ways at once, and, as the boat appears to have straight sections, why not? They soon learn that all is not as it seems. That's what the "developed surface" is about. A fellow interested in this phase of design can soon get the hang of it out of the books, or he can use the barnyard method: Chop out models till a piece of light sheet metal will lie snug without a fight. Don't use cardboard; it's too easy to cheat with; it will bend a little both ways. Remember that this boat requires framing, and that good fits are essential. Many plywood vee-bottoms show the same construction weaknesses as do their flat-bottomed sisters, and for the same reasons.

A plywood, vee-bottomed boat designed for large sheets, as opposed to plywood plank, shows convex sections in places, usually forward, and that is perfectly proper for a design intended for this construction. I really see no objection at all to a plywood vee-bottomed boat, if you can get the kind of craft you want in looks, durability, economy, and reasonable ease of building.

I've found these qualities far easier to come by, however, just building with plank. Good plywood is expensive. Unless marine mahogany is used—finished both sides, not just clear both sides—you will spend a great deal of time in getting a good finish on the work. Fir is troublesome to make look right and then does not seem to hold the finish. Outdoor grade construction stuff has voids that can cause leaks and usually do; these leaks can, in many cases, be impossible to stop without a major operation. Large sheets of any material are awkward for a loner to work with. You should really have tools made for cutting plywood; it helps in the final finishing. The lofting and moulding of the frames is more trouble than making the traditional plank sides

and herringbone bottom. With plywood, you cannot get a fine, sharp forefoot, if that is what's wanted, or a shapely stern. Many designers fall down badly on getting a nice stern on a vee-bottomed boat, at least without a lot of complication. A nice stern can often be had, and a study of many old-time craft in books, pictures, and plans will show it can be done. I feel far less limited using plank than plywood in the design and building of simple boats.

For some brutal uses, where any craft would be considered expendable, I consider plywood superior. It will take a fearful beating up to a point, when the whole craft sort of goes to pieces more or less at once, and it's time to replace the boat.

For the right use and model, the file bottom takes kindly to the sharp stern. This is true even in a rather fast powerboat of easy-driving shape. This hull form is not much understood nowadays, but the originators of the type knew all about it and, once engines became available, used the sharp stern with success. The long, lean, flat-run double-ender, or, more properly, sharp-stern deadrise, can be quite a performer with very modest power. For rowing and sailing, this type works well too, and often a very handsome craft can be turned out. The round, or fantail, stern can also be used with certain models, and, if properly done, can be very good looking.

Just why we see so many ugly and clumsy vee-bottomed boats today is hard to understand. I have heard it stated that good-looking boats are a thing of the past, that no one can take time anymore, and shoddy shapes and workmanship must be accepted. Wooden boats, the few that are made, must be built with all sorts of shortcuts. Steel boats that are wrinkled tin boxes are standard. Cement and glass are expected to look inferior and so on. I differ. Most anyone can tell the nice looking from the ugly, whether or not he knows anything about a boat. A builder who can and will turn out an attractive craft will always have a few interested clients who will beat a path to his door, and, surprisingly, many are willing to pay what they think is a little extra for such work. In the end, paying the extra is apt to be the cheapest way out, for good boats last. This principle seems to apply in whatever material a careful builder chooses. If his boats are good, people soon know it.

It is my opinion, backed by the products of many past builders, that the file bottom can be a most handsome craft. She can be designed to suit, using many bow profiles, many sterns, and many tricks of fitting and trim without becoming overly complicated. Why make a homely craft, when, with a little head work and imagination, you can make her really attractive?

Some of the "tricks" of making any boat look well might be of interest. Naturally you start with a shapely design, though it might be a very simple one, and you stick to it. Fair curves in any boat work are most important; humps and hollows never can look well. A good looking sheer seems to catch the eye first off. Boat shops seem always to be crowded, so that you can't back off and look at a sheer batten. Different craft take different approaches. Double enders, very full craft, and long, lean ones all have different sheer problems. The ideal situation, seldom found, is a boat well out in a field so you can get off from her. If a shed

A large v-bottom hull for outboard power being caulked prior to turning over for the interior finish. Note the placement of the bow staves. Initially upright, they will gradually fan toward the stern. The change from butt to lap at the chine, generally occurring around mold #2, is clearly visible.

roof can be clambered up on, or even a tree climbed, you often see things not apparent from the ground. The usual situation, however, is a crowded shop. When sheering a craft in cramped quarters, I put on the batten, fuss with it, fuss some more, and then go to dinner or knock off, depending on the time of day. Another look in an hour or the next day often shows up "hidden" shapes. If, by chance, the sheer batten will not be in the way for some time, I just leave it there; sometimes, several days later, I

The boat in the previous photo has been turned over and the interior finish is well along. Note the large keel, side stringers, strongbacks, chines, and frames. This is a typical Bay-style large boat with file-bottom construction. The port side frames have been installed and the starboard side is partially framed. Note the larger frames installed in the bow where the flare is greatest. Along with keeping weight in mind for the topsides, these construction elements result in a light yet strong craft. Excess weight will doom a planing craft quicker than anything else.

see fit to change it a bit. Never hurry battening a sheer any more than you have to. After much experience with this sort of thing, you tend to hit it in short order without much fuss. I never cut down a stern or a stempost to exact height while setting up. Some folks do—and lessen their chances if they have to jockey the sheer much. One-quarter or one-half an inch to play with in the ends is sometimes a lifesaver in getting a nice sheer.

An occasional bead and taper on things does wonders in giving a boat eye appeal. Many parts can be made quite attractive very simply by using judgment and imagination. We have all seen wooden cleats, some crude and some quite handsome. They both take the same amount of material and almost the same amount of labor. The handsome ones work better. Clean building, with a few nice touches, often makes the boat. If she is clean and fair, she will be good looking even though of plain finish. Without fairness, something is missing,

and no amount of high finish will make the boat pretty. More likely, it will make her look worse.

A certain touch to any part of a boat's structure is a help in making her look fine as a whole. There is no simple, step-by-step way of showing such touches to any extent on plans, or of really describing them either. Just keep the niceties in mind, have sharp tools, and use your imagination. Each builder's craft will show his mark even though several may build boats of the same design, and this is as it should be. Boats built by individuals are not at all like the usual mass-produced items that flood us, all alike even to the mould marks. Each boat the work of a man who likes what he's doing—this is boat building!

I have little more to add about the lore of chine boats, either flat or vee-bottomed. They may fit your use and pocketbook along with your available skills and building equipment, or you may hate the sight of them and prefer to shoot for higher things. A transition

A bow photo of the same boat showing the harmony of side lapstrake planking, spray rails, and bottom staving in v-bottom construction.

The workman finishing the motor well on the stern illustrates the scale of construction on the 30' fast outboard. Note the ready to install wash-deck frames sitting in the bottom.

type might be mentioned here, though I think for the most part she is quite specialized and complicated. This is the craft with a round bilge forward turning into a chine aft. Many of these craft have been quite successful, though from an economical standpoint they leave much to be desired, at least in the building. If a certain performance is required for a certain use, they pay off. The type has been used many times for rather larger motor yachts and was much used in some classes of wooden military craft. These last were built because it was thought they were needed; cost did not enter into it. Usually these craft had bent frames and were padded out aft to form a chine. I suppose they could be considered semi-planing boats, when they were not overloaded. Most war boats seem overloaded most of the time. There were other complicated approaches: full-chine boats with fully bent frames, webs over stringers, and all packed with wood, just like a wooden airplane wing. These were 40-ton boats, and to turn out one a day complete, with men who had little boatbuilding experience, was a feat. Some of these craft are still around, so the design and building must have been sound in their way. I think no amateur and few professionals will be tackling such craft these days, so I leave them at that.

LAPSTRAKE

The round-bottomed hull may well have been Man's earliest type of boat, being the natural shape of a log. Of course it has progressed from the log to almost every possible variation (and some nearly impossible ones). Since the log—and it's still with us in many parts of the world—about everything has been used at one time or another for covering a frame. Skins, cloth, woven work, reeds, wood in many forms, paper and many materials now long forgotten have been used to make boats watertight. Relatively recently, we have seen fiberglass and cement added to the list. When you think about it, some ancient craft, dating back to Moses and before, were not very different in principle from modern craft. A woven hull covered with some kind of waterproofing, such as asphalt, is not so far removed from a hull of woven glass cloth covered with a man-made stickum. You can be sure of one thing: the old timers used what was available. It was either that or stay landbound!

One of the finest coverings for the frames of small to moderate sized boats is lapstrake planking, well worked out by the Norsemen and not improved on since. Just why and how it developed is well put down in books by those who have made a study of ancient sea ways. I will only point out why I think it's still the finest way of planking certain craft. Lapstrake planking has been used in much larger craft in the past than many now realize. Old photos of Scandinavian and British harbors show many fine lapstrake craft, cutters, paddle tugs, luggers, and coasters.

Many boats used on our coasts in the past were lapstrake, or clinker-built, as it is sometimes called. Boats used for surf work were nearly always of this build. These boats often had to take a pounding on a beach, even with the most expert handling. They could not be too heavy, and lapstrake makes a light boat for her size and strength. Lapstrake was also much used for ships' boats, as the construction stands being out of water for extended periods. If lapstrake boats do leak after a long time out, it's usually not much, and they have a way of taking up quickly. A carvel, or smooth-planked, boat used on the beach can get a bad pounding and spew her caulking, and she is then leaking beyond coping with. A lapstrake boat can take considerable straining and still not leak to the point of being useless.

A small craft which must be reasonably light, one that hauls up a lot, surf or beach boats, some small, fast, motor craft, and, in my opinion, some types larger than we now accept for this method should be lapstrake. Even if a person has an aversion to lapstrake, unfounded or not, he must admit it does offer something, or why would they copy it in glass, metal, and soon, I suppose, in cement? Aside from giving a boat a certain style, it has been long known that laps make for dryness if the boat's model is otherwise good; they are a sort of battery of little spray rails. It's also been said that laps tend to give a fast boat more speed, whether a planing model or a "displacement" craft. This is a point to be argued. Some old timers used to say that if you had two boats built to the same lines, one smooth, the other lapped, the lapstrake was apt to be the faster, but not always. What went on here? Was it a weight difference or the way the water went around the hull? My own feeling is that, assuming a craft of good design, a lot of it may have to do with the lining off of the strakes to suit the flow lines of the hull. This lining off, whether or not it has anything to do with the speed and ability of the boat, is one of the fine points of lapstrake building.

It's now said that the building of lapstrake craft is a most difficult process. I find it by far the easiest

No matter the size of the vessel, "a lap per day, clear round," was the industry standard for planking. This boat took Pete eight days to plank. This little 10'6" yawlboat was designed for Stephen Forbes of Nashawena Island, Massachusetts. Its lines plan appears on page 47.

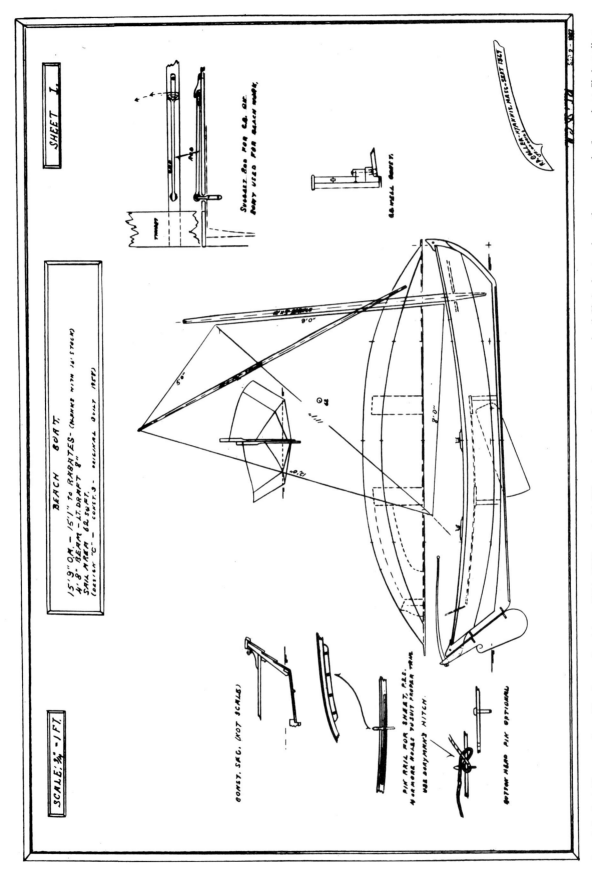

Pete Culler had this to say about this v-bottom beach boat: "This 15'9" vessel with 5' beam is very handy under oars and sail. She's about as dry as they come and a fine seaboat. She's really a rowboat with auxiliary sail, but is quite fast and handy under canvas, being very sharp bottomed. She has a fair sized centerboard and fine sail plan. She is a striking craft." (© Mystic Seaport, Ships Plans Collection, Mystic, CT)

way to build most round-bottomed boats. I say most, for some models are not very well suited to lapstrake. The best general shape, to me at least, follows somewhat the lines of a small Norse longship, without the dragon head of course. She should have a long, easy hull with a thin forefoot, and a thin heel if she's double-ended, though she can be quite full on the rails. Some slight reverse in the garboards I find of advantage, though not necessary. A turn of bilge that is an increasing curve as it comes up from the dead flat to the rail—a somewhat flaring side in other words—is desirable. If she has a square stern, she should have some reverse next to the deadwood. The model can vary in shape and size, yet there should be a definite Norse cast to her. A nice, flowing sheer is essential. Other shapes work well if

of nice model, though a bulbous craft does not. A bulbous boat is not much good built by any planking method.

When lofting lapstrake craft, or any small, shoal craft for that matter, I like to use sufficient diagonal and buttock lines. Waterlines, especially the lower ones, are of little use in accurate lofting of rather flat, shoal boats. Be sure to mark the moulds with the diagonals; these give a good guide to the lining off of plank, as touched on before.

In lapstrake construction, keels, posts, and sterns and their kneeing are no different from those of a smooth-planked boat. Depending on the size, type, model, and available stock, the keel can be scantling with a cut rabbet, or can be made with an apron and lower keel, or batten as it's sometimes

The 15'9" beach boat all rigged and ready to launch. This example was one of a pair built for the Museum of the Sea in Savannah, Georgia. One of the first small boats that Pete designed, he created and built it in the early 1950s in his Hyannis shop for Waldo Howland, who became his employer in the 1960s. The first beach boat was named Java, *after a historic Howland-family whale ship.*

called. Or, a plank keel with a worked rabbet can be built, as in a wherry. The deadwood can be in the form of a planked box, as on a Jersey Seabright skiff, if a wide, plank keel is used, or can be in the form of a shaped wedge with a rabbet. I prefer the wedge, made out of Eastern pine. Work a little reverse into it if the craft's other sections show some. I think all the above are more trouble than the true scantling keel, though if the design requires it, the plank keel in some form must be used. This last is very handy to set a centerboard well in. When using a scantling keel, rather than swelling it to accommodate a centerboard well, I prefer to use the offset well, finding it less work, and very strong.

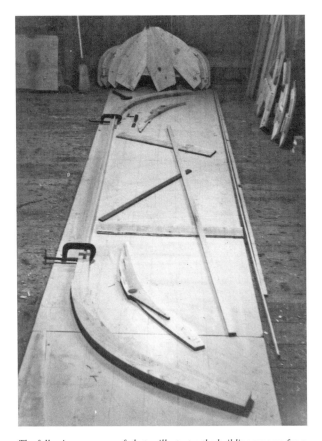

The following sequence of photos illustrates the building process for a small lapstrake boat as built by Pete Culler. The particular boat being built in this case is the 16'8" Race Point surfboat Coskata. *The first photo shows the keel laid down on the lofting to ensure proper line-up, clamped to the stem and sternpost, and all ready to be bolted together.*

An offset centerboard does not affect the sailing of the boat at all, though some folks are prone to think otherwise.

You see many methods of setting up. Upside down is common for small craft, and if they are very small, this is probably the best. Don't fit the last or sheer plank until she is righted, though. I have not yet learned how to get a good sheer upside down. The method of setting up depends on the lay-out of the shop, but for most boats I think I prefer what I call the Norse set-up. The boat is built right side up on shored keel posts, with shores from the moulds to an overhead timber running along the centerline of the boat. The post and stern shore to this timber also. The floor under the craft is nearly clear, which is most handy. The overhead shores battering inboard are little in the way, and, with a nail or two here and there, are handy to store battens on or hang tools from. I hear complaints about having to squat to work on the bottom plank; I find a stool or shoal box helps here. The fact that shores can be used handily from the floor is a big help, and you avoid crawling under an upside-downer at times to see what's going wrong. This Norse method is very rigid, and as work progresses, the craft is never totally adrift from the set-up; when she is framed and the moulds are removed, she's first shored from overhead to the top of the keel, and as she's now fully planked, a couple of bilge shores on each side steady things just fine. I use enough keel shores so they can be shifted when in the way of interior work.

The mould stations should be established in designing the craft, and if they are not, as perhaps when using a design other than your own, they should be established and lofted to. Their spacing should be divisible by the amount of the frame spacing; in other words, 2-foot moulds fit 6- or 8-inch frame spacing. Some designers overlook this. If the craft is not moulded to inside of plank, the difference must be allowed for. I think a person

Keel assembly with the rabbet cut into stem, keel, and sternpost, ready for setup.

doing his own designing should learn to do it to inside of plank, no more difficult than building a boat that has been designed to outside of plank.

In designing your own boat, lapstrake or not, allow plenty of deadwood in posts outside of the rabbet. If it's too much, you can always cut it down; too little, and you get that stubbed-in effect that can spoil an otherwise fine, sharp entrance. Keel and post siding can be far less than many people suppose in light, sharp, lapstrake craft. My rule of thumb is: Twice the thickness of the planking, plus the thickness of the stem bolts, plus $\frac{1}{8}$ inch. Thus with $\frac{3}{8}$-inch planking and $\frac{1}{4}$-inch bolts, keel and post would side about $1\frac{1}{8}$ inches. I often "fetch the bolts" in final rabbet trimming and knick the chisel!

This proportion gives a fine, thin forefoot, and, with the usual wide beard or back rabbet here, it's quite strong. I think many forefoots today turn out stubby on account of not using this kind of proportion. Often the mistake starts in the lofting and is carried along.

In lining off—and some of this will apply to carvel planking as well—first decide the number of strakes. It is better to have one too many than be one shy. Some experimenting with short blocks of wood can be a guide, using the mid-mould to see just what is needed. The width of the stock will be a guide too. Some craft can take fairly wide plank, though the stock available may not allow it. By playing with the blocks, establish

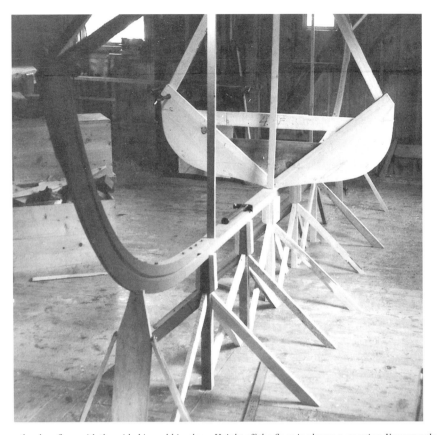

The backbone set up on the shop floor with the mid-ship mold in place. Height off the floor is always a question. You want the boat to be set up high enough to ease the work of installing the lower planks, yet low enough to facilitate finishing the interior when planking is complete. Like everything in life it becomes a compromise.

what lap you will use, and what plank thickness. I find that on classic craft of more or less easy model, 10 to 20 feet long, $3/4$-inch lap and $3/8$-inch plank work well for the most part. Use thinner plank on a small, light boat. If the planks are narrow and the boat well framed, you can build a craft of quite some length using $3/8$-inch plank, say in cedar or some other lively wood. I prefer as much flat grain as possible; edge grain, though the finest kind for decking, tends to split more easily than flat grain.

Rip out battens from any soft wood that does not kink after sawing and of a length to reach around the boat. If the stock is too short for that, I simply splice, using long, slash scarfs fastened with tacks or clinch nails. Battens can also be lapped,

though the bump is sometimes hard to see around and get fair. I think splices are worth the slight trouble, especially for a small craft. The battens can be quite thin, but should be the width of the laps. You only have to batten off one side of the boat; use the more convenient side. I use the side next to the saw and workbench. Batten the sheer first, and the garboard next, keeping the ends well up, as mentioned before. Then put in the rest of the battens, one for each strake edge, being guided by the diagonals. Then stand off and study it from all angles. Little errors will at once become apparent and should be corrected one batten at a time. Shifting one may call for shifting another a second time. I usually do not attempt to have the hood ends forward all the same width, letting those above the garboard be wider than those near the sheer as a rule. Take your time. The object is to have the boat all fair and pleasing to the eye.

Bear in mind, if the craft is a nice, easy model, that which would be the shutter in a carvel planked boat should have very little shape, only taper, in a lapstrake boat. What you are doing, starting with the garboard, is throwing the ends up and reducing the hook in the plank. The hook will increase again somewhat as the sheer is reached, the amount depending on the uprightness of the top plank and on the amount of sheer.

I say again, never attempt to edge-set lapstrake plank. There will be at times a slight unavoidable edge-set when a plank springs as it is sawn out, which it sometimes will with certain stock. This spring will haul back in place with little trouble, as the plank was laid out to the correct shape. Usually

the plank are sawn out in pairs, tacked together, so you just line off one. Before you take off the battens, mark them top and bottom at post, moulds, and stern. These are the marks to spile to, and also "browse off" to when beveling one plank for the next to meet.

When spiling plank, naturally you start with the garboard. As it lies to the moulds, it is spiled just as is any plank that might lie to the frames. The garboard, once on, takes little browsing off, many times none at all, if there is some reverse in the sections. Now here is the rub. The next plank does not lie to the moulds, but laps the garboard. Its upper edge touches the mould, or its middle sometimes touches the mould at the turn of the bilge. The spiling batten must lie the same as the plank to get a true shape. I simply tack small wedges on each mould to simulate the lie of the plank, making sure that the wedges are

All the molds in place with the sheer batten indicating the boat's shape. The molds will be set up square and plumb to the keel. They must be well braced for the stresses of planking up, soon to follow.

The molds are now lined off for plank with battens that are the same width as the laps. The tops and bottoms of the battens are marked against the molds, stem, and sternpost. For a fair planking run, it is helpful to follow the diagonals, which should be marked on the molds. On Pete Culler's boats, the middle plank will have no shape and only be tapered. If your line-off doesn't seem to be working, try adding another plank to your number and line off again. At times, it can be the solution.

no thicker than the plank which was put on and browsed off, and that their points fetch the upper mark of the plank being spiled. The batten now takes a proper lie. Naturally, no wedges are needed at post or stern, as the planks flush out here.

I feel planking in single lengths can be carried too far, and more can be lost than gained by it. Besides requiring wide stock, single lengths tend to produce cross-grain plank in the ends. Well-made butts are, in my opinion, far less objectionable than plank prone to split. The usual butt block is all right in a boat not intended for lightness, and which has a lot of joinerwork inside; in such a craft they do not look out of place. A light pulling boat is another matter, and in her the slash scarf should be used. These can be made either on the bench or on the boat.

This is the way I like to do it. If I can locate a butt on a frame, so much the better. I try to have the butt come in a clear part of the plank, allowing for the stagger of other butts of course. It's no fun making a butt with a hard knot in it! My rule is to make the scarf length the same as the plank width. I cut the scarfs on the bench; with sharp tools, it's simple, once you have done a couple. I join them on the boat, thinking there is less work and less chance of error that way. I use Weldwood glue and fit blocks that cover the scarf, separated from it by wax paper, with all the clamps there is room for. When the scarf is set, I clinch it up with copper tacks. Glue and gluing are subject to much argument. I use Weldwood because it's simple and strong. Some folks say it's no good because it won't stand boiling. If you are going to boil your boat, don't use it! Good fits and plenty of pressure are necessary. I confess I know nothing of gap-filling glues; the kind of work they seem to encourage I have no interest in. When properly made and sanded off, and with the boat painted, the scarfs I describe are often next to impossible to see.

Let's turn to fastening the laps. The dory lap, with galvanized clinch nails, is seldom seen except in dories. Copper rivets are used for fastening laps and are, of course, good. Working single-handed, however, these are sort of a chore. You don't have enough hands, so you resort to some method of holding the bucking iron, such as strapping it to your leg, or hanging it from a line around your neck, letting body pressure hold it to the work. None of this is very speedy, especially when putting in frames hot. For small craft, I like the copper cut nail, clinched, and have not seen any weakness in this method. It's best to clinch across the grain of the plank in soft wood. I find in hard wood, even though hot and wet with steam, you should clinch with the grain to get a good bury of the nail point. On a craft of some size, say over 20 feet, possibly it's best to use rivets. A bigger boat usually calls for a helper at times anyway. The main objection to galvanized iron clinch nails in a light craft is that the heads are not sunk and the clinched ends are never deeper than flush and so are subject to striking with sandpaper, which soon goes through the galvanizing, and rust streaks result. Even so, a boat built this way seems to last a long time. Certainly a light boat of classic model should

Planking is in process, with both manufactured and home-made clamps in use. These plank laps are fastened across the grain using copper tacks in pre-drilled holes folded over while hammering. If the metal is not malleable enough, simply heat them in a metal pie plate and anneal by slow cooling. This softens them nicely. This was Pete's preferred method for lap fastening in small boats. Over time he discovered no weakness using this procedure.

have copper, either clinched or riveted, as the builder sees fit.

Laps should never be glued. Gluing does not allow the plank to "slip" in changes of wet and dry, and so will either buckle or split the garboard, or some other plank. The time-honored way was a dry fit. Many builders just must put something in between; if so, use a bedding compound, like Dolphinite, thinned with kerosene to the consistency of thin paint. It won't do any good, but if it's thin enough, it will do little harm, assuming you do not get chips and dirt in it to prevent getting a tight lap. All these sticky things play out after a while, and some, when done for, seem to leave a sort of dry ash. Much better wood to wood! There have been attempts to "improve" on the fastening of lapstrake craft by using glue-like sealers, short screws, and other short cuts. In the end, they don't work.

Once a builder tries lapstrake planking on a craft of a shape suited to it, he will find it's not the most difficult way of planking boats. You line off, spile, saw out, fit, and fasten, and browse off for the next one. This may sound like a lot. As compared to smooth plank, you do some things about the same way, some differently, and some not at all. Except for the garboard and hood ends, you work no caulking seam, there is no backing out of plank, no fret to get a good edge-to-edge fit, and usually no sinking of fastenings in a very light boat and only the screws to sink in a stouter one. Nor is there any outboard joining in the true sense; I've never met anyone who said he enjoyed this particular operation! And there is no caulking, paying, filling of seams to amount to anything, and not many fastening holes to fill. Even the framing and preparation for it go faster with less work on a lapstrake boat. True, you batten off to get the planking run on one

The hull planked and ready for framing.

The interior showing the steam-bent frames and floors installed. Temporary battens hold the sides together while frames go in and the molds come out. Pete's method for small-boat framing in lapstrake construction was to install the hardwood frames with copper tacks fastened with *the grain.*

Interior finish continues with seat risers, inwales, caps, seats, and sternsheets. These are reinforced with posts and knees. Bow and stern decking has yet to be completed, after which will be sanding and several coats of paint and varnish, with more sanding between coats (sanding seems to go on forever) and ultimately a happy client when the boat is finished.

side with light stuff, but there are no stout ribbands on both sides to bend frame to, no sticking the frame to hold it with nails and sometimes screws till plank comes to it, and no removing all this temporary stuff as you go. You simply frame to the already-planked hull, one at a time, fastening while

hot. The lapstrake frame is also lighter and easier to work with, takes only one clamp at the sheer, and is easy to crowd to the inside of the already-planked hull. Once in and fastened, it's done, complete in itself, finished—unless it broke and you didn't notice in time! I leave lapstrake at that.

CARVEL PLANKING

Carvel or smooth plank is no doubt the most common way of building a round-bottomed boat, and, as a method, has a lot going for it. There are of course various ways of getting a smooth skin on a boat besides a single thickness of plank, edge-to-edge-caulked; all are more expensive than the common carvel method, and are for specialized uses and types of boat. Right now "strip-built" is popular; I think the shape of the craft has a lot to do with where and when to use strip planking. The common idea is that strip building is rather cheap, easy, and rapid. The idea is that you can work to a standard taper and use light strips, either beveled, or hollow and round, done on a shaper. This is fine if you own or can borrow a shaper, but one that can really produce all day long is not a cheap machine.

I feel a sort of spindle-shaped hull is best suited to strip building. A classic hull, especially if of a very shapely model, will soon develop a bad "hook" in the strips, making for much sometimes impractical edge-setting. Then the principle of the master taper strip can fly out the window. My remarks on the lining off of regular plank point very much to just what goes on. All this setting tends to spread the hull and pull the plank away from the moulds. I sometimes think, for some hulls at least, a set of *outside* moulds would be better, not forgetting to have many rolls of wax paper on hand to keep the plank from sticking to them, for strip building relies on some sort of stickum, glue, or gunk along with edge nailing. Jointing off in this mess once the hull is planked is a sticky business and often prone to dulling tools rapidly. If the craft when finished is to show her skin inside, there is much work here to make her presentable; she's often glue-smeared and ridgy.

Just how strip building developed, and where, we can only surmise. Probably it was born Down East when lumbering was in its heyday and strips were free for the lugging off. Winters were long, the old ripsaw was sharp, galvanized wire commons were cheap, and a man needed a new boat. There was no fuss, no complication. Work with what you have; it made sense, and another boat could be built the same way when the first wore out. By the way, a few of these old craft still exist. My own feeling, though, is that strip building, if done well, using expensive stock, much glue, and bronze nails, and involving some of the complications above mentioned, is not the easy or cheap way to build a boat. And it is totally unsuited to some shapes of hull.

Then there is double plank, and even triple plank, the latter having two of the skins on the diagonal. For special use, such as in a light racing craft, or wherever much strength with light weight is needed, these methods are worth their trouble. Some lifeboats used to be built this way and will stay tight out of water, even for long periods. Multiple planking is expensive and time consuming. In the Great War, many small wooden craft were built, using many planking methods. Some members of this splinter fleet are still around and in commercial service. Some were made into yachts, and to my way of thinking did not make good ones. As to lasting, the single-plankers seem to have lasted about as well as the craft with more than one skin.

This leaves us with the old standby, the single-planked, caulked-seam method of boatbuilding, on which millions of words have been written. Why say more? I won't say much, just a few things, long known but often overlooked.

I have seen carvel plank as light as $\frac{3}{8}$ inch in fancy dinghies, but I think lapstrake for such craft is better. Some craft plank with $\frac{5}{8}$ inch, which I think is still too light for a long life. With $\frac{3}{4}$-inch

Carvel planking can be utilized on small craft such as this 19'6" shallop. (George Putz)

Carvel planking can also be used on large vessels like this 40′ schooner.

plank and heavier, carvel planking comes into its own. In figuring plank thickness in these small dimensions, you should consider the amount of backing out and dressing off required for the particular design. On the other hand, you should not put stout plank on too light a frame; problems in fastening and holding the shape develop if the frame is too light. And whether the craft has bent or sawn frames, there is a need for three or four sawn frames right aft, as no amount of stout plank will pull true frames that don't quite make the curve there. In other words, right aft, especially topside, things tend to flatten in.

While it's not often that sizable craft are backyard jobs, because a big vessel is just too much unless the home builder is dedicated, I really like vessels that require plank of $1\frac{3}{4}$ inches and up, with thicker wale strakes and garboards. The latter should be preferably of hard, or semi-hard wood, say fir or hard pine, and she should have an oak bottom. Or, she can be all oak if she's salted. A professional caulker can really button up such a hull. He uses a

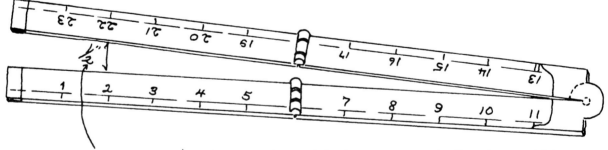

ROUGH METHOD OF FIGURING AMOUNT OF OUTGAUGE FOR ALL THICKNESS OF PLANK, USING 2 FOOT RULE.

SET RULE AT ½ INCH AT 10 INCHES FROM HINGE. OUTGAUGE IS WHAT SPACE MEASURES ACROSS ANY GIVEN DISTANCE (PLANK THICKNESS) FROM HINGE END - EXAMPLE, 3 INCH PLANK IS ABOUT 1 EIGHTH INCH -

"Outgauge" is the width of the caulking seam to be beveled into one of the edges of a carvel plank. Pete used this simple and effective method for figuring outgauge for any thickness of plank.

All planked, painted, and ready for cabin top installation and rigging, the dogbody was designed by Pete Culler for Philip Volker. The example shown in these photos was built by Bruce Northrup. (Bruce Northrup)

choker of cotton, followed by sufficient oakum, and the garboards are caulked complete, but are not hawsed back until all the rest of the vessel is done, including the covering boards. You can hear her tighten up day by day, as the caulking progresses. The day the garboards are hawsed back—the last operation in the caulking—the hull rings like a bell. If the thick garboards and wale strakes are edge-bolted, so much the better. The smells are there, the sounds are there. To use the words of a well-known statesman, there have been blood, sweat, and tears (and once in a while bankruptcy). This, bored reader, is wooden shipbuilding. Few now have a chance at it. If you ever do get a chance, take it up!

I think that those folks who recommend or sell some of the new compounds said to do away with caulking know nothing about wooden boats and shipbuilding. Caulking, by one who knows his job, is what stiffens and ties all the structure together. Before the days of steel strapping, large wooden vessels were packed solid between the frames, especially in the bottom and at the turn of the bilge. The frames were caulked and pitched both sides, then planked and ceiled; planking and ceiling were both caulked, as were all the decks, and there were often three. All this was to tighten up the whole structure, and help it keep its shape for a while. By no efforts and skill of men could every joint be perfect,

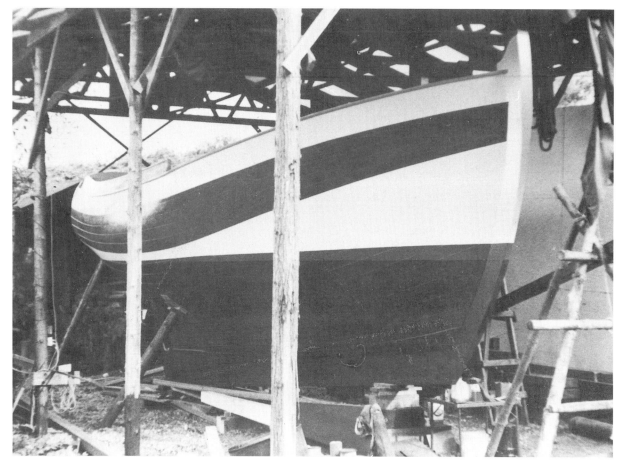

The 21'8" dogbody is a snug little overnight cruiser based on a very ancient type: the square-sterned Chebacco boat. The original was a two-sail boat of medium size that originated from the smaller shallops, or ships' boats, during the Colonial era. (Bruce Northrup)

and this was the way—the only way—a large vessel could be given sufficient strength. Yes, a carvel-planked, single-skin hull should be caulked in the traditional manner, be it a light boat, with a fine thread of cotton put in with a small caulking wheel, or be it a big craft with coarser methods.

No seam compounds I know of last indefinitely. Some of the newer cure-all ones certainly don't last in proportion to their cost. Those in use a hundred or more years ago are still good; some of these are readily available and others are a bit of trouble to get today. Mostly they go unnoticed, as they are not packed in cans with a picture of a boat on them. White lead and whiting make an excellent and lasting seam and fastening-hole filler for carvel-planked

boats, especially those of rather stout model. This stuff is too hard for use in laid decks, and is not the same as store-bought white lead putty. Put dry whiting on a board, like flour when kneading bread, and work up a wad of white lead ground in oil until it can be handled. Don't get it crumbly. I suppose this mix might be 90 per cent white lead. I've known it to last for 40 years.

Underwater, a similar mix, using pine tar and whiting instead of the lead, lasts and lasts. Pine tar is still available if you hunt a bit for it. Black asphalt paper shingle stickum works just fine too; it has a way of "settling in," even in an overhead seam. This is fine in a new craft; there is less to flush off when she sets herself. This shingle stickum is fairly

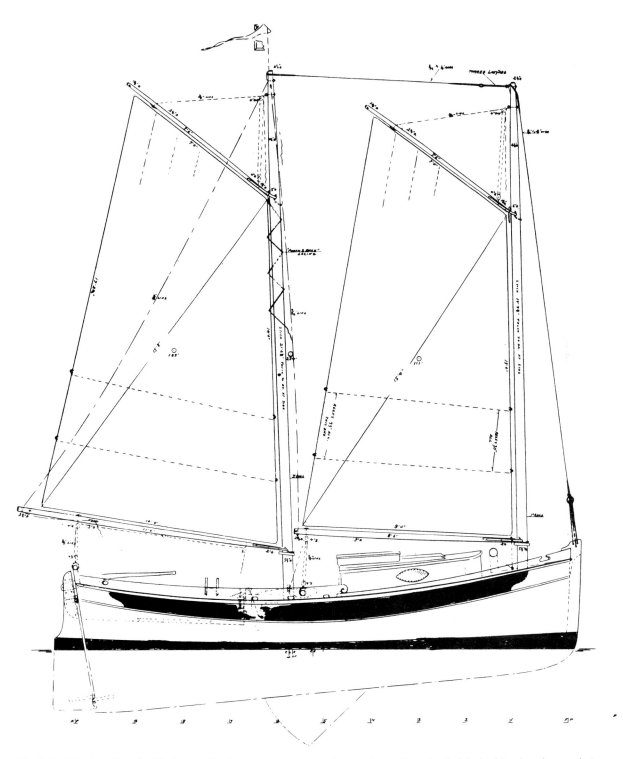

The dogbody is a lot of boat for 21', the waterline being nearly the same as her length overall, yet her draft is shoal for alongshore work. As a concession to her short length, the centerboard and the mainmast are offset from the keel, on opposite sides. This is strong construction, if done properly, and it should present no problems on the water. There is a lot of the artistic in this design. The general shapes of hull and rig are handsome, particularly the bow profile. The underwater shape is remarkably fine, and she is almost certainly an excellent sailer. (© Mystic Seaport, Ships Plans Collection, Mystic, CT)

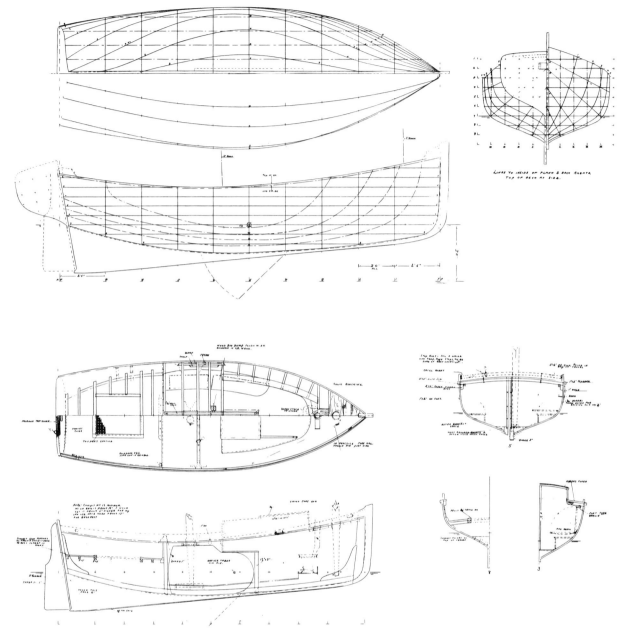

Dogbody (continued). (© Mystic Seaport, Ships Plans Collection, Mystic, CT)

cheap, easy to use, and very durable. There are other things to use, but why get complicated when the above will do the job?

Carvel plank usually suggests bunging or wood-plugging the fastenings. This is fine if the plank is thick enough; if it's not, bungs are trouble. I feel many craft that are now bunged in the interest of having the best are not in the end the best. They may be too light for bunging. A rough rule of

thumb is that bungs should be set about as deep as their diameter, and should not cut the plank through more than a third of its thickness, preferably a bit less. There is no use in cutting a plank half in two, as is often seen. Bungs that fit too tight compress in driving, and this leads to puffing out later. Bungs are set in all sorts of stuff, depending on whether the plank will have a bright or paint finish: glue, red lead, any old paint, varnish, and way back when I

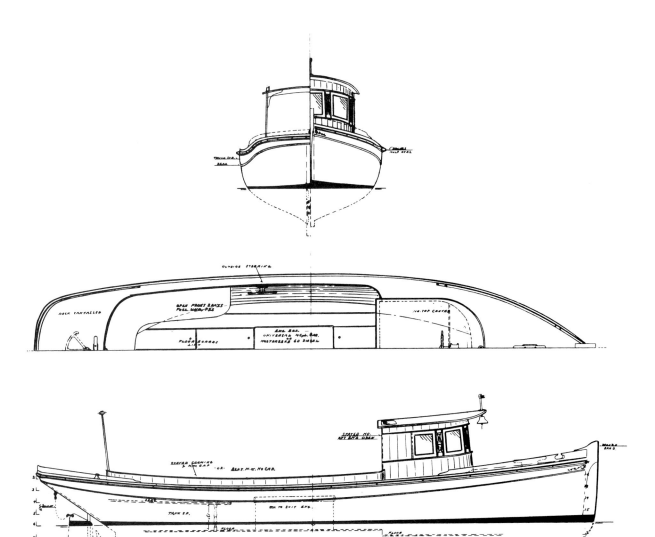

This handsome 24'5" fantail motorboat for inland use was designed by Pete Culler for Peter Burling. The fantail stern is appealing. In addition to its good looks, the stern offers honest function in displacement hulls using modest power, providing good capacity and bearing aft along with a fine run. In fact, it all seems to fall naturally in place once this design is chosen. The fantail stern is famous for steam applications, but works equally well with other power options as long as it is not overdone. (© Mystic Seaport, Ships Plans Collection, Mystic, CT)

learned about this, often in shellac for bright work. Nowadays, it's thought shellac is no good; somehow it seemed to work. Take your choice.

Much fuss is often made over carvel planking, yet it is rather simple. With proper planning, attention to lining off, the right amount of backing out or dubbing flat if she's a sawn-frame vessel, and care in taking the bevels, all goes along without bother, assuming, of course, that the frame is of proper size, well ribbanded, and fair. I've worked on many large craft with very stout plank, and very little use was made of "C" clamps. Often there was no place to put them; the ceiling crew was pushing well ahead of the plankers, and clamps were of much more use to them. Putting the heavy plank in place was nearly all done with shores, wedges, wrain bolts and staves, loggers, chains, and common sense, along with the standard planking dog. Experience on large craft certainly does simplify your outlook on smaller boats.

ENGINES, OARS, AND SAILS

Boats are made to go. I'll take up first what in some ways is the simplest form of propulsion—the engine. Raised eyebrows? Engines are bought as units, either new or second-hand. It's just a matter of money; I don't know of a man who has built his own engine for his boat, unless, in rare cases, she's a steam launch. Internal combustion engines are manufactured and are made very precisely nowadays.

I'm still approached now and then by people who want an old-time, slow-speed engine, new of course. They just like the idea, and so do I. With three or four exceptions, however, there are none now made, and, on explaining these exceptions, the subject is soon dropped, for most folks want self-starting, and may not realize that certain two-cycle engines still made don't take kindly to clutches, reverse gears, and fancy instrument panels. We settle for a high-decibel automotive job—yes, automobiles are where they all come from until you get into big rigs. Diesel, of course, is the best of all, and for good reason, though no one has yet built a quiet one that I know of.

In planning a powerboat, it should be kept in mind that the machinery will be a very large part of her cost and also of her maintenance. This applies to outboards, and with the very complicated installations of all kinds that you see nowadays, power craft can be quite a drain on the wallet. They don't run for free; every mile costs, and usually the faster the mile the more it costs.

Some few folks can build a cheap boat, and being whiz mechanics, can work from a junk pile and have a very usable rig, though it may not meet presently accepted standards or even the law in some cases. Besides, the lash-up is not insurable. Yet most of these inventive craft seem to give very good service, just because the operator knows very well what he's doing.

High speed is always expensive; if there is a real need for it, it is, of course, quite worthwhile. Much consideration should be given to whether or not speed is really needed or practical for the intended waters. There is a saying around my area that great speed is practical mostly in the early mornings only; afternoon winds usually make the water very lumpy. Many people don't like to get up early. There is a lot to be said of a non-planing boat of small power and very easily driven model, yet now such boats are seldom seen, probably because the idea of using the great length required just appalls. A person trying out one of these long ones for the first time is astounded at their easy way of going and at what fine seaboats they are. They make a most economical type of power craft, and, though long, are not big boats, having a modest displacement. The displacement is where the cost is, both the cost of building the boat and the cost of the power to drive her.

There are all sorts of plans of fast, long, narrow craft to study. One of the finest examples was the wooden subchaser of World War I. Her record stands, and for her day she had extraordinary endurance and range. North Atlantic weather separates the pots from the ships. That the principle works in both smaller and larger sizes is shown by the motor crab skiffs in Chesapeake Bay and by the liner *United States.* If you wonder about the *United States* being narrow, take this liner's dimensions and divide by nine. The result is close to a 100-foot steam torpedo boat of Captain Nat Herreshoff's design. The speed record of the *United States* speaks for itself.

Outboard motor boats are, of course, everywhere, and in the smaller sizes make a lot of sense. Boats can be simple, and the taking care of the motors the same, if you don't overdo the motor. Some of the huge washing machines still called outboards make me wonder, and I speak here with some slight experience, having designed successful outboard boats up to 30 feet long, all twin-screw. They work just fine and fill the present desire for fast boats.

I personally don't care for fast boats, though they are very useful and fun at times. They are not at all economical by the hour, though not so bad by the mile when the weather is light. The cost of powering the fast boats I've designed is high, even though these boats use half the power of most outboards and yet have plenty of speed. Maintenance of the power plants is reasonably easy but by no means cheap, and the engines, by their nature, do not live long.

Someone is always suggesting outdrive, which sounds good. I have no idea how many of these are in use. The numbers in boatyards in a laid-up-and-taken-down condition in mid-season puts their durability in doubt. I assume a bronze lower unit is impossible because of cost and weight; the durability of the potmetal ones speaks for itself.

We hear of new types of power plants just around the corner that will revolutionize motor craft. I'm sure they will, when they come. Since my earliest exposure to boating, these wonder engines have been lurking behind that corner; a few have peeked out and then drawn in their horns again. The gas turbine is now with us, but it can only be bought by the taxpayer for his Government. The cost may come down later on. A machine which, from the drawings, looks somewhat like the inside of some auto oil pumps is about to take over the automotive industry, and, doubtless, boats, lawn mowers, et al. We'll wait and see; there may be great things coming for boats.

There is another kind of engine, the steam engine, considered by many motorboat men merely the plaything of nuts. Yet, if you are exposed to the right type of steam engine, you've had it. Steam enginitis is very catching. Those who work with steam are not so much concerned with its lack of pollution—though they always make a point of it—as with the sounds and smells, and just watching an open-crank engine go. Some fellows who do this stuff are so dedicated they build the whole thing, hull, engine, and boiler, while others stick to the machinery and acquire the hull. A proper "steam hull" is classic and much sought after, and if she still has a steam wheel on her, so much the better. A steam propeller, by the way, often has a pitch twice its diameter, and to see a tiny engine, overshadowed by a hulking boiler, simply run away with that hunk of bronze is a sight to behold. Steam

(continued on page 104)

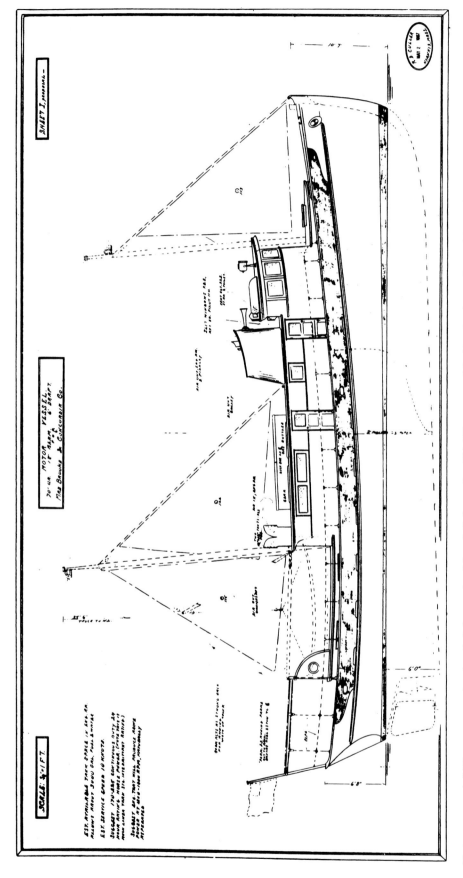

Most power vessels fall into two categories, those built for speed and those built for comfort. This 70' motor vessel for Mrs. Brooks was designed for comfort, with a cruising speed of about 10 knots. The cabin plan emphasizes how comfortable such a vessel could be, with its owner's stateroom, fireplace in the main saloon, and ample crew spaces, and including plenty of room for the hardest working crewmember, the engine. (© Mystic Seaport, Ships Plans Collection, Mystic, CT)

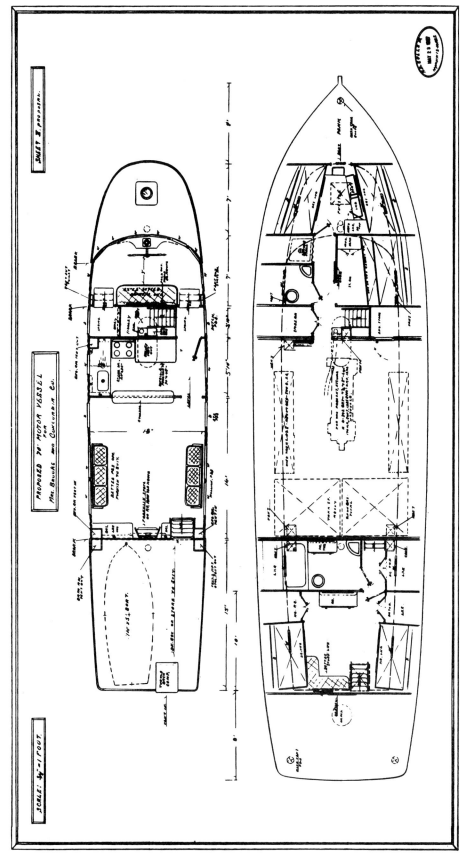

70' motor vessel (continued). (© Mystic Seaport, Ships Plans Collection, Mystic, CT)

(continued from page 101)

jargon is different too: double simples, tandem compounds, in-lines, Wards, Navy K's, Stephenson links. It's awful; don't go near it or you are hooked. I like the smell of soft coal myself!

A more complicated yet cheaper form of propulsion than engines is oars, and I think we should include sculling oars and paddles. The complication is that you cannot buy really good oars off the shelf; it is far, far easier to buy a good engine. I've expounded on oars before, do so now, and will, no doubt, in the future. A good boat requires good oars, and as her type varies, so, to some extent, should the model and construction of her oars. Until you have tried a good pair of oars, it's impossible to realize what you have been missing. Fortunately, good oars are not difficult to make, for those who like a little woodworking, and the stock to make them is easy to come by.

Most oars are made way too short nowadays; they should be at least twice the beam of the boat, often more, and it's difficult to find any long enough in a store. When you do, they are frightening—great logs of wood, often with poor grain. So you grab the shortest, which are lighter, but good for little except stirring a great vat of jam.

You can purchase a stock pair of oars if they are of sufficient length and then work them down. These are never quite right, however; as well as having too much wood in the wrong places, which you can work off, there is not enough of it in others. Greatly oversized surplus lifeboat oars have enough wood so they can be worked down successfully; there is a lot of trimming, but they are often cheap. They are apt to be of heavy wood, and though they may well suit a dory or other working craft when taken down, the stock is unsuited to light, smart craft.

Many lumber yards stock construction spruce, and if you know a yard crew who happens to be the kind who lets you pick—leaving the pile as neat as it was, naturally—some very nice stuff can often be found. A place that has a big turnover is good; if you don't find it this week, go back next. The stock is often wet or damp, so it must be taken home and stored carefully to dry. No matter, it's fairly cheap, so get enough, say longer and wider than your oars require, so you can use the best parts.

Ash has been the standard for working oars for a long time. Good fir also does well for workboat oars, though it has more weight than, say, spruce or some other woods. Sitka spruce is just fine for light oars, if you can get it and want to pay the price. Depending on the use, many other woods can be used, and just because they are not used now is no reason why they can't be. I have a canoe double paddle, which is 75 or more years old and seems to be made of Eastern pine; it's in fine shape and lively.

Built of solid stock, an oar or paddle can be very wasteful of stock. Gluing up, which has been done for a long time, makes it quite easy to build up a suitable oar out of stock of almost any dimensions, saving much material and a little labor. Oar and paddle making, while by no means difficult, is not a fast, machine process, if the oars are to be any good. You make a big pile of shavings, which is, I think, pleasant work.

Proportions for one oar are shown in the accompanying drawing. I feel these are not, and never can be, absolute. The boat, the wood, the physique of the oarsman, the waters to be traveled, and your plain artistic ability and imagination all play a part in just how an oar should be built. Here are some guides I've found to work. To begin with, children often row, and should be encouraged to do so; right away, you are apt to think of a set of small sized oars, but unless the boat is tiny, too, these don't work. A properly shaped oar, made out of the right material and of the proper length for the boat, is so well balanced that any active child can handle it with ease and usually with delight, as the craft responds for him as it should. We need to keep

Two different engine installations are pictured here, an inboard diesel engine for a 40' schooner (above) and a pair of 55-hp outboards for a 30' v-bottom day cruiser (below).

children out of boats of poor model with oars like clubs. One of my Down East friends describes such craft by saying, "They're so bad you can't row 'em, you just sort of pry 'em along."

People's hands being about the same size, the grips on the oar should be about the same length regardless of the oar's length. We are not speaking of big single-banked lifeboats where you use two hands to an oar. A length of 5 inches is about right for the grip. Never use a keg shape, as in a stock oar, but give the grip a diameter of about 1 1/4 inches at the inboard end tapering to about an inch next to the swelled part of the oar, just the opposite taper to what you might think. A very light oar for a slight boat and small hands can be a bit smaller. This is easy to make; you just whittle and feel until you're happy with it. Whatever the finish chosen for the oar, the grip should be left bare. Give it a smooth finish, and palm grease will do the rest.

The inboard part of the oar, between the grip and the oarlock or thole should be large. The idea is to keep the weight, such as it is, inboard. The balance point should be only a little outboard of the leather. Most oars are very blade heavy. Just how you shape this inboard part is, I think, a matter of fancy, so long as you have enough wood for balance. I like eight-square or four-square, but an oversize cylinder is workable. The Turks and other Mediterranean people use a big, nicely shaped swelling.

The oar outboard of the lock should be very light and nicely shaped. There should be a fairly rapid taper to the neck, or thin part at the start of the blade. The loom should start turning to oval right after clearing the leather, with the long part of the oval horizontal when taking the stroke, putting the more wood in the direction of strain. The thin dimension of the oval can be quite small, sometimes an inch or less.

The blade should be narrow, with a nice taper to the widest part, never more than 4 inches, even for a 9-foot or longer oar, and slightly less for shorter oars. A ridge should be formed on each side of the blade, extending from the wide part of the oval and not quite dying out at the blade tip. Much hollow should be worked on each side of the ridges. This combination of ridges and hollow lightens the blade very much, gives it sufficient strength, and, for some reason, makes the oar almost self feathering. Just how the tip of the blade is finished seems a matter of taste. I like a very flattened roof-like angle, relieved in the edges so the blade looks to have no thickness at all, except in the center ridge, which is not touched. This shallow point is nice to

Capt. Pete shows proper oar technique aboard Otter, *a high-performance bateau he designed and built for his own use.* Otter *is pictured in several places throughout this volume.* (© Mystic Seaport, Richard White Collection, Mystic, CT)

shove off with. Some Mediterranean oars have a hollow half-moon in the ends; I suppose this might have advantages in shoving off. The oars of some pilot yawls of the past had almost circular blade ends. Maybe more investigation is needed on this fine point.

Softwood oars require leathers, and store-bought leathers now are way too short, about 7 inches. They should be at least 12 inches; I prefer 14 inches myself. Usually, sufficient material can be had from a worker in leather goods, or if a fellow is going to make several pairs, a tanned hide can be bought. Leathers should be kept lubricated, as should the oarlocks and sockets. I like tallow best, though Vaseline will do. A rowing craft should have a container of such stuff aboard. Cow horns not being available to everyone nowadays, I like to make a thing that looks somewhat like an old-time rigger's tallow horn, of wood, with a plug and lanyard, and keep the goo handy in that. This is part of a well-run pulling boat's gear. Ash or hardwood oars do well without leathers if they are kept greased. Grease seems to work well on tholepins too, though plenty is needed, especially in wet weather.

Who uses tholes now? Not many, yet they work just fine and are traditional to dories. The slight thump of the tholes on a quiet morning is pleasant. Except in one way, they are no different to use than locks. The exception is the simply learned trick of jumping the oar out when coming alongside, to prevent a broken pin or oar. Otherwise, if you can't use tholes, you have not really learned to row. Oarlocks, either of bronze or galvanized iron, are apt to have a poor finish inside. Some work with a file soon fixes this, and though filing cuts the galvanizing off, it's no matter, as the galvanizing soon goes on the inside of the lock anyhow. Use, with lubrication, will keep things in order. On sizeable boats, oarlocks are often too small, usually number ones; I would sooner use number twos that are a bit slack than number ones that are too small. There are not

as many oarlock patterns available now as there used to be. I like what is called the Boston pattern, a ribbed lock with a small side-eye for the lanyard. The lanyard or chain that goes through the socket is a two-handed abomination. Tholes require lanyards through the holes, and these are awkward too, if not rigged right. You need nicely shaped tholes with slightly tapered bottom ends and sunk lanyard holes. Reeve the lanyard from one thole through its hole and up through the second hole to its thole. Use a wood toggle or metal thimble in the bight that hangs down. With the tholes lying inboard, run your hand under them, grab the lanyard, give an outboard toss of the hand and a pull on the lanyard—a natural movement—and the tholes pop in at once. I have never seen this method used, except on my own boats. I'm sure it's nothing new.

Many old craft had some form of wooden oarlocks. Those I've used all work, and like lubrication. If they suit your particular type of boat, there is no reason at all for not using them. It's sort of nice to make your own gear and fittings; they are easily replaced or repaired, often enhance the right boat for them, and, of course, allow a bit of artistic license and imagination.

Some discussion of rowing might be in order. The rowing of shells and sculls is a thing in itself, and there are experts on it, which I am not. The boats we consider here are different. I feel a sliding-seat craft can be unhandy around saltwater if the area is exposed, and I sometimes think spoon-like oars are not worthwhile unless the craft has a sliding-seat rig. I'm no doubt open to some critics here. I have noticed that those trained in shells and sculls who have done little or no rowing in other craft darn near kill themselves in an attempt to pull a dory in any wind, even one of rather sharp model. It's a different kettle of fish. Those who have rowed only dinghies, boxy skiffs, and most of the stock craft, with poor oars, too, find that they too have something to learn about using a proper rowing craft. The

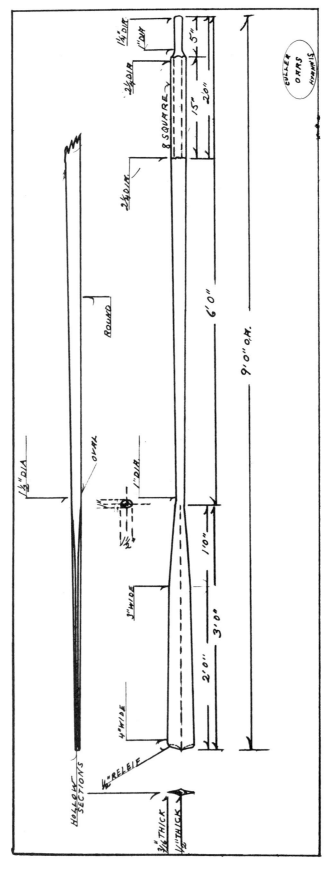

Pete Culler's oar designs are as unique and distinctive as the Culler boats they are used in. I know of no other designer who gave this amount of thought and attention to both flat and spoon oars to be used in his boat designs. Pete supplied his own oars of the appropriate type and length with every boat built at his Hyannis shop. Ordering a boat was how you acquired Culler oars. In order to make his oars more accessible he freely gave away the designs to Mystic Seaport, to various publications, and to anyone who asked for them. These oars are worth the time and effort it takes to make them. The fabrication techniques are discussed on pages 219–233. Pictured here are plans for 9' flat oars. (© Mystic Seaport, Ships Plans Collection, Mystic, CT)

short dory stroke, so often seen when pros pull them, does work. A more sophisticated stroke, if in any wind at all, does not get the best out of a dory, even a Swampscott, and is tiring. I find a smart boat, say a Whitehall or similar easy-moving craft, pulls best in light weather using what I think of as the old yacht hand's stroke—not too much forward reach and a good long pull aft, letting the elbows kick out on the recovery, with the body upright, and a precise, quick feather with the oars just clear of the water. The old-timers seemed to clear the water by about $\frac{1}{16}$ inch, they were so skillful. Many of these watermen used what I choose to call the Battery boatman style of rowing, with their hands one ahead of the other instead of side by side so the grip was in the center of the boat for both hands. Some craft take very kindly to this, and there is less weight of oar on the hands. Try it; once mastered, this technique will move a boat very well, and it's not tiring.

I think variations of stroke in rowing are worth cultivating; they suit different boats, and a change of stroke can be restful on a long pull. It's sort of like the wise old dog, trotting down the road on far-off business, usually going somewhat on the bias, and every now and then changing tacks, no doubt to change the load on his muscles and rest them up. I feel a lot about rowing has been somewhat forgotten and that we must be willing to experiment and re-learn to get the most out of it.

A pulling boat of good model can be a lovely and satisfying thing, even though she may be somewhat plain. Good oars she must have to respond, and it they are nice to look at and maybe have some decoration, they add much besides their efficiency. Usually, if you get interested in pulling boats, you want a smarter boat, or one for more specialized use, and this is good. Having such craft is economical, you get close to the water, life is not complicated, and I think the exercise from rowing does no harm to one in any sort of health at all. In fact, it may do a lot of good, mentally if not otherwise.

To my way of thinking sail propulsion is the least simple of all the methods of making a boat move through the water. It is not that the rigs themselves, particularly in the smaller, classic craft, are complicated, difficult to use, or expensive. The complications come from the wide range of possibilities with sail, the many hulls that can be developed for it, and the wide variety of sizes of craft that can use it. A tiny skiff can be made to sail quite well, within her limits. Sail has been used on craft nearly 500 feet long. The variations in rig to cover such a range of sizes are many. Moreover, rigs are influenced by

A good boat requires a good pair of oars. The options have expanded somewhat since Pete's day, but to acquire a good pair of oars, properly fitted to the craft and capable of powering your boat with a minimum of effort, you must still build them yourself, or hire a willing pro to build them for you. The photo shows spoon as well as flat blades on Culler-style oars. (© Mystic Seaport, Richard White Collection, Mystic, CT)

109

the trade and the local conditions in which they are used. The gear to control all the rigs that have been developed is extensive and, in many cases, elaborate, if the craft is large. Probably no one man has ever become adept at using all rigs, though any trained seaman in sail would not be totally at a loss with an entirely strange rig. He would soon catch on, as all rigs have things in common—the use of the wind and supporting and handling sail with rope and wire. The smaller the craft, the simpler her rig should be.

Sailing, at least under half-way decent conditions, is probably the most pleasant way of moving about on the water, and the mastery of handling several different alongshore sailing craft is not learned overnight. Sailing is not at all difficult, but it takes time, experience, and study. All of it is enjoyable,

though some heavy-weather experiences don't seem so at the time. You tend to learn fast in rough weather, or give it up. True deep-water sailing is a trade in itself. Some may doubt this. Many a coaster of long experience and good record is uneasy, however, when well offshore. Sea buoys, dirty gray-green water, and the sounding lead he understands well. The true deepwater man in the great days of sail, on the other hand, had a great fear of the land. His vessel was not designed and built to find herself suddenly with a strange coast close abroad, and once she made her port, it was not so good either, for there were land sharks about to prey on her crew, stores, and gear. The deep-water ship was a true daughter of the sea. The coaster, able as he was, always had some shore dirt clinging to him. Most of us have to be content with just that.

THE SPRIT RIG

Rigs being so many and so varied, it's well to start with the smallest and simplest. Pulling boats and dinghies, though mainly for oars, can well use a sail, which will much increase the pleasure and range of these boats. Most such craft can use centerboards to advantage, though a board is not needed if the sail is only for reaching and running. The beach boat types are, as a rule, well adapted for sailing. Naturally, a small, open boat, often having a model with little sail-carrying power, must have a simple rig, one that is easy to use, light of canvas and spars, and with the latter reasonably short. The rig should be easily struck and set up, for it's not permanently placed. The common dory spritsail, properly cut and rigged, is the most efficient and practical of all small, open-boat sails. Do I hear great shouts of doubt? Try it and find out. I repeat, it must be well-shaped and cut. Such sails are shown in Howard I. Chapelle's *American Small Sailing Craft*. Anyone can have such a sail with the aid, if need be, of an interested sailmaker.

The spritsail, in its simplest form, has a minimum of rigging. There is a snotter to hold up the sprit. It's just a bit of line, though the way it is rigged is all-important. There are a few robands, or else a lace line, to keep the sail to the mast, and a sheet. The sail should by all means be loose-footed with no boom. The sheeting point is critical, but not at all difficult to determine. That's all there is to it. No sail has less, and the spritsail has the maximum sail area for the least spar length. Any of the other practical small craft rigs require as much or more gear and longer spars for the same amount of sail.

The rig can be taken in rapidly in the event of weather making. If need be, once the knack is learned, the whole thing can be thrown overboard to leeward, still spreeted out, on a slack but fast sheet (don't lose the end!) and ridden to as a sort of sea anchor until such time as it's convenient to drag it aboard, and furl it. A very handy thing to know, yet the knowledge of this trick has nearly been lost.

A somewhat larger craft, say from 16 to 20 feet in length, still of a model that rows well, can have more of a rig. Such boats being longer than dinghies, and usually somewhat sharper, are often very smart sailers and will be used under sail except in calms or just for the plain fun of rowing. Here the sprit rig still works best in most cases, and its handiest form, if considerable sail area is wanted, is the old working boat two-sail rig.

This rig is most versatile and is suited to all kinds of conditions and strengths of wind. The full two-sail rig is the light weather or pleasure rig and its area is suitable for light to moderate conditions. There is a foremast step and a mizzen step, usually in combination with mast gates in the thwarts so the spars can be easily handled in a bit of a lop. There is a third step between the first two; this takes the foremast when the foresail is used alone. This makes the working rig and is suited to moderate to fresh winds. Usually the sail is cut high enough in the foot so the mast rake can be changed a bit to achieve good balance. Often the foresail has a reef so that it's usable in a stronger wind than just fresh. In the event of having to work in a strong wind, the little mizzen is stepped in the middle hole, often with considerable rake.

All this makes a very workable and seaman-like rig, one that is able to adapt to all sorts of uses. The rig is light and reasonably cheap with very little upkeep. The whole rig is struck unless the boat is sailing, except for occasional short stops, such as beaching to clam. If the boat hauls up and the rig can be put in shelter, fine. If she's moored and the rig is left aboard, it should be well lashed to the thwarts; then she can stand much thrashing in bad weather. I find that when leaving the rig lashed in the boat, a sail cover is very worthwhile.

I think cotton sails are far easier to handle in these small boats than sails of any man-made fibers yet developed; these are just too slippery and fluttery for easy use in small boats. If Cuprinol treated, a cotton sail lasts as long as any other. Plain ordinary boat drill used to be the standard for these sails. They do well with a vertical cut and should be roped on at least three sides. This is very much 18th Century thinking and for good reason; this kind of boating is from that era. It is boating that involves the attractive and economical boat, one that has many uses, which will teach much seamanship and be a pleasure for many years. People seem to be seeking this kind of boating, yet it is hard to discover in today's yachting magazines.

The average craft of the size and type we are discussing with a two-sail rig has about 100 square feet of sail. Spars for these rigs are small and light. I'm often asked just how and where you get a wooden spar. The answer is at a lumber yard, unless you are so fortunate to be able to go out in the woods, which is more fun. Sprits for these rigs are about the same length as the mast they work with, and vary from about $1\frac{1}{8}$ inches to $1\frac{1}{2}$ inches in diameter. A reasonably clear 2×4, split, makes a couple of sprits to be shaped up. Spruce or fir does quite well. Masts go from $2\frac{1}{2}$ inches to $3\frac{1}{4}$ inches in diameter, and a 4×4 of the same stuff does the job. Sometimes these little sticks are glued up out of thinner stuff, but with the availability of $2\times$'s and $4\times$'s, it's not worth the trouble. A spritsail mast should not have much taper until near the head; sprits themselves have a taper each way from the middle.

The fittings for these rigs are of wood, and easily made. The few fittings needed have had long development and work far better than fittings that can be bought. These latter seem designed to fit all small boats, and so fit none just right. This is more backward thinking, but the wood and rope stuff is efficient, cheap, looks the part, and, as one of my friends has so often pointed out, "It can all be repaired if something goes wrong at 7 o'clock on a Sunday morn, when all the marinas are closed."

There is a shoulder on the sprit's upper end to engage the becket in the peak of the sail. The spindle beyond the shoulder should be 4 or 5 inches long. This maybe can't be called a fitting; it's whittled on the spar. In the lower end of the sprit there is a slot to take the snotter; a rivet should be driven through just above the slot to prevent splitting. The mast has a round, tapered heel, since a sprit mast must rotate, or the snotter, robands, and all will bind. The foremast needs two or three small thumb

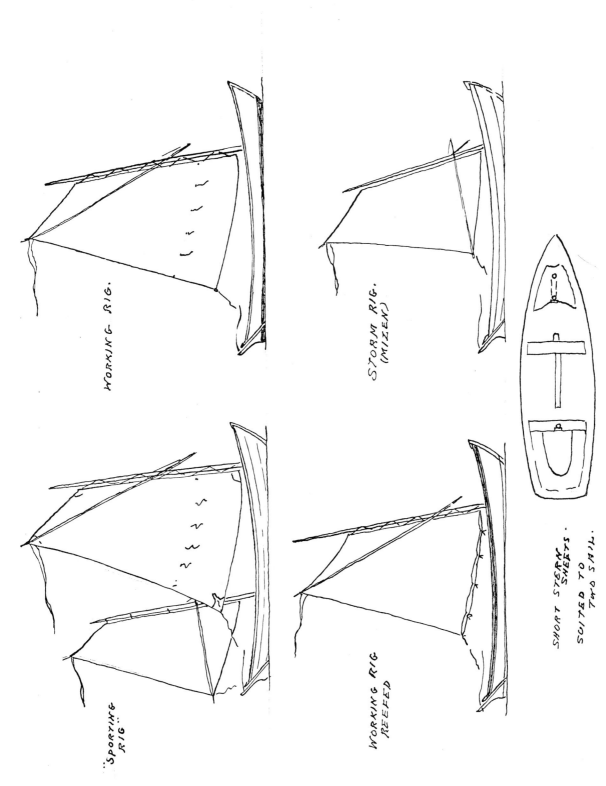

WORKING RIG.

STORM RIG.
(MIZEN)

SPORTING RIG.

WORKING RIG
REEFED

SHORT STERN SHEETS.
SUITED TO TWO SAIL.

This sketch shows various configurations in the old working boat two-sail rig that Pete Culler discusses. Note the mast step locations and a swinging mast gate.

113

cleats for reefing. Each mast has a fair-sized hole about an inch from the head. It's been said that a hole takes no maintenance! If the boat carries the two-sail rig, she will require a fairlead on or near each rail, of wood, naturally, for the fore sheets, which must be double to work around the mizzen. A single-sail boat, or one using the bad-weather mizzen, uses a single sheet.

Mizzens in use as such need some sort of spar to make them sheet properly; some folks use booms, others, short clubs. I like the sprit boom, much used in the past on many craft, notably on Captain Nat Herreshoff's early boats and on Commodore Ralph Munroe's sharpies. This boom is rigged with the inboard end above the foot of the loose-footed sail so it's clear of the helmsman's head; it makes the sail set flat, as a mizzen should, and the sail can sheet to the center of the boat without twist. It's sort of like sheeting a barn door; the sail's draft can be adjusted nicely. The principle is

the same as that used on New Haven sharpies and Chesapeake small craft sails in regard to taking care of the foot. A sharp-headed sail of the sharpie cut can be used as a mizzen on an otherwise sprit-rigged craft, and though this rig saves one spar, the mast has to be quite long to get sufficient sail area, a general failing of any sharp-headed sail.

If the tack of the foresail is set very low in the boat with a high-cut clew, she carries sail better. Many folks don't want the rig low, saying they can't see ahead; you can, better than you first think. It's important in sailing small boats to keep the center of effort low. Some of the rigs now seen on small stock boats demonstrate that this principle has been forgotten, and if you sail in the racing classes you have to go along with tall rigs.

The best way to rig a spritsail on a mast is to use a laceline. The lacing can be some slippery line, rather small, kept greased with tallow, and *not* passed round and round the mast, for then it will

Capt. Pete's dory Dancing Feather *with the sporting rig that is suitable for light or moderate conditions.*

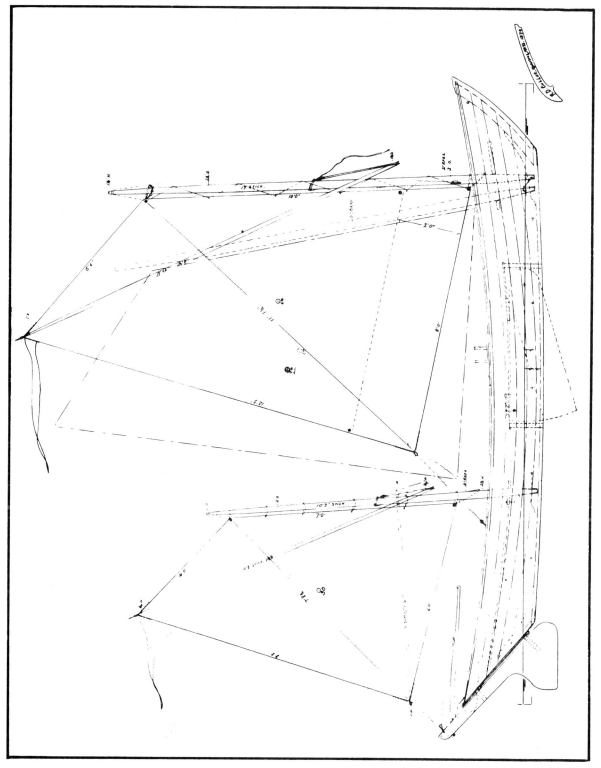

The sail plan for Capt. Charley Sayle's 18'8" dory, which is very similar to Dancing Feather in model and rig. (© Mystic Seaport, Ships Plans Collection, Mystic, CT)

jam. Pass it back and forth, forth and back, and it will never jam. The laceline can be quite slack. A single-part throat halyard is best, with a cleat for it on the mast so it can rotate with the spar. I make fast the tail of the halyard to the throat of the sail so it goes aloft as the sail is hoisted, leaving no line to coil, and just slack enough to belay. A mast loop or toggle with wooden parrel beads should be secured to the sail's throat to keep it to the mast, for the sprit tends to push it away.

I find a foremast from 12 to 14 feet long with sail and sprit rolled up on it to be not at all difficult to step and stow, if the spars are well chosen and shaped. A 16-foot mast is about the reasonable limit and will be suitable for a 20- to-22-foot boat with a two-sail rig. In bigger two-sail boats, or in a sizable

Pete's sharp wherry Seaman's Friend, *showing the sprit rig and its details. Note the arrangement of the snotter.* (John Burke)

boat using a single sail, another kind of small craft sail becomes more practical: the standing lug. We can take this one up later, with all its simplicities.

A sprit foresail of 60 to 70 square feet in area should have a reef, one about two feet deep. Many folks ask just how you reef a loose-footed sail. It's done just the same as one with a boom, with the added advantage that you can't make the mistake of tying the reefpoints around the boom! Assuming the sail to be lowered, pass the tack lashing, stretch the foot taut with the sheet and keep it so, pass the clew lashing between clew and reef cringles, set up just snug, and tie the points. That's it, and it's simpler than with a boom in the way. Incidentally, the laceline needs no taking up when reefing; I don't know why, but the old timers who worked it out knew their stuff!

Some folks nowadays think reefing is too much work or "sissy." Some designers go along with this attitude and turn out grossly under-canvassed craft. Yet the owner will go through all sorts of antics struggling with many light sails, their purchase, stowage, and upkeep, to make his under-canvassed boat go. In a properly rigged craft, you are exposed a much shorter time to the more risky parts of the boat in reefing than you are when tussling with light sails that are out of hand. If you race, you put up with the going thing, be it sensible by your lights or not.

We have mentioned a snotter several times; all it does is keep the heel of the sprit up. If it's not right, the sail won't set properly. There are several methods of rigging the snotter, some quite complicated for the big working sails of the past. For small craft, my favorite snotter rig does just fine. I have seen it nowhere else than on craft I have to do with, though, being simple and practical, it was worked out long ago, I'm sure. Take a piece of line of proper size, say $5/16$ inch for the size craft we are considering. Make a long eye splice sufficient for the eye to pass around the mast and about 3 inches more. Seize in tightly a wooden or brass thimble next to the splice. Then pass the whole rig around the mast, putting the single end and thimble through the long eye. The thimble should now be on the forward side of the mast and a couple of inches below where the doubled line passes through the eye. Naturally this rig wants to slide down the mast; one of the before-mentioned thumb cleats is needed to hold it up. The best position for the cleat can be determined by trial with the sail spread on the ground. The cleat goes thumb upwards on the aft side of the mast. It can be shifted later if not right.

To set the sail, ship the sprit in the peak, take a turn through the slot in the lower end of the sprit with the single end of the snotter, then reeve it up through the thimble, then haul it down. You have a nice little tackle. Peak the sail up well, for things do stretch. Never sail with the peak too low. Hitch the end of the snotter in the sprit slot. There should be little strain on the end of the snotter under a press of sail, so the snotter can be let go immediately if need be. Some methods of rigging a snotter make it difficult, sometimes impossible, to let it go in a hurry.

Sheets are simply lengths of line, single-part for sails of the size we are describing. The old standard belay was a slippery hitch on a half pin under a thwart. A half pin sticking below a thwart or pin rail does not get foul of things, and if a slippery hitch is used, a twitch of the sheet frees it instantly. For snotters and sheets I still prefer manila line. The other stuff is slippery, though it's all right in other parts of the rig, not that there is much more.

Sometimes, if your place of getting underway and coming to is awkward, a single brail can be very handy on the foresail. It can kill part of the sail's drive without slacking the sheet or touching the sprit, and it tends to quiet flogging. A slippery line that won't kink when wet should be used for a brail. Rig it this way: spread the sail on the ground or floor with the sprit rigged. Strike an arc with a piece of string from peak to throat, carrying

it out to the leech, and mark the spot. Here sew or seize a small brass thimble to stand vertically on the leech, just like a reef cringle. Similarly secure three more thimbles to one side of the luff, one at the throat, another about half way down, and one at the tack. It does not matter which side these take, so long as they are all on the same side. Fix one end of the brail to the throat on the opposite side from the thimble there, reeve out through the leech cringle, back through the thimble at the throat, and down along the luff through the middle and tack thimbles. Have enough slack to come back, and some more, to a cleat on the side of the centerboard well or some other handy place that suits. To brail in the sail, simply slack the sheet and haul on the brail, slacking more sheet as needed. A brail is a handy rig, though now seldom seen. The one I have described is no different in principle, though much simpler, than the big brails with many leads used on large barge sails or ships' spankers. I find the brail a most useful bit of gear on a loose-footed spritsail, and it in no way interferes with the usual method of furling, which is rolling the sail up on the sprit and securing with the now-loose snotter. A sail rolled up with the sprit does not blow loose.

All this Old World gear always raises eyebrows. It can't possibly work or be "efficient." It does, however, and if the boat is any shakes of a model at all and the rig tuned, as any must be to perform well, she gives a good account of herself in modern company and sometimes takes over, a wolf among sheep. Then the eyebrows do some twitching! Try it.

An old-time boatyard owner, now retired and somewhat of a sage, tells an interesting story that illustrates some basic differences between "modern" craft and the simple boats we have been describing. The story is totally true: A man, wife, and children with picnic baskets arrive at the waterside for a day's sail in their ultra-modern boat; she's no bigger than a dory, but she has everything. Her owner stores his boat at the yard; the craft is nearly new. The family is put aboard by launch. There is a flurry of sail bags and there is much rigging up, as these craft require. After some delay comes considerable waving; the launch finally spots this signaling and goes alongside. Seems something is wrong with the tiny wire halyard which reeves inside the hollow metal mast; the trouble is aloft. The launch tows the boat to the club dock to see what can be done. No one there really knows what's up, so they send for the rigger from the yard, which is nearby, and he shows up. The boat is jockeyed alongside, wife and children having been put ashore, and the rigger balances shakily atop a piling and reaches with long-nose pliers. No dice; he needs help. His helper is sent for, arrives and they struggle. Still no soap; something more is wrong than they can reach. So they take her to the yard crane and hang a man from a bos'n's chair, for the craft is too frail for going aloft on. This requires the yard launch to tow the boat to the crane and a man to operate it. She's put in position, the great boom is swung over her, the big block lowered, and a chair hooked on. By now it's dinner time and all hands knock off. The Yacht Owner and family sit glumly on the caplog with picnic basket, which has suffered some from the hot sun. They munch from it. The children start to bicker. (Can't blame 'em.)

Finally, the yard gang straggles back, we assume well fed, and go at it again. The crane is a hand-winder. Little Joe is the operator; he's a hot man on a crank and puts the rigger over his work with some dispatch, bucket of tools and all. There is more struggle, sort of like pulling teeth from a sky hook, and it goes on quite awhile. The helper sends things up and down on a gantline; the crew knows their trade. At last word comes from aloft, after the helper has done much more pulling from under the deck, "Can't budge it. Got to take the mast out and unreeve the whole thing." They do,

laying the mast out on horses ashore. Its innards are removed to reveal some sort of kinked thinga-majig. Have to make a new one, which they do with dispatch, as the yard has the latest tools for putting fittings on this light wire and a bin of the doodads. Then the re-reeving starts. A mouse with a string on his tail, chased by a cat, might have taken a pilot line through. There is neither cat nor mouse handy. Finally someone turns up with a plumber's fish, and the job is accomplished. It's now mid-afternoon. The proud owner decides to go home; his wife has been dictating to him; the children are at each other's throats. The boat is buttoned up before quitting time and put out on her mooring with care and dispatch by the yard tow-boat and her man.

Some days later the owner appears and inquires as to his craft's health. He's assured she's fine, at the moment, and is presented with the bill for her recent sickness. Seventy-eight bucks! (This was in the cheap days.) The Yachtsman goes straight up! He lands, running, and heads for the Sage's office. He howls and screams. The Sage looks sad, but there is an interesting light in his eye. He is wise; he is patient; he explains the bill, item by item: rigger and helper teetering on top of piling, so much time; towboat and man twice; rigger and helper for most of the day; crane charge and the cranker's time; wire and fittings (the least of it); someone to run the plumber down and get his fish. The poor Sage has to charge his time somewhere. Besides, the plumber was hard to find; he was under a tank in the bowels of some vessel, it was hot down there, and he was somewhat irritable and had to be talked into lending the fish. The Sage has a way about him; the owner is now willing to admit, yes, the time must have all been there, but, God, all for a 14-foot boat?

This gives the Sage the opening he's been waiting for; after forty years of boating, he's very knowledgeable about these things. "Mr. So and So,

(continued on page 122)

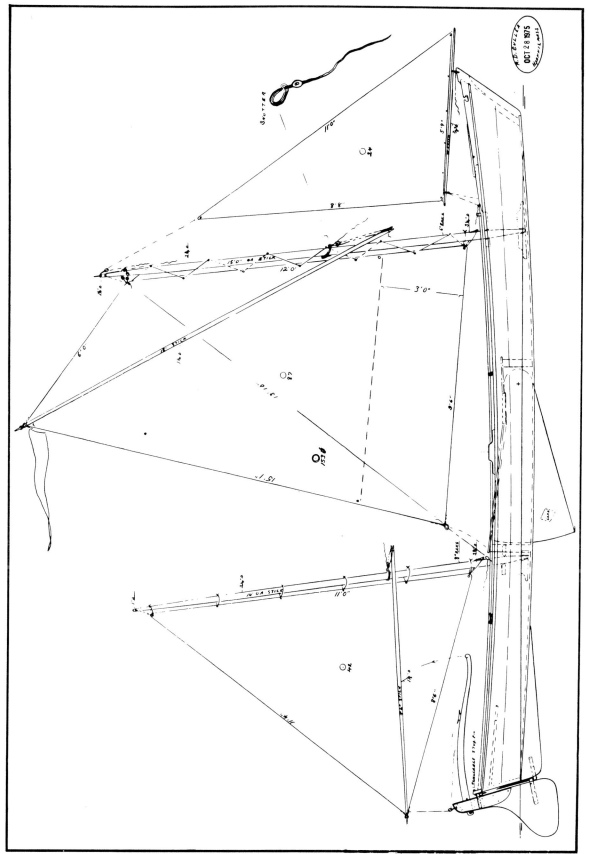

Sail plans for a Sharptown barge, a Bray skiff, and a beach boat (see following pages) all being flat bottom and showing various configurations of sprit rigs. A little study of these sail plans and a careful reading of the text will help the reader in understanding how the working two-sail sprit rig is utilized as auxiliary sail in classic rowing craft as designed by Pete Culler. (© Mystic Seaport, Ships Plans Collection, Mystic, CT)

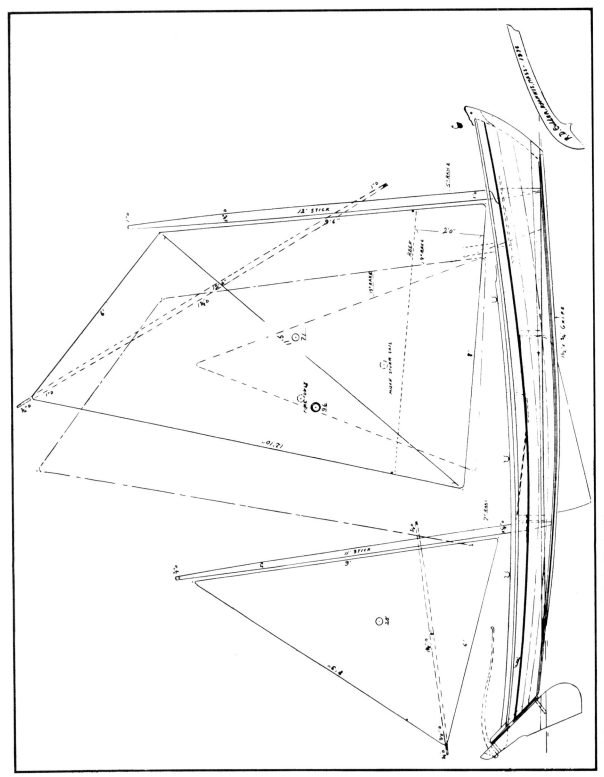

Bray skiff. © Mystic Seaport, Ships Plans Collection, Mystic, CT

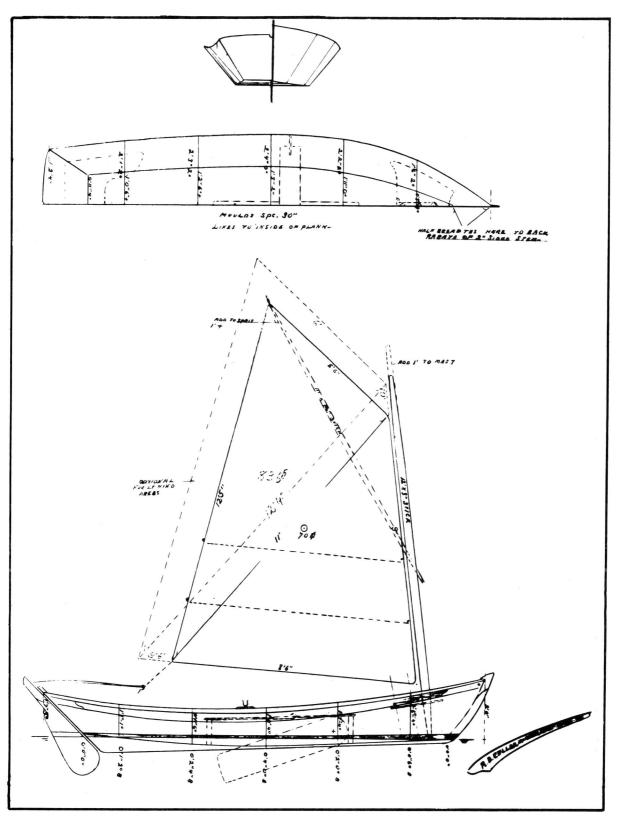

Beach boat. (© Mystic Seaport, Ships Plans Collection, Mystic, CT)

(continued from page 118)

simple wooden craft, yes, of nice model, can be very smart. The simple sprit rig, a plain hole, and a bit of line are so cheap. And these are things you can repair yourself in a few minutes. Something that can readily be rowed if need be (no towboat and man), and something attractive to the eye. It's all so much more fun and you get at the sandwiches before they spoil, and so on, and so on. Maybe another type would be better; come sailing in my Yankee sloopboat sometime."

The fellow does, and gets hooked. The Sage builds him a handsome classic craft, for a good price, but she's a lovely thing. She's smart, docile, can sail herself, and is a witch at working in tight places. The owner preens a bit, for many take notice, even those who don't understand her. If you do or not, no matter; she's good to look at. She was designed by some Cuss from Cape Cod who is noted for his set ways when it comes to boats and tobacco.

I leave the sprit-rigged ones right here.

OTHER RIGS, INCLUDING THE KETCH

In continuing to discuss open craft, which in many ways are the most fun, it may be well to mention another rig which seems to be almost forgotten, yet which is well suited to a boat a bit too big for the sprit rig. This is the standing lug. Like so many working rigs, the standing lug will spread considerable area of sail, yet without the necessity of long spars and lots of gear. With a properly cut sail, the rig has a lot of drive to it.

Unless the boat is big enough for a two-sail rig, and a mizzen is used, the standing lug is loose-footed with no boom. A mizzen lug sail usually needs a boom for proper sheeting, as does a sprit mizzen. The lug requires a somewhat longer mast than does a spritsail, as there is a halyard, single-part for most boats, or with more parts if the sail is large. The sail requires no method of keeping it to the mast; it sets alongside the spar and stands on its own merits. Rigged right, stand it does! The tack only requires a lashing to the mast and a thumb cleat to keep it from riding up. The sheet can be single, or double if the boat is two-sail, and can have as many parts as you feel you need, in practice the less the better. The head is spread by a yard, which should be well peaked up, and this crosses the mast

at a point about a third of its length from the fore end. There should be a small-line serving on the yard where it crosses the mast, to take the chafe. This should be kept greased, in which case it will have a very long life.

There are several ways of keeping the yard to the mast. The simplest is a strap or parrel passing around the mast with a wood toggle to engage an eye. It should have a loose fit. It may have parrel beads in a sizable craft; usually they are not needed. The object of the toggle is so you can easily remove the yard from the mast. Setting the tack adrift makes the whole sail portable; it can be put in a long sail bag if left on board, or can be taken ashore. I like to rig a few permanent sail stops right on the yard so the sail can have a proper stow before removing.

The mast can be left standing, or can be lowered if it is small enough and there is a gate. A lug mast can be longer than that for a sprit rig and still lower fairly easily, as it has no sail and sprit stowed on it. Often the halyard is set up to the stemhead to steady things at a mooring if the mast is left up. Unstayed masts in small craft are quite able to stand for themselves, with the exception that now most harbors have so much motorboat traffic that such masts tend to wear in the deck and step. Even fully-stayed masts take a beating this way in small craft nowadays; something gets a little loose and things begin to wear from the constant thrashing. Some hulls eventually suffer in the garboards from all this man-made commotion. I grant lowering a heavy mast each time a boat is brought to is too much of a chore and has some risk if it's sloppy. I suggest lowering masts in craft with masts no more than 16 feet long. With bigger spars, the rig should be designed to stand, though even so it's wise to keep the rig light and simple enough so that with help

A cat ketch rig on the 25' cowhorn dory Trudi. *This is a rig that has an overlapping main set in the eyes of the boat, while the mizzen, of nearly equal height, is stepped in the center of the hull, with the centerboard box offset to port.* (Jim Brown)

the stick can be put in upon fitting out and taken down on lay-up for some minor repair without calling on a crane. Even on fair-sized open boats of classic model, I like to try to arrange for a gate in the partners.

Setting and lowering a lugsail is most simple. The sail has a single halyard, very little gear, yet a good spread of sail. Reefing is simple too. And it's a rig that can be stowed very rapidly in a hard chance.

The only trick I see to making a lugsail is to realize that, by the nature of the sail's setting, the luff takes a good strain, so that the sail should have a stout luff rope with a little stretch to it. A lugsail stands better and lasts longer if cut vertically.

The dipping lug, much favored in Europe among the sailing fishing fleets in the past, is probably the most efficient sail of all, as long as you stay on one tack! That it has to be lowered each time on going about makes it impractical for pleasure sailing, particularly in narrow waters. A rare instance of its usefulness might be for someone situated in a trade wind belt where he was always making long cross-wind runs, in which case it would pay off wonderfully.

The same comment might be made about the lateen rig; it's fine for monsoon sailing in a dhow but generally unhandy in a small craft along shore. The revised or canoe version of the lateen, as now seen by the hundreds on sail boards, seems most awkward in that on easing it off in a puff, nearly the whole weight of spars and sail is suspended to leeward of the craft. I found that this was so long ago, and the same boat with a sprit or lug rig was much more stable than with her original canoe lateen.

Another rig that used to be popular for some small craft was the sliding gunter. Except that the three spars required were all about the same length and would stow in the boat, there was nothing good about it. The sliding gunter is very unhandy to set and take in and is hard to make set well. Though

this rig was much used for years in naval small boats where large crews were available, its use in small pleasure craft always seemed to me just the wrong thing. The crowded conditions in a small boat make the sliding gunter, with its long, unwieldy club, unhandy and unsafe.

The gaff rig and the Marconi, or sharp-headed, rig are used of course, but where rigs must be portable, there is too much gear to make these practical. And, as mentioned before, any sharp-headed sail is always hard to make big enough unless the mast is very long, just the thing you don't want in a small boat with a rig to be struck.

Craft of a build and design suited to standing rigs, open or decked, or craft large enough to be called cruising boats have requirements different from those of the portable-rig boats, and for the

Everybody likes a Friendship. This boat is 22'4" and was designed by Pete Culler for Knight Sturges for use in Buzzards Bay, Massachusetts, an area that has similar conditions to midcoast Maine where Friendship sloops were developed. The Friendship types are craft of great power and require large sail area and low center of effort. Due to owner preference, Pete reduced the sail area in the final design and in view of the displacement felt the design was somewhat under-canvassed for light weather.

most part the rigs suited to the small craft become unhandy in bigger boats, with the exception that the standing lug can often be used to advantage in fairly large craft. This is not to say that standing rigs, cruising or not, must be complicated and expensive. Just the opposite is true. Keep it simple—simple to build, repair, and use.

In discussing rigs with others in the past, using this approach, the reaction often is, "Will it be efficient?" A properly designed rig will be efficient and will be all that the hull is capable of using. Unfortunately, much money has been spent putting so-called modern rigs on classic hulls that are unable to use the advantages these rigs are supposed to offer. Nowadays, a "modern rig" means hollow spars, currently metal ones, special fittings, and many complications not needed on a handy day boat or small cruiser. Such a rig is expensive in terms of first cost, upkeep, and repair. Unless the craft is a racer, the great efficiency is seldom of much real use. The rig is only efficient by the wind at any rate, and the hull must be made up to it. Once the sheets are started, the modern rigs become real dogs; the farther off the wind, the worse they are. None of them are easy to handle if they have sufficient area without light sails. Usually, if the modern rig has enough area to work well in light going, its center of effort is very high, the area is too narrow on the base, and more often than not there are sheeting problems that require expensive gear to overcome. Often the boat does not steer as well on all points of sailing as she should. Some folks may doubt this statement, but I base my words on having made several conversions from modern rigs back to what I thought were more sensible rigs. The boats were better handling all around, a couple decided to become self-steerers, and all steered better and carried sail better. Some were even better to windward, for they stood on their feet and went where they looked, instead of being hove down and sliding off. The lack of pointing ability of the revised rigs was largely overcome by better sail-carrying ability and easier helms.

For a utility boat, a properly cut sail is of great importance for good sailing and handling. Racers of real experience know all about this; otherwise they couldn't stay in competition. A sail of proper cut, intelligent setting, and the right sheeting, makes the boat go. The trouble with so many high-aspect-ratio rigs (this just means the mast is too damn tall) is that it is difficult to make their sails set properly, and it requires considerable gear to do it. Quite all right for a racer, but not really practical for ordinary use. Why make a chore of it?

Just why you see so many craft now with no topping lift is hard to understand. I suppose it's the racing thing again, but for easy and sensible handling, a topping lift is needed to hold up any sort of boom at all. The lowering of a sail with a boom down on the stern sweeping around or overside is one of the most lubberly sights seen today (along with the present practice of setting the jib first and taking it in last, so the whole foredeck is in a state of menace casting off or coming to). I think I can say, without too much contradiction, that seamanship has degenerated very much in the last twenty-five years. Just why is hard to say. The nice handling of a boat under sail is now looked upon as a difficult thing, and is even at times made fun of. Actually, seamanship is only common sense applied to the tools one uses, in this case a boat. Possibly that's just the trouble; common sense is no longer felt to be needed in our modern society. A fellow gets into trouble on the water and the U. S. Coast Guard will bail him out. And Uncle will look after him in his old age. But I disagree.

On small boats and fairly light displacement boats of two-masted rig, I use simple rope lifts; wire is not needed. Some folks prefer to make the end fast on the boom, lead the lift to a block aloft, then down the mast to belay. Others make the end fast at the masthead by reeving it through a hole with a stopper knot (why use a fitting when a hole will do?),

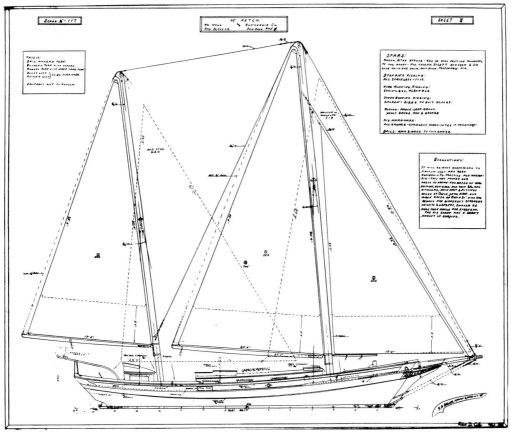

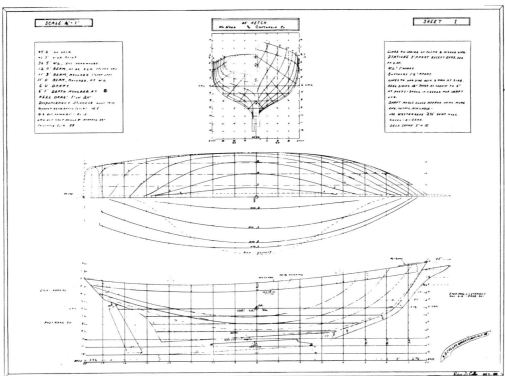

Swan V was Pete's most yacht-like design and for years the pride and joy of William Wood. With a careful reading of Pete's discussion of ketches (on pages 129–134) you will understand what he meant when stating that the rig lends itself to a hull of pretty shape; this sweet-lined 45'2" ketch design is a real gem and shows that Pete was capable of producing a gold-plater when called upon to do so. He usually did not strive for this quality, however, feeling that yacht standards were in no way a prerequisite for enjoyment on the water and that the rigors of maintaining varnish and glossy paint could be dispensed with and more time spent sailing. (© Mystic Seaport, Ships Plans Collection, Mystic, CT)

127

then down through a hole in the top of the boom, and along the underside of the boom to a cleat in a convenient position. This is a single-part rig and is enough unless the boom is very long and large for the size of craft. No sheave is needed in the boom; a nicely rounded hole does quite well. I think it's a fine point whether the lift makes fast forward coming from aloft, or on the boom coming from the boom end; it depends on the particular rig and simply on the owner's preference. The aloft lead, coming to a fairlead and then aft makes good sense in a small boat. In a two-mast boat or small day sloop, having the running end aft would often be handier.

Lifts for large booms may need a two-part purchase, either forward (and this seems a common practice in Europe) or at the after end of the boom, when it then will pay to use a sheave in the boom. Large sloops and fishing schooners in this country mostly used the single lift, often with many parts of tackle on the boom end arranged in such a way as to prevent twisting up; that is, it was done with single blocks above and sheaves set in the boom, all as widely spaced fore-and-aft as was practical. It can be argued whether this would be the best rig on a craft with a small crew. These vessels required large crews for fishing, and such things as lazyjacks were not needed where many hands that knew their work were available.

Coasters were intended to be run short-handed. They used the double lifts, port and starboard, usually in conjunction with lazyjacks, and the purchases were hung under the trestle trees aloft, with the hauling parts leading to the deck. This was about standard, except in the West Coast lumber trade, where they had their own methods. There are few big sloops left, but there are some schooners of modest to somewhat large size by present standards. On these vessels, the double lifts, rigged in their traditional way, are still the thing for today's small crews; they are as important to the handling of the vessel as is her rudder.

A lift on the boom of any size should be frequently inspected and kept in good order at all times, for the breaking of a lift in a hard chance can be a major disaster. Picture most of a crew strung along a main boom, possibly 70 feet or more long, turning in a reef or stowing sail. The lift parts as the vessel lunges into a big one. No one there has a chance. By all means keep a good lift, even in a small boat.

I have had considerable experience with the gaff rig and some of its slight variations, particularly the short gaff using a single halyard for both throat and peak. Some folks think the one-halyard gaff cannot possibly work, but it does, and wonderfully well. All kinds and shapes of boats are not necessarily suited to it. The regular gaff as used on a catboat can be most handy and efficient, and of course on other craft too. There is a lot to be said for the catboat, and at the moment it seems to have a following again, with a catboat association, many builders competing, each with his own version of a catboat, usually a moulded creation. Catboats in the past have often been considered brutish things to handle, especially if of some size. Granted, many things inherent to a very wide hull with a big rig stuck right in the eyes of her do cause difficulty in a breeze. The builders now turning out these boats seem to have made little effort to overcome any of this, except to follow the modern approach of reducing sail area, until the boat is dull in light going. My own feeling is that cats were over-developed for racing up to the time interest in them died out many years ago. This development made for big rigs and very wide, boxy hulls to carry them and produced craft that were not easy to use for ordinary sailing.

Whether or not a person likes a cat is beside the point; he must admit the rig is fairly simple for the area it can spread. I think for present-day use the cat can be greatly improved. I would give a catboat a fairly modest beam as cats go, more deadrise with some reverse in the sections, high, light quarters, and some overhang aft. I would give her generally sharp lines with some slight increase in hull depth, and would use a fair amount of inside ballast, or outside ballast if expense were not important. I'd want a good amount of outside deadwood, and along with the sharper lines a somewhat smaller centerboard and a rudder that was not oversize. She would have a fairly sharp hull of modest displacement. Such a catboat would sail very well with a smaller rig. The gear would be a bit lighter. A lot of the brutishness of the over-developed cat would vanish, and I feel, if the designer had any art in his pen, the boat would be far better to look at than some of the cats now being built.

Sloops never seem to go out of style, though interest in particular types waxes and wanes. The Friendships have had quite a following lately. I much admire the type. Certainly those who developed these sloops knew what they were doing, and the boats very much suited the work they were to do. By nature, the Friendship sloop requires a big rig. There have been some slight variations in the true type recently, to improve them (it's hoped) for today's pleasure sailing. My own feeling is that the Friendship, with the big rig, mast far forward, sharp entry, and heavy quarters, though right for a working craft, is not just the thing for the weekend sailor. Some designers, as I say, have attempted to improve the type for pleasure sailing, notably the well-known Maine designer, Murray G. Peterson, who turned out small, classic sloops of yacht quality. These boats are most docile and handy, and very easy to look at.

My own preference in small sloops is for what used to be referred to as a deep centerboard. Fine-lined and not too bulky, such a sloop does not need an outsize rig to move her, yet has plenty of sail to make her go in a light breeze. The fact that she will have to reef now and then is taken as a matter of course. She would have a gaff rig, naturally, for reasons previously given. Whether she has a plumb

stem or clipper head is mostly a matter of how you feel about it.

A centerboard cluttering up the small cabin is of no matter whatsoever. If the rest is right and she's sweet to the eye and nice to handle, I learn to live with what is below. So many craft nowadays, regardless of size, are designed around a cabin. They look it, too. Some folks seem to care little how well a boat sails and what she looks like as long as the cabin is big, to store beer in mostly. Seems a shantyboat might do just as well.

The idea of a very large sloop is intriguing, though the practicality in today's economy makes you forget it, even though the pictures of great stone sloops and Hudson River craft are fun to look at. What often happens when a certain sloop design becomes just a little too big—that damn main boom you know—is she is made a yawl. Until recently, modern yawls were very popular and had some advantage under rating rules for racing. The original reason for the rig, however, was too much main boom on a big sloop.

I've spent many a year with yawls, both the old type and those induced by rating rules. Can't say as I really cotton to the rig, always feel I'm really in a sloop, though there's nothing at all wrong with that. To convert a big sloop to a yawl to make her easier to handle makes sense. But for me to design a yawl from scratch (unless the client just must have it and no other) makes no sense at all. The cost of the added mizzen, or jigger, as it's sometimes called, is nearly as much as a ketch mizzen, and it gives far less return.

It seems most anybody thinks he likes a ketch, whether or not he knows the whys and wherefores of the rig. The ketch is said to be easy to handle, thus it must be a good rig! The designers of ketches have problems, notably trying to get enough sail area to drive what often is a bulky hull. Beyond a certain point, there is nowhere else to go but up in figuring a rig, particularly when using the Marconi

(continued on page 132)

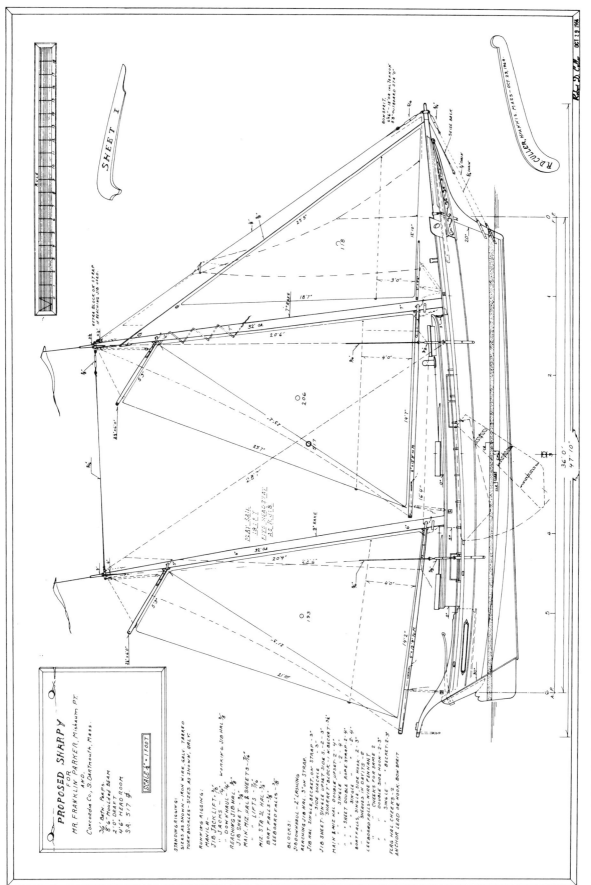

130

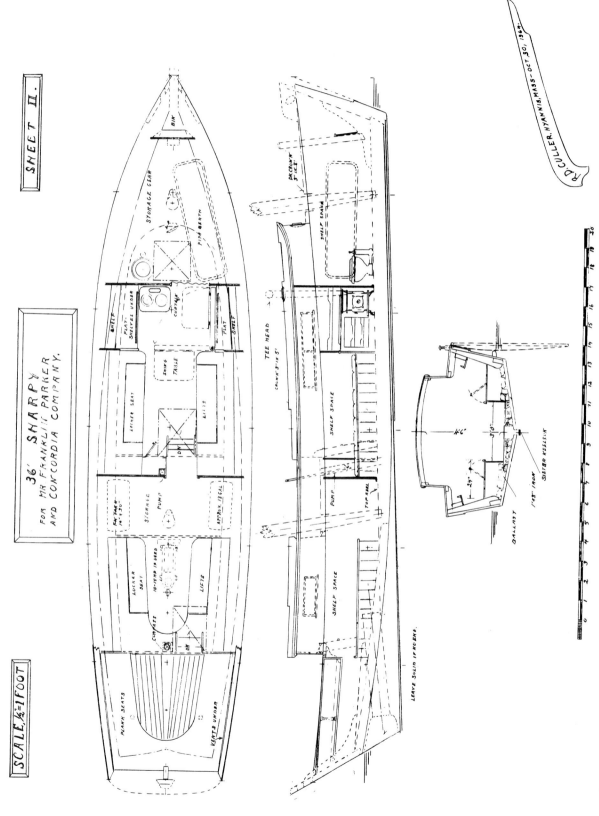

36' sharpie ketch Old Glory. (© Mystic Seaport, Ships Plans Collection, Mystic, CT)

131

(continued from page 129)

rig. You end up with very tall masts and narrow sails that tend to set poorly. Often such a craft is hopefully intended for long passages. These tall narrow ribbons are just plain wrong for such use. Sail area in a ketch being hard to come by, she should have a rather easy-moving hull with moderate displacement. Often you see designs that are just the opposite—deep, wide, and heavy. Combine such a shape with a tall, narrow rig that won't "sleep" on what's probably a bouncy hull, and you have a poor design.

For a ketch, I like a rather narrow hull, sharp and easy of line, not of heavy displacement. She may not be overly roomy and so should have more length than a man might think he needs at first. And she should have a simple rig, which need not be massive, for the boat will move well and not put great strain on it. She needs a strong rig, but it need not be heavy in the sense of having huge blocks and big lines and stays. These are not needed with an easy hull. In other words, I like a fairly "slight" hull, compared to the often-pictured world-girdling ketch, a stout, bulky thing with a very heavy, short rig. The craft should be handsome and delicate of line, for by the nature of her design she's well suited to a pretty shape. Might as well make the most of it!

Now just how do I go about fitting a proper, light rig, with enough area, and keep it simple and handy? I'll tell you what to do, but none of it is original; I never seem to do anything original, unless combining things done many times before may turn up something a bit different. The rig to be described is suited to hulls about 28 to 45 feet long. For shorter boats, the ketch is not necessary; for longer craft, other rigs are better, or so I think.

I like both masts to be solid sticks about the same length, though the foremast (some call it the main) should be of bigger diameter than the mizzen, as it carries more sail. I place them similar to the masts in a Chesapeake bugeye, and give them considerable rake by present standards, but not as much

as in the Bay craft. A bowsprit is essential. The booms are about the same length. Short gaffs controlled by single halyards are light, simple, work extremely well, and get area without undue mast length. A single headsail is all that's needed, even in a 45-foot boat; it should set on a one-third-length club, not a full-length one. Right here I often get noise, for few folks seem to know about this short club. Rigged right, it tends for itself; it was standard in the oystering fleets of Chesapeake and Delaware Bays. Oyster dredges often made more tacks and handled more sail as a day's work than some yachtsmen do in five years. Their gear works if you learn it, which takes all of ten minutes, with an open mind.

Standing rigging should be wire: a jibstay, rove through a bee hole in the bowsprit end to become the inner bobstay; an outer headstay to the bowsprit, backed by the lighter outer bobstay. (This stay also carries the lazyjack iron.) For foremast shrouds, a single one on each side, on craft from 28 feet to about 36 feet, a pair each side on bigger boats. On the mizzen, a single shroud each side is adequate even on a 45-foot boat. There should be a spring stay. Three halyards, three sheets, and three light lifts, and that's about it. The rig has a minimum of wire, lines, blocks, fittings, and ironwork; it has considerable area, modest weight and windage, and of course, simple upkeep and repair. The rig is an efficient driver, and, due to the shape of things, the sails ahead don't backwind the mizzen, a failing of some ketches. If you like light sails, the rig is laid out so that a big reaching jib works well in the fore triangle, and it will fit exactly as a mizzen staysail too. Or you can spend money and have two; it does not matter which bag you grab, either sail will fit, and they are real jazz in light going!

There is one drawback to this sort of rig for those preoccupied with cabin space and arrangements below. The masts must be placed just about so, and they govern the placement of the deck houses, and there must be two houses, unless the boat is on the small side. This, in turn, sets some limits on the accommodations. The layouts I've used vary somewhat according to length of boat, naturally. They have proven practical, offer some privacy and at times necessary segregation, you do not step on the cook, and there is storage space. The bigger the boat, the better the layout.

I find this rig tends to invite self-steering if the hull has it in her. The rake of the masts seems to have a lifting effect on the boat when running off,

the sails "sleep" in light going, and jibing a sail on what's now considered a heavily raked mast is remarkably easy and simple. The sails hoist and lower very easily, and experienced sailmakers tell me it's much easier to cut a well-setting sail to a raking mast. The old timers knew all about this.

The rig has a minimum of standing rigging and turnbuckles. The bobstays can be of chain. The iron work is simple and easily made, and it should be galvanized iron, not bronze. Blocks and running

The 36' sharpie ketch Old Glory, *designed by Pete for Franklin Parker and built at Concordia Co., under a press of sail. Once again, the v-bottom hull shows its versatility in utilization for all types of rig and size and purpose, this example being a shoal-draft, sitting-headroom sailing ketch that looks like a real little ship!*

gear, as mentioned before, are few and simple. There is a minimum of windage aloft. Lacings or hoops can be used to hold the luffs to the masts; I think it's just a matter of preference. The lacings work so well, offer so little windage, and are so simple and cheap that I see no need to use hoops. The sails are so small and light that a twenty-year-old boy, once he "learns the ropes," can handle them with considerable snazz in ordinary weather. The spar-making for such a rig is about as simple as you can find, and the spar material is available.

I don't say this is the only kind of ketch rig. A normal gaff ketch with, say, a sharp-headed mizzen is a seamanlike rig. If the boat is at all bulky, she will need a main topsail to get enough area for light going. If you like light sails, there is the chance for a light jib topsail as well as a mizzen staysail on this rig. Most ketches today are sharp-headed or Marconi-rigged on both masts. For reasons already given I find Marconi sails the most difficult to work with on a ketch. To begin with, the system of rigging requires more stays, fittings, and, of course, spreaders than with gaff rig. Efficient or not, you end up with a lot of windage and more weight than you might suppose. The cost of such gear has gone up considerably too. The tracks for mast and boom, masthead fittings and sheaves for wire, goosenecks, and outhauls that these rigs require, along with all the other paraphernalia that goes with them, are not cheap. Usually there are hollow spars, of wood or metal. Winches, wire halyards with wire-to-rope splices, and a thousand other things thought necessary for such a rig can make it cost as much as a whole cruising boat of simple nature. Even the amount of bronze screws used up on one of these rigs is quite an item.

My own approach to using a true Marconi rig on a ketch, if it's insisted on, is: Sail-hoist to boom-length no more than about 2 to 1; some rake to the masts; a rig generally long on the base, which calls for a bowsprit and some boom overhang aft; and considerable in the way of light sails to help along what is a rather under-canvassed hull in light weather. By now we have spent a whale of a lot of money, and have a rig that is workable and that does not look too bad, but does not have the ultra-modern style. It all works out this way: the Marconi sails are no better than the simple, short-gaff sails, and sometimes not as good when the vessel is under working sail only; the rig is not difficult to handle, but is not as handy as the short-gaff rig; and it has cost far more than the simpler rig would. In case of an accident or repairs of any kind, the Marconi rig must rely heavily on some shipyard. Yearly maintenance is much more expensive. The Marconi rig is not really suited to being left in the boat all winter if you see fit. All in all, the Marconi rig is the hard way to do it.

And that, my patient reader, is what I think of ketches.

THE SCHOONER RIG

We all can't own big boats, yet some of us can, and anyhow, they are fun to dream about. There have been big sloops, big yawls, and bigger ketches, yet to my mind the schooner rig is the most suitable for a big boat. Everybody seems to like a schooner, in dreams at least, yet many folks think of the schooner rig as being difficult and complicated to handle. The opposite is the truth of it. Fewer men can handle more vessel with a schooner rig than with any other. It was the standard rig of coasters, pilots, and fishermen for craft of any size. Though fishermen usually had plenty of manpower and their craft were rigged accordingly, the schooner rig was very handy for them. The vessel could be shortened down for the skipper, cook, and a boy to handle when all the dories were out, and she often took some handling when it breezed up and it was time to pick up the dorymen.

The schooner rig is not suited to a craft under 40 feet long, in my opinion, though a few successful schooners smaller than that have been built. In craft 45 feet long and bigger, the rig comes into its own. I speak not of the rigs of the racing schooner-yachts of the past, a class by themselves with very small foresails in proportion to the rest of the rig, but of the coaster or pilot boat rigs, with a large foresail and a modest mainsail. Such were the working rigs of working vessels. Some say, and I very much agree, that such a schooner rig is the handsomest rig there is, and, assuming a proper schooner hull under it, may be one of the finest sights the marine world can present, next to a fine, deepwater square-rigger.

Some schooner designs of late don't take into account that a real schooner rig must have a suitable schooner hull under it. Schooner hulls can stand considerable variation in general appearance as long as certain characteristics compatible with the rig are not overlooked. When sticking to the true, smaller schooner rig, a main-topmast two-master, or a three-master if you can find someone who can afford one, I find the schooner a very easy rig to work with design-wise. It is no trouble to get plenty of area, yet have the vessel manageable in bad going. The rig is easy to stay, and, though it may look complicated to some folks, is easy to build, and build stoutly, too.

You have a main topsail and fisherman staysail for light canvas, though in a way these are much more like working sails than the light stuff on other rigs. A topsail and fisherman are simple to use, once you are instructed, and there is no going aloft to hand the topsail in small schooners, as is often thought. The old schooner men worked all that out long ago. In large schooners, yes, you had to go aloft and like it, but then these great vessels are sort of out of range for most people and of practical interest today only in that they point out many interesting things about smaller schooners. In a small schooner, say, 40 feet long, I feel a single headsail is all that is needed and is probably more efficient than two under-sized headsails. In schooners 45 feet long and more, the old jumbo and jib with the jumbo or fore staysail set part way out on the bowsprit seems to work best. If the vessel is a flying jibboomer with two-part head gear, this jumbo goes to the end of the bowsprit proper and the jib sets on the jibboom end. If the vessel is still larger, a fore staysail set to the stem-head will work. A fore staysail or jumbo that is too narrow and too small is a hateful, useless thing.

A schooner's mainsail is her real driver. Her foresail is her salvation in bad weather; this sail's performance when it blows must be experienced to be appreciated. Some old schooner men used to say

A real schooner has a lot of headgear and the 52' schooner Integrity *Pete Culler designed and built for Waldo Howland is a good example. Pete carved the billethead and trailboards.*

if they had to go with rotten sails, let it be so, but never the foresail.

There can be several variations, mostly in detail, in the schooner rig, and yet stay true to type, and I suggest strongly to any coming young designer (and to some who are already established) that you stick to the schooner rig as it was. The minute you get away from the traditional proportions, the rig fails to work in practice, though it may look fine on paper.

Probably no other rig in this country has had more thorough development than the schooner. No one knows how many schooners have existed or how many variations have been developed for different trades and waters. Many vessels shifted from one trade to another as economics dictated, but, generally speaking, there were definite schooner types for definite uses. Of course in many cases, the dictates of the trades made the differences slight. Packet schooners were apt to be good sailers if built for just that trade. Very big cargo capacity was not as important as the ability to make somewhat regular passages. Pilot schooners were the nearest thing to yachts in that they carried no cargo. Their work was competitive, so they had to be fast, and they had to be very able, as their area of operation was full of hazards. Land was never very far off, they were among much shipping, and they had to be on station regardless of weather. Many yachts have been based on pilot boat models.

When we think of fishing schooners, we usually think of the Gloucester type, and it was a rather definite type in its later days. There were many other fishing schooner types, however: oystermen, menhaden fishermen, Gulf snapper schooners, Western cod and halibut fishermen, and sealers, just to name a few. And of course there were the coasters. These, in their heyday, were often designed for a particular trade, or maybe two so that the vessel had work in the off-season of one of her trades. Several very definite and useful types of coasters were evolved,

to suit certain cargoes and waters. In the last years of their sailing, most coasters took any work they could get, and many a deep-draft vessel found herself in want, for she could not get a cargo up some rivers, though she had been just fine for offshore runs. All this intensive development of schooners over many years showed what was what, both in hull design and rig. Certain variations in rig suited certain hulls and uses.

Having been so fortunate as to be exposed to the working schooner before she died, and having designed some successful schooners for today's uses, some of my notions about schooners may be pertinent. Let me note that I'm talking about small schooners, say from 40 to 85 feet in length. If anyone thinks these are large vessels, I say they are toys compared to most schooners of not so very long ago. Many folks just don't realize how much boat most working craft were, and, in most cases, how few men it took to work them. I knew an old schooner skipper who ran quite a fair-sized vessel in the Carolina-Chesapeake lumber trade. She "carried 175,000 o' boards," and he sailed her with a man and a stout boy; he being the man—quite a man. In summer, he used an idiot boy because he could get him cheaper!

Say a fellow is planning to have a schooner, a very small one. First he should consider if he can afford it, and if he can devote the time to her once she's complete. And I say right now, if you are able to build and sail a schooner, that's living! Then what about draft? She may be deep, or a fairly shoal, keel vessel, or a deep centerboarder, or a shallow one. You decide how and where you will mostly use her. Personally, I have a weakness for the deep centerboarder, if she can be of some size and other things agree.

If she must be small and of modest displacement because of economic and manning problems, if draft is no great concern, if she will be used mostly along shore, I tend to favor the Chesapeake

(continued on page 140)

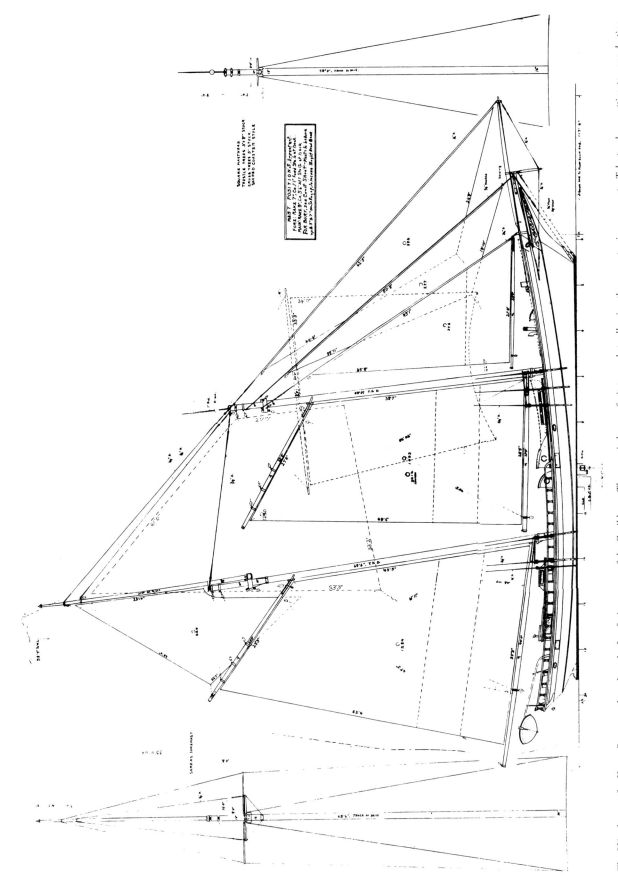

The 82′ schooner for Henry Sears was based on the fast fruit runners of the Caribbean. They carried green fruit to market, allowing the cargo to ripen en route. Take too long getting to your destination and you have a worthless trip. A photo of this design's half model appears on page 40. (© Mystic Seaport, Ships Plans Collection, Mystic, CT)

138

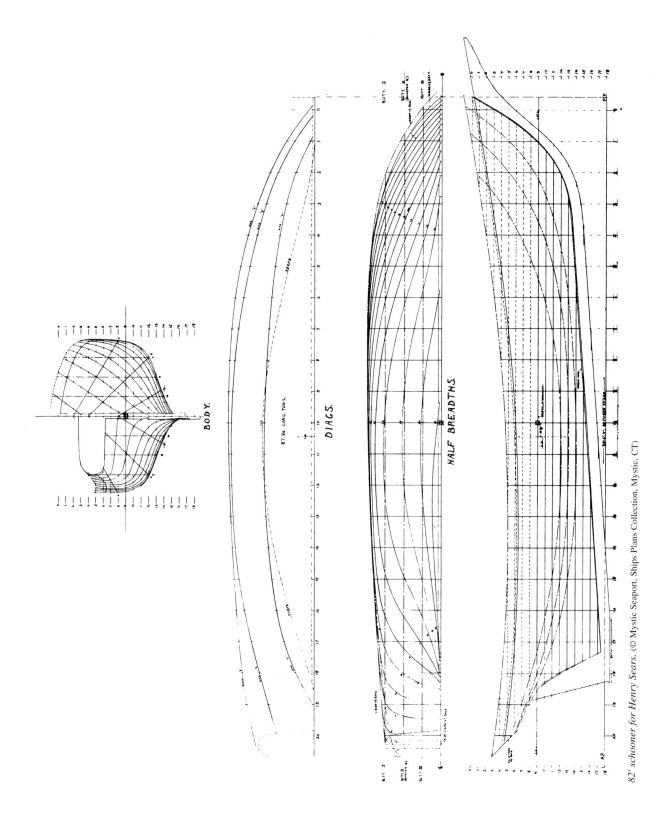

82' schooner for Henry Sears. (© Mystic Seaport, Ships Plans Collection, Mystic, CT)

BODY.

DIAGS.

87.86 LONG. TON'S.

HALF BREADTHS

(continued from page 137)

pungy schooner, though no one else seems to. These craft are descended from the Baltimore clipper schooners and are famous for several things, some of them drawbacks by present standards. They are handsome, in fact can be just daintily pretty, are known as smart sailers, and, if you stick exactly to their traditional form, are not overly expensive as small schooners go. The pungy rig, while very much a true schooner, is somewhat simpler and lighter than most as to gear and fittings. The pungy hull is also simpler than most, though she is very shapely. I've never found good looks to run up the cost in a schooner hull. The pungy has a rather uncomplicated stern, though it may look fierce to one not used to its construction. Though building this stern takes an artistic eye and some adz work, it eliminates framing and a built-up rudder port and simplifies the taffrail work. If properly designed, these craft steer very well, so are suited to a tiller.

The pungy's faults, if you consider them that, for yachting purposes are much the same as the drawbacks these schooners had as working craft. Being noted sailers, they tend to be wet. The draft must be fairly great for the vessel's size and displacement, the latter being quite moderate for a schooner. The moderate displacement leads to a lack of room below; a pungy was never a big carrier. Though she is deep-heeled, with considerable external deadwood, the pungy is high-bilged, and so not an easy craft in which to get real headroom, especially aft. For cruising coastwise where draft is not an issue, and the pungy's draft tends to be no more that that of any keel yacht of comparable size, I feel the drawbacks are of no account, compared to the good points of such a vessel.

Early pilot boats were much like the pungy's ancestors, and as the pilot types developed, I think they, like the pungies, became vessels of a type well suited to use as schooner yachts today. Several of my cruising schooner designs have been based on the late pilot boats, though of course due to present economics they have been much smaller, and hence

subject to modification. I find the stern often used in pilot schooners, with the rudder port coming through a slightly immersed transom, very well suited to schooners of small size. It's strong, good looking if properly built, is buoyant and dry in rough water, and, I think, aids much in getting a nice run aft.

Saying the latter reminds me of the observations of several old-time schooner men. They all more or less agreed, though each had his preference, that a vessel could be full forward, or fine, or somewhere in between, she could be flat-floored or sharp, wall-sided or not, deep or shoal, or have any of the other combinations and variations, and still be a good ship; but not one of these experts had ever seen a vessel with a poor run that was worth a damn! I very much agree, and a designer should cultivate the ability to shape a good run, and should see to it that the builder does not "lose it" in lofting and setting up. These things can happen.

Pilot schooner yachts take kindly to the clipper bow, and also, of course, to the more-or-less plumb stem, which many originals had. It now seems the plumb stem is out of fashion. And by the odd and strange stem profiles you see now in both sail and power craft, including what seems to pass for a "modernized" clipper head, it seems many designers are groping for something they can't seem to find. Howard Chapelle and others have pointed out that the rules governing the design of a clipper head are absolute, though the size, shape, and details can vary infinitely. From the looks of some efforts now, it seems that these rules have been forgotten.

John G. Alden did so much with schooner yachts based on the later fishing schooners that these craft and his work have spoken for themselves. Suffice it to say that they were, on the whole, outstanding, but, like many good things, have gone out of fashion for the time being. Also like many good things, they could be "discovered" over again. Having been much exposed to these particular craft in the past, I still think they have a lot to offer for serious cruising.

A Maine designer, and a very good friend, the before-mentioned Murray Peterson, designed cruising schooners based on the small coasting schooners. These little schooners have been around a long time now, and have proven their sound conception. They are able, and some have done considerable voyaging. Very appealing to the eye, they stand out in any harbor scene and are just plain nice to be around. Possibly a small coaster or packet is one of the best types on which to base a cruising schooner yacht.

(continued on page 146)

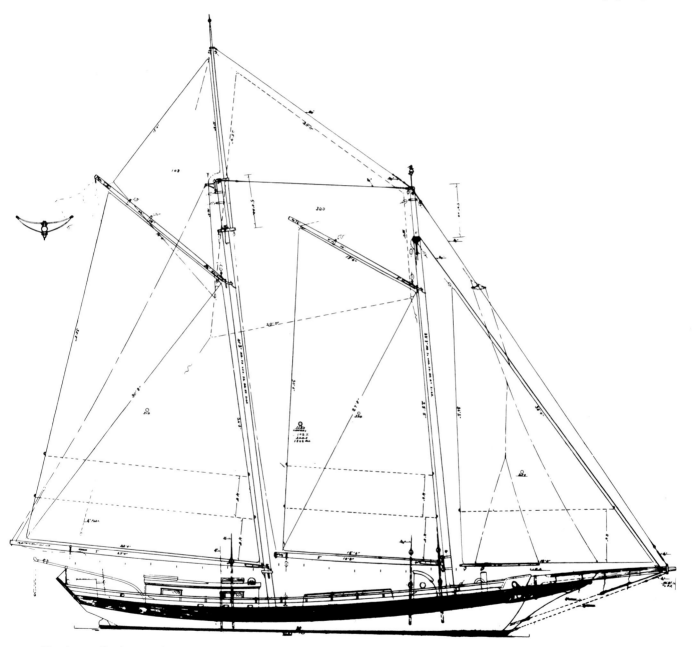

How do you tell a she pungy from a he pungy? One has a centerboard case and the other doesn't. This 45' she pungy was designed by Pete for his friend and neighbor Capt. Eddie Crosby and was based on a keel pungy he had designed for himself in 1963. These vessels were characterized by sharp but short entrances, with greatest beam well forward; a sharp lined, slight displacement underbody incorporating long and fine runs; long heads; and high, thin quarters with the typical pungy double transom. Capt. Pete favored the pungy model even though few others did. (© Mystic Seaport, Ships Plans Collection, Mystic, CT)

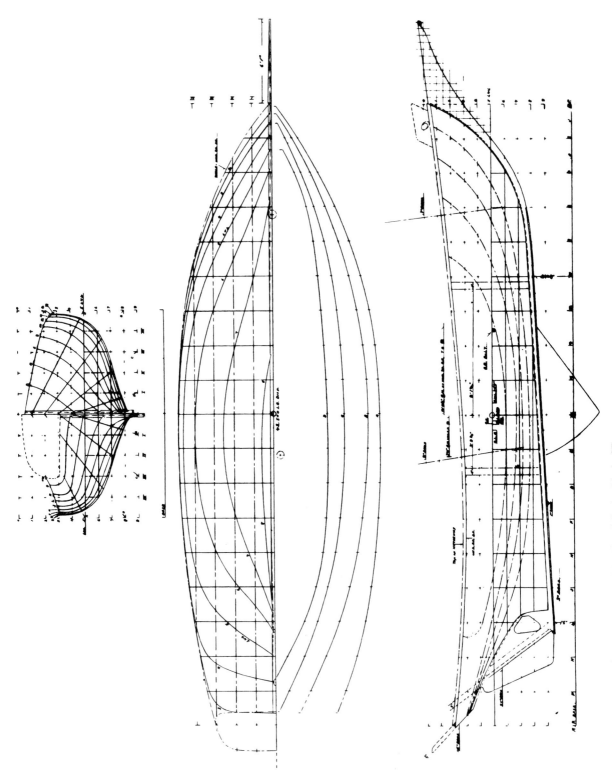

45' she pungy (continued). (© Mystic Seaport, Ships Plans Collection, Mystic, CT)

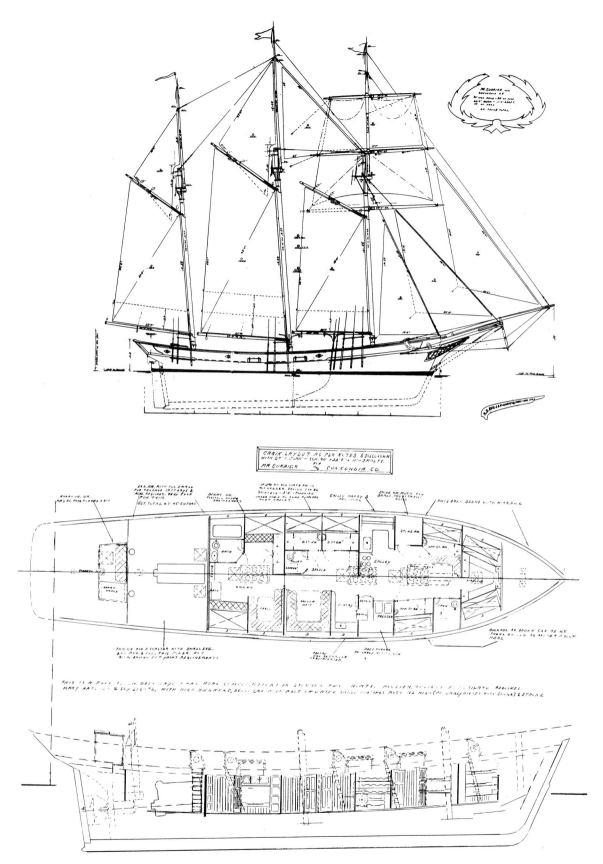

A fine 96' topsail schooner Pete designed for Mr. Currier in the English style. Pete had a medium clipper hull in mind, but it did not proceed beyond the proposal stage; that is a shame because the concept shows a lot of promise. The original intent was to use this vessel as a school ship. (© Mystic Seaport, Ships Plans Collection, Mystic, CT)

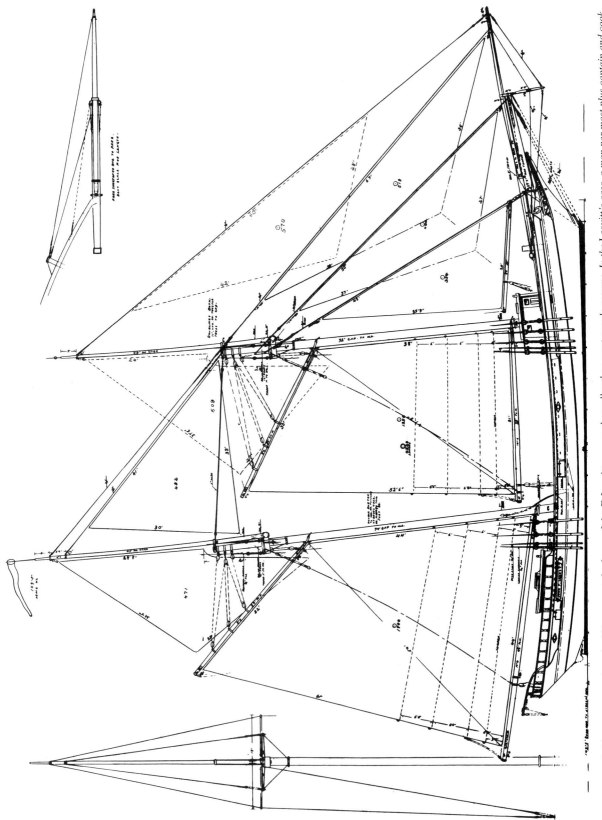

The crew needed for coasters such as the 92' two-masted schooner John F. Leavitt was much smaller than most people assume. In the Leavitt's case, a man per mast plus captain and cook would have been ample. Traditionally, the cook tended the headsails when tacking—that is, all of them. Well thought out gear based on years of refinement made this possible. After all, the primary reason for the development of the schooner rig, its evolution, and its near-domination in coasting vessels was its lower operating costs. The bottom line was based on ease of use and repair. © Mystic Seaport, Ships Plans Collection, Mystic, CT

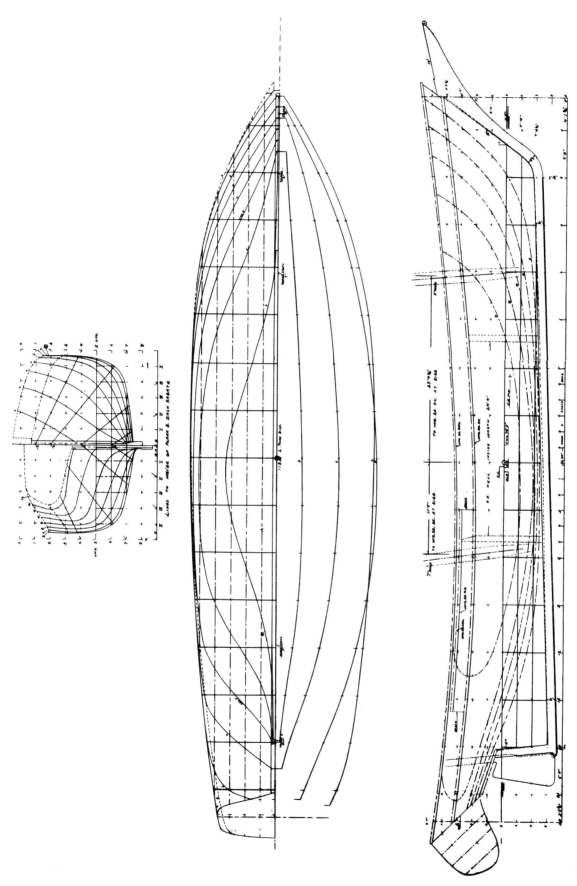

The 92' two-masted schooner John F. Leavitt was a coaster in the tradition of sailing vessels that carried cargo along the coasts of the United States before the advent of passable roads and highways; even into the 1950s isolated practitioners held on, though just barely. Capt. Pete knew more than a few of these diehards, felt sympathy for their plight, and was saddened when the last finally gave up. Naturally, he was receptive when Ned Ackerman approached him with his story of reviving sail cargo carriers with a fleet of three schooners. The Leavitt was the only one built.
(© Mystic Seaport, Ships Plans Collection, Mystic, CT)

(continued from page 141)

By the nature of the requirements of most owners, nearly all of these modified traditional schooners tend to be keel craft. The accommodation is almost always a big matter, and a centerboard in a small vessel is usually felt to offer problems to the arrangement below and is seldom accepted. A designer's lot would be much happier if at least two bunks were left out of these small schooners. It's hard to get across to a client that as these two bunks are intended to be occupied, they bring on other problems of space: fresh water tankage for two more, space for their vittles, and more ice or a bigger electric reefer and more juice to run it, two more tooth brushes, longer towel racks, more lockers for dunnage—well, you take it from there! What often happens is that the vessel's tonnage increases to hold it all, and the auxiliary power and the rig become bigger to drive the bigger hull. By now there has been talk to the point of hoarseness, much paper has been used, and many lines drawn. And then it's finally out to the yards for estimates. It will cost far more than the owner thought, though the designer knew very well it would. More often than not the whole project is abandoned. I have, for the most part, had no luck trying to think cheap for a client, though when he first approaches me, he's very apt to make a show of poverty. Then, once things are started, he's apt to run wild, and nothing will make him see the light, except being smacked full in the face with an estimate! Sometimes, if we are lucky, we start over again, with, say, a small, alongshore sloop.

Launch day for the John F. Leavitt *was a festive and happy occasion and there were hordes of people, media, and very nearly every schooner in the windjammer fleet in attendance to watch a flawless launch on a bright and sunny day by the Wallace Shipyard crew of Thomaston, Maine.* (John Burke)

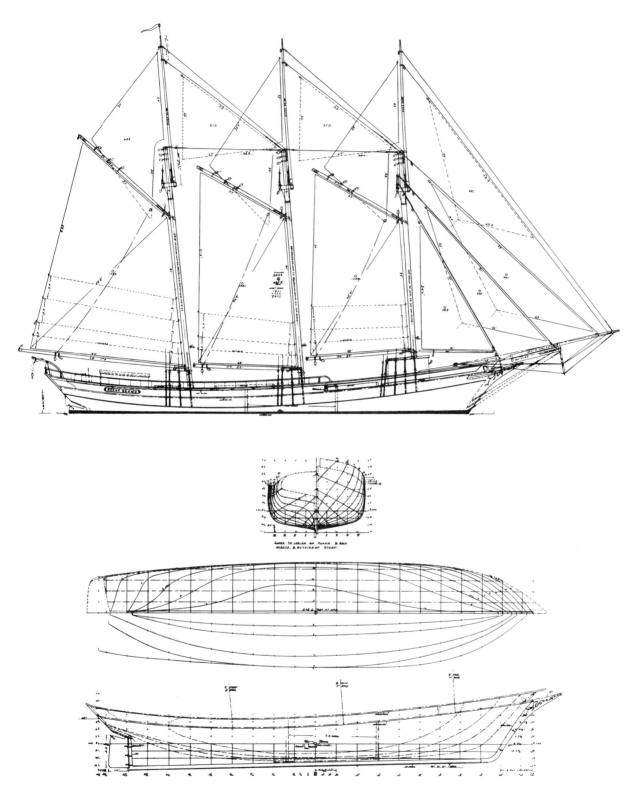

Ned Ackerman planned a fleet of three cargo-carrying schooners. The John F. Leavitt *was one. The* Kathy Brown, *shown here, was to be the second. Although a three-master, its scantlings would have been the same as the* Leavitt, *which was designed for heavy use as a stone carrier. The third was to be a deep offshore two-master, but it did not get put down on paper before Pete died.* (© Mystic Seaport, Ships Plans Collection, Mystic, CT)

Draft can be a big problem if a proposed schooner must use very thin waters. As mentioned before, a centerboard can be much in the way in a small schooner for some uses. A really big craft by today's standards makes the use of a board much simpler, but economics usually knock this idea in the head right off. Yet there is precedent in past schooners for small centerboard craft. Some of them were real old pancakes; just so it was a little wet under foot they could sail, and do it well. If a man is stuck with thin water, he soon adapts to craft suited to it, forgets full headroom, and learns the wonders of a good big wooden centerboard and the way of life that goes with it. In many ways I think it's better than the deep-draft life. Commodore Ralph Munroe, Vincent Gilpin, and others have preached the dogma of shallow draft, so I won't go into it, except to say there is no reason at all to give up schooners and cruising just because the waters are shoal. One advantage of shallow waters is that they are to some extent, still uncrowded. Besides, it's fun to have some guy row over and tell you that you're anchored in only four feet of water, "and the tide drops a foot here." Thank him kindly and look dumb. Cripes, you are only drawing two!

The feeling among many folks nowadays is that these very flat ones are unsafe, that to be any good a sailboat must have a chunk of weight on its keel.

The 52' Baltimore clipper Lizard King *gaining an offing and headed for the Marquesas. Note the square yard lashed down until needed in the trade winds.* (Bruce Northrup)

I have even met people who thought square-rigged ships and big steamers had outside ballast keels! Without going into the technical aspects of ballast, hull design as it pertains to ballast, and the reasons why outside ballast is used or not used, I will say simply that commercial craft never had it. This statement can be qualified a bit by saying a later fishing schooner or two experimented with outside ballast, a pilot schooner or two added it, and certain small working cutters in Europe used outside ballast to some extent in the later days. In this country, at least, these experiments were not repeated.

Many folks have a great fear of capsizing. I think every type of craft built has rolled over in the past and will continue to do so in the future. Some came back, some did not for various reasons, not always the fault of the design.

Since the beginning of boats, shoal craft have been around, and a study of them from early times to the present shows their record to be remarkably good, just as good, apparently, as that of the deeper vessels. Shoal craft have been everywhere, done everything, and it seems, made it pay. Captain Bligh made his remarkable 4,000-mile voyage from the Friendly Isles to Java in an open, shoal boat, the *Bounty*'s launch, granted that he was a master at his profession. Many others have made long cruises in shoal boats also, as in Bligh's case not always from choice. A study of these things makes you aware that the boat, whatever kind she was, did fine; the real problems were grub, water, and exposure. Furthermore, these craft often did a lot of looking after themselves because their crews became incapacitated. If a person is unreasonably afraid of capsizing and shoal boats, he might stay ashore and take his chances on the highways. Freeways frighten me, for I don't know what I'm doing on them. In trouble with some old shingle of a boat, I may not know what's what either, but if she's let alone, she has a way of coming through, and the chance of being sideswiped by some nut changing lanes is slim!

More often than not, the idea of a schooner is, for many reasons, doomed to be always a dream, yet sometimes there is a way. Usually the stumbling block is money. In the past in working craft, the same problem caused the development of a type, with several variations, that was economical to build out of easily obtained materials without necessarily using highly skilled labor. A cheap schooner of this type might be an enlarged sharpie, a pointed-bow scow schooner, a full-scow schooner, or in effect, just a large, flatiron skiff. The records and pictures of them show that such craft were practical from various parts of our coast and the Great Lakes. Some of these vessels were sloop rigged; many others had the normal coasting schooner rig, with the slight variations peculiar to each locality. The idea of such craft might be hard to accept nowadays, but once understood, they make sense for shoal waters and comparative cheapness. Some of these flat-bottomed craft were quite good looking in a businesslike way. So they can be today; it's a matter of the designer's ability and the builder's artistic skill. Nowadays, the sailing ability of a flat-bottomed schooner will be questioned, but many a skipper of a deep-draft boat has found out, quickly and decisively, that with started sheets a scow can leave him behind in short order. By the wind with much of a sea, the flatties did not do so well, yet with her shoalness and ability to cut corners, many a smart scow schooner could just lay the harbor on one tack, and was soon in and to a wharf, crew maybe ashore in the local barroom, while the deeper vessel, with maybe better windward ability, had to stick to the deep water and take hitch after hitch to make the same port, often finishing after dark with a failing wind. Yes, in waters suited to them, these sharpie and scow schooners got around with dispatch.

Many of these craft took more weather than they were really intended for, and in open water, and came through without undue trouble. I remember

Integrity *fully rigged and under power without her suit of sails.* (Norman Fortier photo, courtesy New Bedford Whaling Museum)

one of these incidents well. The schooner was about 85 feet long, cargo capacity about 150 tons. She had a totally flat bottom, though she had a pointed bow with a nice clipper head. In profile, she looked like any other coaster beginning to show her age. Her rig was that of the usual two-masted schooner with main topmast and flying jibboom. She was said to have the most prettily proportioned rig on the Chesapeake Bay. She had a hard chine with fore-and-aft planking and massive logs for chines. Her stern looked like a high-cut skiff stern. She was, on close inspection, wall-sided. Her deck layout was that of the full standard coaster of her period, with donkey engine, davits, motor yawl, and low quarterdeck. She was said to "draw 4 feet light, 6 loaded." Of course her centerboard was a massive contraption. In the schooner trade, fast-failing due to competition from trucks, she was still able to get a cargo, and "trade the rivers" when deeper schooners went hungry. Often she carried road materials, further to hasten her own end.

One winter evening she was struck by a heavy northerly with snow, and lost her sails in attempting to make a lee and anchor. Then she had no choice but to scud. The weather was getting colder by the minute, and the visibility was poor to non-existent. During the night, she was driven out to sea between the Capes, without hitting anything, thanks to the abilities of her skipper, who was black and a licensed steamboat captain. She was now in a situation for which she was neither built nor equipped, and she was aging. She drove off quite a way, when the wind let go, leaving a miserable sea of course. Then the wind shifted to east and built up to a gale. Her skipper and very small crew managed, with some salvaged rags of canvas, to scud her back into the Bay again in torrents of rain. She was found by the Cutter and brought in to a safe berth, and given the opportunity to buy new sails that she could ill afford.

That this scow-skiff hull could cope with all this points out its abilities, for, without intending to,

A powerful schooner hull standing up to a breeze—the Integrity *under sail.*

she was playing a tough game—Winter North Atlantic. I thought this a small epic of the sea, and sought out her skipper. Besides exposure, much work, shortage of stores and firewood, there must have been much mental strain all around, flat-bottomed vessel or no. Her skipper's words were short and to the point. "I never worried for the vessel. If the wind hadn't changed, I don't know where I woulda went to!"

I feel, for the right waters and for the man with the right outlook toward them, these scows or flatties, schooner-rigged for the hell of it and because it makes 'em look very good, have a lot to offer as a cruising boat, sometimes floating home. They are one way of getting about in interesting waters.

And that, I think, is just about enough of schooners.

The rigs I've discussed, from very small boats up to large ones, are based on much development and testing from the economic angle. I've noticed that to depart much from "just like it was" leads to complications not at first realized, for these rigs are wholes, and to disturb one part sets off a chain of problems that ends up by causing none of the rig to work right. If this sort of boating and tinkering with what some folks say are things outmoded does not appeal to you, by all means stay clear of it and stick to something that was developed last night; the originator may well know his stuff, and it could be good. I think going thoroughly modern is so much better than taking something known to be good that you don't really like, then botching it up by trying to change it around into something you do like. If you don't feel at least some kinship with the men who worked simple boats in the past, there's no point in wishful thinking about the kinds of boats and rigs they used. But if this sort of thing does appeal to you, then you've come down with a fascinating disease.

WATER, STOVES, ANCHORS, FUEL, CENTERBOARDS, AND CABINS

There are so many things about boats and ships that no one can ever begin to know all about it, let alone write all about it. There have been Monumental Works on marine subjects; I marvel at the amount of labor it must have taken to compile them. Yet even these books don't and can't cover everything. Each man's experience gives his understanding and approach different meaning. Besides, boats and ships are so specialized. Just the subject of tug-boating can fill books, and has.

I simply give some experiences, ways, yarns, and methods, some of them highly local, all of them to do with boats and vessels I've been exposed to. Making the point again, none of this is new, some of it is useful, and much of it has been forgotten.

When going out in a small boat, with whatever means of propulsion, even for an hour or two, there should be some sort of water jug. You may well stay longer than you think, from choice or necessity. I sort of like odd-shaped bottles, and some of these tend to go with an attractive boat. It's best if the water bottle is protected in some way, and it can be fun to cover it with some sort of ropework. The covering can be fancy if you lean that way, or can simply be some fishnet triced around the bottle or a canvas cover sewn on. Many folks nowadays just grab some sort of plastic jug; it holds water and is not easily stove up, but to me, at least, is not an attractive way of carrying water.

For a long day-trip or an overnight cruise, naturally the container can be bigger, and here the plastic thing may be better. A cabin boat that is small can often use some sort of portable "tank," something to be taken ashore and filled, or possibly several such tanks. Whatever is used, it needs a rack on board so it can't fetch away, and the rack should hold the container high enough to put a cup or pot under, for these things can have some sort of spigot on the bottom. In the past, some of us used new 5-gallon kerosene cans with a small spigot soldered on next to the bottom; these made quite a water supply for a small cruiser. On larger craft with built-in tanks, Monel now seems to be the best. At one time tin-lined copper was the best. Some now say a fiberglass tank is the thing; others say the water from them always tastes lousy!

My own experience is that I've never had any trouble with galvanized iron water tanks, this comment based on twenty-three years using the same tanks. In the realm of tugs and big ships, plain iron tanks are used. My experience was that we cemented the tanks once in awhile. They were big enough to be crawled into, and, upon overhauling, they were drained, opened up, scaled if need be, scrubbed out and flushed, and then cemented. We used Portland cement only, mixed with water about like a thick soup and painted thoroughly on the tank sides with a "cement brush," which was about like a calcimine brush. The water from these tanks was always sweet and clean. This, of course, is only of interest to small-boat men as sea lore.

The water cask is now considered outdated, though I think for extended cruising it could still have its place. It's hard to damage, can be taken ashore in a yawl boat, and is a handy container for extra water or for doubtful water to save contaminating the main tanks, for the cask is easily cleaned out. Like many things used in the past, a new cask has a ritual surrounding its preparation. Get a cask of suitable size, if you can find one now, preferably of oak, and if it has galvanized hoops, so much the better. Cut an oblong hole where the bung is, big enough to put a dipper or small pot through. Or, if you use a spigot on the bottom, leave the bung be, and put a lanyard on it. If you use the dipping hole, put a stout canvas flap over it, tacked on one long side only. Sew a stout bolt or rod into a pocket along the other long side to keep the flap in place. In the past, when harbors were cleaner—or maybe people just didn't care—a wood toggle was put in the hole, line attached, and the cask hove overside and swamped, for it was thought "river water" helped in the seasoning. After a week or so, the cask would be taken on board and washed out, then taken ashore in the yawl to be filled, and then set aside to "go bad." After several cleanings and fillings, this going-bad ceased, and the cask was considered seasoned and fit for use. A chock was made to hold it, and a place chosen to lash it down. It was painted, and often in a decorative way. Such a cask was the water supply for the men in a small coaster or sailing oyster dredger, and it worked. What you did in very cold winter weather, at least what was done on craft I was on long ago, is interesting. The cask was on deck and should have frozen, but did not. A dry salt cod was placed over the dipping hole and a heavy scrap of old sail thrown over all. It worked; don't ask me why; I don't know.

Many large sailing fishermen had big wooden tanks below decks, usually built of cypress, and some deep-water sailing vessels had them too. They were, from all accounts, highly satisfactory. For that matter, many of us remember the old wooden tank that the windmill pumped to. Think about wooden tanks when building a cruising craft and cash is short. I use wooden tanks in my shop, one for quenching, and one as a reservoir for the steam box; they never leak. They are built with a "draw," so freezing does not hurt them.

Nowadays many sizes of metal tanks can be bought "stock," and should be considered in making a design or planning a layout below deck. Nothing is now cheap, including these tanks, which usually have had a pressure test, but there is much saving over custom-made tanks of odd shape. Something that is often overlooked is that a tank way down low, maybe in the bilge in a deep boat, with a long fill pipe will have a heck of a "head" if filled right up, and may rupture unless very stout.

Among other things, water is used for cooking, which brings up galleys, be they a sort of box with small stove and other gear to use in an open boat, or something more elaborate for a cabin craft. Without a stove, there is no galley; with one, it's official even though it may be an unhandy nook, or just a shelf.

Nowadays there are all kinds of portable stoves running on several different fuels. Some are risky in a close space. Each man to his choice; I still prefer the Primus using kerosene. It has the drawback of requiring a priming fuel, usually alcohol. Some curse these stoves, for they never learned to pre-heat them properly.

No one has yet made a cabin comfortable in wet, chilly weather with an open-flame stove. All you get is foul air and condensation, and often a headache or worse. Even a very small cabin boat, if there is possibly space for it, should have some sort of solid-fuel stove, no matter how tiny. These stoves can be bought, but a small stove, or a large one for that matter, can be made of sheet metal, a few rivets, and some stove bolts by anyone handy. It will burn sticks of wood, using sand for a grate. If you do this, remember there is a necessary relation-ship between the draft vent and the stack; examine a few small stoves to learn about this. A miserable Northeast day and one of these stoves is the differ-ence between living and wishing you were home. Some folks say they won't have a solid-fuel stove because it's messy; to some extent it is, but it's "clean dirt." For myself, I would sooner live in squalid comfort than be miserable in bad weather. Besides, you can heat a kettle on a wood or coal stove, make toast, simmer a pot, and do many other things, including dry socks. Such a stove is very nice, too, when tinkering in the cabin on weekends in winter, and for spring fitting out. After a cold morning under a bottom, scraping, it's nice to have a warm place out of the wind to work on the lunch box comfortably. All this is, I think, a very good part of boating. As soon as you do these things all cold and wet, boating is not so good.

Sizable cruising craft naturally have more elab-orate galley set-ups, though getting too elaborate does not seem to bring worthwhile returns. A craft that is able to do some real cruising and have the galley in operation in most kinds of weather is the dream of many. Here again, for certain climates, a solid-fuel stove, or at least one on the range princi-ple with plenty of iron, an oven, and a stack, is needed. In many cases today, such a stove will be oil-fired. In practice, the type of fuel is not the main

thing; it is the slow, steady radiation of heat that is important. The first thing any range needs is a good stack draft; without a good draft, there is nothing but trouble. Many folks may shy away from a good cooking range, though intending to do considerable cruising in latitudes where it's really a must, because of experience with a stove that had a poor draft.

In working up a design for a cruising boat, I often find that the client has quite set ideas on a cabin arrangement, sometimes without realizing just what goes on in use. A sailing vessel has air circulation from aft forward at anchor, and most of the time at sea. This is most noticeable in classic models, maybe because they tend to have plenty of sheer and deck layouts that favor this reverse cir-culation. Most folks want the galley right by the main companionway, basing the choice on "light, air, and ventilation, besides being handy to the deck." My experience has been that this is the worst possible place for the galley in a craft of offshore capability and some size, say 36 feet and bigger. In port, the cook is in a line of traffic; everyone is step-ping on or around him. Some air gets in, and all the hot stuff goes forward. What air tries to get out the companionway because it's hot is bucking the vessel's natural draft. Some pleasant ape wants to sit in the companionway and shoot the guff; he blocks both light and air. His remarks like, "Cookie, what's cooking?" get tiresome. If you give him potatoes to peel, he does it right there.

At sea, having the galley aft is worse yet; there are comings and goings, often in wet oilskins, and there are dollops of spray as the hatch is slid back. Worst of all, under sail, there is poor stack draft with the galley aft. On one tack at least, and more often on both, there is a downdraft from the sails, and besides, there is not room enough for a proper smokehead. The oldtimers knew all about this, and their stove pipes were near the forward end of a cabin trunk, be it after cabin or forward house, and the smokehead was usually in the form of a long tee, from one side of the house to the other, with turned-down elbows on the ends. Iron straps or rods supported these ends and also prevented lines from fouling them. The point was that since the stovepipe was limited in height by the foresail or mainsail, both when set and when stowed, the pipe was made as long as possible athwartships to gain draft. A very long pipe, even horizontal, increases draft, and the turned-down elbows prevented downdrafts from the sail directly above. At the same time, the pipe being as close as practical to the mast, the part of the boom above the pipe did not get very far outboard, even before the wind. This tended to keep those drafts that did come from the sails fairly constant regardless of point of sailing.

There was often a hatch directly over the cook's head. This hatch worked in favor with a vessel's natural ventilation, from aft forward, and the hot air in the galley further helped ventilating. The system is not bucking nature. I have had it pointed out that a galley forward is bad on account of much motion at sea. In practice I've not found it so, at least in designs based on classic models. Having the

galley forward was standard on all sizes of sailing vessels in the past, and you see nowadays many motor fishing vessels whose galleys really are little different from those of the days of *Captains Courageous*, except for the oil range and a reefer.

I think I speak from experience on these matters; it's been said I was considerable of a cook; at least there was never much left, and someone else was usually willing to wash up. I go into such things as galley arrangement just to make it clear that in planning, designing, or having designed a vessel with serious cruising in mind, this kind of thinking can have a great bearing on the vessel being successful later on. No designer or builder can have full experience in all things pertaining to vessels, but they can and should be very much guided by what worked in the past.

Another important factor for the success of any vessel meant for serious cruising is her ground tackle. Many kinds of anchors have been invented, quite a few relatively recently, yet only one or two of the recent ones have stood the test, and these, like all anchors, are not perfect. Each kind of anchor has its best or worst conditions of holding power. We

The galley of the schooner Integrity, *showing the solid fuel Shipmate stove in the right foreground with flue ascending to the cabin top where the coaster-style t-head smokestack would carry away the smoke. In the center of the photo is an alcohol stove sitting on a counter, which has a sink with wood storage under. The alcohol stove would be used in warm weather and gimbaled on the rails of the Shipmate.*

don't seem to have come very far ahead with anchor development in 500 years. Most everyone agrees that every vessel should have a really big anchor and cable of some kind for use when the chips are down, yet the big hook is often very unhandy to put overboard quickly. There was a rule, now mostly neglected on account of "the work," that in seasons of bad weather or in unfamiliar waters, the big hook was always put down first as a matter of course; some used it regardless of seasons and conditions. These men seldom if ever drove ashore; they had no mad scramble during the night to get a too-well-stowed big anchor overboard. Instead, if they felt they needed a second anchor, it could be gotten out calmly and in an orderly manner, as the vessel was not in immediate danger of dragging.

If a wise skipper, thinking this way and having a vessel built or an older one overhauled for some adventure, dumps the ground tackle question in a designer's or builder's lap, it's no big problem. All that is needed is a method of letting a big anchor go, sufficient power by man or motor to heave in and cat it, and a way to stow the cable. It's all been done uncounted times before, yet to fail to prepare for these simple operations in a new craft and then find (if you have been lucky and have not driven ashore) that these things must be done, can be a most expensive proposition. It's better to do it right the first time.

Another sometimes underestimated part of a cruising boat is the fuel system for her engine, if she has one. Fuel problems can mean not only discomfort and inconvenience, but also, of course, sudden disaster. A good many years' working around fuel tanks has taught me many things. Way back, when even big engines were gasoline, or possibly distillate, the first-class fuel tank was considered to be copper, unless large tank size made this metal impractical. I remember no more engine trouble in those days than there seemed to be later on, though the cause of trouble changed. Gas does not smell

now like the old stuff used to, and the old stuff probably was not much good, though the engines used then did well on it. Something in the gas changed, and copper tanks started forming gum. So now it's Monel, and, in some cases, plain steel for diesel oil. For the most part fuel tank installations are now made to Coast Guard recommendations; for certain uses they must be. In some classic boats it's best to have the tank on deck; even though it's covered on top, there can be full ventilation around it. I feel a shut-off valve at the tank, always a good idea, is the thing here. Always use it. Shut down the engine; shut off gasoline.

I've found that shutting off the gas and running the carburetor dry is bad business. Sometimes when the gas is turned on again, the carburetor float will stick and flooding results. Flooding is no good at all with the present system of remote starting; you get ready to fire up and never know she's flooded!

The engine should be very accessible (few are now) and when you start it, you should be right at its side—no remote starting. What happens is, you get right next to it, and smell before doing anything else. The difference between open air and engine gas smell is easily noticed. Look and check things over for a few seconds. What's that juice washing around in the pan? water? gas? If it's oil, check the stick. If all seems okay, fire up. The throttle and clutch lower ends should be handy or extensions put on them. There should be a cut-off valve at the engine too, right next to the pot. Folks running their engines this way have little chance of blowing up. I'm well aware that this thinking will not go over with some folks in these days of Step-On-It-And-Go. Some people bring the auto outlook aboard their boats, but remember that the car has most of its guts hanging out in fast-moving air; that's what keeps it from burning up.

In my distant past, most engines were stem-winders; a few had starters; all had to be cuddled up to if starting was intended. It was all very backward,

I suppose, but we did not know any better. We started and stopped these hunks of iron totally by feel on the darkest of nights, and even made hasty repairs in the dark. In some "trades," lights of any kind were very much frowned on. Some remember when the only beer was known as "3.2." Starting in the dark of a wet and drippy night, we learned some things quickly. There is often a stream of red sparks from the starting gear ring. If the starter cover is not on just so, there is much blue light at the armature. A connection you didn't know was a bit loose sparks a bit. A big-bore "six" with dual ignition has a lot of wires and plugs; the whole business often glowed and crackled till she got a bit warm. Try it some miserable night, in the dark of course.

I still like to cuddle up to start a gas engine, even if it's the most modern type.

Though it's done, I don't care for the siphon pipe tank in a diesel, as, over a long period, or even in a short time if you are unlucky, water and crud collect until they come very close to the bottom of the intake. After a winter lay-up you fit out and try the engine at the dock; it's fine, and you start for the home port. It's early spring and it's windy, with the tide horsing up against the wind. There's lots of thrashing, and soon she gets a blob of the gunk. You clean filters, get going, and soon it happens again, and again. Wallowing in the trough with this smelly stuff is no fun. I know because I've gone around Point Jude this way. It's better, I think, to feed off the bottom of the tank, and catch the mess a little at a time, by plenty of attention to the filters; if it can't build up, it can't cause as much trouble. There is much to be said for the old Navy type of filters, those that are dual in the same line, with separate cut-offs. You clean one while you run on the other. Cooling water filters work well this way too. The system isn't cheap, but it may save piling her up.

Centerboards seem to have nothing to do with fuel systems, yet, like them, they have some relation to making the boat go, at least somewhere near where she looks. Nowadays, and in cabin boats in particular, centerboards and wells seem to be designed mostly to suit the cabin, and not primarily to help the sailing of the boat, or not for strength, simplicity, and ease of maintaining. Therefore, centerboard boats tend to get a bad name in some boating circles. Even in open boats we find some poorly designed centerboards nowadays. In so many craft, open or not, dropping out the board, either ashore or afloat is most unhandy and difficult. There is no need for this. The centerboards in small, open craft can usually be arranged to be removed from either the top or bottom of the trunk; it's often unhandy to lay the craft on her side to remove the board from the bottom. In cabin craft, taking the board out through the top of the well can often be impractical, and few railways now have easily removable sills or a hole under them for dropping a large board. Or, if you beach out, you can't get the board out through the bottom.

The "old way," which now seems forgotten, was simple. We are talking of very large, heavy boards, such as were used in schooners, bug-eyes, and big sailing bateaux, 2 to 4 inches thick, and 16 feet long or longer, but of course the same system works with smaller boards. There was stout eyebolt on the top of the board at each end. The well cap was made to remove easily over these eyebolts, and halyards were dropped down through hatches and hooked on to the eyebolts, along with a stout lazy line to each. The vessel was put in water of sufficient depth to clear the board, a strain was taken on the tackles, the pin, which was a simple affair, was punched out, and a couple of wood plugs driven into the pin hole, one on each side. The board was then lowered clear of the keel, the lazy lines following. The lazy lines then were fished out from under the vessel, using the yawl and a long boat hook. Just the bights of the lazy line were taken aboard the vessel, not the ends, which were of sufficient length to stay fast in the hold. The bights were racked off, or other falls secured to them, and a strain taken. The original falls were slacked off, and naturally the board came under the lines or falls alongside. The board was then hoisted up to the rail against fenders and the vessel taken to railway or ground. At the railway she was hauled with the board alongside. Then the board was slacked down to the sills if the tackles were long enough, or to blocking. The outboard side was scrubbed, then the board was pried past center if need be, and gradually lowered outboard, flat, so the inboard side could be tended. Repairs, if any, followed, and the board was, of course, painted. Also, the well was swabbed out. After launching, the procedure is reversed to bring the board back up into the well. You might think this would take some tricky fiddling, but if the water is quiet, she comes right back where she belongs, hauled up by falls on the lazy lines, with no fuss.

Some craft had the centerboard pin slightly above the waterline when in light condition, so it could be driven out without the usual temporary flood below. To me this is most sensible, and I've designed a number of craft this way. Just why a centerboard pin has to be complicated, expensive, and inaccessible I fail to see. Some present designs show complicated machining, bushings, stuffing boxes of a sort, threads, and what all, often for a 14-foot boat! Small working craft often used a tapered hardwood pin and just a plain hole in the board. Bigger boards had crudely bushed holes, made with just a stout piece of flat iron rolled in a circle without a weld, just a butt, and driven into a tight hole in the board. Sometimes the pin was threaded with a nut, more often not in the large sizes. A big pin would often consist of a stout bolt with a large head and a forelock on the other end. A forelock is simply a punched hole, usually oblong, a big, stiff washer, and an iron wedge, that was driven through the hole to set up against the washer. The bolt head and forelock washer set against stout hardwood blocks,

often square, with thick leather washers under them, and they were quite tight! So much for simplicity, which many centerboarders do not have nowadays. These under-the-floor, hidden boards, while suited to gold platers and racers (where they give much trouble at times), have no place in practical, economical cruising boats.

Centerboard pennants often cause trouble, just because it's not understood what goes on and can happen at times. A centerboard is made to kick up when something is struck, or if purposely used as a brake or temporary hold-off on coming alongside in shoal water. A rope pennant does fine in a small craft and is easy and cheap to replace. If the board is let down below the well, it's very apt to jam the pennant on striking something. I think chain is very bad this way. And even if the board is not lowered too much, chain piles up and once jammed is most difficult. Wire, being stiff, does all right, but needs watching; sometimes it rots out fast. Big coasting schooners used a stout iron rod or "monkey tail" hoisted by a tackle from aloft. This never jammed, which in those big craft would have been a big problem. Rods of various patterns have been much used in small craft, especially in beach boats that tend to get gravel in the wells. I like rods, with one exception; in a fast-sailing boat you like to fuss with board adjustment. If the board is part way up, the rod won't lie down and house properly, and lines get caught under it.

Any centerboard well, large or small, that is totally capped should have a hole in the cap, with a plug, of sufficient size to allow pushing, or even pounding, down the board with a stick if something goes wrong. A stout dowel will do for a small boat; a large craft might sometimes require a stout oak 2x and a sledge. Jamming, from many causes, can happen. If the board is get-at-able, there is seldom much problem.

Many folks think a metal "board" is the answer; I find it not at all so. Some class racers use metal centerboards, so it's the law there, and, like other racing things, you put up with it. Metal boards kink easily or crimp on the edge, and, of course, jam. If they are built stoutly enough not to have these faults, they become so heavy that they require strong mechanical means of handling, usually a winch. This is not an economical approach. For some reason, a boat that has been using a wooden board successfully will not sail as well with a thin metal one, even though the well is narrowed to suit. I really don't know just why this is, except that in practice thick control surfaces, and this includes rudders, seem to help, though just the opposite would seem the case. My experience has been that the very extreme streamlining of both boards and rudders, at least in the ordinary run of boats, does no good and sometimes causes harm, most notably in steering and handling. Blunt, or even nearly square, edges seem to require less area for a given board or

rudder. I find I much prefer a very long, shoal board to a short, deep one. I suppose the long, entering edge has a way of steadying the boat and making her hold on. On the other hand, the very narrow, deep rudder, which is not always practical on a shoal boat, seems to do the most work easily for its size and has less leverage on the steering gear.

Centerboards of my experience in big working craft were not ballasted. Being built of green oak and being heavily bolted they had sufficient weight. In small craft and even in sizable pleasure boats that winter ashore, ballast in the centerboard is required. In small boats, almost any wood is usable and strong enough for the board; lead makes up for its happening to be light. I have made small boards out of almost anything that's on hand. It's best to use narrow planks and plenty of bolts. Wide boards tend to warp in spite of much bolting, whether or not the board is taken out for the winter. Some people put

The interior of Spray *looking forward at the navigation table with the barometer and clock as well as shelves for publications.*

a hardwood shoe on a small softwood board, though I prefer a metal band. Wood end pieces, supposedly to stiffen the board, have, in my experience, been a waste of time. Also, they tend to get loose; the swelling and shrinking of the horizontal planks, coupled with end-grain fastenings, make them not altogether practical.

Plenty of drift bolts, "fastened wild," that is raked this way and that, hold everything securely in a centerboard. You often see drifts in any kind of structure nowadays put in carefully parallel with each other. The trick is to put them in raked all differently fore-and-aft, the only care being to keep them in line in the plane of the board, so you don't "bore out." Many folks think boring for drifts in thin wood is difficult (by thin, I mean $3/4$-inch to 1-inch) yet if approached properly, it's not hard. A straight-edge short enough so it does not foul the drill is clamped to the side of the work; it can also be set to the wild rake, though that is not critical. The electric drill for this job should be of modest speed. The trick, if any, is to have the drill properly sharpened; one side doing all the work throws things off. Take care in starting, for the first inch is the critical one. Feed easily, and clear often. For big bolts, say $1/2$ inch and up, the barefoot auger is used, as it runs the truest. Everyone bores out occasionally. So what? Plug off and try again.

I've used about everything to bolt up centerboards in a pinch, everything except square rod, for I have not yet learned how to bore a long, square hole. I don't care for copper or bronze, as it has little holding power, though this can be improved by putting the bolt in a vice and making sharp burrs along it, similar to those on a coarse wood rasp, using a very sharp cold chisel. Unless these bolts are of hard metal (and then they don't burr so well), they don't stand driving into sufficiently tight holes. Galvanized bolt iron, from $1/4$ inch up, is probably best. Plain black iron rod seems to last a long time in a centerboard for some reason. On small boards

made with narrow stock, I often use 60D galvanized spikes with the heads cut off. These seem excellent and "draw" wonderfully, as they are usually very rough. Softwood should have a somewhat tighter hole than hard stuff, not much tighter, but some. What I say here pretty much applies to building rudders, except that they should be hardwood if possible, and narrow stock is even more important, as rudders get exposure to sun and kick around in an open boat.

Some folks think a centerboard should be of plywood. If you make a plywood board, lay it out to the stiff way of the stock; this applies to rudders, also. Plywood is not pleasant to work; edges tend to splinter, and there is much time taken to "sell the edges." Any metal binding is hard to fasten into the end grain. So the notion comes to fiberglass it. Time and stock are now more than doing it the old way, so why bother?

Since I've said centerboards ought to be designed solely to make the boat sail at her best and never mind what the well does to the cabin arrangements, maybe some thoughts on cabins would be proper. Of course a cabin can be anything from a small cuddy or "hunting cabin," often removable and just a place to get out of the wind and chuck gear out of the wet, to a big layout suited to considerable cruising. Somehow, the light cabin house which can be bolted on in spring and fall, or used in winter, and then removed in the hot months, is seldom seen nowadays. Yet it makes a lot of sense and is easy to build. For land sakes make it low and good looking! Remember, just a while back you did not have any cabin, so don't attempt a palace, just a shelter. Such a cabin much extends the use of many small boats. The Rhode Island Box is of similar nature, just a shelter to squat in when operating an outboard in cold weather with a half lid that folds back so that you can stand up at times. I suppose this kind of shelter has not created more interest because most boating stops on Labor Day, and the usual molded stock boat is not suited to easily fitting them. Most people miss a lot by conforming.

A real cruising cabin is another thing. It requires some sort of drying-out stove (my previous remarks indicate this is not complicated unless you want to make it so) and it has to be tight. Everything else can be poor, but if the trunk and deck are tight, you make out pretty well. Good light is usually essential, except you don't want too much daylight in bunks. I make no fixed statements as to cabin arrangements; some work, some don't. A good position for the stove and the why of it has been mentioned. A cabin to spend a lot of time in is like a home ashore; have it as you see fit.

I've noticed so many times that some of these domains are most cheerful regardless of the time, weather, and other conditions, and remain so even if you are confined below for long periods. Others, with excellent joinerwork, expensive fittings, and all the things you would think would make a nice cabin, somehow fall short, and Cabin Fever develops quickly. On trying to analyze the differences between cabins, some things become apparent. In the interest of a "clean look" and a certain style, maybe, in one "cabin-fever cabin," nearly everything was awkwardly placed. The toilet room was especially unhandy. Somehow things were planned for a contortionist throughout. Simple things, like taking a shave in port with all quiet, or a supper for a lone man, almost become productions instead of simple chores. Underway the set-up was plain hateful; a lee bunk on only one tack, plenty of light, but when sun, skylight, and the usable bunk happened to line up, a watch below in daytime was worthless. And so it went. Nothing was quite right, but all was beautifully built.

I've been in other cabins, some in pleasure craft, some in working vessels, where everything felt just right and, what's more, worked right. Most real offshore craft tended to be not overly bright below. The bunks were quite sheltered or recessed.

A spot of bright sunlight sweeping around below as the vessel plunges is not at all restful to those turned in. Such things are worth thinking about if you're planning real cruising.

Few folks realize nowadays just how nice and well appointed for their time some of the working vessels' cabins were. The larger the craft, the more elaborate the cabin, as a rule, though some of the small ones were pretty nice. They all seemed homelike and workable, their "design" being based on years of experience.

For cruising, much thought should be put into arrangements below decks. A counter that is all wrong as to height, width, and depth, though covered with Formica and shiny metal bindings and all, is no good. A plain pine board that is just right is what counts; you can fancy it up later. Though there may be a cabin plan drawing for general guidance, as the interior is built, the pieces should be mocked up and tried for height, clearance, and usefulness; fewer mistakes will be made. The mock-up can be simple; just a few sticks and small nails, a shoal box, some boards to shim it up, and a couple more pieces of board. Kneel, stand, reach, and try; it all tends to work out.

My usual method of placing a toilet bowl is this: Once the telephone booth is built, I place the pot about where it seems to want to be, block it for height, and then set the boatowner on it. We fuss, shift, and change the shims. Finally it seems all right, and the location and height are carefully noted. When the bowl is finally installed, the fellow is usually happy with it; after all he decided its location himself. Many other items in the cabin can be located just this way, by trial. No cabin plan, even though carefully drawn, can be wholly accurate, due to the fact that such accuracy depends on the craft and her scantlings being built exactly as drawn, which is not quite the usual case. Most builders come pretty close. A designer with much cruising experience tries to show the things that matter in making his drawings.

Some parts are difficult to show. Drawings of some minor detail could get so elaborate as to cost more than just standing by to see that the job is done right, along with some quickie sketches on a board for a workman. Building a good cabin takes some art, like building many other parts of a boat. Staying simple makes it all work better.

Having owned one vessel for over twenty years, having traveled considerably in her, and having made a home and a living of sorts with her, I was much sought out by others planning a cruising boat. Certainly, they thought, I must have worked out many wrinkles, and there were sure to be a lot of "gadgets," which there were not. The craft for her size was a model of simplicity. This was often disappointing to people, and much searching would be done for something that might be considered a wonder gadget. If something caught their eye, it was not really a gadget, but an expedient just to suit the vessel, and probably useless in another. It is so easy for the inexperienced, though well read, to miss the point.

There naturally should be some plan of the basic cabin arrangement, showing locations of the main "furniture." Once that much is installed, the cabin is usable. Some cruising in an unfinished but usable cabin often makes the further details come forth of themselves, and this procedure can save some mistakes. The kind of surface finish you finally end up with comes of its own too; you find where the chafe, finger marks, and sharp corners are.

However it's done, whether plain or fancy, I've found one very valuable method of putting any cabin together. Assuming floor, bulkheads, main lockers, and such are in, I try as much as possible to make everything else as units, which go in with screws, or sometimes bolts, if the unit is heavy. Later on, if changes are made or a big refinishing job has to be done, these units simplify the job very much. Pieces easily can be gotten out of the way of the paint brush, and the units can be taken home for

overhaul. If you have ever tried to remove a complicated glass rack that was built in place (takes more time to build that way) with toe nailing, blind fastenings, and all, you appreciate the unit system. Often taking out a unit is the only way to clean up properly a spilt mixture of molasses, catsup, and, say, black pepper in some compartmented rack. You unscrew it and take it out to plenty of water.

There is one thing I learned in racer-cruisers in an effort to keep a sweet cabin. After a heavy summer of campaigning, these boats get much salt

The interior of Spray *looking aft with her deck chair visible. To the right were two canvas pipe berths that were favorites of children when aboard. Behind the chair were lockers.*

below. There is hasty stowing of wet sails, you often stop up a big, wet spinnaker below decks so as to be ready for the next run down wind, wet oilskins come below, spray gets below, the craft is over-pressed and knocks down, rolling bilge water up into the lockers, and so on. In spite of constant attention she's well salted below by lay-up time. The yard boss knew my methods; he hauled me out near the hose, or arranged an extension. The bilge plug was pulled and the yard watchman was informed that the craft was to stay totally open as to hatches for a few days regardless of weather. All soft goods and linen were taken ashore, washed, and stored. Other gear that couldn't be wetted was taken out; these items were not many, for most things can stand fresh water. A good rousing fall Nor'wester was waited for. It soon came, so full wet-weather gear was donned, including boots, and the hose was dragged aboard with full pressure, the more the better. All current being off and the batteries removed, the hosing started—overhead, down back of ceilings, and from ends to middle, all floor boards up, washed on both sides, and all lockers and drawers. Silverware, cutlery, all stuff which was around loose was dumped on the bunk flats and got blasted. Engine

and wiring were especially hosed down, and finally the stream was sent down into the bilge, being sure to wash every last crumb out through the drain. In all, this took about two or three hours' work, as it was very thorough. All the salt was gone.

Then let the dry wind work two or three days, tidy up, and put the cover on. The wiring never corroded, the engine was free of rust, and the highly finished woodwork glowed; the craft never sweated in winter, and the cabin never needed to be "dried out" for any painting or varnishing or other work. The idea is to blast everything, inside and out, with fresh water, in good drying conditions. The amount of junk that came out of the bilge drain each season was astounding, a great wad of blanket lint among other things. I was of course considered a revolutionary by others who stuck to the rag and the bucket of soon-befouled water and could not possibly reach the places that really count.

So there, patient reader, are a few miscellaneous ways and means of doing things around a cruising boat. As I keep saying, none of these notions is original with me, but, as I also keep saying. I know from my own experience that every one of them will work.

PAINTS, OILS, AND GOO

Since the beginning of boats, there have been paints and such things used to help keep them tight, preserve them, and decorate them. Nowadays, we see almost unlimited products of this nature, nicely packaged in cans, spray tins, squeeze tubes, and other devices. In the not-too-distant past, there were a lot of these products too, not so prettily packaged. Few of these old standbys are still around, or, if they are, they appear in a different guise. I wonder if many were really much good. I also wonder about the new products and try one once in awhile.

The ancient goos applied to boats were what Nature provided. Asphalt was just fine. Animal hair, tallow, gums from trees, and, no doubt, these things combined, were in use. Industrial development brought other materials, most of them still available and still good, though many are about forgotten in the rush to try something new. Most of these old standbys are cheap, and they are easy to use.

Kerosene is the boatbuilder's friend. Plank soaked in it overnight bends remarkably well. Even if you're going to put a plank in a steam box, it helps first to soak the plank in kerosene. The stuff will go right through thin plank in a short time. It

probably is somewhat of a fungicide and seems to be the base of many wood preservatives. It tends to drive the moisture out of green wood. A large, green timber, if heavily soaked in kerosene and then placed in the steam box, though no bending is intended, seems to dry out remarkably well, and with little checking. I'm sure the sterilizing effect on the sap is a benefit.

Kerosene seems to come in three grades nowadays: lamp oil, which is water-clear and doesn't smell like kerosene; stove oil; and something that is quite yellow. They all seem to work on wood. Lamp oil costs the most, but I see no advantage to it, except for lamps and Primus stoves.

I can't imagine a builder getting along without kerosene. I use it, with a very little lube oil added, for whet stones. It's standard for freeing saw blades, hand or power, from gum. It's often used mixed with linseed oil to "drive the oil in the wood." It does. Mixed with melted tallow, it's most handy for keeping machinery tables in shape, and makes for an easy and steady feed. It's also fine for the temporary lay-up of a saw table or similar gear. The metal gets dusty, but there is no rust. This tallow mix, applied very sparingly to clamp screw threads, works just fine. It's also excellent for hand saws in use or laid up, and for any other tool to keep it bright. When working long leaf or any other fat pine, kerosene, with or without the tallow, is a necessity. Without it, tools gum up and become ineffective, and power tools wander and burn. A sanding disk, drum, or belt that gums up can be cleaned easily with plain kero and a wire brush, and this can be done several times. The kerosene seems to have no effect at all on the binders used in today's sandpaper.

Tallow is also most useful and was once much used. Nowadays not many folks know how to come by it or even know just what it is. It's simply grease from the trimmings of meat. Some few butchers still do some trying out. Most everyone eats some meat; the fat trimmings from it, saved and tried out, will make your own tallow. Heat the fat scraps slowly in an iron skillet; don't get it smoking much, if any. Pour off the grease into a container. It will be somewhat dark. Later on, simmer this grease in a big pot with plenty of water for quite awhile; the dark stuff will settle out. Don't boil, simmer. Like all good things, it takes time. Then let it get cold, and the solid tallow can be lifted out. There are, I suppose, three main kinds of tallow that are common. Mutton, which is said to have the best properties of all for some uses; beef, which may be the most common; and that from pig. There are no doubt many others, somewhat rare, and I've had no experience with them. There must be bat tallow, which might be useful in witchcraft!

Tallow is great stuff for adding to kerosene. It has launched no end of ships as grease for the ways. In the far South in the great heat of summer, it's often impossible to keep tallow on the ways, as it simply melts off. Other slippery stuff is then used, sometimes green bananas. No, I'm not kidding one bit! For oar leathers, the steps and partners of rotating masts, and for other crude shipboard lubrication, tallow can't be beat. It's great on gaff jaws,

hoops, mast lace lines and such. It's also good as a grease for serving marline. When working with tallow while rigging, you never seem to get chapped hands or those splits common to much outside work. Most boat gear screams for lubrication; tallow does it.

Mixed with white lead, tallow has been the standard stuff in vessels for years for protecting metal, especially when laid up. For instance, large turnbuckles are packed in this mixture, parceled with canvas, and painted. This mix is also fine for filling rents in big timber during construction; it has the property of "bottoming out" in the crack instead of just bridging and is most easy to work with. In the past, white-lead-and-tallow has been used as bottom paint on iron vessels, as it seems to be somewhat anti-fouling, probably because it wears off as growth forms. Worm, of course, is no problem in a metal hull. Many steam engines and other bright machinery were smeared with this stuff on laying up; it gave fine protection, yet was not difficult to remove when fitting out.

Tallow and slaked lime make a good, cheap, seam filler for some old boat that is past her prime; you know she will need a lot of tinkering with the seams, and the stuff goes in easy and is simple to get out for recaulking. Boiling hot tallow will, more often than not, cure an unreachable leak, such as a split keel, or defective king post, centerboard well, or deadwood. This particular use of tallow takes some experience and knowledge of construction. A few holes are bored in likely places and the hot tallow run in. It seeks out rents, cracks, and worm holes. I've seen the tallow run right through at the start of a pour, which is fine, as you have found the trouble. Slack off, let it congeal, then pour slowly, slacking off again as necessary. When she shuts off, fill right up; you have it licked, unless there is another bad place somewhere along. This same system works fine in a split shaft log. Sometimes the conditions are such that you will want to use a high-pressure grease gun, using grease fittings screwed tightly into holes you think will catch the leak, and for the gun the best mixture is, again, white lead and tallow. The great pressure will tend to heat the tallow. Keep pumping until the stuff shows somewhere. If the pump fetches up, take it slow. Often the goo will begin to show in the most unlikely places, around nail heads, out of end grain of wood, and in seams you thought looked tight.

Though I've used tallow for years, I still marvel at its properties. For some reason that I don't know, it acts as a dryer for an old-time canvas treatment that is famous for its slow drying. A chemist friend can't tell me either, though he knows it works.

(continued on page 170)

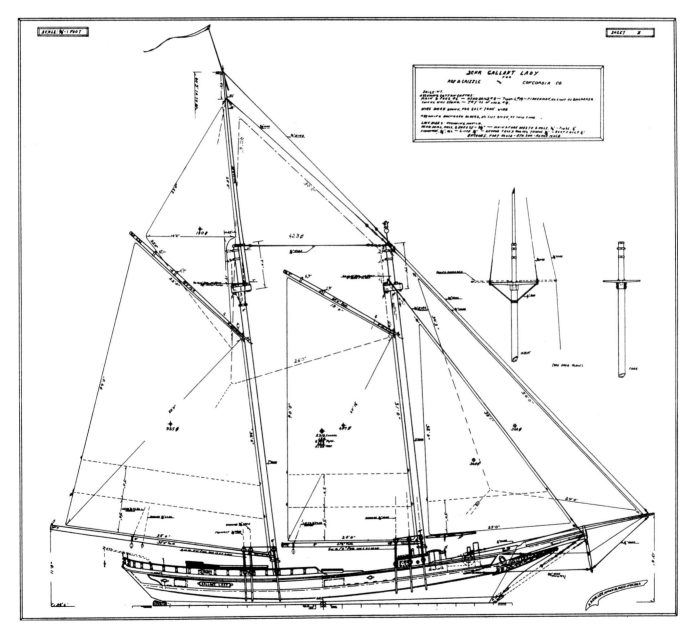

In this schooner we begin to see what is possible with added length and displacement. For most of us, this size and tonnage are out of reach. However, for those who have both the commitment and means, such a vessel must be exciting beyond description. (© Mystic Seaport, Ships Plans Collection, Mystic, CT)

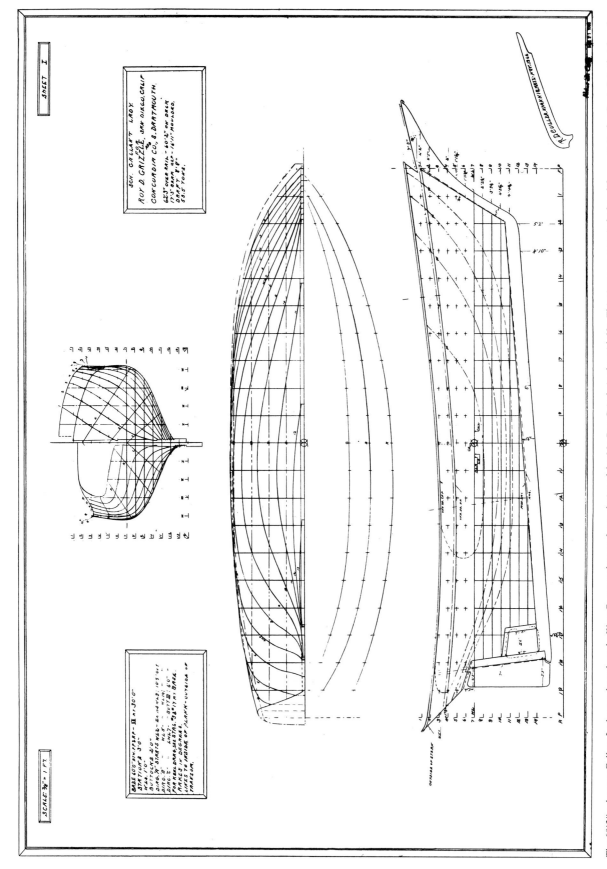

The 60'2" schooner Gallant Lady was based on the West Coast sealers and was designed for Mr. Roy Grizzle in the mid-60s. This time was a period of prolific creativity for Capt. Pete that found all manner of traditional craft designed and built, both at his Hyannis shop and at the Concordia yard. To my knowledge Gallant Lady has never been built. (© Mystic Seaport, Ships Plans Collection, Mystic, CT)

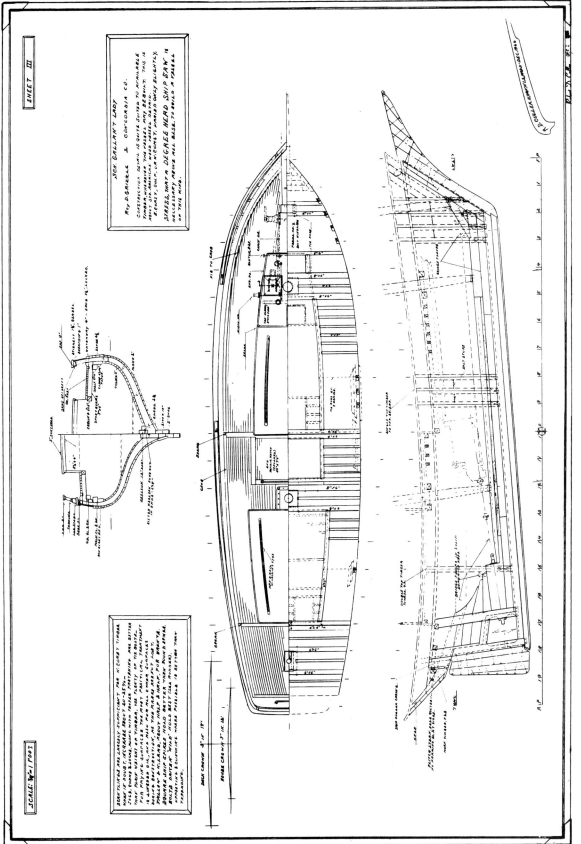

The 60'2" schooner Gallant Lady serves to show Pete's idea of a proper schooner hull. This includes a straight raking rabbet with a clipper head; a deep prominent forefoot; straight keel with drag; a raking sternpost and a short counter with a flat raking transom; generally sharp ends and a good body as well as hollow garboards with much wineglass shape worked into the sections. All of the above points to an exceptionally fine run. (© Mystic Seaport, Ships Plans Collection, Mystic, CT)

(continued from page 167)

It does not get rancid if properly tried out, even though stored for years. I have a "gub" of tallow from a launching over forty years ago. It's a curiosity and sort of ossified now, but it does not smell.

A can of tallow kicking around the shop does not spill like oil, and is just the thing to dip an auger in, or the end of a long drift before starting. When moving a heavy weight, a couple of greased timbers under it makes things go real easy. I know of some yards who move all their craft on grease, though for a sandy, windy place like Cape Cod, it's impractical; ten minutes and the grease is full of grit. Tallow and white lead, or graphite and some light oil make a thread-cutting oil that is not bad at all, if you don't have the real stuff. I use this often in some metal turning, and it's fine for the lathe centers. This same mess, mixed rather stiff, is handy for assembling machinery, especially on threads; it comes apart easily a long time later, as there is no rust. There are so many uses for tallow I just have to keep it around.

Pine tar is another necessity, now little appreciated. Its main use was the protection of rigging, and nothing since developed does as well. It has many other uses, one being around pigpens, which is sort of out of my line. If you put pine tar on the threads of an anchor or mooring shackle pin, it can always be backed out easily even years later, and turnbuckle threads treated with pine tar never seize. Some uses of pine tar seem very odd; one old skipper of a handsome little schooner years ago was always complimented on the whiteness of his paint, and he was quite open about how he did it: one tablespoon of pine tar to a gallon white paint! No one cared to try it, but maybe that's just what he did.

Pine tar is still available; usually it must be thinned. Turpentine or alcohol work fine; kerosene or gasoline does not, unless very hot, which is taking a big chance.

Knowing few folks will be interested in tarring rigging nowadays, I won't go into it much, yet if rigging is to last, it should be tarred. On new craft you can tar several times the first year to build it up; after that, tar once a year each early fall in northern climates, and don't spare it. I've known a vessel thirty-six years old with all original wire and hemp lanyards, all still in fine shape from being tarred. I've seen the serving lifted for inspection on a lower splice fifty-two years old; the rigger said it was a shame to disturb it. This was another monument to thorough tarring. Just how to make up a gang of rigging that will last, in the old-time way, is explained in detail in works on rigging, all of them considered out of date. The rare person wanting to do this sort of rigging will find out all about it on his own and learn many interesting things, and his rigging job may well outlive him!

Some open boats require trimming ballast, not so much for stability, though that comes too, but to get them down in the water or balance against the weight of the crew. Lead costs plenty, is at times unhandy, and can be too concentrated a weight for many craft. For a boat that may haul up often, lead can sometimes be a finger-pinching business to handle. The old sand bag still has a lot going for it. If you want to get rid of the weight, open the bag and let her go. Some localities have only gravel or shingle, but it's just as good as sand. Some folks say a ballast bag filled with gravel or shingle lasts longer than a sandbag, probably because it ventilates better. Being in a sandy locality, I use sand, and the bags are pine-tarred. This tar seems to make them go five or more years with ease. The bags can be dipped or brushed; then let them dry well and they are not sticky. For tarring canvas, pine tar should be mixed quite thin. Any object tarred, ballast bag, rigging, or anything that should be dry to use, should be placed outdoors. Drying in a building, especially in winter, just does not work. Often pine tar is put on too thick; several thin coats do much better. Like tallow, pine tar seems indispensable. I can't see just how a builder or boatman can do without it, or if he does, he's missing a lot.

Black asphalt paper-shingle stickum is readily available and cheap, and is most waterproof. It's very handy for underwater seams and nail holes, and it comes about as near to working in a wet seam as anything made; in fact it will work, though naturally a dry seam is better. Copper paint takes kindly to black asphalt stickum, though most other paints do not; the stickum will bleed through to some extent with ordinary paint, so stay below the copper line with it. Asphalt stickum tends to "settle," even in an overhead seam and in fastening holes, which is fine in a new boat. Any low places can be flushed up later when the craft has found herself. I assume this settling has something to do with the tenacious way the stuff stays in place. With care, and several shallow applications, a very bad gouge in a plank can be furred out with this goo and it lasts. It's very easy to apply, even if the weather is sort of chilly, and it has the property of skinning over fairly quickly.

I've tried other similar asphalt compounds, but that made for sticking shingles seems to give the best results. It tends to flow when bedding down underwater fittings, so you get the fastenings tight right off and a good "bleed" all around is readily apparent. This is most useful stuff. In the past, a well-known maker of bedding compounds had a black one that stuck in wet seams and that was much liked by all who used it. It came in cans with

A schooner ready for paint and finish treatments. Here the vessel has a coat of primer on the hull and will soon receive several more coats of primer before final finishing coats. The fore rigging straps will receive protective metal coatings prior to their finish paint.

his trademark. A pint cost about what a gallon of the shingle stuff does. I think it was the very same thing!

Linseed oil and turpentine are so old and so familiar to most folks that there is no point in dwelling on them. Many things I've mentioned here and in other writings require their use. You will always be using linseed oil and turpentine in various combinations. This is getting close to paints, on which much has been written in the past and is written yearly in many boating publications.

Paint manufacture has changed somewhat through the years, and many paints once much used are no longer around, at least in any quantity. Much is made of paints just for marine use, and in many ways these are fine. Most marine paints tend to a very hard finish, and for good reason. For the most part, they stay white or hold their colors very well. Many are difficult to refinish when that time comes and tend to "build up" through the years. Being hard, many marine paints are difficult to sand, at least to the point of keeping the surface from building up too much. The very high gloss of some of these paints tends to show defects in hull smoothness and, at times, even in fairness. I have no quarrel with these paints, or varnishes either for that matter, if they are used in the right places for the right effect. However, due to their nature, many of these marine paints have a short shelf life once the can is opened and a little used, for they all seem to dry quickly and there is often much skimming over in the cans. Lifting off these skins for short touch-up jobs must remove some of the important stuff in the make-up of the paint each time.

What I now say will no doubt be considered treason, but so be it. For many wooden craft, especially if more or less of classic model and with a fair hull, a high shine, or even a very smooth finish, adds little or nothing and often detracts from appearance. I'm aware, of course, that modern marine paints come in other versions than high gloss. But there is the consideration of do-it-yourself refinishing and the cost of materials. For many more years than I care to count, for exterior use on classic wooden craft, I've used nothing but good-grade, outside, oil-base house paints. The results have been first class; the boats look as they should, are easy to refinish, and the materials are economical. House paint seems to have a longer shelf life than marine paint, and so can be bought in larger cans with more economy. I think house paint is a must on a canvas deck, as, if properly done, there is little build-up.

Every time I bring up this approach, using house paints on a boat, I get a lot of noise from boat owners, paint salesmen, shipyard people, and others. Many boat owners are certainly experienced; I think I am too, by now. Paint salesmen and shipyard guys sell paint, and, to give them their due, they mostly have to do their work in unsuitable conditions and please some owner with shine—maybe his craft is the type for it—so quick-dry stuff that covers is just what they need, especially in spring.

I look at it this way: A fine 8-metre yacht should be dressed in the style to which her type is accustomed or she will look shabby. She is largely a big, unbroken surface of delicate line; any slight defect shows up badly. A classic craft, with much beading, bulwarks, seams that show, and other trademarks of her type, looks dowdy if highly glossed, yet if finished in the somewhat subdued effect of house paint, she looks the part. A 200-year-old colonial house finished in high-gloss marine paint will not look right; it cannot reasonably be made smooth enough. The fancy paint will not "chalk," and when the time for refinishing comes, there is real work to be done. My pitch for house paint is: First cost is less; refinishing is simpler; shelf life is usually longer; it looks fine on the right craft, though on the wrong one it does not.

Protective coatings for the rigging are tar treatments, tallow, and oil. Varnish for the blocks will keep the wood from shrinking and checking and ensure long life. Periodic maintenance will be required to keep the vessel and her rig in good condition.

Some of us still think oil-base paint, usually white, gray, or red lead, sometimes all three in some combination, well thinned with turps, is better as a primer on new work than the "undercoaters" often used, which dry quickly, are often hard, and "drive into the wood" not at all. Many old notions die hard, right or wrong; new ideas come along and require many years of use for acceptance. Some of these never make it, probably because they weren't practical to begin with. Turpentine has great ability to drive into wood, taking some pigment with it. Why, I just don't know, unless turps, being made from wood, just wants to go back where it came from! By the way, pine tar comes from wood too.

Compounds, paints, oils, and similar things can be gone into at length until it sounds like the "Book of Ten Thousand Formulas." What little I've mentioned here has stood the test of time, and works. Whether a person wants to use any of this or not is his own choice; the point is, these things are still around for those who do want to use them.

I think now I have stirred enough paint.

SAILORS, OLD AND YOUNG

To get afloat, for whatever reason, you have to have a boat or vessel of some kind. This means someone, or a gang of people, has to build it, and this starts in a boatyard or shipyard. These places have, through the centuries, developed their own humor, which has often made light days of very heavy work. My experience has been that yards that don't have any humor don't amount to much. Things drag and there is a big turnover of help. Such a yard is generally not a happy place from the workman's standpoint. Just how a yard's sense of humor develops, I don't know, but when you see it building up, things are going fine. Most of the humor is simple, a lot of it is crude, and some is unprintable though very descriptive. Many workmen get nicknames due to their build, way of doing things, or some other oddity, and this includes the boss. Vessels building or in for repairs, their owners, and often their designers all get the same treatment. I think the crowd was unhappy when a him, it, or her showed up that was so utterly normal they could not pin on a suitable name!

I remember "Old Knife Bottom"; everyone dreaded her hauling up, as they feared "dropping her," and once she was hauled, even with all precautions taken, you felt uneasy working anywhere near her. In her long life, she never did fall, though other vessels of flatter model did, in various yards. Having witnessed one "drop," I can say it shakes all hands and the vessel, and it can be fatal to man and ship. If the craft is repairable, she carries the stigma of it the rest of her life. Future buyers view her with suspicion and beat down the price. There are, of course, recriminations all around, a considerable expense to someone, and a lot of work. Most yards manage to live down such incidents, however.

Though there was damage to the vessel I saw fall, there were no injuries. The incident produced some crude shipyard humor. The accident started with a strange tumbling sound from the shores and blocking simply being spit out from under her. There was a great rattling crash as things fetched away below, she bounced and trembled for a spell, and then lay still. It was near sunset. There was a moment of dead silence all over the yard. We knew "Old Up" had been painting under her, no one else. No one wanted to make the first move. Then there Upshure was, about 75 feet away, a big, very elderly black man, slowly turning to look back, paint pot and brush in hand, highwater pants on, not much of a shirt, and toes sticking out of his shoes. A lot of skin showed, and it was the strangest color. One look, and he walked woodenly out the gate into the sunset and never came back, nor the paint pot nor brush either. This broke the tension, and the relief made it seem funny. All hands jumped in and stayed late to straighten out the mess, or at least make a start on it. Nowadays they would demand overtime, and not appreciate the sight of the old black, still in one piece, departing into the sun's glare.

Some vessels get lurid descriptions of their whole hulls, or parts of them. One round old thing became "Missus Bruisewater"; one had "a run like a bucket"; and another's stern was described impolitely. Another craft was so shapely she took the name of one of the country's leading beauties of the time. One regular caller for bottom work was described as still unfinished; someone in the distant past had forgotten to put on the four ball-claw feet!

One dull craft went through the water "like a brick through wet sand," and when it came to going by the wind, another was so close at it that the galley smoke came straight aft and choked the man at the wheel. My, she could go to windward!

One old sailing windbag, named after a political windbag of the distant past, came in to get her seams mended after a long lay-up, for she was going to work again. She was hauled and doctored so much that she was actually quite tight on launching. Then new lanyards were rove and her rigging was set up, the rigger finished about quitting time. Next morning, she was on the bottom, with only the top of her house and her perky jibboom showing. The setting up of the rigging had pushed the masts down enough to open the ancient garboards. Strangely, she was not at all difficult to raise, due to know-how with ancient vessels. Her rigging was slacked up, a very low tide taken advantage of, there was much pumping, and up she came. Setting in the mud had sealed her off. She eventually sailed,

with very slack standing rigging, and made a trip or two, though her days were numbered, as the sawdust and manure ran out at an inconvenient time.

Every old-time yard had access to a shipsmith, and the one I speak of was right next door, on a shell pile hard by the Creek. The shop and its owner were right out of a story book. The building, now long gone to make way for progress, would today be a museum piece; it even had a tree spreading over it and all sorts of scrap and nautical gear sort of propping it up. Its owner, Captain Oliver, was a perfect specimen of an old-time blacksmith. His build was fantastic; he was big all over, and the shoulders, chest, and arms were massive in the extreme. A head with no apparent neck surmounted them. His feet were bad from long years of standing, and he walked with a sort of mincing shuffle. A bachelor, and very softhearted to all living creatures, his oyster tong shaft annex, filled with hard pine shavings, was a home for all the lost, the cast-out, and the ailing cats, kittens, ducks, pups, and others needing help. Every day he went up the street with a great bag of vittles for his charges, and more often than not stuff for the ailing. It was surmised much of his hard-earned money went to some unfortunates in the village, especially children.

This huge, much-liked, and powerful man was, of course, highly skilled. His feats of welding were wonderful to watch; such a shop always had loafers and onlookers. He was also very artistic, and the decorative iron work he turned out was famous, all done with the hammer and forge. I don't think he had ever heard of a welding torch, and if he had, would have cared less. He knew his trade and knew that he did.

Captain Ol liked loafers and visitors and didn't mind their learning how he made things, except for his six-strand, decorative iron rope. This he made in secret. Three, four, and five-strand you could watch being formed, but the six was something special. For heavy work, he employed a powerful black man part time. The heavy thud of the striker sledge and the ring of Oliver's signal hammer directing the blows let the village know something big was going on. He readily admitted that forging an anchor for a 65-foot vessel was hard work for two men, yet he did it. He would not weld with "a new fire," waiting until "after dinner" for it, at which time, and on till quite late, he could put iron together about like working putty, without apparent effort or stress, and

all of it was perfect; laps, butts, splits, jumps, and all the other welds. It mattered not if it was a mast band or a broken truck spring. The flux for all this welding was plain sand, from a small spot on a certain beach; nothing else would do.

Captain Ol was famous for being able to weld six pieces of iron to a seventh, all on one heat, and finish it off too. This he did rapidly, over and over again, when

(continued on page 180)

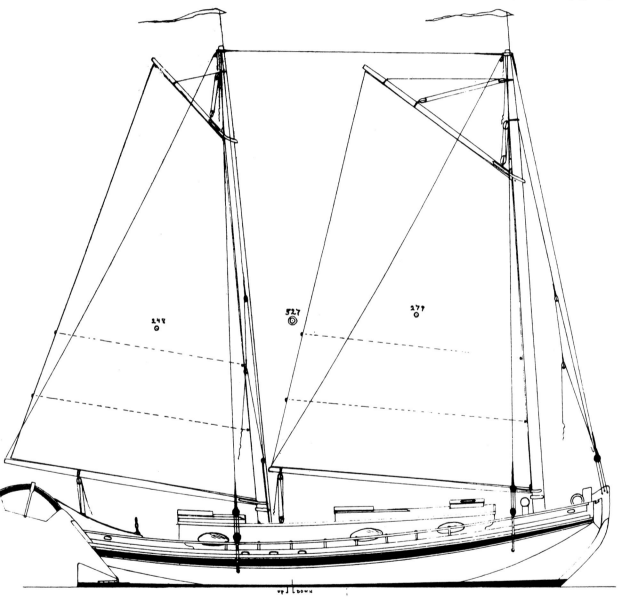

These two designs represent the first and last designs Capt. Pete produced in his career. The fact that they are both scow hulls (and just as beautiful in the Culler style) is thought-provoking. The 32' Periauger scow on this and the following page was drawn by Pete with thoughts of incorporating the gear he salvaged from the sale of his Spray *in 1951. The 45' scow schooner on pages 179 and 180 was drawn for his friend Bob Servais, and the working drawings were on his design table when he died.* (© Mystic Seaport, Ships Plans Collection, Mystic, CT)

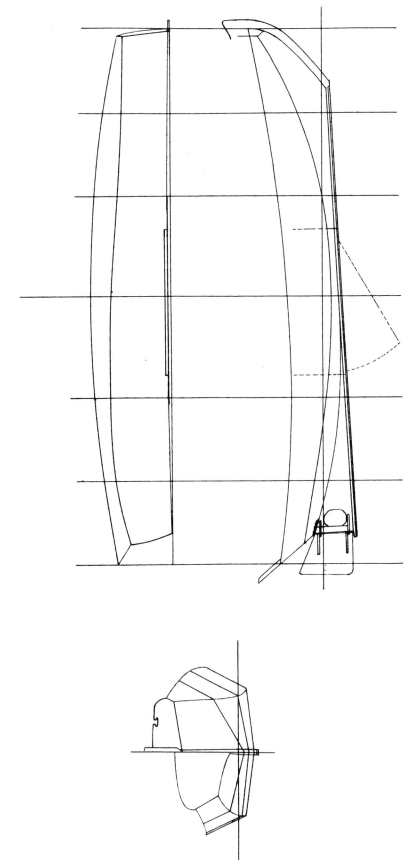

32' Periauger scow (continued). (© Mystic Seaport, Ships Plans Collection, Mystic, CT)

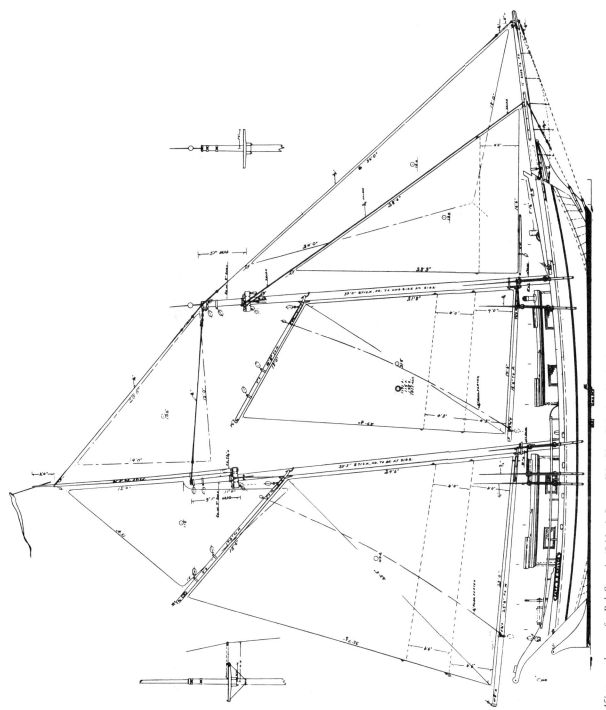

45' scow schooner for Bob Servais. (© Mystic Seaport, Ships Plans Collection, Mystic, CT)

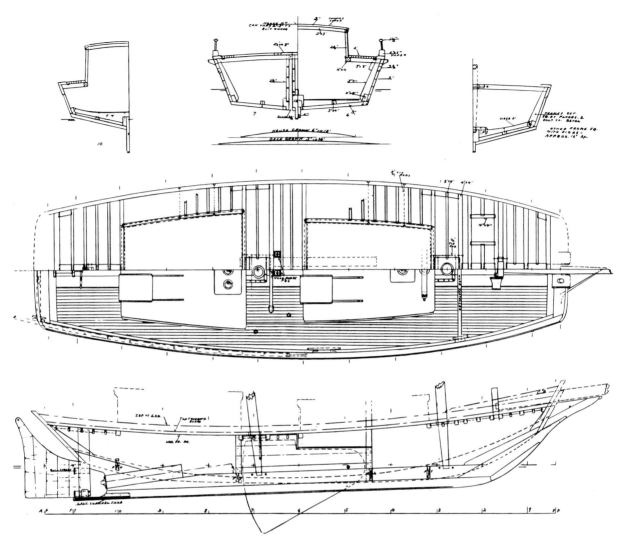

45' scow schooner (continued). (© Mystic Seaport, Ships Plans Collection, Mystic, CT)

(continued on page 177)

making oystermen's grappling anchors, all of different weights and five- or six-prong, according to the fancy of the owner. Though made entirely of scrap, they always weighed as specified when finished! These sessions always drew the crowd. Smiths wear a large leather apron to protect against the flying dross, scale, molten sand, and whatnot that flies in all directions, sometimes twenty feet or more, when making a weld. There is also a loud pop or small explosion as the weld "takes." This six-weld business was a most interesting process, based on a thorough knowledge of the trade, great manual dexterity, strength, and a long reach.

One "observer," not too bright in the head, got pretty close, and, as the first blow of the weld started, received a slug of white-hot in an important part of his britches! This happened long before the days of rockets, but there was a Whoosh, and a blast-off, and a big splash in the Creek. This Brought Down the House with howls and roars of delight. I think this was the only weld Oliver ever botched; he threw down his tools and jigged about the shop, playfully belting anyone within reach. The fellow who went in to cool off never quite lived it down, and, in the retelling many times over, his leap grew to a full 75 feet!

Captain Tom was a "character," and lived up to the part, especially in summer for the benefit of the Rusticators. He had started his career as a Bound Out Boy, that is, he was apprenticed for a given number of years to do as he was told by a tycoon who owned plenty of ships and land. This consisted of considerable experience in the owner's vessels in the West Indies Trade, a big thing in those days.

Tom also spawned numerous children. When asked how many, he said, "Eighteen head, if they're all a' livin'." When asked just how many were living, his answer always was, "Well Sir, I don't rightly know." His abode was tumble-down and his boat not much better. Tom was an oysterman in his later years. He seemed never to wash and was covered with dried mud from the "grounds." When chided about this, he said "erster mud was good for rhumatiz." Maybe it is, for he was a spry old chap. Summers, Tom often built skiffs as part of the efforts of a small boatyard where he was sort of a man of all work. By present-day standards in skiffs, his were pretty good, and he loved to have strangers stop and watch, so he could put on his act. This consisted of much serious "measuring" with thumb, fingers, and hatchet handle, and the transferring of all these dimensions from skiff to board and back again to the accompaniment of mystic symbols in chalk. This chalk came from a pile on shore up the Creek, said to be ballast left by some foreign craft, no doubt from the Cliffs of Dover. Finally, Tom would get a rise out of some Rusticator, such as, "Don't you ever use a rule?" Tom was set for the kill. "Nope, never had no learnin', can't read a rule, but if I'd learnin', and could read a rule, I'd be the best boatbuilder in the Whole Big World!"

Captain Billie was of a different cut. A widower, with family grown and gone, he made his home aboard a tiny, salty craft of his own build. Short, barrel-chested, with blue eyes surrounded by crinkles, he looked the epitome of the old-time seaman in sail. He was self-taught and extremely well-read.

Square rig, coasters in their heyday, oystermen, yachts, he had sailed in most of the best, and had skippered several. He was navigator, seaman, shipwright, rigger, painter, and model-maker of some skill. He was "independent as a hog on ice," as he said, taking a job here or there as the spirit moved and if he liked the set-up, for he had high standards, some of them odd, but nevertheless high.

Captain Billie was helping fit out an extensively rebuilt schooner yacht, having moved aboard temporarily from his own craft to be handy and do the cooking for himself and the straight-laced Marblehead skipper, Captain Jimmie. Among other things, Bill was quite a cook and enjoyed it. This moving aboard consisted of bringing his own skiff, "so as to be independent," and his mattress, better known as a "donkey's breakfast." When chided about this last, for the yacht had the finest of new bedding, Billie said, "I allus done it," with a tone of finality. The two old boys got on just fine for a couple of weeks, and the schooner glowed from their efforts. What with Billie's skill with the stove, life was just good. Then one fine Sunday in early June, Captain Jimmie decided it was time he explored the tiny village. Billie was not interested, as he knew it inside out, and besides, he wanted to work on a model of a pungy that he had under construction. Captain Jimmie was gone a long time, and it got to be way after dark. I think Bill began to worry, and so did the yard owner, as he was keeping a lookout and was my eyewitness to the following goings on.

When finally skipper James showed up, he had considerable cargo; apparently he had found a friend with a jug. Being conservative and careful by nature, he was proceeding with caution, and steering fine. Without undue adventures, he made the yard path, and, though yawing ever so slightly, made the narrow, rickety dock too, and arrived at the piling where his highly varnished yawlboat was tethered. Here he sat down with extreme care, unmoored the yawl, and carefully and slowly worked her directly under his feet. It was flat calm, bright moonlight, and very low tide, with little water under the yawl's keel and all the softest and blackest mud under that. He had a foot or so drop to get into her, so was arranging the maneuver with much care. The moment came to slide in and he started, and then stopped. Something had hooked the seat of his pants! There he hung, unable to slide down, and too far down to pull back. The yawl drifted to one side, and the efforts of Captain James, up or down, were to no avail. He was hung between wind and water, you might say. Suddenly there was a ripping sound as the nail, or whatever it was, tore out of his pants.

Captain James pitched forward on all fours into inches of water, and feet of mud! Then there was much thrashing around recovering the yawl, getting aboard with pounds of mud, and finally making it to his vessel, which was promptly polluted with the mess, as he had to disrobe in the cockpit and clean up as best he could.

Apparently, there were bitter words aboard that night. Early next morning, here comes Billie in his skiff with donkey breakfast, seabag, tool box, and an unfinished model on top of all. He made the very picture of an old-time seaman changing berths. His only greeting was some remark about Marblehead

The 45' scow schooner Vintage *on launch day at the Brooklin Boatyard, Brooklin, Maine. Joel White felt Pete did a nice job designing the cabin spaces on this vessel.*

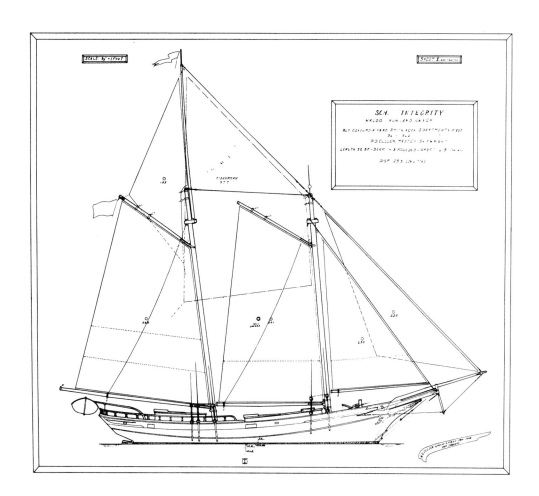

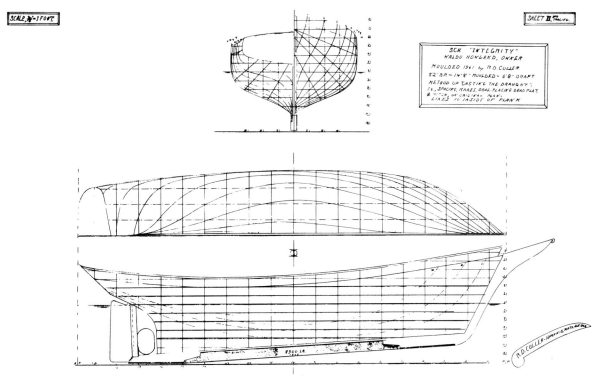

The schooner Integrity *was Pete's masterpiece. He had done "the hull of it," from designing to building and skippering, and always had a soft spot for the vessel. The schooner's tragic loss in an Atlantic storm and under dubious circumstances left a bad taste for everyone who was involved with the boat over its lifetime.* (© Mystic Seaport, Ships Plans Collection, Mystic, CT)

Sots, on which he went aboard his own packet, did a large washing, and sulked the day out. Yes, Captain Billie had high standards.

Many of these old seamen had seen things at sea that they could not explain and seldom cared to talk about. When they did discuss such matters it was with considerable awe, speculation, and sometimes doubt, according to their nature, but always with wonder. They all more or less did agree that such sightings, real or imaginary, had been going on since man first went sailing. There has been much written about this sort of thing, most of it just to make good sea tales, though some serious investigation has been done too, with, as far as I know, no results at all. That these sightings exist, real or not, I have no doubt, for I have been privileged to see some myself.

I was lying in New York lower bay waiting for "a chance along" down the coast, bound South. I was in a nice vessel, well found, had plenty of grub and a good stake after a summer's work, no worries and was not at all tired, for the three or four days' waiting for a wind shift was no chore at all. It was just modest, routine ship's work, regular feeding, and plenty of rest.

Finally, the wind came "down" as expected, with considerable of a squall, and, after the first edge was off, we set easy sail, hove up, and were off. We were two-handed, so it was watch and watch. The wind settled down to stay and eased enough to set the top-sail, and we looked forward to a fine night and a fast passage, which it was. After a good supper, roast beef with the trimmings, and a watch below, I took the deck at midnight. It was fine and clear, though no moon, and a bit of Northern Lights, as it was early fall. The vessel was a noted easy steerer, so there was little to do except pace back and forth and nudge the wheel once in awhile. About a half hour after the start of the watch, I saw a vessel, sailing vessel that is, on our port quarter, about a mile away or less. She was by the wind on the starboard tack, standing in for the beach. She was a full-rigged brig! This was in the

early 1940's, and I knew of no full-rigged brig still sailing anywhere in the world, except possibly one or two in the Maldives trading to India, the last of their kind. What was she? Some new training craft I had not heard of? A night glass being always handy, I took a long look at her. She was about 90 to 100 feet long. Her sails were set to the top-gallants; I could not make out whether she was rigged for royals. A running light shone dimly. She stirred right along, heaving gently to the old southeasterly swell common along that stretch of coast. I judged she would pass a quarter to a half mile astern and thought fit to call the watch below, for there was much interest in this sort of thing on board.

Giving the wheel a slight poke, I slid back the hatch and went partly below to sing out where I could be heard. Just before doing so, I looked in the brig's direction and she was gone. Coming back on deck immediately, I searched long and carefully, with the glass and without, and never found her again. I pondered this the rest of the watch, and many times after, and still do. The brig seemed real, all in order, proper course for the wind, right amount of sail, and I automatically assumed she was bound for New York and had been headed by the wind that favored us. Then she vanished while closing somewhat with our course. She showed clearly in the night glass.

Now, I still don't know what I saw, except that when in sight it was real. Was it a privilege of some sort, a setback in Time; or was it just imagination? Square rig in any form was far from my mind at the moment of sighting. During the war years, I came across a book telling much of Jersey coast history, including accounts of the wrecks there. It noted the loss of a brig in the early fall many years back at about the same latitude, with much loss of life. Was I seeing a re-run of her final hours? I don't know!

Many times during The Years of Strife we had occasion to make places or ports unscheduled and unplanned, usually without charts. This was often a

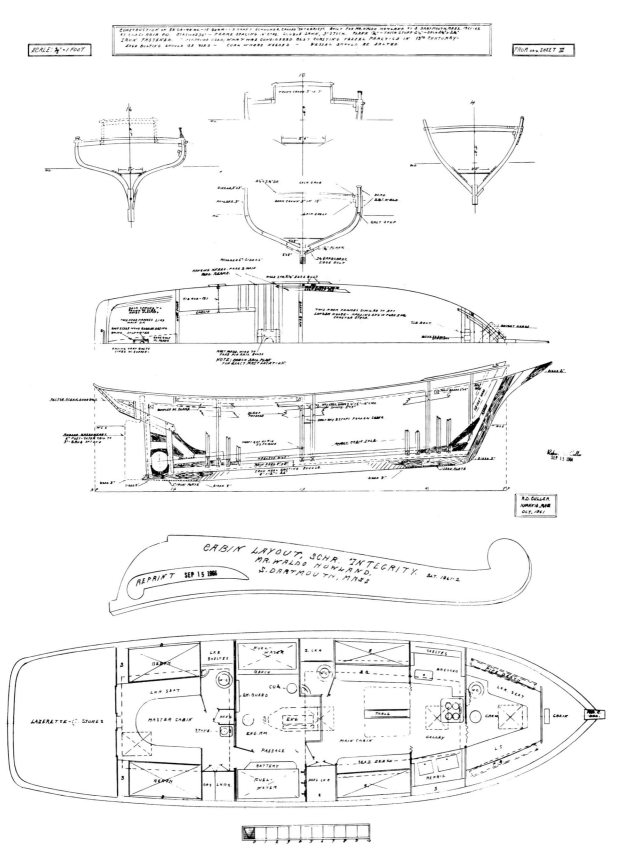

The owner of the 52' schooner, Waldo Howland, named the vessel Integrity *after witnessing the methods, materials, and craftsmanship that went into its building.* Integrity *proved over the years to be a smart, powerful sailer and a comfortable vessel for those who sailed her.* (© Mystic Seaport, Ships Plans Collection, Mystic, CT)

nervous business, though we managed to pull it off successfully each time. On two occasions, it was not difficult at all, however, though the places were just dog holes or mucky creeks. Somehow, without ever having been in that part of the world before, let along in those so-called "ports," entering them seemed perfectly natural. I knew every inch of the places, like my back yard. Both times, my mates on the bridge said, "Been here before, aincha?" All I could say was, "Nope." I was just as surprised as they were.

There are, in the great seas of the world, places known as The Triangles, two that I know of, and possibly more. Many ships have crossed these regions, yet many enter and are never heard from again. Just what goes on in these vast areas does not seem to be understood. Perhaps they have weather conditions that we are not aware of. Some folks think there are other reasons, though they have no idea just what. We still have a lot to learn about the Sea.

Looking back on past experiences at sea, coastwise, and in building, I have fond memories of ships, boats, and those who sailed them, yet as years advance, the idea no longer appeals of long night watches, often the wearing motion of a craft in a hubbly sea, "fog eating," making the land under difficulties, using poor anchorages from necessity with the rumble of chain on a rough bottom, and many other similar things that a sailor must take in stride. They were all right a while back, but not now. There were, of course, the very good times, and these stand out. I think I was lucky. When much exposed to crews, I had very little crew trouble. Most of the fellows were dedicated to some facet of their trade. Many were dedicated to booze when ashore, though it interfered little with their work on board. Apparently I was not born to be blown up in the Forties, though much of my time was spent in floating bombs.

I have experienced no real fires, and no man overboard permanently. The only man who fell off a vessel I was in did so in harbor, and was back aboard again in short order. I had no collisions, or even close calls, though at times there was much hooting and evasive tactics in thick weather. Many times we should have been messed up in many ways and for some reason avoided trouble. Possibly most of those I sailed with felt about like I do; when in doubt stop her, or, if under sail, lay to. Time has a way of straightening out many situations.

When I was young, I was exposed to sailing skiffs and catboats. Now, I find these just as much fun as any vessel; it's my second childhood, no doubt, and made sweeter by a background of varied experience. For many reasons, I still find much pleasure in swabbing out a nice small craft, cleaning her bottom, fussing with her simple gear, and understanding her design, gear, and build. I find I get a lot out of her when we go sailing or rowing. Most good small boats have a lot more in them than most people take the time to get out.

Many folks nowadays say small craft don't offer a real challenge. To take some nice, classic, small craft, with properly cut and sheeted spritsail, around some toy sandspit in what appear to be adverse conditions—there is a favorable eddy if you know where to find it and she works wonderfully in moderate going with only the tip of the board—takes as much experience as driving some hardpressed schooner around some tide-ridden cape, and you don't get so wet!

I think sailing and handling and thoroughly knowing a craft large enough and of a build to be called a "vessel" is the finest of things. Most of us can't own vessels, so we settle for boats, which we can and should learn thoroughly, too. In these days of many small pleasure craft, I'm struck by the short time most owners keep them; people are always buying and selling, and never really learning about the boat they have at the moment. Many folks have never learned to reef and don't know how and when to handle a boat under short sail. These same people also seem to have little real knowledge of the gear they try to work with. Those who go out in protected waters in heavy weather by mistake or to show off soon show their lack of understanding of their craft. Some heavy-weather sailing is good, and often necessary, as it can "air on" at times without much warning. I certainly feel reefing should be learned at once and that judgment that goes with reefing should be developed.

I think much is lacking in the ways of starting young people to use boats today. They are shoved off to a bum start and seldom are set right later on. First should be taught respect and understanding of the value, monetary and otherwise, of a good boat. I think a classic type gets this across, with the help of an elder seaman, better than any. The fact that the young "apprentice" will, much later on, be using way-out racing machines or double-hulled bananas, is, for the moment, beside the point. With a proper start, he will know what to do with 'em when he gets that far.

A classic boat is not easy to arrive at, even though papa is quite wealthy. Her designer has

spent much time on her; the building is quite a chore, though not at all unpleasant. She has considerable "background" even before she is launched, is usually handsome, and is therefore valuable. Cleaning, routine in-commission maintenance, and proper mooring are the first things to master. This is all part of appreciating and getting to know your boat. The craft should be rigged for and be of a model suited to some rowing and sculling. These two should be mastered before any thought is given to sailing. Learn smart and somewhat stylish pulling, skill with the sculling oar, proper shoving off and landing, and the use of the centerboard and how it can aid rowing and sculling. The important knots follow as a matter of course. The painter or the oarlock lanyards need renewing; here is a fine chance for applied marlinespike seamanship.

Oars stowed askew, oarlocks left in, bumps and scratches, these are signs of the "farmer." Besides, when the young man learns to fit out, these bruises can

Waldo Howland enjoys a sail aboard his schooner during the vessel's sailing trials in Buzzards Bay.

make quite a chore of it! When a thorough boat handler under oars has developed, and it does not take long with an interested and knowledgeable teacher, it's time to think of sail, and it will be found that the young apprentice has more knowledge of it than you might think. He has been observing other craft, knows the "fetch" of his boat at oar speed, how she drifts, and something of her turning ability; he has the feel of her. He knows about what a centerboard does, and no doubt has had passengers and coxs'n to try her rudder.

The classic craft should, if possible, have a "two-sail" rig. She is not gotten under way until all the gear is quite familiar. There is practicing at setting and taking in, and there is practice at reefing. Then she is gotten under way under short working rig with the fores'l in the second step, and Old Bill, the teacher, giving a few, now-well-understood pointers. She misses stays a time or two, then it all comes natural, and soon the handling, mooring, landing, and getting under way in many different conditions are an open book. Boy and boat have been out in quite a breeze, under short sail. By now

he knows when to reef, and why. There has been an Expedition with some grub and a small shipmate, and it required the proper use of an anchor, which was long ago acquired while rowing.

The day comes to use the "sporting rig," both sails. It's a fine bit of weather and Uncle Bill gives his blessing and stays ashore, for the boys now know what they are doing. The small mate is now useful, can pull a pretty good oar himself, and is heard to expound on how to do a rolling hitch properly! He already has little use for "farmer" ways.

Comes fall, and the proper laying up is at hand. A clean boat, properly stored, will last. There are many lessons to learn; the sails and gear need laying up too. Then spring, and the fitting out. Things must be right, for this year we are in full charge. That gawky place on the bow needs a lot of work; have to be more careful coming to a dock!

A season or two, and this young skipper, more often than not, gets a summer job on some yacht. He's a useful hand, knowing how to take care of gear and keep a boat clean, and is aware of what

Capt. Pete and Otter *out for a row.* (© Mystic Seaport, Richard White Collection, Mystic, CT)

it's all about in a larger craft. Besides, his former mate is beginning to take command of the small classics that taught him so much.

These boys, with such training, are quite fit to handle a motor launch or big outboard, though chances are they don't care much about such craft except to use and understand them in their proper place. By contrast, the often-seen sight of a boy turned loose in a plastic outboard, his first boating experience, is both sad and somewhat frightening. He never learns what it's all about, and is, unbeknown to himself or his parents, a menace. His boat is never anything to him but something off the shelf, easily replaced.

I think a proper training craft, and she can well do for a family boat for many years later, should not be too forgiving of the young sailor's mistakes. You learn that way. It used to be said in my youth that a lad who could sail some old scow with a packing box leeboard and a home-made sail, and do it well, could, when he got the chance, sail anything. Times have changed no doubt, but the Sea has not. Seamanship is still around too, though sometimes much neglected. Sadly, there are no more good packing boxes from which to make leeboards!

If what I have spoken of in this book is useful to hopeful builders, boatmen and sailors of the present and future, I will consider this small effort quite worthwhile. There is, of course, far more to it than the few things I touch on. I hope what I've discussed, some of it at length, some of it lightly, moves the spirit in the direction of nice boats, their building and handling. That, my readers, is what matters.

(Lincoln Draper)

BOATS, OARS, AND ROWING

DEDICATION

To my wife, Antoinette, who, having spent some years afloat, has been most understanding. Nearly 40 years of nothing but boats and talking of boats, to say nothing of sawdust and shavings tracked into the house, is a lot to endure.

Her answering the phone at all hours, doing most of the banking, and keeping me fed in a comfortable home, have made it possible for me to keep my mind very much on my work.

Some of the courses I steered in the past were doubtful, but there was no opposition; and there were many lonely weeks for her when I was at sea.

I could not ask for a better first mate.

PREFACE

That very much could be written on rowing seemed most unlikely to me when the idea was first suggested and I considered it. On thinking it over, I realized there really is a lot to rowing; I've experienced a great amount personally, and this is what I have chosen to describe in this book. There is a further amount of rowing I have little knowledge of; for instance, I've not mentioned racing except to point out I know nothing of it. Also, I have not gone into detail on highly trained crews in big craft, as I've had no experience with this type of rowing at all. This sort of thing, other than in shells, was going out in my youth; I had a look at its last days, and that's it. Now, with various organizations building large pulling craft, such as seine boats, whale boats, and similar craft suited to group activity, we see a return to the use of rowing crews. Some organizations are even making cruises in such large rowing craft—a welcome way to go in my mind.

I have not gone into camping from pulling boats, quite practical though it is. Enough has been written about this sort of thing—how to do it, what gear to take, risks and pitfalls—about the same advice applies no matter what type of boat or canoe you use. My approach to safety is based on properly designed and fitted out craft, common sense, and a willingness to learn how to handle a boat, which will lead to the true goal—good seamanship.

Whether what I've put down here is of much use to others or not, only time will tell. Putting it all down has been fun for me, as it brings back, almost as if it were yesterday, many happy times with pulling and sailing boats, and also those winters in the shop, when much of the described gear was made, just to suit a certain boat.

May your oars be long and limber, and your boat be good!

R. D. Culler
Hyannis, Mass.

ACKNOWLEDGMENTS

Looking back—over what is now well over 50 years—to how I acquired what I have put down in this little book, I feel I should acknowledge those who gave me great help. On thinking about this, I find that nearly all those of fond memory have pulled their last oar, crossed the last bar, driven their last nail, and, if they were designers, drawn their last line. To mention the names of all those gone would mean little; mostly they were known by waterfront handles, first names, and nicknames. Old Cap (there were several of these), Nick, Mac, Stoker, and so on; I never knew the full names of many.

The few still around that have been much help might be mentioned by name, but I think it would be a disservice to those who went before. Let it be said that many men have been a great help to my efforts to become a boatman, seaman, builder, and designer.

Many of the illustrations in this book are mine, some are from other builder and designers, mostly the coming younger set, some of whom are building from my designs—more success to them.

The very excellent pictures of oars and their detail are by Richard White of West Barnstable, Massachusetts, who spent much time posing and arranging these to give their fullest detail.

THE PLEASURES OF ROWING

Rowing is a fine, simple, and economical way to get afloat and enjoy the water. You are often able to use areas not well suited to sailing or even power craft. Long forgotten as a sport by most, rowing once again seems to stir the interest of many people. However, the majority still seems to think of it as "work," to be avoided if possible. Rowing certainly can be work if you have the wrong boat, oars, and other equipment, which is quite possible because rowing paraphernalia has degenerated since other interests have caused rowing to be more or less abandoned for some time.

Just why rowing now seems more attractive to some people, once they are exposed to good boats and all that goes with them, is hard to say. Possibly, to some at least, it's new and different; the totally mechanical age is fine in some ways, but you can get fed up with it. When rowing, you are very much the master of your craft. It is true that there is a modest skill to be learned, but it is one that is not beyond anyone of reasonable physical condition and aptitude. Anyone who can get in a boat can learn to row. The thing is to have a suitable boat properly fitted out, and capable for your stamina, or lack of it, the waters you will mostly use, and the size of your pocketbook.

In a rowing craft you find that you are closer to the water than you ever were before, no matter how much boating you have done in other craft. You are much more aware of sea and weather conditions, and see more of your surroundings than you ever did before. You get into places, holes, and creeks you never really knew existed. You get a first-hand look at the inner workings of, say, a big ferry slip—when the ferry is well away, of course—and the underside of an occasional big dock. At a certain state of the tide, you find it quite possible to navigate that rock-choked crick that no one goes near, and you discover there is a mile or more of winding, unspoiled stream that few know about. There is a big culvert some way along; keeping in mind the tide, you find you can push through. Another vista opens up—a large, floppy, happy dog, who likes strangers, along with an interesting fellow taking his ease by a small cottage no one realizes is there; a beat-up skiff is moored to the bank, as is some sort of fyke net. You admire the fellow's spread and he your boat—good pulling boats are always admirable. You make a friend and pick up some local lore. You have found a spot unreachable by the hordes and their manufactured, powered craft.

Doug Halleck enjoys a row in an instrument of his own creation. This flat-bottom 13'6" Good Little Skiff was designed by Pete Culler.
(Doug Halleck)

The tide is on the turn; it's time to go. That rocky entrance will be impassable in an hour or so. It's fun riding the ebb down—there are slight overfalls and you find that by backing down or pulling gently upstream at times, you have fine control of the boat, and shoot out between the rocks in fine style. You don't tell just everyone about this fine adventure. Old Ike up there enjoys an occasional gam, but doesn't want a mob; that's why he's there.

There are also days that are "right" for an openwater cruise. Such a cruise is often quite ambitious but easy once you are slightly toughened to it. And then there are exploratory trips to tidal ponds, and among rocks and ledges. More than once I have had a very good couple of hours going up drainage ditches with the making tide across a marsh. It was

so narrow that I stood and poled; so narrow I sometimes couldn't turn the boat, so I came out stern first. On these cruises I never failed to see some interesting thing I've never come across before.

One thing that I've discovered on these inland cruises is the need for a likely spot to beach now and then. You should get ashore to stretch for a few minutes, especially if you are alone, for you are confined to one position in the boat. This stretching is especially important as age advances. Keep as comfortable as possible—rowing is supposed to be fun.

This is only part of what it's all about. In a rowing boat you will have an eye open for all sorts of mild adventures, all of which are interesting and give you a new outlook on areas that once seemed commonplace or even dull.

ROWING CRAFT

I may be talking about the pleasures of rowing, but to row you have to have a boat. Rowing is very economical boating, once you have acquired the boat and gear; if you have not as yet, the amount you can spend, plus the waters you will mostly use, will very much govern the type of boat you get. Though I've done no end of thinking about it, there seem to be only four ways to acquire a boat—get a stock one, have her built, build her yourself, or find a secondhand one. At this time, really good pulling boats of whatever model are not at all plentiful secondhand, and at the present state of the rowing comeback, you seldom find a stock boat, off the shelf; that time may come, but when it does, your choices will still be very small. Another option is to do without, which makes no sense, is no fun, and gets you nowhere. Fortunately, for many waters, and with no expectation of very way-out performance, there are some fairly economical types to build. For more specialized use, there is no answer but a fairly expensive first-cost boat. No really good boat, rowing or otherwise, is totally cheap.

You soon find, using your own steam to move a boat, that she must be of excellent design for the waters intended and must be fitted with the proper gear, oars being the most important. Until you try serious rowing, it's hard to imagine that oars must be good and suit the particular boat—this latter is every bit as important as fitting the proper propeller to a powerboat. There used to be some fairly good manufactured oars that could be bought in a wide selection of lengths. No more. Today's store-bought oars are as decadent as so-called modern rowboats. This is simply the result of lost past knowledge, what is now a small demand, and the tendency of present mass production to downgrade a product.

But let's leave oars for later and discuss suitable boats, the designs of which can vary widely, yet provide good pulling performance. First, when choosing a craft, a prospective oarsman must decide the thickness of his wallet and how much he wishes to thin it down. It's often a good idea to start simple, providing the craft will suit his waters; if she does not, she's expensive no matter how cheap the first cost. And let it be said right here and now that long length, modest to narrow beam, and very modest freeboard—enough, but no more—are essential to all good rowing craft of whatever type; these are the characteristics good boats pretty much have in common, regardless of type.

A smart dory built by David C. King of Wiscasset, Maine. There are two rowing stations and a rudder yoke for multi-person rowing; with such an arrangement this flat-bottom craft could range far.

How long is long? I consider anything under 16 feet, except for boats for very special use, as not being able to get the full potential out of a good pair of oars and a man's not necessarily good back and arms. In many cases the boats should be longer than 16 feet; just how much is a matter of type and waters. As this is pleasure rowing, whatever type we discuss will be a clipper version, for the working rowing craft of the past was often designed to carry big loads; if it was not intended for this, it was lean and sharp so that it went about its business with maximum ease.

It is said that all boats are a compromise, which is probably so. It has been my experience that any compromise in rowing craft shows up very quickly in your arms and back. You soon develop an appreciation of really good design, and wonder at the very common sight, nearly universal it seems, of some large internal combustion engine trying to push some ill-formed motor craft out of the continuous hole she's in. Well-designed rowing craft match the power to the boat and avoid that sort of situation.

No matter how well chosen the boat, any boat, there will be times, not very often maybe, when she will meet conditions where she is not at her best. The boat and even the oarsman can suffer a bit. Though heading into the wind and sea is by far not ideal rowing, a long, slim gig with a very fine entrance would not find the going too difficult, unless the passage was long. A Swampscott dory would not go nearly as well, yet if one had to beach in a small surf, a Swampscott would make simple work of it; the gig could well slew around and swamp under the same conditions.

An Atkins flat-bottom 6' punt built by Kolin Boatworks. This little rowboat would be a handy craft in protected water or as a tender to a larger vessel. (Kolin Boatworks)

No particular boat is going to do all things well, whether she is a simple, cheap one, or a very high performance craft. This is all the more reason to consider well the conditions the boat will mostly be expected to be used in, realizing that at times, from choice or weather change, the boat might meet conditions she's not exactly suited to.

We must consider that in the past, when rowing was a popular sport, congested motorboat and vessel traffic in most harbors was no big thing. Now, as most of us know, weekends in the summer in most protected waters, at least in the latter part of the day, produce a seething mass of fast boat traffic with the attendant wash, which is more of a menace than wind-made seas, as there is no order to it, and none either in the minds of those operating these fast craft. As nearly all the boats are misshapen, some of the wakes are terrific. Anyone who has attempted small boating on the western end of Long Island on a weekend will know what I mean—disorganized disorder. If I had to live in those parts, I think I would confine my nautical activities to sailing toy boats in a quiet pond, if there were one to be found. This man-made confusion has had some influence on the design of some of my

small craft; I don't like it since I'm essentially designing a survival craft, rather than a proper pulling boat.

I get around congested waters this way: I go out very early in the day, before the nuts are out. The air is cool and pleasant for pulling, and I surmise where the wind will come from and how strong it will be so as to have it fair for return (sometimes I goof). If the tide is right, I go up the gut and see Old Ike, maybe more than he wants, though he's never said so.

FLAT-BOTTOM CRAFT

We start with flat-bottom craft, of which there are many different types. There have been all sorts of variations and combinations of flat-bottom craft, some of the past very good; sadly, nearly all of those of the present, pretty bad. Probably the simplest flat-bottom model in many ways is the square-ended type, what some call a John boat now, usually

A round-bilged Norwegian salmon pram photographed in her native Norwegian waters. (Waldo Howland)

18'8" dory for Capt. Charles Sayle, built and designed by Pete Culler. The sail plan for this dory appears on page 115 and a photo of the boat in the water appears on page 70. This hull has a flat bottom.

A 9' round-bilged Concordia pram, built and designed by Pete. The plans for this boat appear on page 6.

West Coast surf dory built by Kolin Boatworks. This boat has a flat bottom and is a specialized rowing design suited principally for surf work. (Kolin Boatworks)

The 11' v-bottom peapod was originally designed for a small Tancook schooner by Pete Culler early in his design career. It is a smaller version of the 15'9" v-bottom beach boat, which appears on page 82. (Dave Hill)

undersize and made of metal. Such a boat is generally a poor and ineffectual craft for our purposes. This was not always so; in the past, there were some excellent models, all of wood naturally, and of good length and very modest beam. That flat-bottomed, square-ended craft can fill the bill for some waters there is no doubt; they have for a long, long time. Consider the junk and the sampan—we can learn from the Orient, where manual propulsion has been a fine art for many thousands of years.

Yes, the square-bowed craft, sometimes called a butthead, square-toe frigate, or swim bow, if of first-class model, can be a very suitable craft for smooth rivers, ponds, and protected waters that tend to have little wind. Some models are able enough in fairly sloppy going, but the nature of the bows of most of them makes going into a head chop no pleasure. However, some of the swim bows developed in the Orient seem much more developed for heading into

a chop than those we have produced in the West. These Oriental square ends can vary from the narrow sampan type with a dory-like "tombstone," to a wide shovel bow, and all in between, using various appropriate rakes. It's a matter of the designer's skill in making an easy-moving craft out of a few simple lines—not always an easy thing to do.

Flat-bottom craft are economical to build and use simple materials. For a pleasure rowing type, some effort should be made in building to keep down the weight yet have a durable craft. One fault of all flat-bottom craft is that, by the nature of their simple construction, they tend to be heavier than more complicated round-bottom craft.

Pointed-bow, flat-bottom craft—flatiron skiffs, sharpies and such—are the next step. They are easy to build, but it is hard to design a good one. They have most of the good points of the square toes, and some advantages of their own: a little better

(continued on page 205)

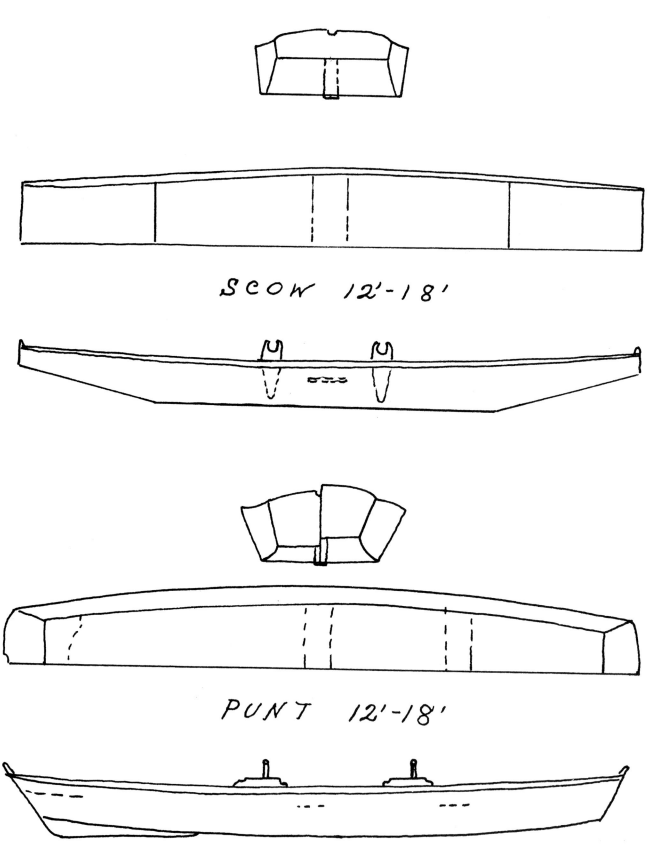

SCOW 12'-18'

PUNT 12'-18'

Flat-bottomed boats.

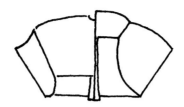

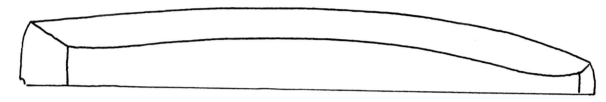

SAMPAN - 12'-16'

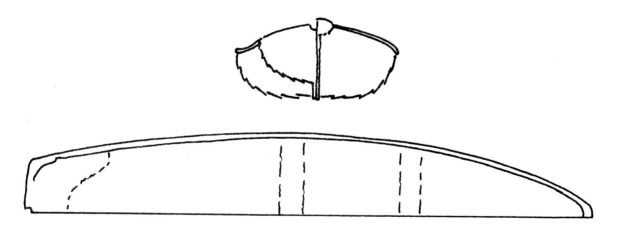

PRAAM 10'-16'

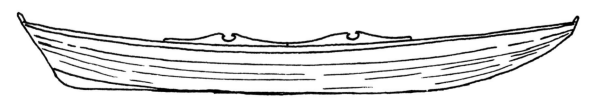

More flat-bottomed types.

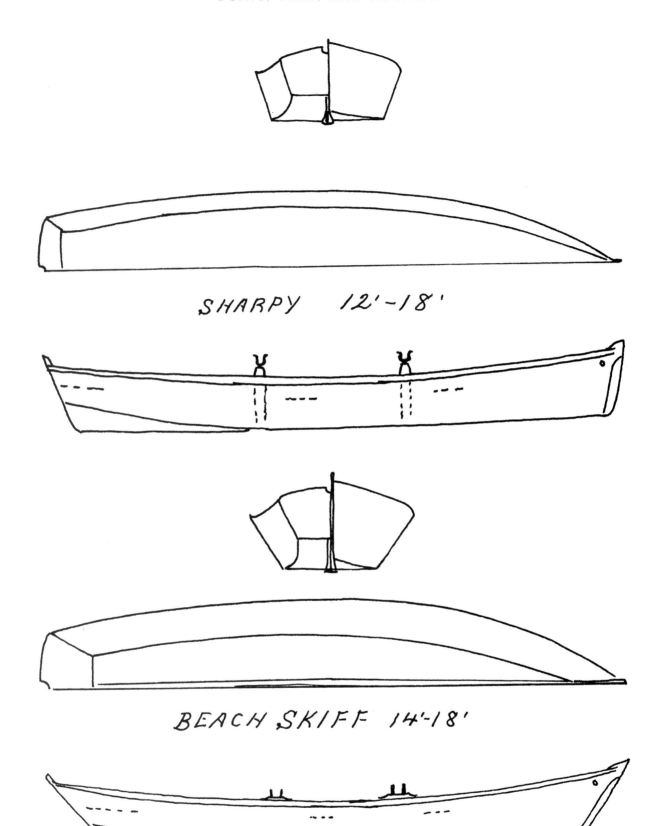

SHARPY   12'–18'

BEACH SKIFF   14'–18'

Still more flatties.

(continued from page 201)

performance in a head sea, but not very much. Slapping in much head sea slows any pulling boat down. This is the price you pay for a simpler craft, though if such a craft is used in the right waters, this slapping is next to nonexistent. I very much suggest that any pointed-bow, flat-bottom craft be designed with a good flare, keeping a very narrow bottom; the boat will row and look better and have a great reserve of stability, even though she may seem more tiddly than a box-like craft when light.

Bateaux, dories, half-dories, and other flat-bottom craft that seem related to, or were developed from the dory, each in their own way make useful pulling boats, if properly designed. Here again, I emphasize that they should be of finer model for pleasure rowing; they were originally designed as working craft and should be modified for recreational use. Obviously, one would not copy a big lumberman's bateau for use as a one- or two-man pulling boat. This also applies very much to the standard Banks fisherman's dory, which is not a satisfactory craft for pleasure rowing. Some semi-dories for rowing were developed in the past, and are good, but in no way are they like the modified versions for outboard motors we see today; these last row about like a window box full of daisies.

The Banks dory has one good application besides its original intended use—it makes quite a good surfboat in experienced hands. The Swampscott dory is another matter. Swampscotts, at least in my experience, seem to come in three distinct models—ordinary, semi-clipper, and full-clipper model. The differences among them are not immediately noticeable to the casual onlooker, but the similarities are quite obvious: they all have flat bottoms and rounded sides, the round being very pronounced in the clipper model. As is, they are quite nice rowing craft, make excellent beach boats, and work well under sail if need be, with a centerboard, of course. Though somewhat deeper than most

rowing craft, Swampscotts are quite nice rowing craft with little weight in them; the very narrow bottoms cause very little slapping unless the boats are stark light. Though I have a very soft spot for a really good flat-bottom skiff, I think that, of all the flat-bottom craft, the Swampscott may be tops and the bateau next, if well designed—these last were sometimes, and can be again, round sided.

Due to their traditional construction, which is different from that of skiffs and sharpies, dories can be somewhat lighter than other flat-bottom craft, but not much. Some weight is an advantage in some waters; other waters may require a craft of fairly light weight. One thing is sure, weight you don't need is simply more weight for your oars to move, yet a boat so light that it blows about in open water becomes quite unmanageable.

VEE-BOTTOM CRAFT

Almost everyone has heard of vee-bottom craft, yet we see next to nothing of them as pulling boats; fast motor craft and some sailing craft, yes, but rarely a pulling boat. Vee-bottoms tend to be heavier than round-bottom craft, so this should be kept in mind in designing and building; don't overbuild a vee-bottom. Though many don't realize it, these craft are not as easy to build as they appear. The idea of straight sections makes it seem that the construction would be less complicated than that for round-bottom craft. This, I assure my readers, is very much not so. There is just about as much labor and boatbuilding skill required, though of a somewhat different nature, as in building a round-bottom craft. Possibly this is why you seldom see vee-bottom, rather high-performance rowing craft. There just may not be all that much advantage gained over a smart, round-bilge boat.

It's well known, however, that a vee-bottom hull, properly designed, can be quite fast; I think there are good possibilities here to create an exceptional pulling boat. I personally could not turn out

(continued on page 209)

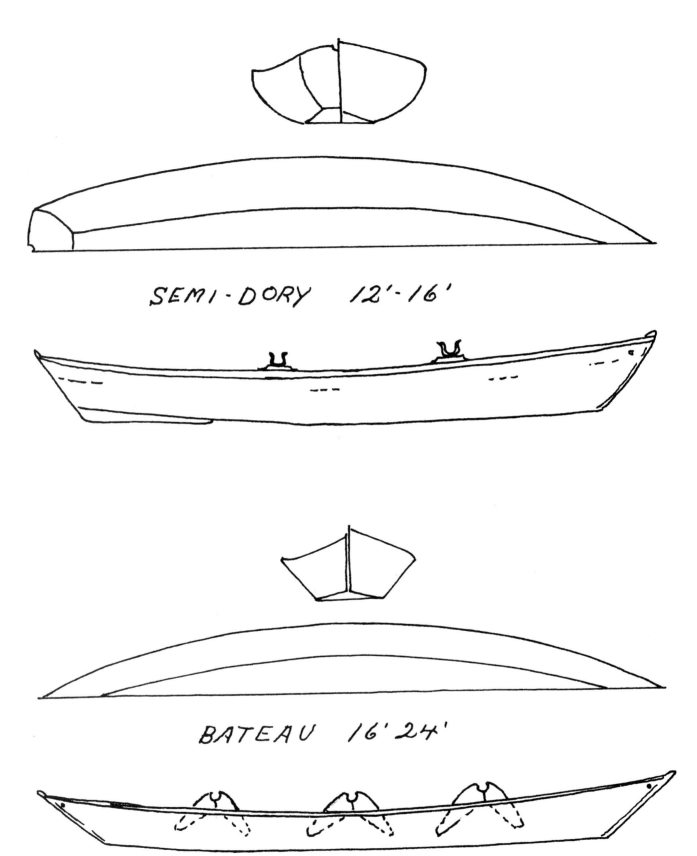

SEMI-DORY   12'-16'

BATEAU   16'24'

Dories; semi-dories; and bateaux are all flat-bottomed designs with a common heritage.

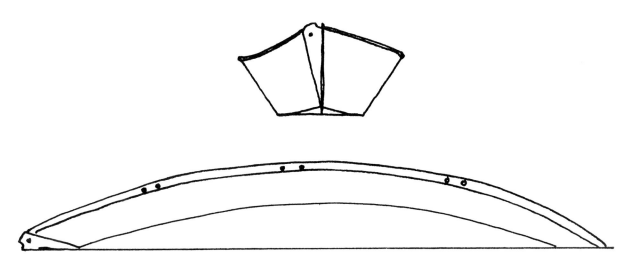

BANKS DORY 16'-21'

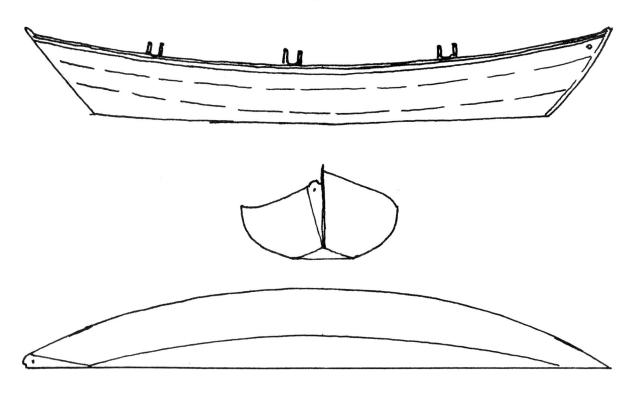

SWAMPSCOTT 15'-21'

More dory types. The Swampscott dory is about as "round" as a flat-bottomed boat can be.

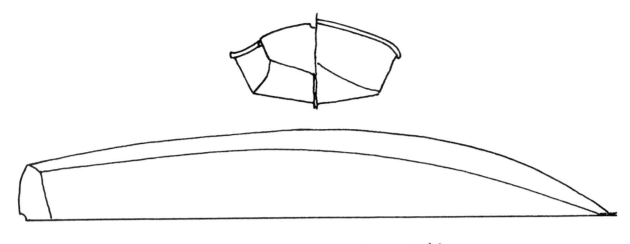

VIRGINIA VEE 14'-18'

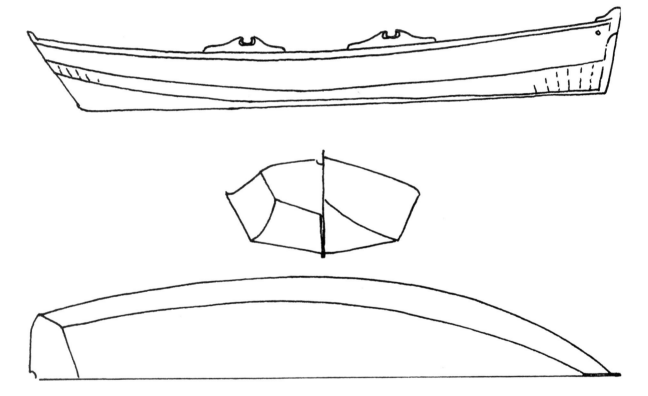

OPEN WATER VEE 14'-18'

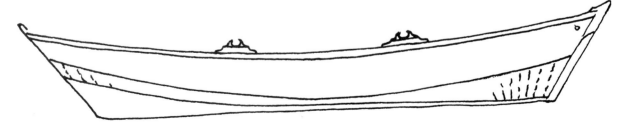

V-bottomed boats.

(continued from page 205)

a suitably modeled craft using developed surfaces, so as to use plywood in the usual sense; maybe some other designer can. Using normal framing and planking methods and using aircraft-type plywood as plank (because of its excellent grade and the very thin sizes available), a very nice boat could be built. But it would also be expensive. The other choice, and may be the simpler and cheaper one, would be to use the traditional cross-plank herringbone bottom. Though this construction is somewhat heavy, even with sophisticated building, the extra weight is in the right place. Some may feel this type of bottom does not give as smooth a surface as fore-and-aft plank. I have said many times before that, if the job is well done and the plank smoothed up, I have never been able to notice the difference in handling, and herringbone planking does give a very durable bottom that is clean and easy to maintain inside.

I would like to see more work done in the designing and building of somewhat way-out vee-bottom craft for pleasure rowing. The results could be pretty good.

ROUND-BOTTOM CRAFT

Round-bottom craft have been the most used for easy rowing. The various models have an almost infinite number of variations. With the renewed interest in classic craft of all kinds, the small comeback in rowing, and the wide publication of lines, pictures, and descriptions of these craft—notably by the *National Fisherman* of the work of John Gardner of Mystic Seaport, and the writings of others—a complete description of each round-bottom type is unnecessary. Nearly all models, though mostly developed from working craft, have evolved into clipper versions. Some, such as guideboats, fast pilot yawls, and a few others, seem almost to have originated in the clipper form, simply because their work demanded it; a fast type was required to begin with, and became more refined to do its job better.

Those very definite types that have undergone a long evolution have, as they went along, been accorded their own construction methods as well. A real guideboat is built a certain way, a Whitehall its own way, a wherry its way, and so on. Each method was worked out simply because it was the best way to build a certain craft using local materials. You will find occasional building methods, even in old boats, that don't quite follow this pattern. I have seen a fine yawlboat that must certainly have been built by a whaleboat builder; her construction was almost exactly the way of a New Bedford whaleboat, though the model was far from it. I might add that she is nevertheless a good boat, and has lasted a long time.

With the renewed interest in classic round-bottom craft now, it is quite likely that present builders, both professional and amateur, will be varying the traditional construction somewhat to suit available materials. I see no harm in this, providing a careful study has been made of the older methods, and it is fully realized why the craft was built the way it was originally. You should be cautious about making changes, and well know what you are doing.

I make no suggestions as to which of these many excellent round-bottom craft is better for pleasure rowing; they are all good, each in its own way and for certain conditions. Most are surprisingly able, much more so than their often-delicate lines would indicate.

I think a coming oarsman should make a study of these craft and choose, being guided by all the data available, which might best fit his needs. Some of these craft can be quite expensive, though the return from them is very great; others are not so costly to build. For the homebuilder, once he's built a simpler boat, be it a sharpie or flattie skiff, building many of these round-bottom craft is not nearly as difficult as it might seem. Basing my observations on my own work—and I've built many boats—I find building a really good flat-bottom boat costs about two-thirds of

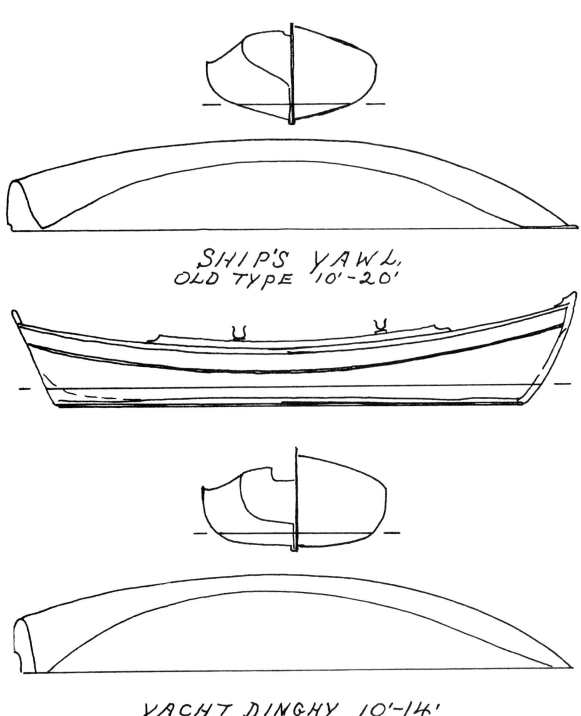

SHIP'S YAWL,
OLD TYPE 10'-20'

YACHT DINGHY 10'-14'

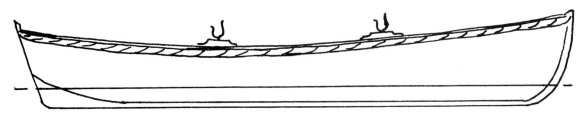

Some classic round hulls.

The 16'8" Race Point surfboat Coskata, *a round-bilged open craft designed and built by Pete Culler for Robert Caldwell and the Nantucket Lifeboat Museum.*

what most round-bilge craft cost; a good vee-bottom boat costs just as much, sometimes a little more, than the round-bottom boat. I provide here a rough rule of thumb; there are so many variables that the proportions cannot be wholly accurate—just a good guide.

FINISHES AND MAINTENANCE

If a pulling boat is to truly satisfy, no matter the type of craft or how you get her—home-built, pro-built, or secondhand—she must be good looking. This quality, if the work has been properly done and attention given to detail, will almost be automatic—nearly all traditional rowing craft are handsome, each in its own way. And finishwork is not necessarily the touchstone of a good-looking boat. It's very noticeable that, at various gatherings of nice rowing craft, the nicely shaped and pretty ones get the most attention. This does not mean that all boats should be highly finished; high finish has its place, though a plain, neat finish, with some artistic touches and the proper choice of colors, makes just as much appeal as some finely varnished craft. How you will finish a boat depends on her type, where she will be mostly used and moored, and whether she lives at home when not in use or is exposed to the elements on a mooring.

A boat that harbors at home should have a shelter, which will very much prolong her life and simplify her upkeep. The best shelter is an outbuilding, with no heat in it, of course. If you don't have one, it pays to build a shelter. Mooring a boat out in the water, if the situation and the waters allow, has much advantage for some craft, though there still will be need of a winter shelter. A proper canvas cover and frame like those used on big yachts is good if no building is available for winter storage; and if the craft lives on a trailer, it's a good plan to make a cover that protects this to some extent, too.

Naturally, a trailerable boat much extends the possible waters you can explore; using a trailer is almost standard practice these days. Most know how to handle them, but here's a hint: Be careful to prevent your boat from drying out on the trailer. During a 200- or 300-mile haul in dry, hot weather at 50 miles per hour or better, one heck of a lot of wind goes over the boat; a craft can dry out badly in a short time, some more than others. The extent of drying depends on materials, construction, and color of paint. Imagine yourself back there in the boat during such a tow; you would be dried out too! For much long-distance trailering, I find a boat painted white outside, with very light colors inside,

(continued on page 217)

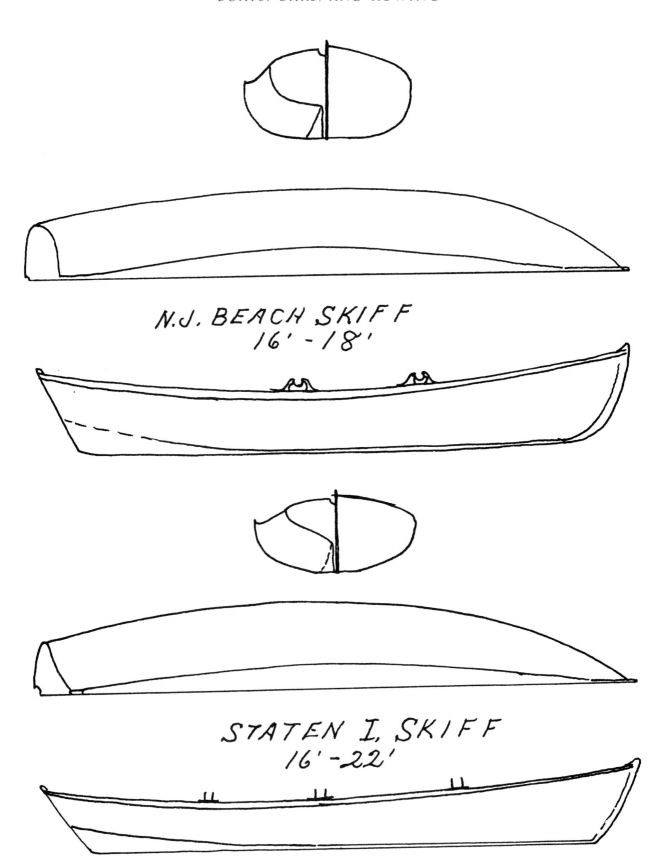

N.J. BEACH SKIFF
16' - 18'

STATEN I. SKIFF
16' - 22'

Round-bottomed boats, again.

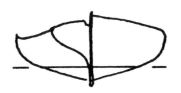

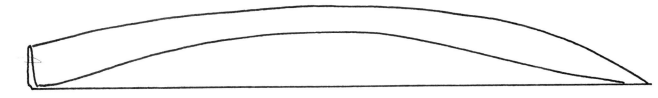

WHITEHALL 14'-23'

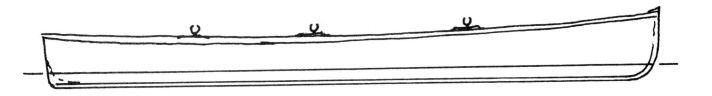

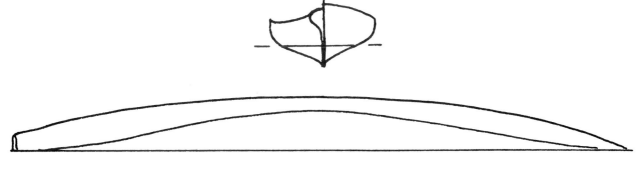

SHARP GIG 18'-30'

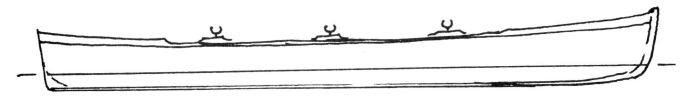

Two fast and efficient round-hull boats.

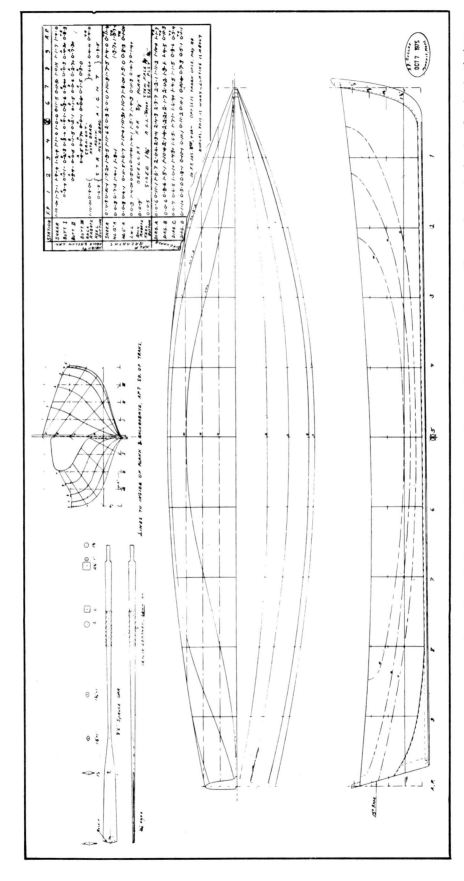

The 20' clipper Cornish yawl designed by Pete Culler for Clayton Lewis is a round-bilged open craft and would be very fast under oars. There are three rowing locations for trimming the boat according to how many persons are aboard. (© Mystic Seaport, Ships Plans Collection, Mystic, CT)

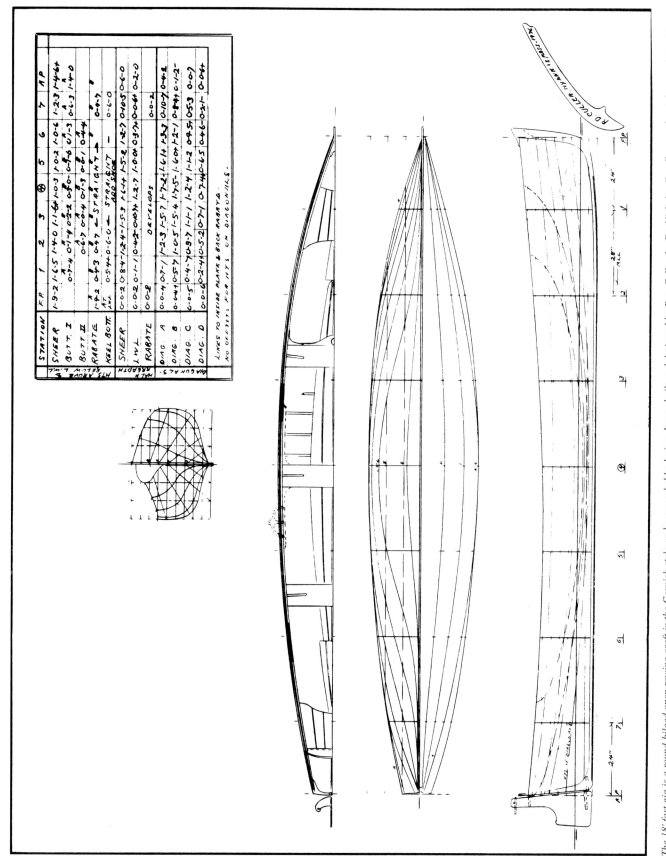

The 18' fast gig is a round-bilged open rowing craft in the Cornish style and a remarkable design. It was built and designed by Pete Culler for Dr. Nicholas Freydberg and weighs complete with gear 152 pounds. (© Mystic Seaport, Ships Plans Collection. Mystic, CT)

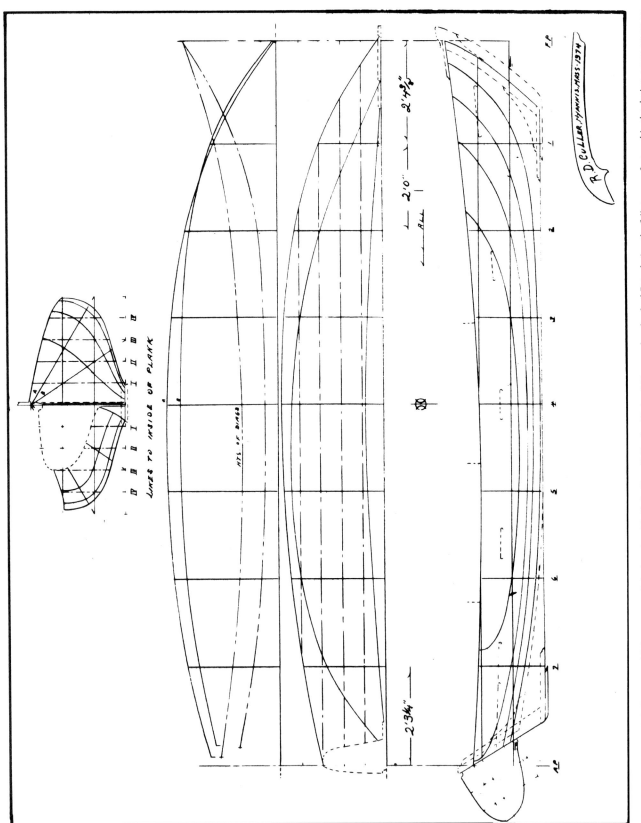

LINES TO INSIDE OF PLANK

HTS. OF DIAGS

R.D. CULLER. HYANNIS. MASS. 1974

2'0"   2'4½"

2'3¼"

The 168″ Staten Island skiff is a round-bilge open craft designed and built by Pete Culler for Richard Hovey, who also had Pete design the 34′ steamer featured in the design commentary on page 352. (© Mystic Seaport, Ships Plans Collection, Mystic, CT)

Maintenance is just one more component of seamanship.

(continued from page 211)

suffers the least, or not at all, especially if the boat is of lapstrake construction. Some varnished craft seem to dry out rapidly. And no matter the finish you use, there are some roads that will make a mess out of your boat. If your towing rig is an oil burner,

it will deposit some goo on the boat. I'm sure I don't have all the answers to trailer problems, but just mention what I've observed.

A few fortunates may have to use beaches where there is some small surf, even in good weather. Surf is

The 18' fast gig ready for sea trials showing the extensive use of natural knees that is an integral component in the Cornish boatbuilding style, which promotes light weight with strength. Pete Culler discusses natural knees as a boat construction material in the article on page 319.

fine once you get experienced in it, and use a boat adapted to surf and beach work. The boat will get sand in her, often seaweed, and will be a bit messy at times. This is just a way of life on the beach; the mess can be cleaned up. For beaches, I like a drain plug in any boat other than one so small and light that one man can turn her over and back with little effort. I also find a drain quite worthwhile for a boat that harbors at home. It allows me to wash her down well, inside and out with a hose, and swab off any smears while they are fresh.

There is no totally maintenance-free boat, advertising blurbs to the contrary. If you don't care for boat maintenance, don't have a boat, for upkeep is part of the game. If gone about with common sense, maintenance is part of your enjoyment. Some of these pulling boats take more care than others—a matter of construction and finish—but none of it is much of a chore. A clean, well-maintained boat is a pleasure to be in; good order in any craft is a part of seaworthiness.

Finish the boat in a style suited to her type and use, and keep her that way.

OARS AND OARMAKING

We can no more row without oars than we can without boats. In some ways oars are nearly as unlimited a subject as boats, since there are so many possibilities of construction, shape, materials, size, and length to suit various boats, not to mention some of the stuff that must go with oars to make them work. It seems next to impossible to buy other than very bad oars now; if someone is making really good specialized oars, I hope he comes forward and tells us about it.

As many know, I've been making oars for some time, since it's the only way I can have good ones. Descriptions of my building methods have appeared in other publications, notably the *National Fisherman,* and at Mystic Seaport, where they have made up a blueprint of my design methods, with suggestions and directions for making your own. This print is available from the Seaport at a very nominal sum, and very much with my blessing. The print shows how-to for a pair of working oars, the model of which has given much satisfaction to many. I will take up the subject of more sophisticated oars as we go along.

But before going into the practical aspects of oarmaking, let me say something about the time involved. One should be able to devote time to any worthwhile project, not that it has to be full time, unless you are working professionally. In reckoning my time, I don't really count my time picking stock. I look for likely boards when the chance offers and put them by, especially if they are wet, as they usually are. Assuming my oar patterns are already on hand, it takes me about half a day to lay out, saw out, dress, and glue up a pair of oars. Shaping takes a day, plus an hour or so for sanding; varnishing, painting, and leathering take a total of about another day—an hour here, an hour there over a period of days while things dry.

Spoons take a bit more time; a lot more if you want to make a way-out pair, different from any you have done before.

I can make good time because I've made many oars, and I am still foolish enough to put in nine-hour days, with none of the coffee breaks, time for washing up, prolonged lunch hours, and all the other fringe benefits of organized labor. True, my oars take time and are expensive if ordered made; I note that organized labor makes *no* oars that can really be called such.

OAR STOCK

Before building any oars, we must consider available stock to make them from. There is much wood available from which to make good oars. The use of some types of wood is now forgotten, or maybe these varieties were never used simply because other stock was available and there was no need to use them.

First the hardwoods. Ash has been standard for working oars in this country for many years. For many rather high-performance boats, I think it is too heavy and not necessary. For surf work and with some dories and other craft that will have a lot of rough going and heavy work, ash is a very good choice. Often, if the locks or tholepins are kept well greased, ash oars can get by without leathers. Occasionally, ash is available from small mills, at least in these parts of southern New England. I've seen oars of oak, though rarely; they tend to twist and warp and are not a good choice for hardwood oars. Sassafras, if you can find it (look around in small mills) makes a fine oar, though you seldom see a pair now. I've noted other hardwood oars in foreign lands; boatmen there build with what they have—we must consider that here, too.

If you feel your craft is suited to hardwood oars, I see no reason why some woods other than ash are not suitable, as long as the wood is not overly heavy, is stable, is somewhat resistant to splitting, and will not warp easily. This last quality, warping, is not uncommon with some cuts of ash, an oar that changes shape while lying on a thwart in the sun. An ash oar, if it warps, usually curves in the direction of pulling, and will often warp back again if you turn it over. An oar that tends to warp in the up-and-down direction of the blade is a most frustrating and useless thing.

Some softwoods tend to warp, but generally speaking warp less than some hardwoods. You sometimes get involved with a poor piece of wood in oarmaking, in spite of trying to select properly.

It's best to junk it and try another. Gluing up, as is now often done, tends to prevent some warping, but even here, you sometimes have bad luck. I've seen good oars of Oregon pine, used where that wood is common; here again, it's a matter of selection of stock. I suppose Oregon pine might be considered between hardwood and the real softwoods, and oars made of it would need leathers for long life.

Spruce of various kinds is more or less the accepted wood for light oars; Sitka spruce is just fine if available to you, though expensive. So-called Northern spruce, the wood common in the Northeast, has been used a long time, and there are variations—black spruce, white spruce, red spruce, all of which

Three examples of Culler spoon oars, their finish and decoration. Note that all three have been fitted with hardwood tips to protect their ends. Installing these tips is discussed in the text.
(John Burke)

seem to be lumped under "lumberyard spruce." All spruces are very light-colored wood and look alike. It's said, and I find it very much true, that black spruce is superior for strength, but I, and most others, can't tell one spruce from the other, once sawed; I must see it in the bark. In my oarmaking I find that determining the type of spruce I use is a fine point I don't have to worry about.

For high-performance spoon oars, as well as plain ones, I've used Northern white cedar (Maine Cedar, upland cedar, arbor vitae) and found it excellent. I've also used swamp cedar, which is good, though if there is a choice, I prefer the Maine cedar. Eastern white pine, if the grain is chosen well, makes quite a good oar, though you never hear of it being used—I don't doubt that it was once used in the past.

You can well combine two or more woods in gluing up, both for looks and to get a certain action and strength from the oar, or you can simply glue up because of the stock on hand at the time. Gluing up and choice of grain have much to do with the working of an oar. If you use solid stock throughout and if the plank has edge grain through the blade and up the shaft, the oar will be stiff—sometimes a requirement, sometimes not. An edge-grain blade can possibly be subject to splitting. If you use flat grain, the oar will have more spring and may be less subject to splitting in the blade (we go further into protecting blade ends later). Gluing up with, say, three pieces—a center one of flat grain for the blade, with side pieces of edge grain—is apt to give a fairly stiff shaft and a springy blade, a good combination for some craft. Gluing up with three pieces or more, totally edge grain, will give a very stiff oar, too stiff for my liking; the gluing plus the edge grain gives a very rigid structure. One thing about an overly stiff oar: you can usually work it down quite thin, thus lightening it considerably. In boats with any pretentions to high performance, light oars are always welcome; the more wood and weight you

have to move, the more power, your power, it takes to move the boat. We will, as we go along, get into oar balance, but from now on keep in mind that any extra weight in an oar that is not earning its keep is excess weight you have to move with your own steam.

It is also well to keep in mind when making oars, designing them, or working over an old pair, that there is no cut-and-dried method to follow. Instructions cannot be put down precisely, every proportion to a small fraction of an inch. Wood of the same kind varies; boats and people do, too, as do the conditions you will row in. In other words, it's impossible to give very exact plans, like those for making a motor part or those for some lathe work. Oars are alive, or should be, and this is what you strive for. I hope you will use a little art and imagination when you make them. The guides I give are only guides, though based on oars that work. The variations are up to you.

PATTERNS

I find it well worthwhile to make patterns for oars. Simply take a board of sufficient length, better too long than too short, anywhere from $3/8$-inch to $3/8$-inch thick and of sufficient width, and draw the profile of the oar on that. First—and this is important—strike a straight centerline the length of the board. I use a chalk line, then blacken it in with a straightedge and pencil. Naturally, you need this line to lay out from. It also serves another important purpose: the pattern can change shape when it is sawed out, or later on when it is stored on the rafters of the shop. If the pattern goes out of shape, you simply sight the drawn-in centerline back to straight, tacking the pattern to the stock you are laying out on.

I have several patterns around of different sizes and models of oars, though with a bit of juggling one pattern can do for several lengths of oars, widths of blades, and other parts too. I don't like to carry this juggling too far; if the proposed oar is of a different model than the pattern on hand, I make a new pattern.

You will have to decide the one big difference among oars before considering patterns, stock, or anything else: Will you use spoon blades or flat blades? If the boat is smart and fast, spoons will no doubt get the most out of her. However, it's good to have a nicely made pair of working oars for some conditions, and if it's a first pair of oars you are making, it may be best to start with these. Once you have made a pair of flat-blade oars, there is really little more to making spoons—more time, but not more difficulty. Once you get your hand in, spoons, way-out shapes, and all that goes with them, seem no more difficult than plain oars.

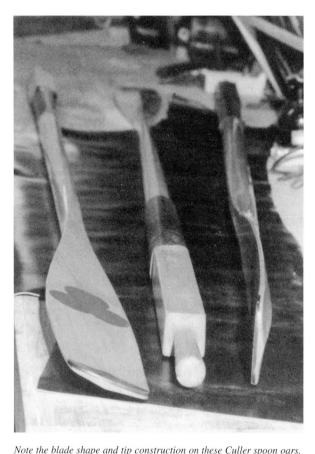

Note the blade shape and tip construction on these Culler spoon oars. All unnecessary weight is removed from the outer ends of the oars and the inboard sections are left relatively heavy so that, hopefully, the balance point is inboard of the oarlock. Pete talks about this consideration in the text. (John Burke)

USING YOUR STOCK TO ADVANTAGE

The next decision is—and this is usually settled by the stock available—how will you prepare and join up your stock? Generally, oars for the boats we are considering here have shafts next to the grip of from 2 inches to $2\frac{1}{4}$ inches; the latter dimension is plenty big enough, even for a 10-foot oar. The whole oar can be made of a solid piece, which is often hard to come by. You can use a hunk of stock that is 2 or $2\frac{1}{4}$ inches in actual thickness, with sufficient length and width (these last two dimensions pose no difficulty). But to get your actual thickness, you may have to work from a 3-inch piece: 3-inch "lumberyard measure," that is. Our big-time lumber industry feels the buyer should pay for all the waste, which he does. If you are handy to a country mill, though, you can often find boards measuring an honest 2 inches, rough.

Besides the troubles getting solid stock, working from a solid piece is wasteful of wood, though not necessarily of time. Working up thinner stock, and then gluing, takes time, but doing it on your own time should be cheap. If it is not, find a pro who knows how and pay his price, which will be cheap in the end, though very expensive to begin with.

I find that for a plain oar the simplest way to make oars with presently available stock is to use spruce boards that will finish about $\frac{3}{4}$-inch thick. Here is where the pattern is most handy for judging what you can get out of a board, and how well you can avoid defects and knots—very small pin knots don't much matter except for looks. For instance, by using an 8-inch board (actually $7\frac{1}{2}$ inches), you can cut the center part of the oar from about the middle of the plank. This will leave two side pieces that, if cut to your pattern, can be glued on each side of the center piece, which goes on to make the blade. These side pieces won't go all the way down the blade, which is fine, since you will have far less wood to work off. Just be sure there is enough wood to go partway down the blade, so the oar isn't too thin where the shaft narrows into the blade.

What is called ledger board or fence board in my area is actually Northern spruce. As lumber prices go now, it's cheap, so get enough so you can work around defects. Picking over what often looks like a knotty pile will occasionally turn up some quite clear boards, providing the lumberyard lets you pick, which they might do if you leave a neat pile after rummaging.

Some oarmakers use a 2-inch-square piece and glue on side pieces for blades. This is okay if you must do it, but I think the $^3/_4$-inch-plank method is much better. Using the three-board method, there are all sorts of possibilities of combining different woods without requiring complicated or unattractive glue-line patterns. Some recent glue jobs I've seen were done by people who didn't take into account how the finished work would look, especially if that work were varnished.

Here I digress a moment to growl about some pet peeves. I find many people now go for anything that is "laminated," whether there is good reason for lamination or not. They seem to have the idea that lamination is a hallmark of quality. This is not necessarily so; in oars, and many other things, the less lamination the better. Picture an oar made up of quarter-inch-strips—possible no doubt, but it can't help but be ugly and stiff. Some makers of wonder glues now boast that you can get by with all sorts of poor fits—even if you can't it's a sloppy looking job. I also note that many people, though comfortably off in many ways, at least they eat well and spend large amounts for a gas-eating car, are quite chintzy when it comes to using wood; some pro woodworkers are too. Get enough stock and use it freely. Pinching around with defective and scant stuff never produces a good job. That wood is expensive now, we all know, even the so-called

cheap stuff; it's simply inflation. Wood is plentiful, self-replacing, biodegradable, pleasant to work with, and nice to look at. Use enough good stuff; you will waste less in the end. To my thinking at least, trees were made to use, especially for boats, along with some discretion and common sense, do-gooders and worrywarts to the contrary. An aging tree, like most of us old duffers, is apt to have a lot of defects in it, and if let go, becomes worthless.

But enough grousing. The three $^3/_4$-inch-plank method does not do for spoon oars. Some people go right ahead anyway by cutting the side blanks to the full pattern shape, which gives them enough wood to work the spoon part. This always produces a very unattractive oar, unless the blades are painted, because you must break through on the hollowed out side into the glue line.

For spoons I like to use two 1-inch (after dressing) planks, both cut to the full oar-blade pattern. I work these to a $^3/_4$-inch or $^7/_8$-inch hollow, which is quite sufficient and does not break through the glue line. On the back side of the blade, due to the ridge and the very sharp angle that it makes (it even has some reverse curve), the exposed glue line takes the shape somewhat of the waterlines in a varnished half-model. Such a glue line is rather good looking and is quite a help in getting the oar shaped evenly on both halves of the ridge.

Having mentioned the effect that the run of grain—flat or edge—has on the action of oars in use, it might be well to point out some other aspects of grain in laying out stock to be glued. Much of what I have to say is obvious, except if it is forgotten, you can have a lot of bother. For instance, two pieces of wood side by side with opposite grain can cause much aggravation when planing, worse when roughing out. You may not be able to avoid mismatched grain totally, but it should be carefully considered when matching up stock. Sometimes, using what you can get, in spite of good planning, you have to fight poor grain all the way. The only way to tackle the job is to take it easy and work along with the grain as best you can. While you're at it you might consider the foolish statement I've made more than once—that making oars is a lot of fun!

Some spruces, some cedars, and other softwoods often grow in a spiral. This is quite noticeable on the stump, but once a tree is sawn up and board edged, it can fool the unwary. In picking boards, look at the plank to see if it is already developing a twist, then look at the plank edges. If there are slight checks and grain running at a rather sharp angle to the run of the board, the plank came from a spiral tree; it is no good for oars, so keep picking over the pile. A board from a spiral tree, if used, will have awkward grain no matter how you join it, and a finished oar made from it may well keep twisting.

Most lumberyard stock is damp and some is wet, so it pays to pick your stock in advance and dry it carefully. Yards having a lot of wet stock on hand most of the time have a big turnover, so if you keep close watch on things, you will on occasion find some almost clear, straight-grain, common-run spruce boards. Grab them, even if all does not go for oars—spars and other stuff soon use it up. By the way, small-boat sparmaking using the same stock is really very little different from oarmaking.

Using the three-plank method for working oars, there is no reason why, if the idea appeals and it's suited to the boat, you can't make oars with a hardwood center, with softwood outer pieces, or reverse it and have the hardwood outside. You could also combine some softwoods, which I've done with success. Some of these combinations are quite attractive due to the different colors of the woods, and they allow you to use each wood's mechanical properties to the best advantage.

There are many other variations and possibilities for joining wood to make oars; there are oars with hollow shafts, with ridges in back, with ridges

in front, and with all sorts of specialized combinations for pure racing craft, which this story is not at all about. Such racers are another world and are for those who know much more about that aspect of rowing than I do.

TOOLS

Now having all this good wood around, there is the matter of having tools to work it up. Your selection of tools can be simple and minimal, though some few tools not now very common can much ease the work. Having stock in the rough is a small matter; I lay out and saw my stock in the rough, either putting it through a small power planer, or dressing it by hand—either way, you are planing much less stock by doing it after the parts are cut out. You can rip your stock out with a hand ripsaw or a hand electric saw, helping this latter in the tight places with a handsaw. Some use the electric saber saw, for that is what they have. It will do the job but is not really suited to such work. Since I have a good bandsaw I do nearly all the cutting with that— I think it is by far the best tool for the job. If you don't have one, perhaps you can borrow the use of one. Mine seems to get borrowed a lot for all kinds of cutting.

Many will use a drawknife for the rough shaping; this is fine, though for some reason I can't explain I've about totally given up the tool for this kind of work, and most others, finding a small slick or a large framing chisel with a long push handle much better. The ordinary iron smooth and block planes are used where they will work. A couple of gouges, one of large radius, come in handy. Also useful are a spokeshave and a rasp for working around the grip and down around the neck next to the blade.

One gripe I hear from those making their first pair of oars: "How do you get that hollow on each side of the ridge on the blade?" First let me say that this hollow is most important; the ridge gives

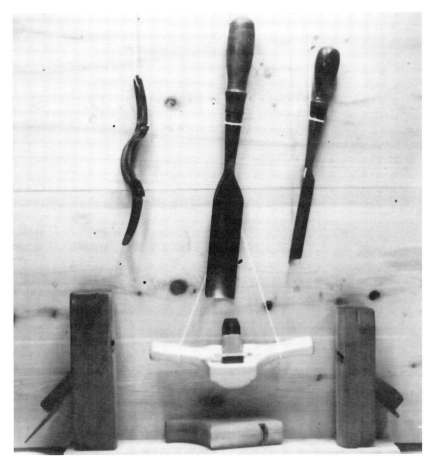

Some tools used in oar shaping. Use what you have and find what fits. Pete Culler talks about the use of tools for oarmaking in the text.

sufficient strength to the blade, and the wood that was in the hollow serves no purpose. You want to remove that extra wood so the oar will not be blade heavy. The natural shape of a proper oar, or a misfit one for that matter, tends to put the weight outboard, so you want to do all you can to overcome it partially. A wide-radius, outside-bevel gouge works fine in the hollow for roughing out; a small, round-bottom plane and a round-bottom shave are good for finishing. Right away I'm told that these latter two tools are next to impossible to find—not quite so. Any small, wooden, smooth plane can be easily modified as a round bottom. These are still available, usually in a battered condition in what used to be junk shops, though now

the shops have fancy names and such planes are quite expensive, considering the rickety condition of most and that they are of little use other than for the above-mentioned work. I don't run down wooden planes that are good, but most used ones now are not worth much.

It's no big deal to make a round-bottom plane about 6 to 7 inches long from scratch. You can use part of a very heavy file for a bitt. You do not need a cap iron for this sort of plane with a thick bitt, nor do you require fancy slotting for the wedge—simply put a pin across in the right place. You can even make the plane in two halves, cutting most of the slot with a fine saw, finishing it with a chisel, and gluing the two halves together. A fine smooth plane for fine work is

225

one thing; a shaping plane that is quite adequate for oarmaking is something else, and will work well.

The round-bottom shave is often seen in secondhand shops, people now being sure it's a carpenter's tool. It is not, but said to be part of a leather-worker's outfit—if that's so or not, I don't really know, but I do find it just right for the hollowing part of oarmaking. The Stanley Tool Catalog for 1934 shows no round-nose shave, so it well may be a tool for other than the woodworker. Using the same methods as for making a simple round-nose plane, I've built a shave of wood, using part of a power hacksaw blade for a bitt. This rough tool works well, too.

The smoother and truer you can get the oar with cutting tools, the less sanding there will be. I try to keep sanding to a minimum, but, when the time comes for it, I use a power sander with #80 open-coat garnet paper. The one-third-sheet orbital or the so-called powerblock sander work equally well. There is then some hand sanding to do; you can go as far as you like on this, depending on the finish desired and your ambition.

Holding the work during shaping and finishing can be awkward. Unless you are building oars in quantity—and there seems no point in that—there is no need for an elaborate hold jig. Just how you hold the work will depend on your shop, workbench, and other factors. You can do all your work on almost any bench that does not wobble, using C-clamps and wood pads. My own method, worked out by trial and error, is based on a bench with two wooden carpenter's vises (homemade) about 7 feet apart. I clamp my work in either one, depending on what part I am cutting and the run of the grain. I often have the grip end of the oar in one vise and nail a plank to the bench; the plank sticks out somewhat for the oar blade to rest on. When the oar is almost finished, I use vee blocks and cloth pads to avoid bruising it. My holding methods are neither complicated nor scientific, simply handy and comfortable.

WEIGHT AND BALANCE

You should consider the weight and balance of your oars before gluing up the component parts. Once you have six pieces sawn out for a pair of oars, using the three-piece method, and these pieces no doubt will all be out of two or perhaps three boards, it's well to weigh the pairs before any gluing. A common household scale is all you need. It usually turns out that one group of three parts—the center with blade and the two sides—will weigh more than the other group. If so, simply shift the pieces in various combinations until you have sets that weigh nearly alike; it's unusual to be able to get them exactly equal. For instance, two heavy side pieces might be combined with a light center piece.

Spruce oars will seem frightfully heavy in this roughed-out state; don't dismay, they lighten up remarkably fast as you work them up. This pre-assembly matching of parts for weight will give you a good start toward a nearly matched pair, both in weight and dimensions, when finished. Finished oars are seldom exactly matched though, but usually are within an ounce or two of each other.

How much should a pair of spruce oars weigh? It is always a guess—$5\frac{1}{2}$ to 6 pounds for a pair of unleathered, ready-to-varnish $8\frac{1}{2}$- to 9-footers is not uncommon. Such oars in ash, though carefully thought out and worked up, may go 11 pounds bare.

GLUING

I left gluing in detail until now, for this requires what some feel must be a jig. For me, a jig is not necessary, since I have just enough clamps. I glue up both oars at once, using the edge of the workbench for one, as the bench is not long enough for two, and a pair of flat-top sawhorses for the other. The horses have to be lined up straight with wedges, as my floor is uneven. All surfaces used for glue work should be covered with newspaper, for glue will run out of the joints. If glue does not run out everywhere, you are not using enough. It's a good idea to put paper on the floor under the work, too.

Always cover both sides of any gluing surfaces with glue, not just one side—be liberal with it. This is one of the tricks of successful gluing. Match the pieces and secure them with a thin brad at each end

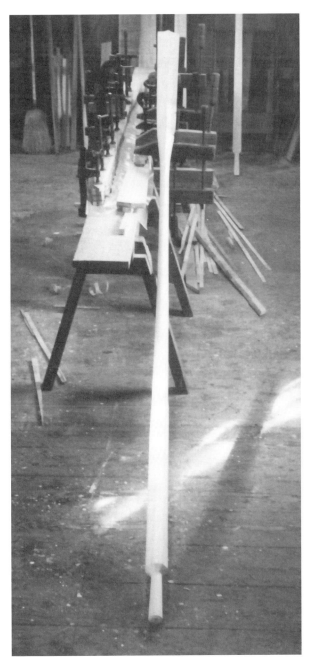

Clamping pressure and plenty of glue on all faying, or joining, surfaces is essential. Don't spare it! Take care to keep the work lined up, straight and level.

to prevent "creep," which must be avoided in glue work. Put a small clamp or two temporarily across the three pieces (assuming you are using the three-piece oarmaking system) and draw them into line. This is most likely necessary because, when you sawed out some of the pieces, they sprung out of line somewhat. Sight down the work to be sure it is straight, and line it up with a clamp, pulling down on the horses or bench. Use pads under the clamps, of course—I use long strips of scrap. Keep adding clamps, all there is room for, or all you have.

I said use all the clamps there is room for. Why? Because it's necessary with the kind of glue I use. Many have said that my glue work is excellent most of the time. I think good glue work at least requires good joints, and in oarmaking there is nothing at all difficult in getting good joints; with a clean-running power planer, the joints are accurately machine made, and it's very little more trouble to get the same results by hand dressing, as it's all flat work.

Wait 24 hours for the glue to set up, assuming you have maintained the proper temperature, and then pull the clamps. The paper will stick to things—no matter, tear it off, what remains will be removed in shaping the oar. If this does not appeal to you, use wax paper instead of newspaper; it usually peels right off.

You can use any glue you wish that is more-or-less water resistant. I use Weldwood, single mix, and no other; it gives the least noticeable glue joints for brightwork. Resorcinol does not work for bright finishes. It leaves a purple line that is very noticeable in light woods; it also creeps into the grain to some extent, which is not at all attractive. Most will want to go the epoxy route—go to it. It is said that you should not use much pressure with this stuff. Some of your wood will not be quite true once it is worked up, especially if it stands around a few days before gluing. If you do not use much pressure, the epoxy will gap fill (said to be its strong point), but it will not totally close the joint at times either. The resulting bond is quite strong enough from what I'm told, but it won't look like a properly hove-up joint.

Any of these glues are stronger than the wood they bond when properly used, and no one really seems to know accurately the aging and life expectancy of any under various conditions. My feeling is that no glue lasts forever. But, by The Great Jackscrew, the way I do it, it's *got* to fit, warped stock or not, assuming you use enough clamps, centered and squared with the work. Some say the glue I use is not waterproof. I don't know, but I invite inspection of a pine mooring buoy I've been using for nine years. It was glued up out of several pieces with Weldwood. This test is still not conclusive, however, as the buoy has up till now shown no sign of falling apart.

As long as you use glue that has been commonly used in boat work for some time, I think it matters little the type or brand for oarmaking. If you are looking for handsome work to be finished bright—and a really nice pair of oars should be finished so—my methods and materials will do the job. No doubt some others can do as well using different methods and materials.

SHAPING

I now take up the actual shaping, as I do it; no doubt there are other satisfactory approaches. The idea here is to get a handsome oar that works well in propelling the boat. It should have sufficient spring and be as light as seems practical while still having sufficient strength. A heavy, dull boat requires a stronger oar than a light, fast one.

While shaping, as the final size is neared, you should check the oar on a scale several times to see how the weight is coming along. Equally as important as weight is balance. I like the balance point in the oarlock a little below the leathers, as little below as I can manage—I'm referring here to 12- to 14-inch leathers, not those short, store-bought things. I go further into leathers later on.

I like my oars square in section between the grip and where the leathers start; they roll around less in the boat and help keep the weight inboard. I try to avoid blade heaviness at all costs. Some prefer an 8-square rather than a 4-square section. This is fine, but you are losing weight where you don't want to. You can have it round here, too, but to get proper balance requires gluing on extra wood to make up the weight. Making it square is far simpler.

I dress the square section first, checking it with a try square, then chamfer the corners a little. Then I work up the complete grip, by eye and feel, fully finishing it, including sanding. Next I strike a centerline on both sides, starting about where the square will start turning to round (at the leather), and right down the flat side of blade to its end. Where the square is to stop, based on my pattern, a plan, or a notion, I lay out an 8-square slightly beyond the leather; from here on you fudge with a straightedge down to the neck, which should be a pronounced oval fore and aft at right angles to the blade. How much of an oval is a matter of judgment. Have plenty of wood; you can always take it off. The up-and-down section, where there is no pulling strain, can be 1 inch thick or somewhat under (keep thinking about weight). I lay out a centerline on the edges of the blades, then another set of lines to give about $3/16$-inch blade thickness at the edges when finished. At this time I also cut the blade end to the shape I favor, which is a shallow, roof-like angle. Some prefer round or other shapes for their blade ends.

I now cut down the 8-square and work it into a round until just below the leathers. Keep in mind the thickness of leathers to be used and the size of the oarlocks you are stuck with. There is a limited selection of oarlocks available now, but more on this later. Next, I work down the shaft, developing the start of a ridge at the centerline right off and keeping it increasingly pronounced. After I work down near the neck, it's time to turn to the blade,

228

working much hollow from the ridge. As the blade develops, it will be quite apparent how to work it into the ridged shaft. Take your time here.

When the first oar is fairly well shaped out and still covered with plane and shave marks, most of them rather bold, I put it aside. I then work down the other oar in the same way. When this is done, I compare the two for equality. I check for heft, put the blades on the floor and try for spring, and lay the oars on a scale for weight. If they are still pretty heavy, one especially so, I determine where more trimming is called for.

Finally, after much fussing, things will seem about right. At that stage, I set a sharp plane, shave, or whatever tool fits, very fine, and go over all that has not been fully finished. This very fine dressing will save much heavy sanding.

Sand as much or as little as you want; it's a thankless job, but does enhance the finished work.

SPOON-BLADE OARS

When I make spoons, I prefer to use two 1-inch (finished) pieces laminated together, though they can be built up other ways. Shaping from the grip to the leathers is no different than that for straight-blade oars. From the leathers down, the ridge is all on one side of the oar; it doesn't quite disappear at the blade end. The section at the neck is much like the shape of a church window, which is possible because the oar is used one way only. This ridge is a buttress for the blade. Rough out the shape of the spoon, both sides, on a bandsaw, but be sure the work stands plumb at all times, or you can undercut and spoil the blade.

Though I show what I consider a good shape in a spoon or regular blade, I'm sure there is room for artistry and experimentation here. Many don't agree with my notions about narrow blades, feeling they are not getting all the grip they can on the water, or more simply, "their money's worth." My ideas on blade design go like this: a heavy, though

good, rowing boat in open water needs rather long, narrow blades, and, if the water is at all sloppy, not too long a stroke—this theory is about the same as that behind towboat propellers, that is, narrow blades with a flat pitch. I also feel that narrow blades are much handier in a chop. A fast boat using spoons can have somewhat wider blades, but if this width is overdone, you have to lift the oars more to clear the water—a fine point, maybe, but I notice its effect while actually rowing. How much hollow—both up and down, and across the blade—you put in a spoon is, I think, a matter of the boat and the oarsman, and is open to some experimentation.

I use a pair of hot spoons in a hot boat. As an experiment, I tried these oars in a Swampscott dory—it was a total failure. They cavitated just like a fast wheel on a slow boat. The dory could not get away from them. This was interesting, so I tried my ash dory oars, which are quite nicely shaped working oars, twice the weight of the spoons, on the hot boat. This was another failure in a different way; the hot boat kept running away from the oars, and I was getting bushed trying to keep all that wood up with her.

There are many other little experiments I've tried. Some worked, some didn't. The good ones I try to pass on here. There is no doubt that oars should be matched to the boat, and, to some extent, the oarsman; he at least can adjust somewhat, even change his ways, when he finds a good combination of boat and oars. The oarsman must be willing to find out how to get the most out of them. I notice some people hate to change, even though the boat may go better and easier because of it.

OAR-BLADE TIPS

To protect the blade ends, I tip my spoons. I never use tips of any kind on plain oars, finding them unnecessary. In the past, factory-made copper tips were available; I doubt if they are now. I don't care for metal tips on any oar; they simply mar a nicely finished boat, and I can't see that they do much good. I tip spoons with hardwood, the grain running across the tip. Walnut and locust seem best for oar tips—they are hard, yet carve well, do their job, and look quite snazzy.

This wooden tip business, and there is nothing new about it, seems to throw people into a tizzy—inlay, extreme wood-carving skill, violin making, much ooh and aah—their fears are all rot once you look into it. To begin with, the way the grain runs in the tip of a spoon is very much in your favor; there is little danger of breaking under.

Here's how I go about a fairly simple (though the result seems complicated) operation: The shape I use is my personal preference; there are all sorts of other possibilities that can be used without changing the job mechanically. Strike a centerline on a piece of cardboard, fold it, and cut out one half of the design, making it slightly larger than the tip will ultimately be; when the cardboard is unfolded you have a nice template. Take the chosen hardwood, about $\frac{1}{2}$-inch thick, and saw a piece out as marked from the template. Fair up the inboard edges—the outboard edges and those overhanging a little don't matter; they can be trimmed off later. Saw the hardwood block lengthwise. You now have two pieces somewhat less than $\frac{1}{4}$-inch thick, with two faces dressed. Put these down on the oar tip, carefully centering them, and mark around the inboard part with a very sharp pencil. Be sure to mark these pieces with a code—say A and B—so you can later tell which oar they belong to, thus preventing any error. Now is the time to cut the blade tip. Support the blade tip on a shallow vee block and a cloth pad, cutting straight down about an eighth of an inch with a thin, narrow chisel. Then remove the rest of the wood using a chisel or very shoal gouge, working in from the tip. I usually mark a line on the tip to indicate the eighth-inch depth.

The bed for the hardwood does not have to be dead flat, only nearly flat and fair; clamps will pull

it into place. Try the blocks. If they now fit but are still pretty thick, take another saw slice off them to save whittling. When gluing the tips on, cut a couple of softwood blocks more or less to shape to go on the back of the oar tip to take the clamps—on the hardwood side, marring does not matter, as you have plenty of wood to work off. Once all is right, glue and clamp. I use three or four 2-inch C-clamps here, which provide plenty of pressure. When the glue has set, trim off the excess wood around the tip, and cut the tip down to grade with a shallow gouge, finishing the job with sandpaper. As you can now see, it's pretty easy work compared to a fiddle.

FINISHES

Whatever finish is used on the oars, the first coat should be on and dry before you put on the leathers; leathering done after the first coat prevents marring any high finish later on. What finish you decide to use is a matter of the kind of boat the oar will be used with, and just plain what you prefer. No finish you put on will last forever; it will have to be renewed. I make a few suggestions: for a working boat, linseed oil and turpentine is good, or you can use Val Oil. I like painted blades on working oars, even though the shafts might be oiled. Painted blades pep up the whole thing. For this I suggest using some color that is on the boat, either the inside color, or that of a wale strake or the topsides.

For a more yachtlike craft I much prefer varnished oars, either varnished all over or partially, with the blades painted, sometimes in a decorative way. You can paint the whole oar if you want to, but this makes an oar look drab. Though few seem to understand this now, I always use and recommend at least six—yes, I said *six*—coats of varnish, well rubbed down between coats with fine white oxide paper. This paper is for varnish and paint, not for bare wood. A six-coat varnish finish will last, even with a lot of exposure, so yearly maintenance will be much reduced. I'm sure that the many varnish failures commonly seen are caused by a poorly prepared surface and not enough varnish—spar varnish, not urethane, which seems to give trouble for this use.

Decoration on oars dates back a very long time. The idea of it is similar to the feelings that resulted in elaborately decorated steering wheels or tillers—they are important parts of the craft and are to be revered; oars for a pulling boat share this importance. Some decoration is also a form of identification. Markings might signify the boat the oars belong to, or her mother-ship, or often the oars' place in the boat. Matched pairs of oars should have matched markings. Multi-oared craft might have the oars numbered or otherwise marked to indicate their used position in the boat. Naval craft, pilot yawls, whaleboats, and others were marked this way. Whaleboats, by the way, seem to have been oared lopsided, since they pulled five oars, yet they really were perfectly balanced, as they pulled two long oars on one side and three shorter ones on the other.

I always decorate my oars or at least have some device on them, even if they are a single pair in a working boat; if there are two pair, they should be marked as pairs. A chevron device is good; it can be single, double, or in some cases triple, and it can be varied in shape to suit one's fancy. If blades only are painted, with or without a device, the point where the paint ends on the shaft can be treated in a simple decorative way; a couple of methods are illustrated. This sort of thing was common in the past, a sort of folk art, and I think the custom should be encouraged now that pleasure rowing is again becoming interesting.

I've heard it said that all this decoration is an affectation and waste of effort, since it takes time and is "work." When one is young, jumping about from one endeavor to another, it may seem there is never enough time. As I approach my dotage, there seems to be plenty of time for the good things—those things that don't matter just plain don't matter, and they didn't get that way because they offer no monetary gain. Some wonder what rowing gets you in this world. It gets me things no person or government can give at any price; try it and find out. And by all means decorate the oars, even if the first attempt is no great artistic feat.

LEATHERS

Oar leathers should be 12 to 14 inches long, as mentioned before, and sewn on; tacking on makes a fracture point, and leathers wear out, so you soon ruin a good oar with tacks. Sewing seems to be a great mystery to many, yet it is not. I simply use sail twine, waxed, which every boatman should learn to use, and the stitch is simply the rough-and-ready sail-repair stitch called the herringbone, or the baseball stitch inside out; yes, as kids we used to make our own baseballs. I suppose this, too, is now a "lost art."

Some soak new leathers before sewing them on, having carefully fitted them first; they shrink tight in drying. Some leather when wet can be difficult to work, for the stitches tend to pull through in sewing. Take care. If the leathers are put on dry, there is less risk of this, but later on the leathers may become loose and slide down. The first thought when that happens is to tack them—don't. Simply smear the shaft with contact cement and slide the leather back into position and let it dry. I've had very good luck with this simple solution.

One question I'm often asked is, "Where do you get leather?" As anything else that's not sold in chain stores, you have to get out and look for it. There seem to be a lot of people working in leather right now; asking one of them about sources usually turns some up. If you are going to make many oars, ask where the leatherworker gets his supplies, and get a whole hide. Some hides are quite thick, others not so much, so use your judgment if you have a choice. Substitutes have been tried for oar leathers. I've tried some myself. None work like leather, provided it is kept well lubricated. Fiberglass has been tried, and it's a real bum and soon cracks for obvious reasons. Very heavy canvas works for a time, so does serving with line, but the time for both is short. The store-bought rubber sleeves are way too short and add much friction between oar and lock. I've looked for the answer for many years and found it—good leathers of sufficient length, sewn on, and kept well greased. As

noted before, you can get by without leathers on hardwood oars, if they are kept greased and the locks fit.

Almost everyone has seen oars badly worn below the way-too-short leathers. There are two good reasons for this: first, an alternate rowing position in the boat does not agree with leathers put on to suit the primary position, and second, people row differently. Some row cross-handed, or one hand before the other; others hold their hands side by side. Naturally, such variations will not agree with

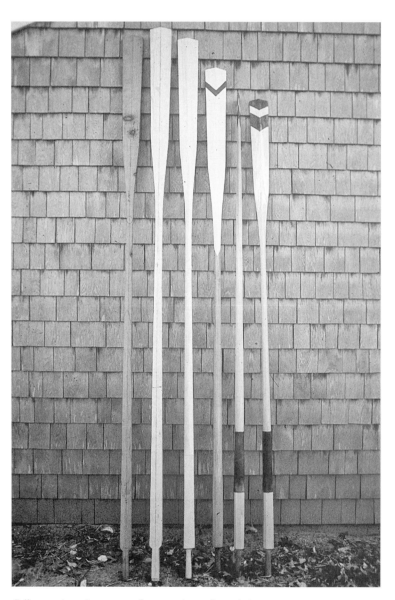

Culler oars in various stages of construction and completion. (John Burke)

232

short leathers—the store-bought kind are only about 7 inches long. So, to repeat, make your leathers long.

I always stress lubrication, which is essential for easy rowing and preservation of the oars and leathers. Either tallow or Vaseline will do quite well; forget neatsfoot oil and all sorts of leather oils. This is more or less a crankshaft you are lubricating. Use enough—be a bit sloppy with it—this is a bearing surface, not a bit of harness or a pair of boots you are polishing. And don't forget to put some on the oarlock sockets.

All this might seem a lot of work to go from boards to a finished pair of oars, ready to use, and in some ways it is a lot to get something that will make a nice boat perform. There is no other way, however—nice boats require first-class oars. Even a poor boat goes a little better with proper oars. Using manual propulsion, you soon find that a man, woman, girl, or boy develops very little power, especially over the long haul at a comfortable pace. A craft for such use must be carefully designed and suited to the waters—and this includes oars and all the other equipment that must go with a good pulling boat—if you want to get the most out of her with a minimum of labor.

You can always buy a bigger engine for some ill-shaped motorboat, in the hope that it will improve her performance, though it seldom does. In rowing craft you have to start with things about right, designed and built into the craft and her gear. There is very little you can do about a boat that does not pull well, except get rid of her. If the boat is good, and the gear is bad, at least you can junk the gear and start over. Good rowing gear is what this tale is about.

OARLOCKS AND OTHER ROWING GEAR

A good boat and fine oars are not quite enough; the oars must have some attachment to the boat—oarlocks, oar ports, tholes, or pins of various sorts. At one time there was a wide choice of oarlocks over the counter. No more. With the advent of the bicycle, motorcar, and other mechanical devices, all creating new interests and naturally turning people to other recreational endeavors, the demand for such hardware decreased. Many different patterns of oarlocks were discontinued. There were little or no sales of specialty locks, so the lines were dropped. Now only a minimal choice of types that still sell can be found.

Let it be said right here, by one who is always trying to find what is needed for good pulling boats, the present choice is very bad. Yet there *is* a small demand for specialized patterns. This has forced a few builders to make their own, or make patterns and have them cast, finishing the rough castings in their own shops. The demand has also caused an occasional—what might be called a backyard—industry to turn out some oarlocks of far better design than the standard fare. Since the market is small, this is a labor of love, and the oarlocks so produced are more expensive than the limited choice of stock manufactured ones. At least these special ones are good, each in their own way, and they work.

Right now, at least in my experience, you are limited in size to #0, which is only suited to dinks and very little boats; and #1, which is what many of us make do with, though it's somewhat shoal and narrow for a decent pair of oars. Though #1½ is a useful size, I've not been able to get any in a long time—they are totally discontinued, it seems. Still available are #2s, which are a bit sloppy for some craft, but better than #1s, which are a little tight. I find getting #2s no easy job; they are listed in catalogs at times, but the marine store does not stock them, and they have to be ordered. Sometimes this brings on problems. The store supplier does not want to do business for less than a dozen pair, and the store feels it will never sell them. In any case, there is a long wait. Sometimes there are hard words, and the builder, determined that he's not going to spoil a nice boat because of present business methods, storms off in a huff and makes his own. They are usually pretty good, as he's mad enough to do a fine job, just to show those uncooperative apes what can be done. The sad thing is that the apes will never see them, wouldn't appreciate his efforts, and, if they did, don't care anyway.

Stock patterns available now include a couple of models of side-mount sockets and the flat-mount sockets, some of these tapered, some not (that is, tapered for the shank of the lock). Also to be found are round-type locks that stay on the oar, using a leather "button" to keep them on. I never cared for these in a real pulling boat and have never seen them used on such craft; for a small dinghy, maybe they serve well. The standard horned type is still available in ribbed or plain pattern, sometimes with a lanyard eye. You can also turn up the horned type that is built into its side-mount plate and hinges down when not in use. This type is no doubt good for a dink, but it is heavy, noisy, and unattractive; besides, it is not easy to mount strongly on a real rowing craft. Another oarlock occasionally seen is the patent-swivel, which hasn't much of a shank and is kept in place by flanges on the mounting plate. This plate is not really a socket, so it's easy to mount this solidly as it has a good base. I

These are special oarlocks made by Capt. Pete for boats he designed and built. The extended oarlock is for Otter *and is shown with a lanyard and some ancillary gear: a wooden bailer and a tallow horn.* (John Burke)

Custom-made metal outriggers for Quitsa Pilot. *Note that oarlocks can be used normally when the outriggers are flipped inboard with the built-in hinge.* (Ben Fuller)

somehow never took to this model, finding it somewhat awkward for quick work coming alongside.

Still available is the North River pattern, which is similar to the guideboat pattern. It features a pin through the horns and the oar itself, so the oar cannot be feathered. The North River usually uses a side-plate mounting. That these work for the intended use, there is no doubt; they have much advantage fishing, but for most rowing you want to feather the oars, and you can't do it with these. If you have a fine guideboat, she will no doubt have them, but for the kind of rowing I do, feathering is a must.

A lock you can still find occasionally is the type with one horn higher than the other and the shank slightly out of center with the horns. This is a well-thought-out lock that has been around a long time with slight variations. I'm not sure, but Capt. Nat Herreshoff

might have worked out this design, like many good things. I once had a pair that were said to have been made by the Herreshoff Manufacturing Company. Somehow, the oarlocks had the mark of it, being very nicely shaped and finished, with just enough of the best metal to do the job well and take overloading, and not one bit more. Fortunately, there is at the moment a dedicated maker of these who has possibly improved their shape. There may be other small makers of specialized oarlocks that I don't know about. Let us hope they come forth with their products.

There is still available the ram-type lock, with fixed horns on a plate. Many now will look with doubt on such a rig, but these oarlocks have stood the test of time—the principle of their use may go as far back as the use of oars. The ram-type lock is easy to mount stoutly; one pattern has been used in

Jersey beach skiffs for years—very practical for the right boat.

Materials for today's oarlocks are now either galvanized iron or bronze, and most seem to be some sort of a drop forging or casting. In the past, many old craft had oarlocks of black wrought iron, which did not rust much. I think the choice of metal a matter of one's fancy and what you can get. The size and shape is more important than the metal. I've used galvanized iron locks and sockets off and on for years, and they go a long time without much rust, assuming you use the boat often and keep things greased. In the past, bronze oarlocks were highly finished; some even were nickel-plated. Now, for the stock ones, the story is different. They are very rough, and often, though they are supposed to be matched, you find them either to be very slack or to bind in the sockets.

A few words of warning based on experience: when buying any stock oarlocks over the counter now, check to be sure that the shanks fit the sockets properly; I've found more than once—in fact quite often—that they don't fit correctly. You often have to pick through a bin of locks and sockets to find a set that really match. Also, some sockets are not quite the same design in the same bin. The stock gets low, an order for more is put in, some clerk then consolidates what's still there—sometimes things are not just alike.

An old-time marine catalog makes you drool, with its wide choice of locks and sockets, all in different sizes to suit all craft. You can't get most of them now, but the illustrations can give you some ideas for making up your own. It is no great project to make patterns of some unavailable type that suits your fancy and have a small bronze foundry cast them, you doing the finishing. You can find small jobbing foundries around if you inquire; sometimes, with luck, you may find that they have an old oarlock pattern they are willing to cast for you. They don't like to make up just one pair, so plan to take all you may ever need and hope to dispose of a few more to other classic boat buffs.

There are all sorts of other devices besides metal oarlocks for securing the oar to the boat. They were in use before metal oarlocks were invented and many are still in use in various parts of the world.

Rowing is no mystery for these Norwegian children. Note that tholepins are being used and that the children are sitting side by side, each operating an oar. This requires teamwork! (Waldo Howland)

These all work well—in most cases they are just as good as metal locks for some craft, and sometimes they are superior. One advantage of these devices is that they can nearly all be made by the boatbuilder, the exception being the later Navy rowing port liners, which were cast bronze—to make them is as much trouble as making metal oarlocks.

Just how far back men started rowing, and what their first gear was like, we don't know for sure. It's well known how boats were propelled in ancient times in the Mediterranean and in Norse waters; boats in both of these areas relied very much on oars. Closed-top oar ports were used in large craft and continued to be used until fairly recently, as maritime history goes; no doubt they are still around in distant places in big craft, as an auxiliary to sail. Oar ports with open tops in smaller craft are very old, and of various designs; they were common in naval cutters, almost a badge of the type, until oars were given up by navies, which seems recent to me, for I well remember the naval pulling cutters. Open-top ports were also often used in some pilot yawls and ships' boats.

The early Norse way for holding the oar to the boat—and no doubt a good one, for the Norse were real oarsmen and seamen—was a natural grown chock ahead of the oar, with a hole and thong to help retain the oar. Southern craft used a pin of wood for the oar to work against; this pin was usually mounted on a block, with a strop used to retain the oar. In my youth on the West Coast, this method was common among fishermen from Italy, except, and I think I remember correctly since I pulled this way many a time, the oar worked away from the pin, pulling on the strop. Properly adjusted, the pin and strop was a good rig, especially for standing-up pushing, which was the common way. On the West Coast back then, a fleet of big skiffs and dories coming ashore from a moored seining fleet, the crews hailing and joshing each other in the various lingoes of the Mediterranean, was a fascinating sight. There was usually a race of sorts in progress, and much skill was demonstrated in handling the craft.

One small-craft version of the oarport was simply a stout wash strake in way of the oar, with a slot in the strake shaped to retain the oar. Another version was similar to an oarlock—two nicely shaped chocks of wood forming horns to retain the oar. There were many variations of the same principle, some removable and some adjustable. Some very large pilot yawls used what was more or less the naval oar port, but their ports had shaped covers on lanyards so they could be closed under sail. These craft were totally open, had large rigs, and were often pushed to the limit with large crews as live ballast and sand bags as movable ballast. These boats possibly required the very height of skilled seamanship, for they were open boats that were sailed and rowed in difficult waters in all weather.

I think the gear I describe here should be studied well, and considered, though not necessarily used for present-day rowing craft. But if a device fits your type of craft, use it, for you can be sure that it has passed the test of time. Nothing should be condemned as out of date, but understood and applied where it will work.

Tholepins are still in use, and many people are familiar with them. In the past some pins, notably those used in Europe, were often oblong in section, shaped on the inside to suit the oar, and fitted in sockets shaped to them in the rail. Some tholes used a fairly high chafing block if the boat was low; sometimes the forward pin was higher and stronger than the after one. The dory-style thole was in late years a turned wooden pin, fitting in a bored hole in the rail. Dory tholepins always used lanyards—all tholes should have lanyards—but there are few other absolutes in tholepin design. There are many slight variations in the shapes of both the round- and squarish-type tholes—some of this design work is very good, based as it is on what works and what does not.

These days I've often heard it said that people can't possibly row now with these contraptions, simply because they have never done it. I've tried nearly all of them; you can too. If you have to learn anything over again to use oar ports or tholepins, it's no big undertaking. It doesn't take long to master the simple art of jumping an oar out of a thole or port when coming alongside. Once you learn it, you'll realize it's the best way, even if you have swivel oarlocks. You'll probably wonder why you never thought of coming alongside that way before.

There are all sorts of adaptations of the various ways of holding an oar to suit certain boats and for special uses. For instance, Maine peapods were used among ledges for pulling lobster pots, and the rower found it convenient to stand up. So peapods were fitted with iron oarlocks with extended shanks to raise the oars to a comfortable position. All the work—rowing, sighting, and pulling the pots—was done standing up, so this was the logical way to rig the oars. Other low craft were often rowed standing, or the oars were too low even when the rower was sitting down, so the lock or pin was mounted on a block of suitable height, a common thing in many small craft. There were also some very special arrangements, such as two horns of different heights on the same shank. Just how you apply all these variations depends on the type of boat you have and what fittings you choose. I give some suggestions based on my own experience, and these are by no means the only ways—just one man's notions.

Oar ports in the naval fashion are usually not suited to smaller craft; the oars are simply too low for use. A raised wash strake the entire length of the boat can be used to follow the naval fashion, but do you need all that freeboard and windage? Usually not. Sometimes a wash strake with ports in the middle half of the boat will work, especially if the boat has great sheer and is low in the middle. This same principle might apply with tholes if they seem too low; in other words, you can mount a raised continuous block on the gunwale for them.

I often use continuous, instead of separate, blocks for standard oarlocks if I think the boat will

look well with them—some boats do, some don't. Separate oarlock blocks can be strong and handsome, but more often you see them ugly, short, and weak. Whitehalls, and some other well-established types, used blocks, and they were works of art. Done correctly, small pieces of gear can enhance the beauty of a nice boat. There is room here for a person to explore much nicer shapes than we often see now on what passes for rowboats—classics should have the best in all respects, for looks as well as durability.

A nice craft from the period when good oarlocks were common should no doubt use metal locks; though not apparent, such a boat was probably designed with their availability in mind, and, too, the lock makers then no doubt knew what she required. A smart dory does just fine with tholes; I think to keep the type pure she *should* have tholes, especially since her shape is most suited to them. A fast gig of an early model, or one based on the British pilot gigs, might well have the tholes oblong in section and shaped inside. Of recently built craft, I think the *General Lafayette,* a fast competition gig, built at Mystic Seaport under the direction of John Gardner, is a very fine example of the intelligent use of tholes. This boat is on exhibit and is worth any rowing buff's study. Let us hope she goes afloat on occasion, for she is a fine, extremely fast craft.

A Norse type may well use what was the custom—a shaped chock and thong, or tholes, as are often used in them now. A Latin type will be right using the pin and thong. Some of these southern craft are most interesting, and a few have been imported. It takes a bit of judgment as to just what you use; if possible, suit the boat, and I realize that the pocketbook may enter into it. But then again, poor taste and a fat wallet can make an awful mess.

I leave to the last a mess caused by bad judgment and poor taste—a nice enough Whitehall with, of all things, white nylon oarlocks and sockets. The locks spoiled the whole thing. I've not seen any of

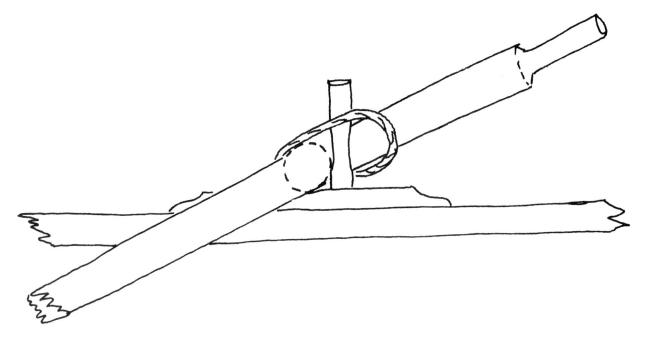

THE MED., LIGHTERS,
U.S.N. ROWING LAUNCHES,
MANY OTHER.

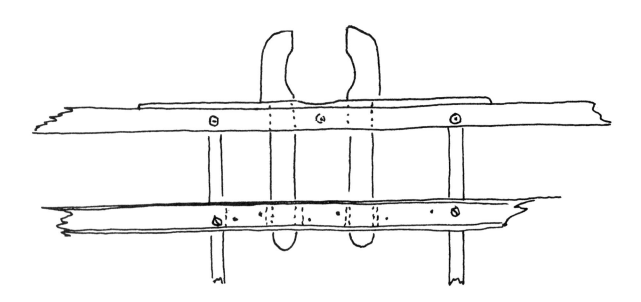

NORTH; GIGS, WHERRYS,
GALLEYS, OTHER.

This drawing by Pete Culler details various ways of holding an oar to suit certain boats and for special uses. These drawings are referred to in the text.

these nylon rigs recently; let us hope they went where bad things should go.

LANYARDS AND SPARES

Oarlocks, other than those attached to the oars, will require lanyards, as will tholes or pins as well. Some pins are totally fixed in some working craft, but I think this is apt to be unhandy and cause trouble, especially if you go alongside other craft or even a float or a wharf. Lanyards are, of course, to prevent loss of the rowing gear overboard. I've seen many lanyards that consisted of a piece of any old twine or chain, and I've seen all sorts of makeshift rigs. The system of a piece of cod line connecting a pair of oarlocks and running one to the other across the boat is a poor thing, something to trip over. I much prefer lanyards of some nicely made cord or marline, neatly made up, yet properly secured to the thwart stringer in a way that allows them to be removed simply. I often spin up marline that is too small to be used singly to form a nice-looking lanyard. In fact, many things required in a pulling boat are best secured with their own lanyards; if the boat fills due to a storm or accident, you don't lose the gear, and, barring a catastrophe, it's secure and not underfoot.

The little chain lanyards with metal toggles often seen on stock oarlocks secure the lock well enough, but I find that it usually takes two hands to get the lock in—one hand for the chain, the other for the lock. If the boat is jumping a bit, it's quite awkward. In other words, I don't care for a lanyard that goes down through the socket. With tholes, the lanyard should go through the holes in the rail or block, to prevent chafe. This can be quite an unhandy arrangement, too, unless the lanyard is rigged as shown, with a toggle at the bottom. Once the knack is learned, you can pop them in with one hand. This system is seldom seen, but it does work, at least with round tholes. With square- or oblong-section tholes, it does not work for obvious reasons, and I know of no way to make it work.

Lanyards might be there to prevent loss, but they can't prevent breakage, which is possible, though rare if things are well made. It pays to carry at least one spare oarlock or thole; a pair is better. Failing this, any sort of metal pin that will fit in the socket or thole hole will get you in, with the aid of a bit of line. This is good to know about, but having spares of the real thing is so much better. Assuming the oars are good, many get along quite well without a spare oar, but for any long-distance rowing in open water, it's only good sense to carry a spare oar that matches those in use, or better, another matched pair. Besides failure of oarlocks, pins, or an oar, there is little else that can go wrong in a pulling boat, unless she's so old and tender that the bottom falls out and she leaves you. You can also leave her, accidentally, but safety in general we take up later in the chapter on using the boat.

THWARTS

Thwarts need some discussion, for without them you can't do much unless you stand. They are important for other reasons, too, for they keep the boat propped open and otherwise contribute to the strength of the craft. The placement of thwarts is critical and subject to some argument. Fore-and-aft placement is a matter of design and how the boat will be used, mostly and occasionally. A boat that mostly pulls single, with an occasional passenger or two, is one thing. A craft that will pull both single and often double, with or without a coxswain, is another. These variations, and a few others, are the designer's and builder's headaches.

The height of the thwarts is most important, and in craft of from 12 to 18 feet in length sometime cannot be perfect, due to limitations of the boat. I've set thwarts as low as 7 inches from the bottom in very shoal, low-sided craft; this is not the best practice, but, if you have room to stretch your legs nearly straight out, it is quite workable. The height from the thwart to the rail runs 6 inches, more or less, in most boats—when more height is needed, oarlock blocks will work. I find thwarts located at 10 inches from the bottom and 7 inches from the rail a fairly happy medium, though mostly I don't quite make it, due to the design of the boat, so fudge out in various ways.

The standard thwart width when I learned the trade was 8 inches for flat-bottom skiffs, and the oarlock sockets were set 12 inches from the after edge of the thwart. This is a norm to work from, but it is by no means ideal. Many fast working yawls and gigs of the past had thwarts only $6\frac{1}{2}$ to 7 inches wide, and I think this has a lot of merit—there is less wood to step over and bark your shins on in getting about in the boat. I also prefer a thwart that is narrow enough so you can hook your butt slightly over the forward edge. Even though there might be a good stretcher for your feet, this hooking over of your butt gives you a firm grip on things, especially when rowing in a seaway, even a slight one. It's quite apparent that the old-timers who used these craft as a way of life knew what they were doing.

I find that many boats allow the grips of the oars to be too low, almost in your lap, which is awkward in many ways, poor application of your power, and just plain unhandy in any sort of a sea. I like my grips to come just about under my rib cage; if I am in doubt when building a new boat or converting an old one, I simulate a thwart, using a box or some blocking, fake up some oarlock blocks, and sit in her with an oar or even a long stick, taking into account where the water will be and fussing around with the set-up until I think it will work. It may never be perfect, but usually, using this method, I arrive at about the best you can do with a given boat. I'm sure that a person's build has a lot to do with thwart location; a person who is thick in the lower regions is going to crowd things more than the string-bean type. A very short person may not have much reach in his arms, let alone legs, and a really long person always has trouble finding a place for his lower ends. All this has to be taken into

consideration—even the stroke the oarsman favors, though this last can be altered if you can convince him that a change will make the boat go better. Somepeople do have bad rowing habits, which they often developed from using poor boats; bad habits can be eliminated, but it's often not easy.

The rough rules of thumb for placing locks and thwarts that I have given are just that—rough guides, somewhere to start. You can work from these, and, with a little trial and common sense, you can make the boat go pretty well and feel right. If, after some use, things don't seem right, try to figure out what's wrong and make the necessary alterations.

FOOT STRETCHERS, OUTRIGGERS, AND SLIDING SEATS

Foot stretchers, or chocks for bracing your feet, have to be fitted by trial. Some are made adjustable in fancy boats. Yet there are craft that, for some reason, don't really need them—at least some oarsmen in those boats don't need them. In those cases, some part of the boat, such as a frame or floor, seems to do just as well as a stretcher. The model of a craft will determine whether you need one or not. If you don't use a stretcher, it's well to note any wear that takes place where you put your feet. Wear on the planking as you brace against a frame, for instance, would indicate that a stretcher of some sort will be an improvement.

Stretchers for small craft should not be too elaborate. You don't need a bulky piece of equipment to trip over. By their very nature, some rather way-out pulling craft are somewhat cramped for other than just rowing room. They are not always easy to get in and out of, or to move about in. Many of these craft can be somewhat tender by wide, flat, skiff standards—all part of getting a high-performance boat, and something you quickly get used to. In any pulling boat, and especially in the high-strung ones, it pays to have places for the gear to be stowed properly,

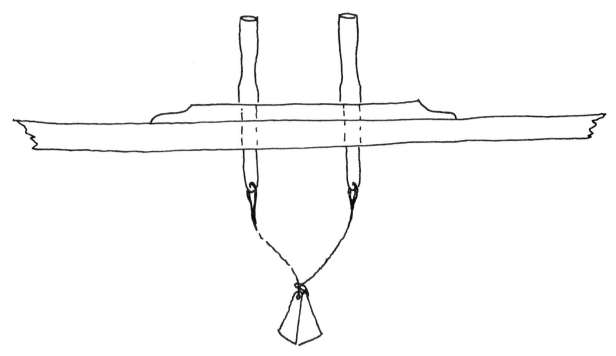

USE OF THOLE & 'LOCK
LANYARDS.

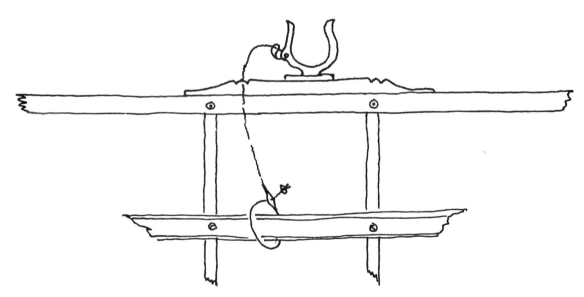

Pete Culler drawing showing the manner of securing tholepins and oarlocks from being lost overboard. Pete Culler discusses this in the text.

and to have things planned so that there are not a lot of things to stumble over or come adrift. This is just one other form of good seamanship.

Some narrow craft should be fitted with outriggers to get the proper length of oar to do them justice. Fitting outriggers is an art in itself, and for the boats we consider here, the gear should be kept as simple as possible. As I said before, I know little of pure racing craft. The hulls and gear for these craft are very specialized; those wanting to have a go at competition rowing must pick it up from those who know about it. The type of rowing we consider here and the waters pleasure rowing craft use are more or less unsuited to pure racing craft. I bring this up partly because of my lack of knowledge of racing, and partly because high-performance pleasure rowing boats have borrowed, to some extent, from the racers—for instance, pleasure craft are seen at times with way-out oars, but not nearly as way out as those for a shell. Outriggers, too, have been borrowed from competition craft, but are not nearly so extreme. I think pleasure-craft outriggers, where needed, should be modified a great deal to fit the job at hand. They should readily fold inboard for just pleasure rowing.

I have installed sliding seats in plain pulling boats; they do provide some advantage if the boat is fast and you want leg exercise. They cause complications for the placement of oarlocks if the boat is to be used without the seat at times; they also are a variable to consider in determining thwart height. In any sort of seaway I consider sliding seats a menace. I don't like to be laced into a fixed pair of shoes (which is required to make the seat work) in any boat, especially if the water is a bit sloppy. For the right boat, the right person, and suitable conditions, the sliding seat pays off. For the kind of rowing I do, it does not.

SCULLING GEAR

Nearly every boat I have built, with the exception of double-enders, has had a sculling slot; the double-enders can well have an oarlock socket blocked out to be used in place of a slot. Personally, I like the looks of a slot, besides admiring its practicality and simplicity. For those who don't like them, an oar-lock socket can usually be placed in any stern. In this country, the slot is usually in the center of the stern; in many other countries, notably the Bahamas, it is offset to port for a couple of good reasons—to account for the method of sculling, which is different from ours, and to allow the oar to be used with a rudder in place, so a sailing craft can be helped out in a calm. Regardless of locality and tradition, I think any small sailing boat should be rigged this way. I don't know which came first, the off-set slot or the stroke of the oar that seems best suited to it. However, I can say that the Bahama method, once you adapt to it, is far superior in most boats to the accepted Yankee method.

Sculling should be learned. It does not take long to master and is most practical in confined situations, or just for the fun of it. You can move a far heavier boat by sculling, slowly but steadily, with less effort, than rowing. I think the reason sculling has fallen into disuse—so much so that some think it may nearly be a lost art—is about the same reason that rowing fell into disfavor—short, miserably shaped, so-called rowboats. A short, fat, dishlike hull wobbles badly when sculled, though an experienced man can get her along reasonably well. Craft built on the gig, Whitehall, or real ship's boat model scull just fine, as they track well. The Bahama dinghy, an excellent sculling boat, is simply an adaptation of the old ship's boats, a model hard to beat for general use.

Most craft we consider here will scull well enough with their regular rowing oars. However, a genuine sculling oar is special. For the best results, I find such an oar should be in length about $2\frac{1}{2}$ times the beam of the boat. There are various patterns, the oriental type being the best, especially in big craft, since they were designed and are handled by experts. Around the Orient, there are local variations

(continued on page 247)

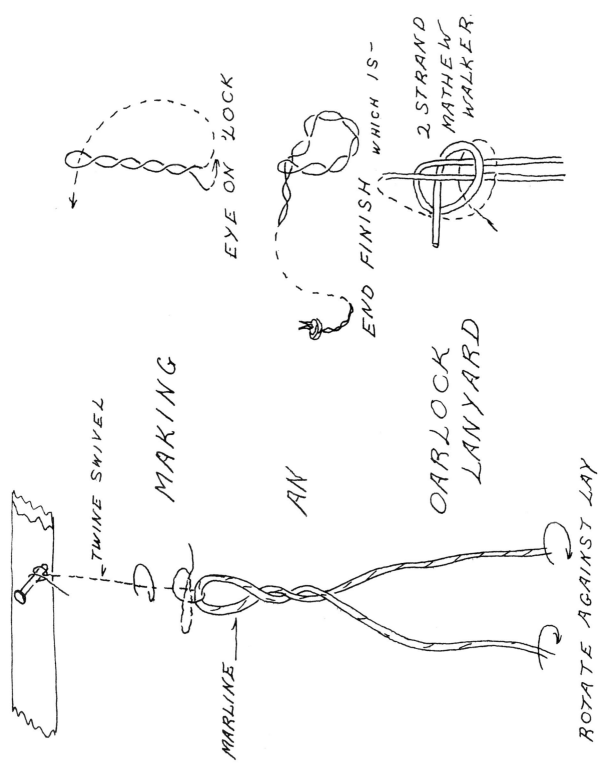

MAKING AN OARLOCK LANYARD

TWINE SWIVEL

MARLINE

ROTATE AGAINST LAY

EYE ON 'LOCK

END FINISH WHICH IS —

2 STRAND MATHEW WALKER.

Pete Culler drawing showing how to make lanyards from marline. Refer to the text for further details.

245

Thwarts on this 18'8" Swampscott dory rigged for sailing have mast holes cut into them and brace the centerboard well (top). The just-for-rowing 13'6" Good Little Skiff (bottom) has simpler requirements for thwart design. Both these boats were designed and built by Pete Culler.

(continued from page 244)

of the sculling oar. European and American boat-men seem quite happy simply using a steering sweep; the Bahama boatman has his own pattern, one which I very much favor. It is simple to build and shaped in such a way that once you get your hand in, it seems to almost work by itself—at least the feathering part. It is most suited to small craft. However, if it's mostly rowing you do, I don't suggest carrying a special sculling oar; use a rowing oar. But I do like to have a good sculling oar around for those days when the only urge is to mess about among the docks, slips, and moored boats.

I think the ability to scull is part of safety afloat. If you lose an oar, you might find it difficult paddling in a sloppy situation to try and pick it up. By sculling with the oar left on board (assuming you do not have a spare), you have much better control of the situation.

This lost oar business brings up ways of preventing yours from going overboard. None of the commonly used methods are totally foolproof. The usual way is to put a "button" of leather at the top end of the oar leather; some substitute a fancy turkshead, or a "mouse" of some kind—a mouse is a built-up serving, often decorated. I find these things tend to hang up when sliding the oar around in the boat. I have also found that an oar built square from the leather to the grip, if planned properly, is its own button. None of these methods can be totally trusted if you let the oars trail, perhaps when you are trolling and need both hands for a strike, or when you simply let go to fill a pipe. Lacking a stopper of some kind, I often pull both oars inboard in the locks, right across the boat, letting them rest on the gunwales.

If your activity at the moment requires frequent letting go of the oars, and if you want to avoid losing them, I give a method I've not seen since boyhood. As far as I can tell, it was worked out by a professional boatman I knew. Old Cap had perhaps a dozen craft—Whitehalls, skiffs, and an odd one or two. These craft were water taxis and were for rent. Old Cap was a sharp seaman and sharp at business; he did not like

to lose gear, and, since he rented boats to "farmers who come down out of the brush to get afloat," he made sure the gear stayed with the boat. And when the oars were taken ashore, lines, locks, and all were just wrapped up in a handy bundle, which stayed together. His method was this: The oars were all ash, leathered, but had no buttons. They were old, somewhat worn but sound, and were always well lubricated. At the neck, just where the blade begins, there was a very stout piece of cod line, rolling hitched and marline seized besides, but very neatly. This line was led up the oar and was of such a length as to allow the line to be hitched and seized to the neck of the oarlock. The length of the line also allowed the oar to lie in the lock nearly to the upper part of the leather. With a long leather this gave enough slack for holding the oar and rowing. The oarlocks had an iron side eye, and another lanyard went from the eye to the thwart stringer, where it was made fast with a toggle and loop for easy removal when the gear was stored. This was a neat and seamanlike rig, with all the old fellow's marlinespike art apparent. The whole business could get overboard but not get away; somehow, the balance of the rig gave it very little tendency to unship. I think this is a fine rig for those who fish or pull a pot or two under oars.

ANCILLARY GEAR

I have discussed the gear that is essential to row a boat: oars, something for these to work against, such as locks, pins, or whatever, and the placing of these devices and their use. You can do little or nothing without all of the above; yet there is other gear I consider necessary for the pleasant and safe use of the craft we consider.

It was said in the distant past that you should not go any distance in a boat without a water jug. I certainly agree, especially since I well know that it is possible to be out longer than you plan. Just how you carry this water, and in what, is a matter of personal preference, but carry it. I like a conveniently shaped bottle covered with ropework myself, as it is in keeping with the boats I use.

For lubrication, I carry my grease in a wooden horn, one like an old-time rigger's grease horn, though mine is made of wood. Carry your grease any way you want, but carry it. The wooden horn looks good, does not break, floats, and is of a shape easy to stow.

I like to carry a small ditty box or bag, with some twine, marline, and any special stuff your particular craft might require. Don't overdo the extras—just carry the things you may really need. I always carry a pocketknife at all times, ashore or afloat, and feel that matches should be on hand on a boat trip, if you smoke or not. Once in a while, though rarely, the ability to build a fire can be a lifesaver. Take that ability along. A well-built lighter in good order may be better than matches, since ordinary dampness may have less effect on it.

Naturally, if you are going any distance and plan to spend the day, a lunch is needed, though this is entirely up to the one who is going to eat it. Take enough to eat, a snack near the end of the trip can set things off just right. Though I've never needed a whistle and seldom need a compass, I like to include both in the ditty box if I am going any distance. The weather can turn thick, and these items can come in handy.

To carry an anchor and a rode seems to some to be an affectation. I think it's a matter of the waters you are using at the moment and the length of the cruise. To go ashore on some deserted beach, just dragging the boat up a bit, is folly. Lay out an anchor on a good scope and stomp it in. Strange tidal surges can develop from various causes, float the boat, and leave you marooned. Don't chance it. If you are in an area with fairly big tides, especially with offshore wind, the craft can be anchored off a bit while you

Small-boat compass types. On top is a board-mounted compass that swings under a thwart when not in use. The small compass is of Swedish make and dry. The lower compass was homemade by Capt. Pete and dry. It worked very well.

Ancillary small boat gear. That to the right of the swab belongs to Otter; *to the left and including the wooden bucket belongs to* Dancing Feather. *The items include rope-covered water jugs, wooden scoops, tallow horns, a lead line, and oarlocks with a ditty box resting on the shelf.*

explore ashore, yet the boat won't get grounded too far out. When crossing open water, if the wind or current overpower you for a time and your steam runs out, an anchor might hold your ground till things improve, thus possibly saving an unintended trip to Spain. Except for river work, or waters so confined you can beach at any time, I think carrying an anchor and a long, light rode is only good seamanship. What type of anchor you use is a small matter, so long as you carry it. I like a very light sand anchor, myself, the kind quahoggers used to use in this area. This type holds in sand, marsh, and stony ground. For harbor work around wharves, rowing in coves, and short inshore exploring, the anchor is of no use. For offshore work, you won't use an anchor much, but when you do, you will be very glad to have it.

A lead line is another bit of gear I've found useful—it's seldom used to be sure, but very much so when I need it. My line is a copy of a full-size one;

it's more or less a cod line with a stout sinker and is wound onto a wooden reel. Mostly I use it because I am just curious about the depth of water in a certain spot, and I can't reach bottom with an oar. A time or two in the past it has been a help in thick weather. With this little lead line, a pocket compass, a watch, and a knowledge of one's strokes per minute, you can be quite a coast pilot if overtaken by really thick weather. If, at this point, any of my readers don't know what I am driving at, I suggest they read *The Riddle of the Sands* by Erskine Childers. I make it a point, when overtaken by fog, to stay as much as possible in water too shoal for motor craft, but if your piloting does have to take you across channels when the weather is thick, it is nice to have the gear on hand to make the passage safely and without delay.

A rowing craft's ability to navigate in water often too hazardous for other craft makes it one of the safest craft to use. The risk of collision, explosion, or fatal grounding—the Big Three Dangers for most craft—are nonexistent for pulling boats. Collision with bigger craft is simply avoided by staying out of their reach—maybe not possible at all times, but almost. I think falling overboard should be kept in mind as the big risk in rowing boats and should be constantly guarded against. If a fall overboard should happen, I repeat what has been said millions of times, yet is still ignored—*STICK TO THE BOAT*—she's your best bet!!

It's understood that you carry the proper lifejackets required by law and obey the navigation laws, which include having a light to show at night in accordance with the rules for rowing craft under way after sunset, if you either intend, or are apt to be delayed into darkness.

Though not really needed, I think a small sail and very light spars are good equipment to carry in any pulling boat when she's taken on a cruise longer than, say, a short harbor row. At present, the use of such a sail seems little understood, as people right away think of centerboards, rudders, and much gear. Many pulling boats do have a rudder for use when a coxswain is along. Such a crewmember was customary for some pulling boat types—others never used them. Some boats are suited to a centerboard, which is fine, and many very sharp craft have considerable lateral resistance without a board. Nearly all are not great sail carriers and don't have to be, as they move easily. I think we should reconsider and learn again how to use these sailing rigs, which, instead of making a sailing craft out of a pure rowing boat, are simply auxiliary to it.

If the craft is up to becoming a real sailer, such as a Whitehall or similar craft, that's fine, too. One of my nicest pulling boats is also an excellent sailer. However, what I call a traveling sail is most useful for any pulling boat. All you need is a rig that is small, light, and simple, to make the most out of a fair wind. You find that in planning a row, you can often put your craft in a weather position under oars so as to take advantage of a slant of wind for the next course. This is only good sense and good seamanship. Most often you can plan a day's cruise so you end the passage home with a more or less fair wind. This does require some understanding of local weather, which should be learned no matter what kind of boating you do. Weather and tide observation is all part of being very close to the water in small craft propelled by oar and sail. You tend to learn fast, for any errors can't be easily corrected by simply opening the throttle. Planning around the tides and working favorable eddies are all part of pulling-boat seamanship.

Just what type of sail you use for your traveling rig is a small matter, as long as it's light and handy. I've used loose-footed rigs—sprit, lug, Chinese lug, and sharpie-type sprit—with success. Your choice is a matter of your preference, your particular boat, and stowage; science and efficient design are overshadowed by practicability.

The fast gigs, smugglers' gigs, and pilot yawls of the great days of the past were so smart to weather under oars that sail was used only when the craft could lay the course under sail. No centerboards were used—a very sharp craft, especially when deeply laden, had sufficient lateral resistance of her own. We would do well now to take note of these past methods and apply them where practical to pleasure rowing.

NOTES ON ROWING

Having gone on at length about the gear for rowing, we should now consider actually doing it. As mentioned previously, you might well have developed some bad rowing habits in years past, perhaps because you used poor boats, or perhaps because your rowing was for short hauls, a means to an end, like going aboard another boat. If you are rowing in boats built for rowing, just for the pleasure of it, it is most important that you row the right way. Especially when cruising, you will find that correct rowing practices will help you to go easily, and save effort and general wear and tear, both to yourself and the boat.

There is no right stroke for all boats, all conditions, and all people. I think a cultivation of various practical strokes is needed, not only to suit conditions, but also to change the pace of rowing longer distances. I won't go into the actual motions of the oar; they are shown in some books, and occasionally again and again in magazines. Most people, even though they might never have rowed, know more or less the principles of it. Instead, I will give some observations based on experience, much of which was picked up when I was a youth. I learned

by watching and aping experts, most of who were professionals of some sort—boatmen, yacht hands, fishermen, and surfmen.

If you find, after trying other ways, that you prefer to row with your hands side by side, the oars just clearing each other, then that's fine—nothing wrong with it, go to it. Most pros of the past pulled with their hands overlapping, one ahead of the other; this allows a bit easier pulling for a given length of oar, or, to look at it another way, it allows slightly longer oars for the same boat. It also allows you to shift things slightly to rest some muscles—you can row with your left hand aft of your right hand for a while, and then use your right aft of your left. You would be surprised how well this works on a long pull.

I prefer not to use too long a reach forward with the blades—the lighter and faster the boat, the more reach I use; the heavier and slower, the less. A very long reach wastes power. You should sit straight, as if a board were down your back, and, if the boat is at all smart, take a rather long pull, kicking your elbows out as you feather. On your recovery, bring the blades forward again, no higher above the water than is necessary to clear the water. On the pulling part of your stroke, lay back a little, but just at the end of the stroke, as you feather the oars, straighten right up. This was a common and stylish stroke used by professionals—their boats always went well but easily. It's a stroke that is very nice to look at, and once you get the hang of it, it's the very best for light- to moderate-weather work. Meet some rough water, however, and the stroke must be different.

In any sort of choppy water and wind, especially if you're headed into it, you soon find of advantage a shorter stroke, one much like that observed by pros in Banks dories. Let it be said right here that rowing in a lot of wind and sea is no real pleasure, though at times you may have to do it, not from choice, but because it suddenly airs on— you have to cope with rough conditions until you make a lee. A shorter stroke also requires more strokes per minute—not many more, but some. You want to keep the boat moving steadily if slowly, rather than have her lose headway between strokes.

Speed of stroke under any condition is a thing each must work out for himself, depending on his stamina, the boat, and weather conditions at the moment. I find, for myself at least, that 28 strokes per minute is about right for distance rowing, though I change my speed and stance slightly as I go for reasons already given. Keep in mind, however, that I am now what they choose to call a senior citizen (I much prefer the term Old Man, dirty or not), and I use a rather high performance boat and spoon-blade oars.

But more on rough-water rowing; I'll return to the matter of strokes per minute later.

Running along with a fresh beam wind and sea, a boat will roll some. You have to watch the sea and your oars—it's easy to catch a crab in such a sea. Some craft want to luff under these conditions, which makes more work for the weather oar; a few boats occasionally want to run off. Quartering seas produce similar conditions, only the boat's response

Doug Halleck rowing in the 13'6" flat-bottom Good Little Skiff Mary, *which he built to the design by Pete Culler and named after his wife.* (Doug Halleck)

The great drawback to the normal rowing position is that you can't see where you are going without a lot of twisting and turning. This is an 18'6" flat-bottom Good Little Skiff, designed and built by Pete Culler.

is not quite so pronounced. Running dead downwind is easy enough; you can run this way in quite rough conditions, as it takes little power to keep her moving. Here again, many craft want to luff; sometimes it pays to row from an after rowing station if there is one, thus raising the fore-foot. If a passage *must* be made downwind in really rough going, it pays to tow a drag—what you rig up depends on what you have on board—a long line, perhaps terminated with an unstocked anchor might be most handy. You will be going quite fast enough, probably too fast; with a drag, the idea is to let her drive, helping her go more or less straight with the oars.

If you go single in a dory, Banks or Swampscott, of say 16 to 18 foot length, you should have three rowing stations. Dories are excellent craft once understood, but brutes until you learn to trim them. In light weather, row from the middle station. In any sort of headwind, use the bow station, and the craft will weathervane with her high stern

downwind, which will enable you to make quite fair going of it to windward. If you're going downwind, use the after station, and she will track quite well. I've heard many inexperienced people cuss dories simply because they did not know about using the rowing stations to advantage. The same technique can be applied to other craft to a lesser extent; if they become difficult to handle, try some variation of the dory trim method.

Some boats, especially dories, benefit in the trim department by carrying a ballast bag. The "dory stone," stowed right aft at the tombstone, is a common sight in Banks dories used alongshore. I prefer a canvas bag of sand or shingle as ballast in most boats. It does not bruise the bottom and does not shift. It's said that shingle rots a bag less than sand, as it ventilates better; either way, the stuff is cheap, and you can chuck it over to lighten ship if need be.

Certainly, for open water pulling, feathering the oars is the only way to go and should be learned at once, if you don't already know how—there's nothing like cutting down on all the windage you possibly can. If, as often happens when learning to feather, the oar keeps jumping out of the lock, it's almost never the fault of the lock. You are simply allowing the blade to enter the water at an angle that is too close to 90 degrees. You should drop the blade at an angle that is shallow enough to allow you to feel the grips trying to rise; your downward pressure on the grips makes the blade dig in, and the result is downward pressure on the locks. How much downward pressure to apply is a matter of practice. Obviously, the answer is the least you can get away with, for overmuch downward pressure is power wasted, since it is not moving the boat ahead. The weather, the boat, and your skill will soon tell you how much pressure to use. It will vary slightly with conditions.

Actually, once you become somewhat skilled, it's quite possible, and easy, to row against a single pin or chock without a strap, thong, or other retaining device, as long as sea conditions are moderate. Plain dory tholes have no device to keep the oar from jumping out; their use is based on learning to row properly. Many of today's stock oarlocks are so shaped that they tend to make an oar climb; in my experience at least, tholes do not. I personally prefer

tholes in many ways over some poor oarlocks, knowing that tholes do have some slight drawbacks—mostly they wear poorly.

For some reason, I find a good pair of spoons, assuming the boat is suited to them, somewhat better in rough going. It is not so much in the propulsion department that they excel in rough water. Rather, they seem less prone to catch the tops of the seas, or, if they do catch, they do it with less fuss. When driving downwind, or through a narrow gut, spoons trailed aft to clear obstructions can control a responsive boat quite well if you simply twist the blades in the locks and resist their desire to swing in or out—the curved blades act fairly well as rudders. Another useful trick for running a fast-water gut, as you often must do in regions of very fast tides, is to face the boat upstream and pull into the current. You have very good control of your direction simply because you can prevent the boat from going as fast as the water over the bottom, and can tack her from side to side with little trouble. Besides, you are facing downstream and can see what develops ahead. (All of this assumes that you have room to swing the oars, of course.) Backing downstream while rowing against the current avoids the headlong rush of a paddled canoe and doesn't require fast work to keep her headed. In fact, lumber bateaux were handled

Dr. Freydberg tries out the 18' round-bilged fast gig designed and built by Pete Culler. This design has a sliding seat in accordance with the owner's wishes.

This 18'6" flat-bottom Good Little Skiff is enough boat to carry her way nicely between strokes. This boat was originally designed and built by Pete Culler for Waldo Howland for his use in Florida waters.

just this way when the waters were not too narrow for the oars; being sharp at both ends helped the bateaux in this situation, too.

I use a double-ended bateau and find that, in working confined waters, especially if conditions are moderate, I can often go stern first and push on the oars rather than pull on them. This allows me to see where I'm going without getting a crick in my neck, and permits a welcome rest from regular pulling. Even in open water, if it's calm, I often turn around and push for awhile as a way of resting my pulling muscles and putting other muscles to use. In a calm, almost any smart boat seems to go about as well stern first as head first.

Push rowing, facing forward, is of course common in working boats, and a good thing to learn as a change of pace. A standard Banks dory goes well this way without modification, for she's deep enough so the oars are not too low, especially if the oarsman is short. Some fishermen used to put a board across the gunwales and sit on that as they rowed facing forward—this provided about the right height for rowers. A gunwale board can be applied to other craft occasionally, but most really smart boats are too low for it and don't need it. I've even knelt on a cushion and pushed, simply to have a change of position for a spell on a long trip.

I think many inexperienced rowers start out too fast. When going for a row—either a short or long one—it pays to start out with a very modest stroke. It takes awhile to limber up, though you may not think so. After awhile you can pep it up a bit to a comfortable pace. By experiment, find out what your pace is. I've done this many times by watching the bottom, counting strokes against a measured mile, counting strokes against paced-off stakes along a straight sand beach, asking an observer to time me, estimating the distance (with the aid of stakes) between dips of the oars, and I don't know what-all. These so-called tests show what I can do and attempt in comfortable conditions; they are not speed trials, and they are always done in light weather so as to be more or less consistent. But remember that the boat must have a clean bottom at all times if she lives afloat, or the time trials will be for naught.

What have I found out from my time trials? For me and the boats I use, it goes about like this: Any boat that rows reasonably well will go about her length between dips of the oars; this fetch between dips will increase with the smartness of the boat and the fineness of her model—it can be very great in way-out designs. All this is based on a comfortable rowing pace; I say nothing about sprints, which are another matter and have little bearing on overall comfortable performance. Of course, your results in your boat might be something else again.

Awhile back I mentioned the number 28, which seems to be a good number of strokes per minute for me in one of my smarter craft. I don't think the number itself matters much. Simply find a number of strokes per minute that suits you, your boat, and your gear, and that is comfortable for about one mile of rowing. The importance of this is simply to know your own pace in light weather and to be aware of what you can easily accomplish without over-exerting yourself and perhaps getting yourself into trouble. It's not unlike figuring in advance the fuel consumption of a motorboat when planning a trip, or the bunker supply for a steamer—only in this case it's your own energy that produces the steam. Incidentally, my 28 strokes per minute for a pulling boat seems to equal about 56 dips of the double paddle (a dip each, port and starboard, counts as two) for very nicely modeled wooden canoes of somewhat shorter length than the pulling boat.

But this brings up an entirely new subject, which rightfully belongs in a chapter by itself.

DOUBLE-PADDLE
CANOES

Canoes may seem out of place in a book on rowing craft, but they occasionally show up on our cruises and excursions, and are ideal for certain waters. I have no fixed mind on the subject, and, as a result, I use both canoes and pulling boats. I look at both types about like this: A canoe has less than half the weight of a pulling boat, though the canoe will be shorter and narrower. A double paddle is at least half the weight of a pair of oars, but you must carry the entire weight of the paddle at all times. In a canoe, you face forward and see where you are going, which is much better than rowing backwards in narrow, winding waters. The advantages of a pulling boat are considerable, too—the weight of the oars is nearly all taken by the oarlocks, and the body movement of the oarsman is slower, though more of it seems to be used. As described previously, in a winding stream with a pulling boat you can always avoid difficulty by going stern first.

It boils down to this—the pulling boat has it hands down for straight-away travel with minimum effort, and is less confining to the body for changes of positions. The canoe has it for narrow waters, portability on shore, and use on some tiny body of water that calls for exploring but is hard to reach with a bigger boat. Not being able to choose between the two, I decided to have both a pulling boat and a canoe, and I still can't say which one I love the most! No one craft is going to do all things perfectly; there is no universal boat, which I think is a most happy situation, for, if such a craft existed, she would be a most uninteresting thing. With a boat that would do it all, to me there would be no point at all in boating.

Now that I have come out in favor of canoes, I must make myself clear on my own outlook on them. Stock canoes and kayaks, readily available in many different makes, sizes, and materials, are not what I refer to, though these certainly fit many people's needs. I think they are great for those who want them.

To me, a person who has no interest in surf work, really fast water, long camping trips, competition, and little other of what these craft are best fitted for, they have no appeal at all, useful as they might be. Besides, I know little about them.

What I refer to as a canoe is what many now call a Rushton canoe, though there were many other builders of the type at one time. I became interested in these late in life after I found they are an adjunct to a good pulling boat. Since I designed and built my own Rushton-type canoe, I'm often asked why I would tackle such a difficult project when you can buy a cheap pack canoe right off the shelf. The answer, like so many to other simple questions, is not so simple. I like to design and build boats—the building of these ultra-light canoes is *not* the difficult project everyone thinks it is. In fact, it's much less time consuming and uses less material than the building of a worthwhile pulling boat. My present canoe and bateau took the same number of hours to build, though the bateau took twice the material. The boatbuilding skill required for both was the same, only different methods were used. Once I tried a wooden double-paddle canoe against all store-bought models I came across, I, for one, could go no other route.

I can also give you a strong argument for the double paddle. Once you have learned to use a well-designed double paddle, you wonder why the single is still in use. After designing and building many paddles, I have found, as with oars, that there are few, if any, really good paddles being made. True, some of the manufactured varieties are great for paddling over rocks, but, for easy cruising, they miss badly for the most part. As far as weight goes, the custom wooden paddles I cotton to are usually lighter than the manufactured ones—not always, but usually. The matter of weight becomes more important as the years catch up with me, so I stress the careful engineering of double paddles—a two and one-half pound paddle becomes quite heavy after a day's cruise.

To me at least, all boats should be good looking within the limits of their type. I can't say that I find any manufactured canoe now built downright handsome—some are plain ugly—but all this is just a matter of my own taste. There is no doubt in my mind that a handsome wooden double-paddle canoe is not only a nice thing to look at, but also a joy to use.

My somewhat limited experience with Rushton-type canoes does point out a few things: If you lean toward design, they are not difficult to do as long as you are guided by what has worked in the past and recognize the very tight limitations within which you must work. Well-designed double-paddle canoes "track" much better than factory-made ones as a general rule, and they are excellent seaboats as canoes go. Some are decked, but, the way I use such craft, I feel a built-on deck simply adds weight and complicates maintenance. I find that a snap-on canvas deck is all that is needed if you like to travel in the rain or in the cold months. Such a deck also turns away all the seas you should ever encounter, assuming, of course, you are smart enough to recognize that these canoes are not intended for heavy weather conditions.

These little Rushton-type hulls are of an ageless shape, about as easy-going for their size as man has ever developed. If a person has to go the store-bought route for his canoe, there are some pack canoes that do the job well, though if you ever use a real Rushton type, you will never be quite happy with the store job.

SOME BUILDING TIPS

This book is not intended to be a work on boatbuilding, but I've said that these wooden canoes are not nearly as difficult to build as they seem, so it might be well to back up my statements with a few pointers, in case you might want to build a double-paddle canoe. It has been said recently that no one now has the skill to build a Rushton-type canoe—that such boats *are* being built, and quite well, is apparent if you look around a bit. Anyone who can build a pulling boat, even one of a simple model, can, after that experience, build a canoe if he really wants to.

The now well-known book, *Rushton and His Times in American Canoeing* by Atwood Manley (Syracuse University Press), shows the lines of several double-paddle canoes, as well as much other

A fine example of an amateur-built 13' Culler double-paddle canoe, with Debbie Halleck paddling it in a beautiful setting. (Doug Halleck)

information on their evolution and building. A number of new canoes have been built right from the book. If you lean toward design, be guided by Manley's book and be guided by the limitations of such little boats. But do what else suits your fancy, just as long as you don't design a hull that is too wide or too deep.

Many Rushton-type canoes are true double-enders, so you can simply loft one quarter of the boat, which takes very little space, can be done on plywood on a workbench, and saves crawling about on your knees. The mold-making is simple; if you use five molds for a true double-ender, you will have two pairs of identical molds. Easy lofting and simple mold-making cuts out a lot of work customary in other boat types.

I'm well known for my preference for building lapstrake boats right-side up; most of the time I keep the craft on the stocks almost to the final finishing. If you prefer upside-down building, at least put the sheer on right-side up. Using either method, have a rigid setup and provide some way to hold the light stem and stern posts true, as they do not have the stiffness of a stout pulling boat stem. Setting up, rabbet cutting, etc., are in no way different from other boats, there is only less of it and the work is lighter. Tacks, some rivets, small screws, and glue are all the fastenings required, and, if you use the best of copper and bronze, might go as much as 3 pounds in a 12- or 13-footer.

Planking for a Rushton-type canoe should be cedar, upland or Atlantic, not over $\frac{1}{4}$ inch in thickness or a shade less. The number of strakes can be 6, 7, or maybe 8, depending on the size and model of the canoe. If equipped for planing on the job, I like to get my plank out of $\frac{3}{4}$-inch stuff, split on the table saw to make a pair. This gives you a boat with matched pairs of planks, which at one time were said to make a superior boat. I still think they do—besides, ripping two planks from one makes the job easier. If I can't make a plank in one length because

of short stock on hand, I don't worry—slash-glued scarfs are simple to make in the light stuff. Hand-dressing split planks is not all that difficult, but if you would rather avoid the chore, you can have your entire plank dressed at a mill. The latter is the more wasteful way of doing things, but, because of the size of the project, there really is not much waste to worry about.

Framing these little boats does require steam bending, which in this case is easy because the parts are so small and everything is easy to reach. Any device that can produce boiling water or steam is all

(continued on page 263)

Interior view of Capt. Pete's 13' double-paddle canoe Butternut.
(John Burke)

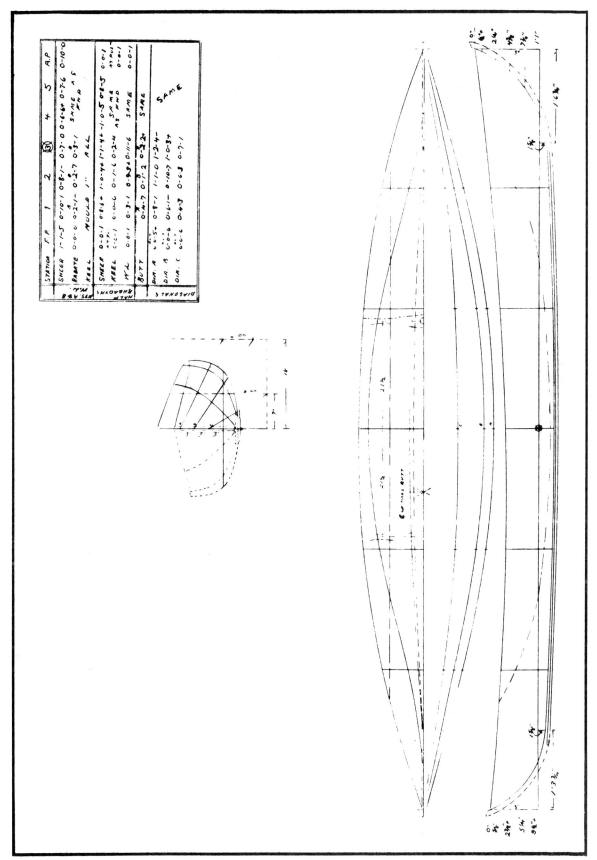

The lines of the canoe Butternut shown in the previous photo. (© Mystic Seaport, Ships Plans Collection, Mystic, CT)

Two fine double-paddle canoes, both built by Dr. John Roche. The one on the left is Cymba, *a stretched-out version of* Butternut *designed by Pete to accommodate two persons. On the right is a Rushton Wee Lassie.* (Ben Fuller)

An auxiliary fully battened lugsail works fine on Butternut. *This is Pete in a fresh breeze sailing in Lewis Bay just outside Hyannis Harbor.* (John Sherwood)

George Kelley with one of his canoes. George was a long-time friend and collaborator of Pete's. George was principally responsible for sparking Pete's interest in light craft and double-paddle canoes. (Richard Cahoon)

(continued from page 260)

that is needed. Most models of canoe require a steamed garboard, and once in a while you will find a model whose shape dictates steaming for other planks. Canoes, being sharp at both ends, allow a planking technique that is useful for those who have never yet steamed or hung a garboard. The technique is to put the garboard on in two lengths, with a fore hood and an after hood. You will have less to handle doing it this way, and you can simply use a scarf to join the two pieces. After you gain experience, you will be able to put on a garboard of any length in one piece.

I personally don't frame my canoes Rushton style, which calls for narrow, closely spaced frames. I use wide, flat frames spaced wider apart, but this is just my preference—either way makes a good boat. I'm sure the old-time builders of wooden canoes knew more about framing than I do, but the wider framing works well for me.

After planking and framing a Rushton-type canoe, the rest is simple finishing up. Always keep in mind the goal to achieve light weight, so use light stock—when in doubt, use cedar. Final weights will vary somewhat, even in boats of the same design. A 10- to 11-foot canoe, which is about as small as most people want to go for a one-man canoe, may weigh about 30 to 35 pounds. A-12- to 14-foot canoe, which is about as big as a one-man canoe should go, will weigh 38 to 44 pounds. Some builders can shade these weights a little if they use light stock and keep their wits about them, but it's very easy to get too heavy quickly if you don't watch out.

Some advice to weight watchers: No matter what you do, a canoe will use $2\frac{1}{2}$ to 3 pounds of

263

fastenings. The paint and varnish on my 13-foot canoe added three pounds to her. Varnish is lighter than paint, but white paint on a hull prevents drying out better than varnish, especially if the boat is car-topped. Obviously, your planking cedar should be well dried and well varnished or painted, or a combination of both, and the canoe, properly stored, should be tight when you use her.

My double-paddle canoe designs don't follow Rushton for a reason. I took into account that the boats would be used in waters now cursed with the wash of motor craft, and this wash is usually more confused than natural seas. I suppose this might be called defensive designing; I don't like it, but the boats get along well in man-made bedlam when they have to and avoid it when they can. The changes I made do not seem to affect their ease of paddling or handling.

I prefer rowing, and sailing if the boat is suited to it, but I would not be without a classic wooden double-paddle canoe.

A CRUISE IN A PULLING BOAT

Assuming you now have a suitable pulling boat, the proper gear, and proper stowage for your gear in the boat, and that by now your muscles are somewhat adjusted to more or less regular use of the boat, I will take you on a day cruise. Our cruise is not wholly imaginary, for it's about like those we take in these parts. To get a cruise started, there is some discussion and planning of such a cruise among those locally interested in manually operated craft, which often includes both canoes and pulling boats. A tentative date and waters are chosen; the choices are often governed by the time of year and the tides. A day or so before the event, there is much discussion back and forth, especially in the evaluation of the weather. In the past, through luck or good guessing, we have had a pretty good record in hitting the weather about right.

The day comes, and an early start is always made. Boats and oarsmen begin arriving at the chosen launching site. Sometimes there are many, often there are just a few—it does not matter, since the whole point is to go when it is convenient. That we would have a big gang, a group operation, or a mass outing is not the point at all. Anyhow, we launch

and start drifting off. Some craft have a single occupant, simply because that's what they are intended for; others may have passengers and crew, who take spells at oar or paddle.

The tide has started to ebb and the wind is a light land breeze offshore. Once under the bridge some suggest we take a look up that creek over to port, as these waters are all interesting and there is plenty of time. One cruiser sets his sail, but the wind is too light and the sail is soon taken in. The pace is slow and pleasant—those who have done much of this don't rush it. If some of the younger set are along (they are much encouraged to come), they will have their own boats for the day, as they will dart here and there, burning up the steam of youth. Later in the day they will simmer down.

After working out of the creek, a couple of boatmen think they can get a lay downriver by pulling up into a cove, and the breeze does seem to have improved slightly. They try it and make it, because they were able to get a stronger puff just when they needed it to clear the spit. The maneuver didn't amount to much speed, but it was fun. By now, those who have not seen the tiny child-size Rushton canoe in action before marvel at her ability

You can range far with two rowers taking turns. Pictured here is Waldo Howland and Glenn McNary aboard the Pete Culler designed and built round-bilged 18'6" pulling boat Punch *on sea trials.*

to keep up with the fleet with ease, and even run away from it at times. No one knows why, but a longer version of her is only a little faster, if that; she only has more capacity. A cruise such as this is a fine study of how well-shaped craft go through the water.

The harbor entrance is near, and there is a passage back of the dunes to another bay. The land wind is now very faint. Someone suggests an outside passage from one inlet to the other, as conditions are ideal for it. There is some discussion about when the sea breeze will set in; the consensus is that it will not appear for awhile, so offshore around it is. This is taking no chance at all, as the area seldom gets a real sea swell. The big risk is from the fast motor craft now starting to pour out of the inlets for whatever their business is offshore. Almost without exception, these craft make no attempt to slow down. The passage is narrow here, and, though we keep out of the way, we do run the risk of being thrown on the jetty, or being swamped by the man-made backwash from it. The operators of these craft

stare down at us from high flying bridges in a be-fogged sort of way. It's always a great point of discussion—once we get clear of this sort of "civilization"—as to whether the people who man these motor craft are boorish, stupid, or ignorant. The more tolerant among our fleet think these operators suffer from ignorance; the fellow who just got a lap full of water thinks otherwise. Being irascible myself, I lump them all under the label of idiot. Seriously, it's a real problem that has to be dealt with; further boating education and the encouragement of more courtesy, both ashore and afloat, seem to be the only answers, and both will bring very slow results.

This "outside" passage is most pleasant, and the boats settle to an even pace. This is fine, because those pulling double for the first time tend to set a pace that is too fast. The stroke oar should set the pace, which should be on the moderate side, and the other oar should follow it. By using boats the size we consider here, in light to calm weather, I doubt that rowing double is all that more efficient—fun, yes, but unless the boat is heavily loaded, or it's blowing hard, and the oarsmen are practiced at doubles, I think you will do just as well or better by spelling each other at singles. I also think that, for best results, a coxswain is needed to steer pulling doubles. Sometimes, in one of my own boats with three in her, which makes her well laden, we pull two oars—one oar to a man, plus a coxswain, spelling each other all around. Not a bad way to go on some days in some boats.

This is a most interesting aspect of rowing, so allow me to digress further for a bit. I think pulling with more than one pair of oars becomes more practical the bigger the boat. Boats should be from 16 feet on up. I can see the possibility of using boats up to 22 to 28 feet, and perhaps even 30 feet long, for crew rowing, if, and this is a big if, such craft are owned by a club. At one time, there were many rowing clubs; some are still around, though they are more or less dormant. In England at the present time there is a revival of interest in the old pilot gigs, many of which have been restored and put to use by rowing clubs for regattas and races. Even a new gig or two has been constructed. I think this is a fine way to go, and hope the present revival in rowing will encourage the formation of clubs to use larger boats. These big, fast craft are quite capable of coasting passages and hopping islands with little or no risk. That this sort of rowing was once common, there is no doubt. At present, schools that specialize in seamanship and outdoor living are undertaking some expeditions. The Massachusetts Maritime Academy, Outward Bound, the Mystic Seaport whaleboat crew, some Sea Scout groups, and a number of individuals I know or have heard about are doing some extended rowing, with more planned. I think this is great and urge such activities to continue, realizing we older

The round-bilged 16'8" Race Point surfboat built at the Maine Maritime Museum, with a full crew aboard. Note that the sculling oar can be used on either side of the steering yoke. (Lincoln Draper)

fellows should stay in the sheltered cricks ourselves. But, back to our cruise.

By now, we are about to enter inland waters again. This inlet has no jetty, simply a wide entrance with a dredged channel. We work out on the flats, as it's quite smooth, thus avoiding any close encounters with big craft. We note there is a slight ebb still running around the entrance spit. There is a nice beach and dunes just inside, and, though the tide is down, there is some clean sand for beaching. This is the spot for lunch, a dune ramble, or a nap. Boats are grounded and moored properly, as the tide will soon be on the rise. Some of the lighter craft are simply put up in the grass by the many hands available. It seems quite hot on the beach, but some observer says the sea breeze is striking in, and sure enough we find it quite pleasant up on the edge of the dunes. There we have a fine view out into the Sound, where sailing craft are coming to life after the morning calm.

This is all very pleasant, and soon an hour is gone. It's time to clean up the site, get afloat, and head for the little river, which, from the past two week's wet weather, should have a considerable freshet in it. Since we have a fair wind and now also a fair current, some set sail, and it's not long before we are in narrow waters. The color of the water changes, and there is noticeable ebb. We are in fresh water. This is narrow going in some parts. The flora and fauna take on a different look, there is tupelo and holly in places, and we approach an interesting marsh with a structure at the head of it—a pumphouse, for we are up into cranberry bog country. This is the head of navigation, even for canoes, so all hands head downriver. In the lower reach, there is quite a breeze funneling right up, so we face some smart pulling until we are around the bend, where conditions then become more or less fair for the home stretch. Those who have it set sail, some taking a canoe in tow. Some of the very lean pulling

Capt. Pete and crew with the round-bilged 18' fast gig Quitsa Pilot *at the Mystic Seaport Small Craft Workshop. During his lifetime Pete Culler faithfully attended every one of these workshops, always bringing his latest creation to share and never failing to delight those in attendance. He was an inspiration and the standard by which all other attendees were measured.* (Ben Fuller)

boats are extremely fast with a small sail and the wind broad on the quarter, and they are soon way ahead of the rest. We are part of an Old World scene, something out of an old print or painting—these handsome little craft going about their business.

What we really have been doing is circumnavigating a large island situated in inland waters bounded by dunes, creeks, covers, and small streams. The returning fleet will end its cruise at the landing it started from, without any back tracking. As we straggle in, the wind is now fresh, the tide is coming fast, and there is a surge from harbor traffic. We snatch the boats out as they come in to avoid a pounding, and take our time loading, each helping the others. We allow as how it's been a fine cruise, finished just right. Someone always has part of a chart along; mileage is toted up—just about 11 nautical miles, not allowing for all the twists and turns. Each goes his way, now thinking of another cruise in other waters. There's time enough to get home and wash the boat leisurely before supper.

I leave it to my readers to determine if this is fun or not. To me, it always is, even if it rains.

(Chris Wentz)

ARTICLES

OLD WAYS WORK

In these modern days of wonder materials, new methods and what seems at times total reliance on the chemical industry, it may seem strange, not to say foolish, to urge going back to some of the more simple things of the past. Many of these apply to boats and vessels, as well as finding uses in other applications.

Just why should we go back? The main reason is, old ways and materials work, are for the most part readily available, not expensive as things go now, usually are nontoxic (some may be even somewhat digestible!), are easy to use and are a satisfaction to work with—something which is not always so when using some packaged thing out of a spray can. There is no problem of disposal for instance, which can be a danger with a spray can. I always wonder what trouble one of these things might cause when I send an empty on its way to the dump. Personal notion only. I feel anything in a spray can is just a way of doing an inferior job quickly and paying the price of the contraption to boot.

Linseed oil, and I refer mostly to boiled oil, is a most useful thing to have around a boat, shop, shipyard or any place things are built or repaired. Cut, added to or mixed with some other simple things, it can do a lot. Cut with kerosene "to make it drive in," it's a fine primer for new, exposed woodwork. Turpentine can be used just as well, but kero is cheaper if it's to be used in large amounts. Some say a paint primer is better, and in some cases it is; but where marks and figures can be lost by covering with paint, as is common in boat work, oil and kero do just fine. Nothing is more irritating, to me at least, than when work has been carefully laid out, marks made so no mistake is apt to happen, then some dope paints them out!

A gallon of boiled linseed oil, a pint of turps and a pint of pine tar, mixed, preferably when the oil is warm, is what I call "deck oil." This is fine for unpainted decks of working craft, inside of skiff and bateau bottoms that are unpainted, and, in the past, bottoms of log canoes. The same mix is also fine for a starter coat for wooden spars and other woodwork that will not be painted very soon. Wooden cleats, pins, ship's blocks, and any other small wooden items soaked for a month in this stuff become extremely hard in time and nearly weather proof. It's good for the bed of an elderly pickup truck—puts new life in the box, which then outlasts the rest of the rig. Apply to a dry box, under a blazing sun, and don't spare it, and it does real business. Another, and lesser coat, later on finishes the job.

A much used and aging boat trailer can be a discouraging sight—you are going to paint it but don't get around to it. Long drawn out business to do it right anyhow. Probably needs sandblasting. So if she's real bad, bang on her with a hammer enough to get the big rust flakes off and follow with a good blasting with a hose to get any salt out of all the corners, then let dry. Pick a dry nor'west day, if possible, and tuck the deck oil to the rig. It seems to like some rust and runs and penetrates where no paint ever can. A second coat sometime later is a good idea. Not pretty, but it sure takes to rust.

This, of course, applies to any metal work. If you do metal work requiring heat, when the job is done and still hot, say a black heat, quench it in the oil and you have even better protection. This was an old-time smith's trick and as explained to me by an old master at it, "heat opens the pores in the iron and it drinks in the oil, which immediately oxidizes under the heat." If it's so or not, I don't know, but it works!

I feel timber for bent boat frames takes steam and bends better if soused, say the night before steaming, with kerosene, cut with just enough oil so the kero stays around for a spell. Certainly kerosene has the ability to penetrate dry, or reasonably dry wood, as a simple test will show; kero, or something very similar (mineral spirits) is the base for many wood preservatives.

Some old-timers claim kerosene alone will drive the moisture out of green wood—my experience has been that it does to a great extent. No steam box being handy, a plank well soaked in kero, say overnight, will usually bend into place when, if left dry or even soaked in water, it might not go without breaking. Personally, I rely on this method very much, with or without steam.

To get back to using this deck oil mix on metal. A mooring which is pulled up and hauled ashore for the winter rusts and scales rather badly, much salt being in the iron. Here again, what's needed is a good pounding and much washing with fresh water under pressure, then a spell of drying and a coat of oil, which bites right in and carries things till spring, when the mooring is far less messy to handle.

Pine tar now seems unknown to most people, yet it's quite commonly available. Put a dab of it on a mooring or anchor shackle and the fitting will unscrew with ease years later. Same applies to turnbuckles, galvanized iron or bronze, or any outdoor screw thread. Total submerging over long periods seems to have no effect on pine tar. (Naturally, shackles for serious work should be wired.)

Tallow seems now to be totally forgotten as a shop lubricant, or for the same use on boats and vessels. Many people don't seem to know just what it is anymore, let alone where to get it.

Some butchers still try-out tallow, but it's very simple to make your own, as all it is the fat scrap from meat melted down and cleaned up. Trying-out fat scraps slowly is no chore in an iron skillet—most kitchens tend to produce waste fat anyhow. To clean it up, simply simmer it very slowly in a large amount of water. This lets the dark burnt stuff, salt and other impurities settle out. A long simmer is good, then let it cool and simply lift the congealed tallow from the water in chunks. For places of chafe, say oarlocks, gaff jaws, mast hoops, etc., nothing seems to work so well. This was the stuff of the days of sail. The cook set aside what the ship did not use. He often sold it on making port, unless the skipper was a tight-fisted sort, in which case HE got the graft.

For shop use, I mostly dilute tallow with kerosene so it can be used in an oil can; say, a good big tablespoon, melted, poured into a pint or less of oil. Nothing does quite as well keeping power tool tables in good shape while insuring an easy and steady feed. For sawing heavy timber, it's the next best thing to proper rollers.

I use tallow a lot for the dumb center of a wood-cutting lathe, and it's useful in metal turning and thread cutting with these additions: some white lead and enough tallow added to oil to make a thin paste. (Note that now white lead seems to go on the "No" list, like bootleg whiskey.) Powdered sulfur will do the same job. This is not the best cutting oil, but it's pretty good, and you can get by if the manufactured stuff is not on hand. In fact, some old-time machinist books go into detail on making cutting oil. Though a small matter, I find modern auto lube oil not too good for some shop work—it's intended for high-speed bearings under high heat and somehow does not have the slip that the above mixes have for crude work.

Modern quick-dry paints have some very good points. "Skinning over" once a can is opened is not one of the good ones. When about to close up the can after use, clap the lid partly on, and carefully blow a long breath into the can and button it up quick; this is supposed to displace some oxygen. It's by no means perfect, but does help some when working out of the same can every day or so. I imagine a breath smelling strong of onions and tobacco might be just the thing.

Most people have some interest in wood, varying from passive to very active. A large number are sort of in between because they think wood is hard to come by, especially if exotic. So much good stuff goes to waste, just because it's misunderstood or can't be seen for the trees! If you tend to look up instead of always at your feet, you may often spot a few boards, long forgotten, stored overhead in a barn or shed where it's had a good cooking for years, being close to the roof. Often it's some very interesting type of wood, or just pine boards. Sometimes it can be had for the asking, or a very small sum, since it may be cracked, warped and way too dry.

If it's likely looking stuff otherwise, get it, then put down sleepers, level both ways, outdoors. Stick and stack the stuff carefully, weighed down heavily and put on a good cover—tar paper will do, but fix it so it won't blow off. Cover so ends and sides get plenty of air.

Put down this way in the fall, and going through till April, the pile will pick up its moisture content again and much of the warp will be pressed out. The result will be a lot of quite useful wood. The rents will still be there, and other lumber defects, but it's now pretty nice stock.

Not including lumbering operations, trees are being felled all the time—for firewood, clearing land, house lots and "developments." Much of this goes to waste. These tree destructors nearly always spoil any possible knees, for they saw at the elbows, never clear of them, for a crooked knee is most unhandy to throw into a truck. A good lookout, your own tools, the right approach and you may be allowed to help destroy a likely apple tree, cutting it properly so as to save the knees and often getting a passable piece of trunk for real timber. I've found if you explain just what you are after, most tree-cutters will cooperate to a great extent—they don't quite understand it, but if you don't slow things up much they go along with it.

Nice apple, cherry, locust, walnut, elm and many other woods are excellent for so many projects, and all of these take kindly to use in boats as well as cabinet work. Often someone's woodpile can turn up likely stock for all sorts of parts and fittings, at no cost for superior material. All it takes is a sharp eye, a rag-picker's makeup and some know-how to work the stuff up, and this last is not at all difficult to learn.

Let's assume you've acquired a chunk about 3' or 4' long, and 12" or more in diameter. It can be split lengthways with a chain saw. Then it's quite possible to saw it through quartering with the aid of a table saw or a hand electric saw, partly finishing it with a hand or band saw. If the bandsaw will take something more than 6" it will do the whole job, and of course quarter sawing can be continued for all of it.

274

Smaller diameter stuff can have a flat hewed on one side with an axe, no chainsaw being handy, and finished up as before. It's not the hardest work to do it all with hand tools, provided they are sharp. Locust is especially good—handsome to look at, shrinks practically not at all, turns well, takes a nice finish and is excellent for pins, cleats and anywhere that strength, durability, along with good looks are required. Apple is excellent for knees—nothing quite like it—as apple as well as pear grow crooked by nature. Both have handsome

grain, hard and durable, but require some drying. The common elm of New England is very hard and tough, is not a handsome wood. Still it makes fine wood bull's-eyes, deadeyes and things requiring great strength. A usable knee can often be got out of a crotch.

All sorts of wood turn up on woodpiles—it's a matter of locality. Occasionally one finds ash, walnut, tupelo, and others that are considered very hard to come by. I have made mallets and got knees of mulberry from a woodpile, and nice stuff it is. Some

Capt. Pete's Swampscott dory Dancing Feather, *which was neither built nor designed by Pete, but who made it his own by applying the "old ways" to the boat. This included removing the outboard well it came with, and adding a centerboard and mast partners to utilize various traditional rigs he would design and build for the boat. In addition, he fit the dory with tholepins for rowing and built proper oars to use with them. And he gave the boat a traditional color scheme with paint, oil, and tar treatments to assist its preservation and transform it into a classic small boat for all who saw her.*

old railroad ties from certain parts of the country are walnut—which is quite durable. Really old Cape Cod light poles are often chestnut. Cedar short stuff, to be worked over, is now available from most fence companies in the New England states. Cherry of various kinds is usually available for the taking where trees are being removed.

Old buildings coming down may have excellent timber, and some big craft have taken benefit of the big hard pine timbers, professionally resawed. There is also much good smaller stuff: hard pine, cypress and excellent trim pine. Occasionally walnut and cherry come from what was once a first-class dwelling. Nail and bolt holes there are, to be sure, but boring out and bunging take care of this. I've seen very nice wide pine tables made from an attic floor probably 175 years old. Graving pieces of various shapes and colors of wood covered the rusty nail holes. No one was the wiser; they thought this gave considerable charm!

Usable iron and steel go to waste like wood these days. Much excellent tool steel hits the scrap pile. Working tool steel brings to mind the picture of a craftsman of much skill and training—few think they dare attempt it. Yet, to make simple things takes little skill; more skill develops as you go. Besides, the stock is junk, and free, so you can afford mistakes in learning. For one thing, I refer to worn-out files; they come in all sizes and shapes, from tiny to big old soakers. These are prime stuff for some tools, and in small and modest sizes, at least, are easily worked (you will spoil a couple at first) with readily available heat.

Anything, including a gas stove, which will give a red heat on modest-size files is adequate. More heat than this, and you can easily burn and ruin this type of steel. If you lack regular blacksmith tongs, a big stout pair of pliers will do. Also needed is a hammer, any hammer, though there is often more than one, so one may be more suitable than another. A chunk of iron, more or less flat on one side—a short piece of rail is OK—will serve as an anvil. A grinder, and a cold chisel to cut off a hot end, will get you started. Later on, if your interest holds and increases, a small forge may be wanted.

Two very useful tools require no heat at all. The first is what used to be known as a bearing scraper; few scrape bearings anymore, but I find this item much used in my shop as a deburring tool. Simply choose a three-corner file, worn out naturally, or more than one so as to have different sizes, and grind all three sides, fore and aft, not sideways, until the teeth are entirely gone and the edges are sharp (they will be very sharp). The tool can be whetted on a stone for fine edge. Put on a wooden handle— you may want to tape the point for two-hand use. This whole operation has taken only a few minutes. It can even be done on a water stone, though it takes longer. This is a fine tool for deburring any sharp metal edges, and in some cases scraping of soft metals, and has cost nothing but time.

With the second tool, you start as above, and here you may want three or four sizes. Grind the file, then grind around the tang near where it thickens, and break off—the file is usually soft here. What you now have will fit nicely into a standard three-jaw electric drill chuck; if the file butt is too big, reduce it by grinding, and try and remove the same amount on each side. This makes a red hot and rapid tool for drilling out loose knots in say, cedar planking. The sharp point searches out the run of the knot, and the tool leaves a clean, tapered hole, just what you want for plugging. It's also not a bad drill for boring thin stock if you don't happen to have the real thing in the proper size; a stopgap to be sure, but it gets the job along.

While on the subject of drills, if small holes are needed and a drill the right size is not on hand, various sizes of common nails, with the heads cut off, points beaten cold to a spear shape, and then ground to approximately an included angle of 90 degrees, with some back relief, will do the job. Grinding can control the diameter. Being soft, they don't last, but often get the job done.

I hang on to sail needles with broken eyes. Being quite hard, they make fine small drills, especially for clinch fastening light lapstrake boats where plank is so thin the common copper tack is used. A small wood stop on the needle controls the depth of bore. The hole is tapered, which is just what you want for a tack, so it completely fills the hole, leaving no slack on the inside. Of course, you can grind standard drills to a taper, but then they don't suit another job—the altered sail needle is all you need.

Flat files come in various sizes; occasionally you get a real big one, often much rusted. These are big enough and long enough to supply stock for a couple of plane irons—narrow, smoothing or rabbet. Many craftsmen end up making planes, and John Gardner has written much about it in *National Fisherman*. Plane irons are hard to come by; good wood for them is not, as mentioned earlier in discussing the availability of wood. One of my best working planes is elm—not pretty, but very hard.

For a smoothing plane iron, take the biggest flat file and grind off the tang. Half way along its length, grind with the edge of the wheel all around it, at least halfway through. Put it in the vise at this point and a sharp blow on the upper half will break it off. You now have stock for two irons.

Now grind off the teeth. The pattern does not have to totally disappear except near what will be the top of the cutting edge—if this is not smooth, naturally you will end up with a serrated cutting edge. If the rest of it feels smooth to the hand even though the pattern has not been totally removed, it is sufficient. One end will have a taper. Keep this up in the plane and square off the lower end with the other piece, round up the soft tang end and square the other. Then grind the square ends to a plane iron bevel.

This is a lot of grinding but worth it. A big, powerful grinding wheel is an advantage, especially with a rather coarse stone, as it makes less heat. Have plenty of water for quenching. Some will say this file stuff is too hard for plane irons and will chip and be difficult to whet. Not so. A little judicious "burning" in grinding will sufficiently soften the edge.

It's said a plane won't work without a cap iron. With a thin iron, this is so, but these extra-thick irons don't need any. Being very stiff and rigid, they hold an edge.

I have several planes of various models made this way. I have found out this: Besides cutting the throat and wedge ways, as explained before in *National Fisherman*, and to suit the thickness of the new iron, I like my smoothing planes at a 50 degree angle. Lengths simply suit the fancy, and sometimes the particular block of wood—this goes for the general shape, too. Some manufactured wooden planes are very uncomfortable to hold and work with. I frequently put a wood handle and knob on even a smoothing plane. The German horn instead of a knob is good, too. The bed in the block for the iron to rest on should be dead flat or very slightly hollow—never rockered even a little or the plane will chatter. I like to grind the bevel on the iron only slightly less than the angle it makes with the bottom of the plane—just so the heel never drags. And grind it HOLLOW, using the natural round of the grinding wheel. With the above bevel, a 50 degree angle, and the plane otherwise right, there is a great deal of metal backing the cutting edge, which lasts and lasts with no chipping unless you strike an open knot with sand in it. This ruins any edge.

Rabbet and beading planes can be made the same way, using smaller flat files. I find the narrower-than-standard, lower-angle smoothing plane superior to the standard angle and width for most work, especially spar work. Imagination can run wild with designs and models of planes and other special use tools.

To get back to files as source of material for other tools. Now we need some heat; red is enough. I have, through the years, collected some good carving and light-work cutting tools, mostly English and very good. Many needed much restoring. Still, there were shapes not on hand I felt need of (or maybe it was the need of just making). Small files do fine here, and again I say only a red heat—too much and some of this metal turns to mush. While a forge can be used, it requires some practice with its use, as you have at hand far more heat than needed. Gas stove, wood or coal fire, propane torch, any will do fine. After all, in far-off places forging is still done squatting in the open before a small charcoal fire, bamboo bellows, all very primitive. But nice work is turned out.

Heat and hammer, heat and hammer, as this light metal does not hold heat long, and beating it when it's too cool can break it. Small paring tools—straight, skew, angle, vee—can be made as well as gouges of all shapes, and bevels. Lengths are made to suit, and in all shapes, bent, half bent, spoon, etc. No limit. Finish by grinding.

Now the matter of cutting edge. Grind to shape and whet, and then try for hardness. Some of this material is air hardened and you may find things just right. If not, brighten up the working end and experiment with heat and water. Watch for the color near the working end. This is not a how-to on tempering—if you have gotten this far, you will no doubt pick up the rest. Most old machinist books go considerably into tempering. For such wood-working tools, I use a color somewhere between light and a dark straw. Simply experiment until you get an edge that will hold.

Now, if you get taken up by this sort of thing, and a forge is available, possibilities are unlimited, as is the stock to work with. A garage which works on big vehicles often has broken truck springs out back. This is prime stuff for big tools. Need I say more?

Often some sort of wood-turning lathe is around, or a beat-up metal one is converted for wood. Actually, a homemade wood lathe of considerable ability is not difficult to build. Many have no doubt seen small lathes in museums that were built aboard sailing vessels on long voyages, notably whalers. Cutting tools for such machines I make totally from files, usually just by grinding and fitting a stout wood handle, with a pipe or tubing ferrule. The handiest ferrule stock for any tool handle is common galvanized steel electric conduit—it comes in several diameters and scraps are readily available.

I am no great ecology nut, or maybe I always was without being aware of it, as the word was not known in every household when I started in. The various approaches above mentioned have been a great source of satisfaction, and give a feeling of independence. Knowledge of being able to work over what appear to be useless things can, at some time in one's life, be a real life-saver. My preaching along this line is often not taken seriously, for now many consider it "work," something to be avoided at all costs. Idling away at the boob tube may be some people's idea of living—after all, their set is the most expensive in the neighborhood. Different ships, different long splices, but somehow I feel they miss a lot.

BOATBUILDING...USED TO BE

Based on considerable experience, I've found that frugality has its strong points. Some will take issue, which is fine, but time has proven that the economical way is a pretty good way. I'm reminded of the country auctioneer, starting off a session—the bidding tends to drag at first, everyone sitting on his hands. Finally some wag bids a quarter, and the hoary and instant rejoinder is, "Can you afford it!" This is supposed to bring down the house.

Acquiring a boat, by whatever means, usually starts with some sort of dream; dreams, by the way, are cheap. By the time it's felt something really concrete must be done, it's well to consider: can you afford it? Then you usually reconsider.

The success of any boat-owning is to have a craft to suit your means, and if she has to be small and simple, she's usually more satisfactory than a boat that's a strain to own. A rule of thumb, used when I started in, still holds today. To build a boat costs more, and takes more time than you think; usually about twice the usual estimate, so it very much pays to start thinking simple right off.

The point is to keep your mistakes to a minimum, no matter how you acquire a boat. This rule applies whether the boat is home-built, partly built by a pro and finished by the owner, or a totally professional job.

However the boat is built, a proper lofting job is essential. I know of nothing better to get a craft off to a good start, be she a skiff or a sawn-frame vessel. I have read opinions of some who think too much is made of lofting. It's been my experience that a hasty and sketchy lofting job "to save on hours" has always taken more hours later on to straighten out, much to the disgust of an experienced workman who may be on the job. True, an experienced loftsman knows a few tricks and can prove out lines quicker than the less experienced, but he's thorough, for he knows the pitfalls.

Having come this far in creating a boat, it's assumed it was decided long ago what she's to be built of. For modest craft at least, wood is the most likely to be available and the most readily worked of all materials, shortage jazz and all that to the contrary. If one has the abilities and equipment, or can afford to buy the equipment, steel has a lot going for it in larger craft and for certain uses. It is not economical or easy to turn out a very shapely and handsome craft in steel. But wood and steel can be worked anywhere in any climate. Those who have worked wood and steel in big yards know all about this.

Fiberglass is, of course, the Now thing, yet for one-of-a-kind craft, and building where you must, it falls on its face. (I hear all sorts of static building up.) Controlled weather is essential, and a mold is long, drawn-out work. For instance, quite a good building is required, especially in the Northeast, and some control of humidity is necessary. Why build a mold which takes as much time as a finished boat, and then have yet to build the boat? This is neither sensible nor economical.

If you are going to build many hulls, you are competing with Big Industry, and can't afford to. If you are only competing with the guy across the creek doing glass, he's probably going broke, and as Ralph Wiley, the noted designer and builder recently pointed out, it makes no sense to compete with *him*.

Aluminum as a medium to build boats with has certain advantages for certain craft. Knowing well a builder of racing boats who uses this stuff, and being aware of his skills and the vast amount of equipment he uses, I say it's not the way to build simple craft, at least for now.

Ferro-cement I admit to knowing little about, although in a modest way I've tried to educate myself to it. This last has been most discouraging, as I've not yet met a man who really knew what he was doing. Many of these admitted to their ignorance, and a few others quoted wisely from printed matter. They didn't really know either.

Those boats I've inspected, mostly unfinished (they seem to more or less stay that way), were lumpy, strange in shape, and in some cases really out of shape. A new one, afloat, said to be built by pros, had every disease known to medicine; galvanic crud, pimples, boils, flakes, rudder falling off, you name it. And it cost a mint of money; nothing simple about it. Someone should have been sued,

except they probably had nothing to sue for. My little experience with ferro, all looking and no building, makes it seem that it's the hard way to come up with nothing, at least from the average man's standpoint.

So if you have never built a boat before, and want to try and will have to learn, you might as well save your money and learn with the most versatile, workable and very much available material—wood. At least it's had a bit of testing; how much, we don't know for sure; maybe 6,000 years, in boats at least.

Like all materials, wood has some weaknesses, one being that it's impractical to build a vessel much over 300' with it and still be sure of holding her together. I have before me a stock list in pounds for a 252' wooden vessel of the past. Among other things, there were over three million lbs. of lumber in her, and 58,000 lbs. of fastenings. Large wooden vessels have been built by the hundreds and hundreds, and there is still wood enough for most practical boatbuilding purposes, even for craft of good size.

Of the world's resources man keeps digging into, wood is the one that most tends to replace itself if let alone for a spell. Man can even help it along. I think there is more tree planting of many kinds now than, say 100 years ago. That we waste wood and sell it out of the country for a big buck, there is no doubt, but some useful kinds are ignored by all. Wood is bio-degradable, which is more than can be said of some products. When you are done with a wooden boat you can always break her up and burn her, thus heating the shop while you create another. Or save some of the better stuff and build a rocking chair.

I have very little knowledge of big-time lumbering operations, but quite some experience with small local mills, which is where most small-time boatbuilders get their stock, directly or indirectly. Nearly all the small-mill operators I know like trees, and for reasons more than just what they can make from them. Some people may doubt this and feel lumber dealers are just a bunch of tree butchers, but if such doubters would work along with these lumbermen for a few months, they would soon see. The work is often brutal and very risky, but something about it gets to you if you can stand the gaff. There are certainly easier ways to make a living. A number of lumbermen have admitted to me they always feel a twinge, quite unexplainable, when they fell a prime tree. I know little of the pros and cons of clear cutting and selective cutting; it appears the lay of the land and type of forest have a lot to do with it.

The lumbermen I'm acquainted with all agree that trees can and do get beyond their prime, and then are on the way out, like all living things.

One excursion into the woods with one of these men, to look at spar trees he had located, was most instructive. There were three fine trees that looked suitable. One apparently hearty specimen the lumberman was doubtful of, as he thought she might "have gone by." We took the three, and he was right, the suspect one was not fit for a mast, although it made some good boards.

Anyone using much cedar, swamp or upland, knows the bigger trees often show heart rot, especially in the lower part, where you thought to get some real wide plank. Seems to me the Lord intended for man to build boats, and provided the trees for them, and no doubt He expected their use to be gone at with common sense and discretion.

In these days of huckstering and buying everything "Off-The-Shelf," acquiring material for a boat can be frustrating if you have never done it before. Yet it's simply done just like it always was. You look up a small mill and take your problems to its proprietor. He's willing to listen and can give you some pointers while he's taking your order.

For such an important thing as a boat, you don't usually get good lumber at once, off the pile. Careful figuring, consultations, and an order is put in, to be filled when and how the mill man can. There may be some suitable logs on hand, or maybe they

are stacked along a lumbering road that's impassable until it freezes or there is a long dry spell. Cedar swamps are usually only accessible during a real cold winter.

For the small-boat builder, the mill may have an interesting pile of "shorts" around, and occasionally some quite exotic stuff. Some of these places have a small clientele of cabinetmakers, so often ash, hickory, cherry, walnut, and other nice stuff may be on hand. Someone is always looking for tupelo to make rollers.

Don't expect to find the woods you read about in yachting books at these small mills. Teak, mahogany and marine plywood they don't have; these are "imports" from away. So what else is there to build a boat out of? Well, a standard dory, built by a good dory-builder, is a masterpiece in its way of the use of simple and economical boatbuilding materials. They last quite well, and are simply pine, oak, spruce where it's available, and not much else. Note I say "available," for trying to build out of what's difficult to get is not sensible. If for some reason a gold-plater is required, and I make no comment if such a craft is sensible or not, then timber from far off has its place.

Open, or partially open, boats tend to ventilate easily, so timber that might not be quite suitable in grade for a decked craft is quite usable. I think good fits and construction that tends to prevent leaks and the lodging of fresh water is more important here than is the use of some wood noted for its durability. Sloppy build, and the best of teak and Honduras can soon go bad.

Keeping any boat really clean adds many years to her life. In the Northeast at least, the eastern white pine is one of the finest woods, usable in many ways. It makes a fine schooner mast, or good planking, and wonderful decking as well as cabin construction.

Oaks there are many kinds of, white being considered tops; yellowbark quite good, and various others. One can get in lots of arguments about oak. Some say anything else but the two mentioned above is "red oak"; maybe it is, but some kinds are very dense and heavy and have been much used for shipbuilding.

Spruce is great stuff. Black spruce makes fine spars, and some other kinds make good planking, some of it very suitable for very light lapstrake craft. Ash is often available, and although not considered durable in wet, closed spaces, it makes good framing for some small craft as it bends well and is quite hard. Cedar is always usable, even though most of it requires much boring and plugging of loose knots.

Lumber from small mills should be ordered round-edge, or what some call flitch-cut, that is with the bark on the edges. You save the price of edging, have more wood to work with, and are able to work the curves of a plank to the grain. I find it very irritating to get boat plank out of square-edge stuff. There is much shifting of the spiling batten, trying various boards, looking for the extra inch you need—and you can darn well see where there was a nice extra bit on the butt, if some fool had not ordered it edged. Most imported lumber or that shipped long distances is square-edge, for it takes up less space in a car or ship.

Personally, I hate to plank with what is many boatbuilders' favorite import: Philippine mahogany. It is always square-edge, often has a grain that is hard to finish, is hard to see marks on in a dark shop (all shops seem to have a dark place), and some of it seems very porous and open. You can blow through quite a length of it, and it often has a dark straw-like look. Iron fastenings tend to rot it out.

But why use galvanized iron? Well, bronze screws now cost nearly 10 cents apiece retail, small ones at that, and that fact may make you consider the economic sense of it all. This is one reason for my distaste for Philippine, which is really not a mahogany anyhow.

Of course, at times you find some nice, real dark red, very hard and dense stuff (you can't blow through it like a straw). This is real good in the right boat, in the right spot with fastenings to agree with it. I guess my distaste for Philippine may stem from early exposure to Honduras and Santo Domingo mahogany, which are the real things. What few scraps of these I still have are apt to be part of an extension fence on power tools. This real mahogany does not wear, is slippery, and seems to stay straight for years.

Oregon pine is, as far as the East Coast is concerned, an "import." Many people think this a poor boatbuilding wood. A little delving into the history of it, which I will not go into here, will show it's one of the finest if used with common sense and in the right place. Construction grade, as sold in lumber yards, can be used with some picking over. At a premium price, it can be had in very long, clear lengths, and the shipping cost is now frightful. Naturally, you do a lot of picking over in the cheaper grades.

Of course, everyone thinks of doing it with plywood, but the going price of it, either poor grade or very good, makes you think twice. The good grade is none too good; any lesser is apt to bring troubles later. Besides, just what shape of craft you can build with it economically is limited.

Having worked plywood by the mile in war years, I now seldom touch the stuff. It has shaping limitations, high cost, awkward handling for a loner, problems in getting a good finish, it's dulling to the tools, and when you get the job done, it still looks like plywood. There's no satisfaction at all in it. Besides, to do a really good job with it takes more time than with boards. If this be treason, well—.

There are, of course, many other readily available and good woods for simple boatbuilding. If you live far south, cypress is still around, and loblolly pine. Maine offers, besides other woods previously mentioned, Norway pine, and plenty of hackmatack, a wood apparently little understood now. There is locust in some places, and this is fine for wooden fittings, having almost no shrinkage. It can be used green and is said to last forever. Knees can be got out of most of this stuff. Most of the parts of a felled tree that are wasted, just trimmed off and left, can usually turn up a knee or two, and sometimes many.

Recently a man nearby, who was supposed to know something of trees, was sent out looking for an order of knees. After days of tramping, so he said, he could not turn up one; possibly he was too busy watching out for snakes.

Some time back I had occasion to order timber for a schooner. I visited an old-time mill man and gave him my story, then asked could he supply 50% of it "compass timber." His faded eyes lit, he did a double take, and immediately said yes. He knew sawing for vessels, and although the rickety mill looked very poor, when the loads started coming to the building site, it was just great. He took the trouble to bring his bill in person, so as to see if I was happy with it. I certainly was.

Putting a wooden boat together takes some sort of fastenings, and, as previously mentioned, bronze is now very expensive; bought in quantity it is less so, but still very costly. What we used to refer to as "yellow metals"—copper, bronze, brass, etc.—in the form of fastenings, rod and plate, are all very dear now.

For very light lapstrake craft, yellow metal is still the thing to use, as the fastenings, though many, are light. The smaller the fastening, the more it seems to suffer from corrosion, probably just because there is not much there to begin with. A big iron bolt or spike can become fairly rusty without losing much of its strength, and the rust does not seem to affect its holding power.

Except for very light, high-performance craft, I strongly suggest the use of galvanized boat nails, ship spikes where there is enough wood, and

galvanized iron bolts. Where drifts are practical, they hold better than a screw bolt. Over-long and odd-length bolts can be made from drift rod with the aid of a die set, stock nuts and clinch rings; this is the way it always has been done.

In some places you have to use galvanized screws. If practical, I avoid it when I can. Although long out of style, when the chips are down, one can use the old-time trunnel, called a wooden peg by some. This is an excellent fastening where there is wood enough.

This approach to fastenings has, in recent years, been much looked down on, yet in the past it was the standard way. I've worked on many a boat, and have owned a few built this way, and the life

Capt. Pete's shop in Hyannis, Massachusetts. This is where he built small craft up to 20 feet for Concordia Company. All of Pete's design work was done here as well. (© Mystic Seaport, Richard White Collection, Mystic, CT)

expectancy seems to be 30 to 50 years, depending on the use and care such a craft gets—far longer than most people now ever keep a boat. Until a person has had considerable experience in tearing apart and rebuilding old craft, he has no real knowledge of the value of galvanized iron fastenings.

I hear yak as to how old craft all had wrought iron, and that's why they lasted. Ha! The Bessemer process was around when the Brooklyn Bridge was built. Wrought iron in vessels, in the memory of anyone living, is rare, and then only for special use and usually at government expense.

A boat built of simple, modestly priced materials will last if—and this is the rub—she is well joined and fastened, ventilated, does not leak in the topwork, and has good and understanding care. What helps this last is a craft suited to her use, of good model, and handsome to look at, even though she be just spruce and fir. I don't see how anyone can love an ill-shaped box.

One last blow at fastenings. For some reason no one can quite explain, there is sometimes rather rapid failure of good bronze and copper even in a craft that has no electric stuff in her and which gets good care. What goes on no one is able really to say—whether it is the wood, the batch of fastenings she's got, or the waters that float her. Nearby, other less fancy craft seem to want to live forever. It's blamed on using soap on the screws, sweat on the builder's hands, tobacco juice and witchcraft.

Boats use some paint and other compounds during building, much in finishing up, and a great lot during the rest of their lives. I have little knowledge of the big-time paint industry, although I've consulted with local paintmakers. The thing is pretty fundamental; you use good materials and get good paint at a price. Chalk and water are cheap, and don't make good paint.

For what it's worth, I'm known as a pretty good mixer of colors and blender of paints, and my application of them is not bad. There are some things you

can do, many of them now forgotten, and some things you should never do.

Unless the craft I'm working on is a very yachty goldplater, I never use so-called boat paints, except on the bottom. This has been my practice for a long, long time. I'm often chided about it, yet the years, and the way the boats look and last, bear me out.

By now, I certainly feel I know more about painting a boat than most paint salesmen. Most classic craft, and all plainly finished working craft, look much better without too high a gloss paint and take to the older standard colors very well. I don't know what color "Coral Sand" is, or any of the other fancy names now used on color cards, but I can create a good Coast Guard buff, French gray, spar color, or any other working craft colors without trouble.

In other words, I only use good grade oil paint, sometimes called "house paint" (Oh yes, I hear the howls!). It seems that if there is not a picture of a boat on the can it costs less. Besides, house paint is so much easier to refinish and has less build-up, very much less if you do a lot of scrubbing. Also, there is much less waste as the stuff does not skim over while your back is turned, and it's easy to apply neatly.

If you must have paint that dries at once, in keeping with all the other instant stuff today, there is plenty of it around. One reservation about paint cans with boat pictures—right now, I'm using a very satisfactory varnish with a picture of an old-time battlewagon on it, Admiral Dewey style, with guns blazing. I'm quite aware most marine paints now are made to be put on in quantity by pros, in lousy spring weather, boat after boat, in a rush. Considering the conditions under which they work, the painters turn out pretty good work, though they "lose one" now and then due to a shower, and have to go over it again.

Going along with paint are various bedding compounds, putties and surfacing cements. I use only two or three, as I've found the others wanting in many ways. Plain black shingle stickum is just fine under water, or anywhere a black stain does not matter, and it's cheap. In spite of laws about it, white lead still is the best for some things, and if I understand it right, can be had for industrial use. I think red lead is the same.

I use considerable glue in a year for a small shop, but little of it goes into hull construction. I see little gain by using it thus, and often much complication, bother, and expense for no real return. Glues are good for spar work, if they are hollow, for repairs, and for what may be cabinet style work. I've long ago found using much glue in simple and plain boatbuilding is the expensive and complicated way to do it, new notions to the contrary.

True, when short or thin stuff is all that is available, there are times when it pays to reconstitute such scrap into usable pieces, usually backing it up with fastenings. Or, some piece is difficult to bolt up and keep clamps on at the same time, so you simply glue it, let go all clamps when dry, and fasten conveniently.

Most small shops where there are cold winters cannot heat well enough for big gluing jobs, so if it's to be done, it's saved for the warm months. I have no objections at all to gluing the right things at the right time; however, little gluing is required in simple craft, and the massive use of it is expensive and time consuming, with little real return for the effort. In fact if such a craft won't hold together without glue, she won't for long with it.

Some while back I saw a plain, flat-bottom, straight-sided sharpie that was strip-built, at least in the sides. She looked unhappy about it. Owner and builder are unknown. If the glue and strips, already milled out, had been acquired free, maybe there was a point, but if it was all bought and worked up, what a waste of time. Of course, there must have been a lot of sawdust left to spit into. The craft's model cried out for good wide plank glued up by the Lord; He's pretty good at it.

All boats, even simple ones, need fittings of some kind, and it is often one of the big expenses. Yet, much of it can be built of wood, backed up in some cases by a little metal. The U.S.S. *Constitution* and H.M.S. *Victory* have mostly wooden fittings. Both craft were capable of going anywhere, and doing all sorts of hair-raising things. Both are worth a visit and much study.

Bowsprit caps that will fill a truck, and deadeyes that fill a wheelbarrow are things to marvel at. Some folks will say you can't do it that way now— if so, our civilization is truly in rapid decay. Good locust, white oak, and some other woods, plain old New England elm especially, some art and imagination, and fittings can quite well be made, and often outlast the store-bought stuff.

In my mind at least, it's quite possible to turn out a sailing craft, even of fair size, almost totally of wood, rope, and small bits of metal—rudder fittings being the big item—and have her quite sea-worthy, handsome and a smart sailer. Such craft are durable and easy to repair. There's nothing wonderful about this; that's the way it used to be. If for some reason economics of the times make such boatbuilding necessary, it can be quite well done again, in whole, or in part.

In the past, both rumrunners and slavers were built plainly and without frills, for the risks were great; yet the nature of the trades demanded good design and a strong build to stand hard driving. I think where an economical craft is wanted, lessons can be learned from many of the past building methods.

If you are able to build a craft of really high-class construction, it's just fine. Some models and uses require it, and in the small sizes, say in a Whitehall pulling boat, you don't get the best out of her unless she is built as they were. They are expensive, in hours at least, even if the amount of material in them is small.

Way back, the East India Company built very durable and lasting ships. It had large resources and totally controlled the trade. Then some upstart Yankees began horning in with smart, fast and cheaply-built ships of good design. The race for trade was on, and the old teak wagons, so carefully sailed, began to lose out to hard-driven spruce and pine.

One should build within the economical good sense of his pocketbook, and the times he finds himself in. Without doubt the standards set by Herreshoff and Lawley, and I should include Nevins, were some of the finest, and other noted builders tried to keep their work up to these. Such a thing is impossible for most boatmen now. World conditions with their monetary shakes, shortages real and contrived, a tendency of some to panicky outlook, plus the burden of taxes make "The Old Days" impossible.

As Howard Chapelle so ably points out in his *American Small Sailing Craft* (he has considerable foresight, so his remarks count more now than ever

before), there is a boat to suit anyone's pocketbook, and she need not be a slob, nor be built in the most expensive way. That she must suit the use, I say again, and whatever type she be, the owner must learn to live with her and understand her ways.

I have met many people who just won't adjust to some craft other than what they have been used to. Personally, I find it most interesting to learn the ways of some good boat, especially a type with which I've had no experience. If she be a well-tried classic, so much the better, for there must be much to learn about a well-developed type that has made her place in boat design and history.

Mystic Seaport has been making quite an effort to restore, or reproduce, craft of the past of whose handling and sailing we know little. I think in many cases such a project would also be quite practical for an individual, as for the most part these craft are economical to build, rig, and sail.

ON ROWING
AND BOATS

Finding a suitable craft takes a bit of doing, although by no means is it impossible. A patient and understanding search is apt to turn one up (my present dory being such a case), and failing that, one can be built, or a very ancient one restored. One is aware not all have the skill or time to do this, but when done this way it is most satisfying work. Also, not every rowing craft is suited to all waters, and some understanding of this is needed to make a wise choice to suit one's own conditions, and how one is to work from the shore.

In some cases the craft must be quite portable, and in many cases auto transportation for the boat is a "must"—this last naturally widens the "cruising ground" a great deal.

As to cost, you rightly state it takes some money, and due to what is now considered specialized construction, the price sometime seems high, especially if one is not a born tinkerer. However, proper care (which is really no chore since this is very simplified boating) and the more or less traditional building of these few odd craft tend to make them very long lived. Their storage problems are simple and their equipment small. Several well-loved craft of this kind I know of are 30, 40 and even 75 years old, still going strong. There is a moral of some kind here, in that their design cannot be improved on for their intended use.

One is often struck by the first cost of a fully-equipped outboard with some pretensions to speed, and the cost of her future maintenance as well as well as depreciation, especially if just used as a joy rider. The returns seem small and the exercise not of the right kind, either physical or mental.

Even when small craft are well moored, a big storm with much rain can swamp them—this to a sophisticated outboard is a major disaster, while the pulling boat with her gear stowed and lashed in a seamanlike way is in business again in a few minutes, with the aid of a wooden bailer and no harm done. And, if the place of mooring is not of the best for real gales, the pulling boat is much the easier to pull ashore out of harm's way.

As to types, pulling boats seem to have one thing in common. Usually they are fairly well built and of good model—not high sided, and all rather lean—beyond that we all know they must vary to suit local conditions. Like all compromises, a design that tries to fit all conditions is not much of a boat in any.

Oars, like many things that have been machine made for long periods, have degenerated to the point where they are more or less unsuitable for use in a good boat—however, one can still find, with much picking over, "stock" to work over a likely pair into something usable. Even then, things sometimes are not right, and really smart craft need oars designed and made for them. One does not try to operate a smart sports car with a tired truck engine, or fly planes with machinery suited to digging rock.

A man really develops very little power in rowing, at least at a pace he can comfortably keep up. A well-shaped boat and excellent oars to suit her, and, in light weather at least, one often feels he "can row forever."

I have found the flat-bottom, various forms of vee, round, both smooth plank and lapstrake, and various combinations, all quite good for rowing as long as they are of good model and suited to local conditions.

My real love is the extreme Whitehall lapstrake construction, although I feel she's not ideal for beach work. This, to some extent, depends on the beach, conditions and vandals who might cause damage. Given the right conditions, this type is about tops, next to a double-paddle canoe or scull.

At present I'm making out very well with a rather lean Swampscott of excellent model, which makes an extra fine beach boat. Many beach boats in the past carried a small spritsail, and while this is off the track of plain rowing, is quite practical and a useful addition in some locations by much increasing the range and pleasure of the boat. The added weight of centerboard, rudder, if any, and the spars (which should stow within the boat) often is of real advantage, as for some localities a pulling boat should not be too light.

One might say, of all the rigs so far devised for this sort of use, the common doryman's loose-footed sprit-sail works the best, and like many well

17' sharp wherry designed by Pete Culler. (John Burke)

tried things, adding any modern improvements to it just seems to louse it up.

It is said now to be a very inefficient sail, but properly cut, out of the right material (somewhat of a lost art), and properly rigged in the boat, its simplicity, short spars, lack of windage, ease of handling and stowing, one's ability to relieve what is often a tender boat when over pressed, make it overcome its so called weaknesses so well that nothing else equals it. Like many good things it requires a bit of simple learning.

As to materials for building, as you point out production is small, therefore, mostly the traditional methods will be the most economical, at least for professional builders. I see nothing wrong with experimenting with new things for the home builder, so long as he understands the requirements of his locality and pulling boats in general.

Example: Recently a couple double-paddle canoes were built from plans of a very well known and able (also progressive) designer.

One followed his ideas in detail—this is a fine craft, with almost endless life of her as boats go.

The other got fiberglass happy on the wrong project—result, the last is so heavy and cloddish she will get little use, and with it no care. I assume her life will be rather short in spite of good materials and a lot of work. Oh yes, she cost more, too!

One must use one's head in applying new notions to old dogs.

The design angle is interesting, and I hope some contribute some good and interesting craft. From here it looks this way:

I doubt if few, if any, designers can produce models of pulling boats any better than those of the past, when rowing was the means to work small craft. Certainly the boatmen of those days made it as easy as they could to suit their local conditions. Above all they were not dumb or stupid, and the development of their craft was long, careful and salted with generations of experience.

Fortunately, a lot of this has come down to us in the way of plans, models and writings. To turn one's back on it all would be stupid in the extreme.

SAND DOLLY

Many people I know are intrigued by the Seal Island skiff, or wheelbarrow boat, from Chapelle's *Boatbuilding*; I know I am too. Its appearance again in *Mariner's Catalog, Vol. 2* (page 100) has stirred a thought about it I've had for a long time, yet never put to use in an actual boat, because there has been as yet no need. However, building a long, light, fast pulling bateau some time back, I found a need for some sort of wheel or dolly for handling the boat on shore. The wheelbarrow boat was considered, but found not practical in this case due to the high performance I expected from the boat. There was much time spent sketching what I thought might be an improved wheelbarrow boat, just for the fun of it. I still find these doodlings around in odd corners now and then.

The bateau called for a different approach, since I was contented with a sandy beach, very long, though light, craft, woodshed harbor when home, pickup truck, plus advancing age. I developed the sand dolly, and it works very well. As can be seen by the drawings, none of which are to scale, the contraption stays in place by tripping past its center, and then the weight of the boat keeps it in place. I got this notion from a two-wheel dolly

Allan Vaitses of Mattapoissett worked out some years ago. The frame is oak; the wheel shaft and spacer rod, which the boat rests on, is electric conduit. Note that a tie bolt goes through the carrying pipe. Wooden washers keep things apart for clearance. The roller is simply three 15" disks of cedar, made up about like an old wooden ox cart wheel— two outside disks and a center one. Cedar slats are nailed on the disks, with space between. Padding is used at the boat's gunnels. The boat is 3 feet wide, and the dolly frame is $2\frac{1}{2}$ feet, so it jams at the proper place.

The idea was to build the boat lightly, strongly, and simply; anything you move by armstrong should be light, also modest in size to stow when not in use. The weight of the boat is 92 pounds without gear, maybe 110 pounds equipped with the sailing rig and sea stores for the day. There seems to be 31 pounds, stark light, on the end you lift; about 40 with all the gear. The slats of the roller are dressed round, like barrel staves, so she rolls smoothly on pavement. Grass or soft sand makes no difference; on small stones and shells she rocks. This was fun to work out and build, but the true wheelbarrow boat has kept bugging me.

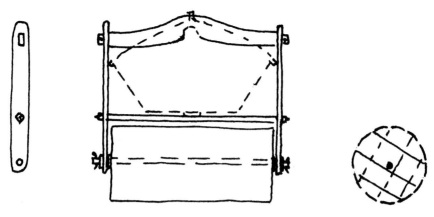

Details of the roller for the sand dolly.

The conceptual drawing of the sand dolly.

The 17' bateau Otter, *all set up with the sand dolly. Note the snotter and sprit on the sail rig.* (John Burke)

WHEELBARROW BOAT

Though the Seal Island skiff no doubt worked fine for the intended use, I thought I could do better than have an iron or wood wheel in a rather turbulent well forward. Any boat should be designed for its intended use, and being portable, the vehicle it may use enters into its design. I picture a skiff about 12 feet long, 4 foot beam; many may think this a bit narrow. Pickups and station wagons take this width, some will take a bit more; 12 feet will give about all the overhang you want with the gate down.

The craft should be of fairly light construction, say lapstrake sides, modest oak frame, bottom splined, cross plank for tightness on shore, for she's an out-of-water, live-at-home boat. I would paint the bottom white, whatever other colors are used elsewhere. The wheel should be about 2 feet in diameter of $^3/_4$-inch oak, drifted up like any centerboard, and with a metal tire. The centerboard well should be built about like any other, except with slotted sides as shown, to take the iron strap over the wheel. This strap should have a thimble seized on top. The drawing shows the well sides slightly expanded to show the detail better. In practice, the strap (of, say, $^1/_4$-inch $\times$ 2-inch iron) rides in slots, free enough to move up and down. The rope lanyard carries the weight of the boat, acts somewhat as a shock absorber, and adjusts the height of the wheel. A pin or wedge of some sort will no doubt be needed if one wants to secure the board all the way up. Naturally, the amount of wheel exposed below the bottom to roll on can be adjusted.

Here is where I borrow from the Chinese: a wheel with an axle well up in the boat, and well aft, should lighten the load and balance, like an oriental wheelbarrow. The raked stern is to keep things clear of one's feet, as well as to make the boat dry and able aft. The barrow handles can be the subject of artistic tinkering; I think an iron rod across them will add strength, enable one to push with his body, and will be a sheet traveler besides. This last, though the sail should be loose-footed, allows for a big rig in an attempt to smarten things up and overcome somewhat the failings otherwise. I think little craft need a big rig, and can use it, for they carry much live ballast for their size. You can always reef if it blows, but to be dull in light weather is no fun.

(continued on page 295)

Starting with the conceptual musings in the article, watch the evolution from the sketches, to the finished design, to the boat that was built. This was the typical progression for Pete.

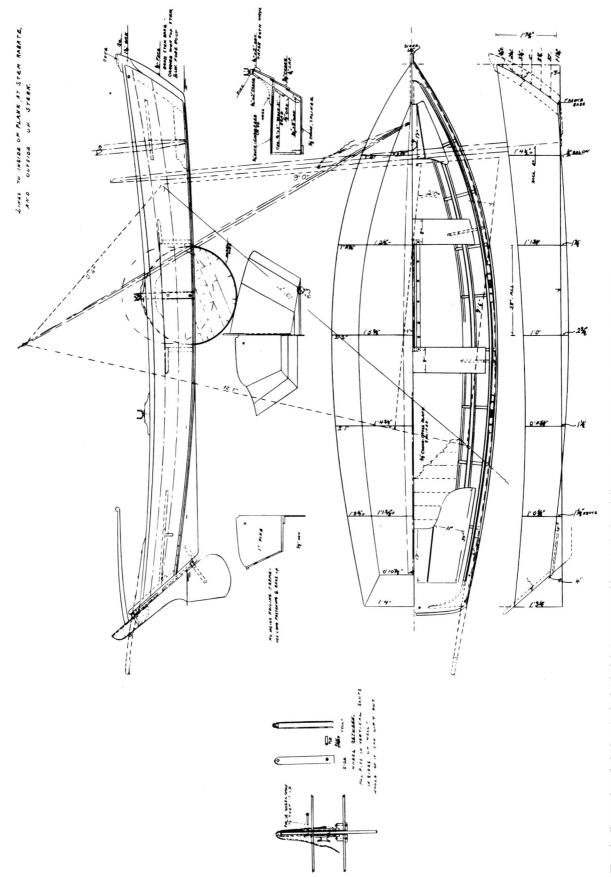

The wheelbarrow boat fleshed out in the finished design as a capable rowing/sailing skiff. (© Mystic Seaport, Ships Plans Collection, Mystic, CT)

Jim Odell of Lowell Boat Shop, Amesbury, Massachusetts, works the 14'6" wheelbarrow boat in to the dock. (Joanne Burke)

(continued from page 292)

Whether I ever get to developing such a craft is a moot point; I hope what I show will stir others to it. No detailed dimensions can be given; you work it out to suit, which is where the fun is. How it will all work only trial can tell. I do know if you hit the beach with the wheel well down under a press of sail, she might run out and capsize on dry land, which would be something new. You could possibly get cited for a motor vehicle violation.

WHAT MAKES
CLASSICS REAL

Being a designer and builder of classic-type small craft, I'm often asked the why's and how's of the many bits of gear for these boats, as well as about the methods many think make these look so well. All of my methods are pretty much the way they used to be done, for those ways work and are for the most part the most economical. There is a lot on record in various books and pictures about classic craft; I sometimes wonder if these works are studied as closely as they should be. To cover all the details of different classic boats and vessels is more than a lifetime's work; many items no longer apply to today's use of boats. On the other hand others do, and it's well to know how to take advantage of them. Being so vast a subject, I touch on just a few things.

The poor stemhead finish on some classic craft, or the lack of it often strikes me, though the boats were otherwise thought out and well done. Occasionally I see this on an old boat; more often on a recent reproduction.

I give my own notions on stemhead design for what they are worth. I never make two quite alike; I think different models of boats require different treatment. However, there are a couple of rules that I use. I never cut a stem-top level, nor quite with the sheer; rather, I pitch it up some, the amount depending on the boat, and it looks right. Model, stem profile, stem siding, and sometimes just what wood is available all enter into my decision. Naturally, you treat a heavy, bulky craft much differently than, say, a wooden canoe. The few examples shown are simply a guide; I've used these, and wide variations of them, on many craft. I also nearly always use the square-sided stem near the top, going to a taper as shown, even in a light, portable boat; this gives good landing for the gunwales and false bead, if any. In fact, this thinking is part of the finishing of all my craft; a little thought, art, and nice detail can add much to any boat. A book on the subject could be written, with large-scale drawings and measurements in detail, which would spoil the whole thing, for then the boats would all look alike, just like in a motorboat show. Better that each builder does it his own way, so long as he does it, thus leaving his own mark.

I'm often asked about stem boxes, bending frames, timber for bending, and other connected items, for I seem to have quite good luck with bending, especially in lapstrake craft. Most boatbuilding books

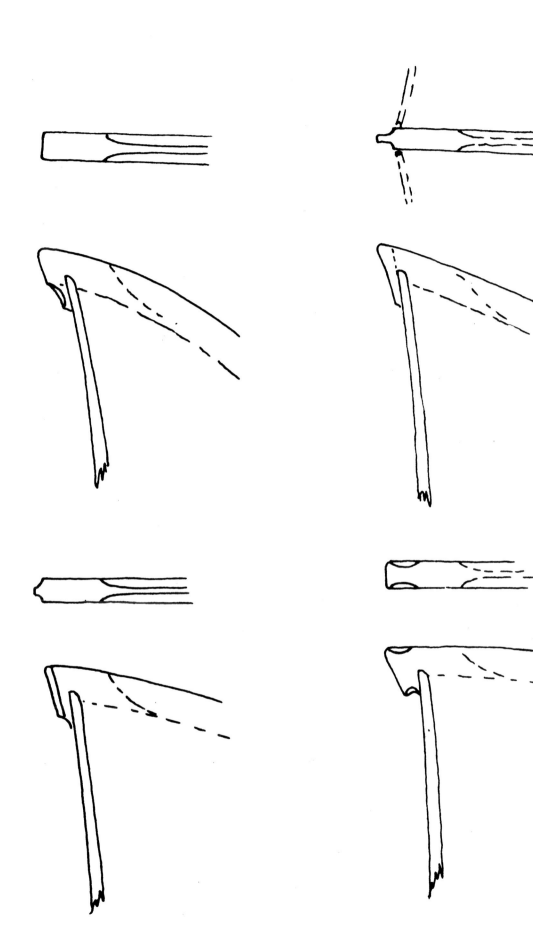

A few stemhead designs.

have good diagrams of steam boxes; I've built them with a plugged pipe stuck in a stove, five gallon tin can, abandoned tank, all sorts of rubber hose scraps, and anything for a box, from stove pipe, tin air ducts, and wooden boxes of all sorts. I even once used an abandoned motorboat exhaust line. The important thing is not the gear, but plenty of wet steam. This is achieved by having the so-called boiler below the box, and the box tilted, so condensation runs back. Softening frames by boiling requires a real rolling boil. How you heat the water is a matter of what's available. At this time I have a boiler, or rather stem generator, for it carries no pressure, of my own design; the box is simply a leftover duct from a shipyard sawdust blower, because it was available. The boiler was expensive, and its only real advantage is it's very free steaming. It uses little wood, so working alone, I'm not too much of a slave to the firebox, and it can be made to heat the shop. It was fun to build, with the aid of a welder friend.

Assuming you have plenty of wet steam, the important thing, to me at least, is the choosing and milling of the bending stock. I speak here of oak, though some other stuff bends well if you can get it. White oak is said to be best. One of my friends, now 90 years old, has probably bent more mast hoops, plus other stuff, than any man I know. He told me more than once that he preferred "swamp white butts"; I think he really knows. However, you bend with what oak you can get more often than not, and I, for one, can't really tell how well a certain oak will bend until I try it, though some oaks have a great reputation. Or, maybe I can, for I do a lot of picking. Most builders insist that really dry oak won't take steam and bend well, and, generally speaking, maybe they are right. On the other hand, I've had to use dry oak that had been overhead in the shop 10 or more years, and it bent like cooked noodles; granted, it was sawed, and otherwise right, at least to my notions.

This sawing right and preparation of stock is important. I don't care for square-section frames in small craft, or larger craft if they are to be bent. Fastenings tend to go too much down the center of a frame, often splitting it. Though it does not seem so at first, square-section frames don't cant and lay snugly as well in the ends of a boat. If practical for a boat that will be fastened, I prefer a frame at least twice the siding as the moulding in lapstrake craft; more moulding if it is carvel (very much depending on the size of the fastenings), say a proportion of three to two or thereabouts. Many don't agree.

So, looking at the oak log flitched up, I want it sawn so the plank will dress to the siding of the frames—in other words, you can usually plane to a good, full $^3/_4$" from stuff sawn 1". Many saw to the moulding of the frames, allowing for planing of course, and I think this is wrong. I use plank #1 for the worst bends, and #2s, too. Sawing plank #1 from the edges in, say to get $^3/_8$" dressed for a light boat, you find these pieces are all flat grain, which is the easy grain for bending. Planks #3 and #4 are treated the same way, though used for the lesser bends, where they work fine. Planks #5 can be used for bracing or to fire the steambox. Note the illustration of the plank on the flat, and the method of lining off; that is, you line off from the sap edge in, shifting the line now and then if need be, to follow the grain. You get some small wasted wedges this way, and one larger piece in the center, to be discarded, but you seldom break a frame.

I have seen in the War years a large yard running fine flitch through a big power-feed gang saw, one every few seconds (until they learned better). It was all prime stuff, but all coming out cross grain, and, of course, the stock has been sawn the thin way of the frame. They thought they were "in production"; they were shortly—in production breaking frames, for most were cross grain. The pile of discards was monumental. When you consider the waste in man-hours, timber, and steam, no wonder

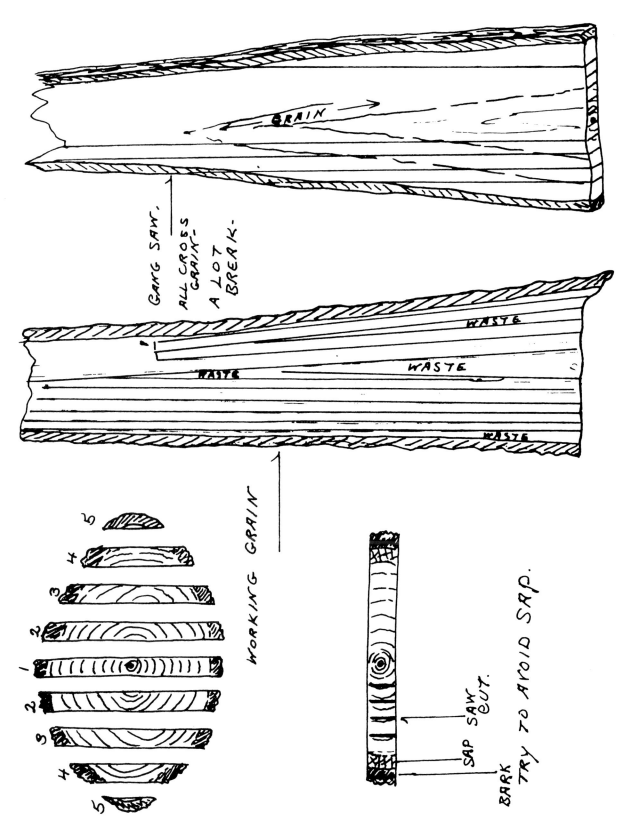

GRAIN

GANG SAW.
ALL CROSS GRAIN-
A LOT BREAK-

WASTE
WASTE
WASTE
WASTE

WORKING GRAIN

5
4
3
2
1
2
3
4
5

SAP SAW CUT.
BARK
TRY TO AVOID SAP.

Sawing frame stock.

war is expensive. Of course, there was a great and noisy show going on in the mill shed, all available to the eyes and ears of the Government inspector; he did not know what he was doing either. I still see this going on today in some yards, though naturally on a much smaller scale. It certainly pays to think about it a bit, and cut up the Lord's timber the way He grew it.

All sorts of things have been added to the water used for steaming to help soften the oak; some put in some antifreeze, which might raise the boiling point. I use it, more to keep from having to drain off the water in the winter—it may help. Soft soap, salt water, and detergents of various kinds have been used. No doubt something that keeps the frame hot longer gives you more clamping time. Some pre-soak the frames, especially if the wood is dry. My favorite is splashy-painting the frames the day before steaming with kerosene that has just enough linseed oil added to keep things wet for a spell. I think it does a lot of good. I'm sure it does no harm, and I seldom get checking later when the frames are well dried. Some say steam drives the oil in; I think it does, for there is a noticeable difference in the sanding and painting of steamed oak as opposed to non-steamed oak in the boat.

Grain is important when choosing wood for uses throughout a boat, including her joiner work; look at each piece of stock to see how best to use the grain. You will do a lot of modest dry bending; flat grain always bends better and is less liable to split. Edge grain, or stock very close to it, always wears better for a laid deck and is the way of least shrinkage. Even when gluing up a paddle or an oar, study the grain; trying to finish two opposite grains at a glue joint can be frustrating.

Nearly every stranger to my shop asks me right off what type of glue I use. My answer is: not much in the boats themselves, and plain old water-mix Weldwood at that. These same visitors are apt to ask the same thing again if they visit later on, for they think they may not have heard right. However, I seem to go through 15 or more pounds of Weldwood in the course of a year, most of it going for spars (if built-up), oars, paddles, and some joiner work.

Naturally, the wonders of glue are discussed, and my notions on it come clear (I'm sure many think I'm nuts). I've been using the above-mentioned glue since The Big War; those days we used it by the barrel and learned a lot about it. I've found that all the standard available glues, including the indoor types, such as "white glue" and old hide glue, if properly used, temperature considered, good fits made, and material used that is glue-able, are stronger than the wood, at least when the glue is new. I have not found much data on glue aging, and what I have does not go beyond five years. My feeling is that glue weakens with time; how much and how fast depends on the conditions surrounding it. These conditions are very hard to pin down, as you are not there all the time to observe things.

There are many wonderful new types of glue; you read about super space-age stuff. In practice, so far, these are often hard to come by, expensive, and maybe unhandy to use in boatyard conditions. All glues I have used so far are touchy about proper temperature, and this is a big boatyard problem in cold climates. In the distant past, down South in the summer, we did things with glue at 90° to 100° that I could not attempt in my climate now. Some woods just don't glue well. The poorer oak with more open grain—poor for boats, that is—seems to glue well when dry and in small sizes. Swamp white butts, the greenish gray stuff, almost as hard as some tools, won't glue for long, and in any size. It lets go quite soon. I think the finest glue available, even the stuff that is said to hold two tons with one drop, will never hold such wood; if it does, the wood simply lets go close to the glue line. In other words, the finest glue cannot overcome the nature of wood; therefore, glue will always show some failure with certain wooden structures.

I've not specifically mentioned epoxy, which seems to come in several variations; I've heard of many failures with it, and I think they happen because many think it's a cure-all and will do anything. I think it fails because too much is expected of it. Advertising that claims epoxy is the answer to every problem partly may cause this. The writers of these ads maybe have never glued anything much bigger or more complex than a postage stamp in their whole lives. Glue work is after all a matter of common sense; a maker of glue cannot build that into the product. My dislike of glue in hull works is based on the belief that a well-built boat does not need it, or very little of it. Clamping up some work is very time consuming. It's very easy to get chips or dirt in a hull joint when making up, and this is the start of a bad glue job. The temperature is usually not right in the winter in most shops in the Northeast. There is often much difficult cleaning up to do after things are set, which is hard on the tools and their temper. Glue that drips on the floor, bench, and tools eventually has to be removed. Many times, a joint by its very nature will not take to glue—it's mechanically unsuited. There just might not be enough surface to make the glue line work for long. Expansion, contraction, and other causes make it let go.

On the good side, glue is most handy to fix some error. A place that starts to splinter—we all have this happen—can be saved by glue. Stock otherwise too small can be reconstituted with glue. Slash scarfs in light planking can be glued, and here I always back it with fastenings. Backing any glue joint with fastenings is good practice; it may prevent trouble from getting a start. Some odd-shaped things, once clamped up, are difficult to fasten properly with all the clamps in the way. Some clamps can jump off during the fastening process and you can lose the line-up. My method here is to clamp up dry, put in a couple of pilot screws, or brads if the work is small, take apart, glue, line up with the pilot fastenings, and clamp. Later on, when the glue is dry, let go the clamps and bolt the piece at your convenience—a better and easier job all around. In the past I've used this method for assembling complicated stems for 85' hulls with great success; they were awkward to line up, and more so to bolt, without jarring something askew. Though they were of fairly dry Honduras, the pieces were large, and I doubt the glue did much good after a few months, but it allowed a very thorough bolting job.

For making oars, paddles, and small, built-up spars, and doing certain joiner work, all to be finished bright, glue is great—Weldwood particularly, as it gives the least noticeable glue line. The stock you use for this work must be dry, and is usually of a kind that glue takes to. This sort of work requires good fits and plenty of pressure, the more the better. Some say now that good fits and pressure are no longer needed; the miracle gap-filling glues do it all for you. In any shop today, even a very small one, the glue joints are largely made by machinery, and the little hand fitting can be learned without difficulty. Pressure is part of driving glue into the wood, at least with the kind I use, and pushing the excess out—there should always be excess for a good job.

I admit that I'm very backward about glue, though my joints are often better than most. When I do have a rare failure with glue, it's simply because in haste I did something that I really know better than to do. I also admit that I know little of using gap-filling glues; from what I see at some of the present-day boat shows, I don't want to learn.

I'm often asked about spritsails, which are most handy for small craft that must have a rig that is easily struck, say for rowing or hauling up. Many now think this rig is out of date, inefficient, and unhandy, when just the opposite is the case. To me, at least, nothing is out of date that works well and suits the boat. The spritsail is most efficient; the most, I think, of all, considering the simplicity of its gear, stowing, and cost, its ease of handling (sure, you have to practice a bit), and its ability to drive a well-shaped craft without pressing her. If the rig does not work, it's the fault of those who made and rigged it.

Though not to any scale, the rig shown here is based on about a 12-foot mast. A smaller mast will lighten things up a bit; a larger one will beef it up. Proportion in boatbuilding is a very necessary knack to acquire; I don't know of any definite rules for proportion on these classic craft, except that if something looks right, it is right. A 12-foot mast is suited to 65 to 70 feet of sail. A 3-inch diameter mast is a norm here, a bit less, say $2^3/_4$", if the stick is a very good one. The mast should have little taper till near the head, where it should taper rather rapidly. Note that the heel tapers rapidly from the mast thwart to the heel and it is round. The mast must be able to rotate, or the snotter and sprit will bind. This is often mistake number one—the mast is made with a square tenon and the whole rig is loused up. This rotating mast has other advantages. There is no sweat getting things lined up when you step it, and one can come to a landing downwind simply by letting the sail blow out ahead of the boat, which is a very good way to take the sail in, instead of having it flogging in the boat. More about the handling of these sails later.

Stock for making masts can be fir, spruce, cedar, pine, or what you can get, so long as it's reasonably light. The red cedars that end to take over abandoned fields or cleared land are common in many places. They make fine small-boat masts, though few know about this, thinking they are not "clear stock." Of course they are all knots, yet are therefore almost unsplittable and very springy. I can assure you that the boat does not notice all the little knots and seems to sail better with a mast with a bit of spring. Picking out a spar from these trees takes a little common sense. Place your head right in among the branches (very many, you find), and sight up the trunk, looking for a straight tree. If

there is a kink or a cleft, look for another. Or, you can glue up these little masts out of thin plank if you can't arrange it otherwise, simply by stacking, then sawing to contour, eight-squaring, rounding, etc., like making any mast. I taper the head and heel of the mast to about one inch. Somehow, though I make them always, the grown stick that was once a little tree appeals to me more; there is a certain rightness and charm to it, and my imagination says the boat goes better with it. The sprit is a simple stick; a split 2×4 can make a couple. Use $1^1/_2$" diameter in the middle if the stick is limber; as thin as $1^1/_4$" if it's a stiff one. Taper the sprit to about $^7/_8$" at the ends. Note the shoulder on the head of the sprit to fit the becket on the sail. This shoulder should be about $^5/_8$" diameter. The heel should have a nicely smoothed slot for the snotter; do not forget the rivet to prevent splitting.

The "gear" for this rig is as shown. There is very little to it, but every piece is important in its making and placing. The mast hole in the thwart should be rather slack, and the mast should have a piece of leather tightly sewn on and kept well greased to take the chafe and let the mast rotate. Don't tack the leather on, as this makes a fracture point. Note the thumb cleats; make them only big enough to do their work of holding the tack from going aloft and keeping the snotter from sliding down. This last can be mistake number two—a snotter that keeps sliding down will never allow the sail to set. The hole in the mast for the throat lashing is to keep the whole sail from working down—in other words, it ensures a reasonably tight luff.

Nothing I do or make seems original, though the snotter as shown just may be. There are several other snotter-rigging methods, some for quite big craft, used in the past both here and in Europe. Some that are shown in recent designs (yes, others now design an occasional spritsail) would seem to jam under strain. What I show here may be original and works very well, at least in craft the size

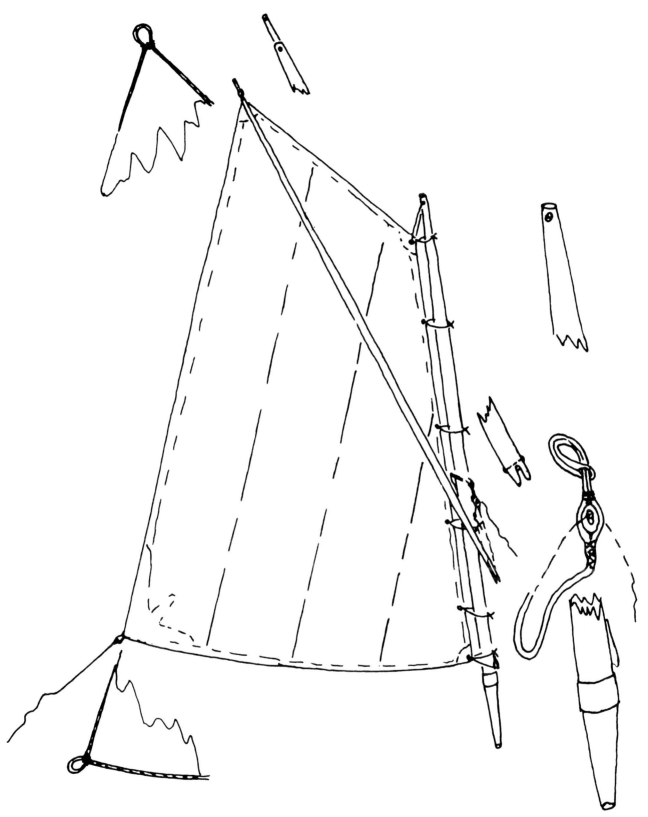

Sail and sprit details.

we are considering, say 12 to 20 feet. It's simply a long eyesplice of sufficient length to pass around the mast at the snotter thumb cleat, and of a length when in position that the thimble, of wood or metal, hangs a couple of inches below the cinch. Note that the thimble is jammed down on the splice, and a very tight seizing is put on above it. The line should be well stretched; even so, you may have to tighten the seizing after some use. I prefer a wood thimble; oak will do, though locust has more charm. A brass one will work as well.

To set up the sprit, simply pass the tail through the slot and up through the thimble. You now have a little tackle. Set up the sprit till there is some wrinkle in the sail from the peak to the tack. This is the same as setting a gaff sail. Pass another turn in the sprit slot, double the stray line, and jam back of the now-tight snotter. A pull on the end of the tail will free things in a hurry no matter how much strain is on it. I prefer manila line here, say about $^1/_4$" to $^5/_{16}$", over man-made fibers, which are slippery. Another turn may be needed in the slot, and a hitch besides, which I don't care for.

Sail is kept to the mast by lashings and the old, out-of-date robands. The tack lashing can, and should, be tight, so the sail is against the mast. The throat lashing should be somewhat slack in the horizontal part. Robands the same, so the sail takes its natural lay without anyone putting undue strain or pucker in the sail. The robands are, if braided line, passed through the sail eyelet holes, then middled and seized with a bit of sail twine. They should be long enough to come comfortably around the mast and be tied with a square knot. If laid line is used, omit the seizing and simply middle, then tuck one end through the strands, draw taut, and tie as before. Personally, I like my own sails to stand well away from the mast at the luff, thinking they are less affected by mast turbulence, and therefore more "efficient." It's many little things like this that make these sails work so well.

Note the small hole just below the shoulder at the head of the sprit, which unships at times when sail is being handled. I simply pass a piece of marline through this and loosely through the sail beckets to prevent unshipping. This should be snug enough to keep things in place, but not so tight as to bind things up. This may be an original device, too. Unshipping at the wrong time can be most annoying and awkward. Though in actual practice you seldom take the sprit out of the peak, I use a slippery square knot here, about like a shoe-tie, for the time you may want to take it out. Though not indicated on the drawing, I like a long, narrow peak pennant of some colorful, light material, seized or sewn to the peak of the sail. It adds not one jot to the boat's sailing, but I think it dresses things up wonderfully.

The sail is probably the most important part of the sprit rig, which is why it has to be backed up by the proper gear so recently described. It's assumed, too, that a good sail has a smart hull under it. There are some sailmakers around who can cut and have an interest in such classic sails. There are also many more who don't want be bothered with them. If you don't want to make your own sail, and have trouble finding the right man, look around. One good source I can recommend is E.W. Smith, Union Wharf, Fairhaven, Mass. I will not go into making your own sails, even though I make my own, but give some general pointers I found to work well. I prefer cotton for these sails; man-made fibers are, up to now at least, slippery, noisy, and awkward to handle in small craft. The old, standard 2:50 boat drill does just fine. Treat it with Cuprinol or any other canvas treatment you like. Most of this stuff can be colored, and russet, tan, or deep cream colors look well on a classic boat. Besides, they show less dirt.

A sail is more durable and sets better if narrow panels are used; that is, use the brightseam if the cloth is wide. The sail should be cut vertically, or with the seams running up and down, parallel to the leach. Remember, this sail is of another era, so you cut accordingly, and, by golly, it sets! There should be good drive in the luff, quite a round foot, especially in the loose-footed version, and what round one dares put in the head and leach is based on his abilities as a sailmaker. Though taped sails are the thing now, I like the sail roped on the head, luff, and foot, going down and up the leach a bit and ending in the traditional rat tail, forming the beckets for the sprit and sheet on the way. I like the beckets leathered, or at least served. Using the modern tape, you begin to foul up around the beckets, so do it as it was and all works out. The leach usually has a double cloth, and here the sailmaking art comes to the fore. One needs a leach that does not curl; not all sailmakers can do it well.

To digress a bit from spritsails: Small cotton sails, unless storm jibs or trysails for larger craft, don't need leach roping unless you just want to see if you can do it. One of my own spritsails is roped on the leach, just to see if I could do it. Any sailmaker worth his salt will tell you that roping a leach so it does not curl, and using no battens, separates the men from the boys. Mine curls a little, sometimes.

I've heard jazz that a spritsail must be hard to handle; it can be, like any other sail, if you don't learn how. Learning is not much of a chore; it consists of forgetting most of the methods that go with modern rigs. Drawing the sail plan for a sprit rig is a matter of having made a study of "how it was," and what worked. Chapelle's *American Small Sailing Craft* (W. W. Norton, N.Y.) has much good data on this. Rigging up for the first time should be done flat on the ground. I like my clews cut high, and tack low, and lash it that way on the mast, so it's almost down on the thwart; the boats go and carry sail better this way. I've heard it said that you couldn't then see under the sail; you can, better than you think and is it nearly as bad as the modern genoas, which all up-to-date craft now seem to use? The genoa is a sail that now almost touches the deck all over.

I think some rake to the mast is good for a spritsail; that's a matter for the designer. You can even rig for changing rake, of which more later. I put my tack thumb cleat just clear of the mast leather, as low as possible, even though I may not lash the tack quite that low. The snotter thumb cleat should be placed by trial on the ground—as low as will still give sufficient drift for the snotter setup. Again, don't get the robands tight; it's better to have them on the slack side. Now start the furl by taking the sprit out of the snotter, place it about parallel to the mast, keeping the head taut, throw the clew over the sprit, then roll the sail up in the sprit to the mast, keeping some upward pressure to the peak, so all will be smooth and tight. Pass the loose snotter around the sail and mast and clove hitch it; coil the sheet and make it fast to the snotter tail. You are now ready to ship the mast, assuming the boat is ready. The sail will roll much better next time, when it's in the boat and upright.

Step the mast, and see that all is otherwise ready. Unfurl and set the sail, and she's ready to go, assuming a more or less proper sheeting location has been worked out. Here, another mistake can crop up: in most craft of modest beam, locating the sheet just inside the lee rail is about right, though it will take some trial to get the fore-and-aft position just so. Sheeting any loose-footed sail is somewhat critical. I often build a long pin rail on each side, with several holes along it, so various positions can be tried. The cut of the sail, the weight of the wind, and your course in relation to it can make some further adjustment necessary.

Having come this far, many leave the sprit rig at that, yet there are handy variations to be described. For instance, a long, slim boat often takes kindly to a two-sail rig, at least on light days. My own preference here is to have the boat somewhat overhatted

A two-sail rig, with a sprit boom on the mizzen.

with the full rig, so she does well on light days or in the early morning, using the foresail only in a step slightly farther aft, with more mast rake in the usual better breeze later on, when the mizzen has been struck and stowed. The mizzen alone, with even more rake and the centerboard lowered more in most cases, can become a storm sail by using the after fore step. This handy setup, which was common in two-sail boats of the past, is one I use myself, and find most versatile. I find a reef in the foresail most handy at times, two-sail rig or not. This means some variation in rigging, though slight.

Some think you can't reef a loose-footed sail. Well, you can. A two-sail rig requires a double sheet on the fore, for obvious reasons, and I prefer to send it through a fairlead on the rail before going to the pin, for handiness in stays. A reef, which should have a reef pendant and tack lashing rigged at all times, requires a halyard, and a second position lower down for the snotter and an additional thumb cleat. It's a matter of design and experience; when using a reef, things must be planned so that, with one turned in, the sprit will not be so low as to strike the boat's thwart or rail. A rule of thumb I use is that the sprit should be usually about the total length of the mast, and I make the rest of the rig agree with that. Another rough rule is: assuming a 12-foot mast, the hoist of the sail should be 8 or 9 feet, the foot, 7 or 8 feet, and the head about 5 feet. The head should be about perpendicular to the "chord," that is, a line from throat to clew. All this is rather loosely gone at, varying the layout of the sail to suit the particular boat. What looks right is right.

The brail as shown is an extra, but one that I think is very worthwhile. One can "come out of it" if it suddenly airs on, and get properly snugged down without much of a battle. It's handy when running downwind to a beach to brail-up and let her blow in. In some instances it is handy when getting underway, as it saves a lot of flogging. Rig the brail as follows: Use a slippery light line, say $^3/_{16}$" diameter

(it must be slippery to render properly). Splice the line in at the throat cringle on one side of the sail and reeve it out to the leach through a thimble seized there, or a stamped brass eye will do. The proper position for these points is at the ends of an arc struck from the throat to the leach, the fixed point being at the peak. Then reeve the line to a thimble at the throat on the other side of the sail, to a thimble about halfway down—this is important, as without it, a slack bight of the line can foul the sprit. The line then is led to a thimble at the track, and from there to some handy cleat within reach, say alongside the centerboard well. When not brailing, the line is kept very slack, or it will spoil the set of the sail—hence the slippery line. I grease my line besides. Very likely, this is the place for nylon.

The mizzen, if used, is about like all the above, except it is small. The boom, really a sprit boom, is needed for proper sheeting, as we are running out of boat aft to sheet to. Often a becket and thimble on the rudder head is the sheeting point. The sheet then leads to a cleat or pin on the tiller. A second snotter is, of course, needed for the boom, and it should *not* be rigged to the foot of the sail, but somewhat above it. The best position is found by experiment. The reason for this is that it makes the sail set without any twist or boom rise. A mizzen should set flatter than a fore. With two sprits and snotters, the sail being otherwise right, you can make it set as you wish. And, here's the real point—with no twist or rise, the sail can trim to the center of the boat, which is usually the only option, unless you wish to build a bow traveler, or use the Norse push stick as I do. In other words, the sail swings more or less like a bar door. Some prefer a sharp-headed mizzen with a horizontal sprit, sometimes known as the Chesapeake canoe rig. Either style works fine. The sharp-headed mizzen requires one less spar, but a much longer mast for the same area.

Which do I prefer? I use both in the same boat, depending on my mood, and sometimes both at once, not using the fore, but placing one mizzen in the forestep. This is a low, powerful rig when it blows fresh and I feel like taking it rough and wet.

At the risk of repeating some of the above, I will now discuss the handling of the sprit rig, using my own craft and her place of mooring as an example, knowing your mooring is apt to be different. I work off a protected sand beach where the slop is seldom more than knee-boot high, most of this made by motorboats, unless there is a real gale on shore. The boat is a two-sail Swampscott dory and is kept afloat, moored to an anchor off shore, and hauled out to it by an endless line, a method that works well in this location with a moderate tide range. The prevailing summer wind is off shore, and there are no real problems with wind from east to west by way of south. The sails chosen for the day, sometimes all three, are taken to the beach, boat hauled in and grounded (her other gear is always in her), rig to be used, or combination of it stepped, and sails set, sometimes with the fore brailed. She's floated, unhooked from the haul-out pendant, and we drift clear, dropping the board and shipping the rudder, trimming her for course and wind. Sometimes, if it's handier, she's gotten underway with the fore only, setting the mizzen later if wanted. With wind northwest by the way of north to northeast, it's on shore, and another method is used, same as with all beach boats in the past, with slight variations due to location and size of boat. If the wind is very light, the rig is laid in the boat, and I make an offing by sculling out to where there is drifting room to make sail, which consists of lowering the board, shipping the rudder, putting the tiller in a becket, stepping the rig, and making sail. It's surprising how much windage stepped spars make when sculling or rowing, even in a light wind, so the spars are never stepped unless it's dead flat at the moment.

When it is blowing a bit fresh on shore, here is another approach: The rig is stowed in the boat, the haul-out line is held double (for that prevents overhauling) and is overhanded from the bow till she's pretty well off the beach. A short strop that is rigged for the purpose is slippery hitched to the haul-out. The rudder and board are attended to, and the proper amount of sail is made for the conditions. Yaw is watched, and, when she takes the right cast, the slippery hitch is let go and she's off. This can be done in a small gale once you get the knack and can work fast without hangups. After all, for a few moments you are in the classic difficult position of the sailing vessel, all in miniature—lee shore, got to get way on quickly, and, if you get a header, a fast tack is necessary because you must, not that you want to. Certainly, these little boats teach pretty good seamanship without undue risks; you get very handy at doing things that help much later on in big vessels.

Making port is, for the most part, quite simple, though there are pitfalls. Beating up to the beach, I make a point of overstanding the mark, as the wind tends to get puffy close in, with many headers. I keep good way on so as to overcome the drag of the board as it hits the sand and so she sticks when she hits, instead of blowing off. Doing it with a fresh beam wind, especially if the current is with the wind, I hit the beach at a fair clip (it is mostly sand) to keep from being driven along sideways into a dock or other beached boat. Even so, she will often slew around, taking a list off shore and heading more or less into the wind.

In light, onshore wind, I simply let what sail is on her blow out ahead, rotating masts, you know, and let her run gently in and ground. In moderate to strong onshore winds, I come-to more or less, well to windward so as to have time, stow the mizzen if it's set, brail the fore, and wipe her off for the beach, keeping my weight way aft so she drives well up. I step forward when she grounds, which jams her so she seldom slews around. The gear is stowed, and she's washed and hauled out for another day; that is, hauled out on her mooring.

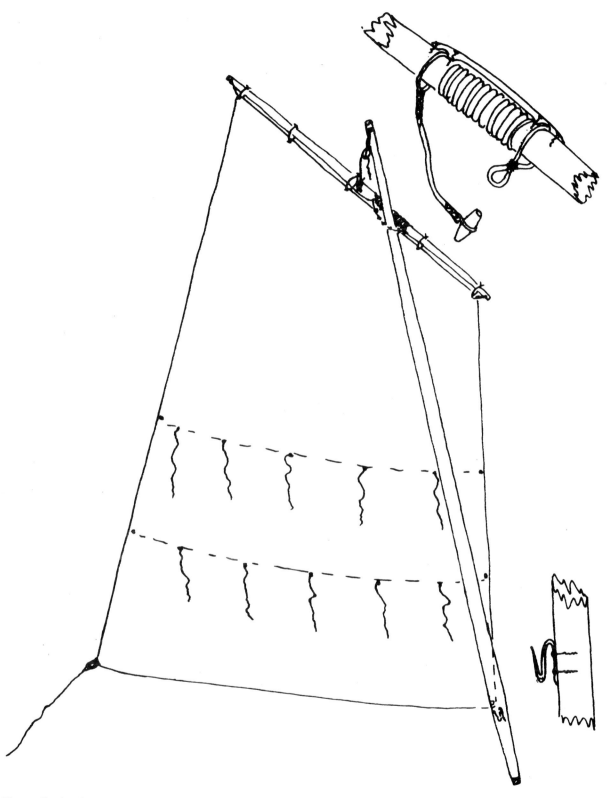

The standing lug rig.

When taking in the fore underway, the sheet is, of course, slacked. You must slack it if you brail, too. The boat will lay about side-to-wind, helm down. If you have a mate, he can head her downwind if need be. In either case, the snotter is now well within reach, and the sail is clear of the boat. You gather the sail to you, rolling the sprit in it (this last is most important, as it helps take wind out of it, and a sail rolled around a spar can't blow out). To stow a sharp mizzen, simply release the sail from the snotter, never the clew, up-end it along the leach, and start rolling. You can, with a bit of practice, take such a sail in when you have no business to be out, which is what I call a sensible rig.

Though I probably should have included it with the rest of the gear, I leave to the last a method of rigging so revolutionary that many with considerable experience just won't go for it. One wants to avoid all the clutter he can in a small craft. A reefable spritsail requires a halyard as mentioned before. This requires a cleat as shown. The halyard has to be about twice the hoist, or a bit more, so when the sail is fully set there is a line to coil and do something with. I simply make the tail fast to the throat; it goes aloft out of the way and acts as a downhaul in case of a hangup—and that's it, self stowing!

This also brings up another shunned bit of gear, the "forth-and-back" lacing, which slides better than greased robands. I know we usually lace back and forth, but you have to go forth before you can go back, hence the name for it. Done this way, it does not jam, as a 'round and 'round lacing does. A stiff, rather small, greased line is the thing to use for lacing, and don't attempt to snug the sail to the mast. Let it take a natural and slack lay. For some reason I can't explain, taking in a reef requires no taking up of the slack. Simply let the slack gather near the tack and forget it, as the sail sets fine. This method, which is hoary with age, also works on quite large craft, and is of course much cheaper and easier than hoops. I dare anyone to try it!

There are other simple rigs for open craft. I think the standing lug rates high. Its slight disadvantage is that it requires a somewhat longer mast to give the sail a proper shape. This, in the end, weighs no more as far as stepping or unstopping goes than the shorter sprit mast, as it has no sail and second spar bundled up in it. The so-called advantages of spars stowing in the boat I find over-rated. The spars can well stick over the stern if need be when the boat is not in use. When rowing with the rig struck, any rig, the spars are usually stuck well over the bow or stern to give room to man the oars anyhow. As shown, the gear is most simple. The sail made about as for a spritsail, though I like a rather stout luff rope, as the peaking up of the sail depends entirely on the luff coming taut first. Without a tight luff, the sail will not stand. It is capable of some adjustment, depending on the exact position of the halyard, which can be experimented with. Here, it is better to have a non-rotating mast. Use a square or oblong tenon, or the halyard lead may work to one side, then not work back. The tack can be lashed to the mast, but I think the British lugger hook is interesting and handy; it should have somewhat of a twist fore and aft so you can put the fastenings in. Any number of reefs is practical though often a small storm lug is carried, complete with yard. The sail is bent to the yard with throat and peak lashings, and the robands mentioned before. The yard should be served or leathered where it crosses the mast; this about one-third the distance from throat. I like the becket and toggle as shown, and then the sail can be rigged or removed easily from the mast. A single-part halyard is simply rolling-hitched to the mast; if the sail is large you can add more purchase, using a lower block to a strop with a toggle for easy removal. The halyard block strop simply goes through a hole in the masthead. You can use a cleat if you wish; however, holes are cheap.

I think this is enough sails and gear to make any classic boat go.

FISH OIL, SOUR MILK, AND STALE BEER

Fish oil has been used in paint, especially dark colors and barn red, since way back, and I think it still is. Drawback is that it's very dark, so it can't be used in light paints. I assume you use it about like linseed oil, and it's maybe more durable. Could be the chemists now take the good out of it and make fake butter and vitamin additives. You might write the Geo. Kirby Paint Co., New Bedford, for the real dope.

I don't know about ox blood in paints, though it might be about like the old casein paints. Sour milk was used; also stale beer. "Red lead mixed with butter-milk or sour beer is a good mixture for a funnel, laid on quite thick" (from Todd and Whall's *Seamanship*). How's that for a dilly? I've found ochres in building supply places for coloring cement, though none there realize you can make paint with it. I simply eyeball proportions; if you make it too thin, it won't cover. Some dryers are usually needed, though both boiled linseed oil and fish oil tend to be dryers. Recently, the lead dryers have become unavailable here—you are supposed to buy the latest coldwater paint invented

last night. Red lead in itself, mixed when practical with another color, is a natural dryer. Yet we are not allowed to have it. I'll bet that, with a bit of digging, fish oil can be turned up. After all, that's partly what pogie fishing is about: oil first, scrap for fertilizer second. Another Todd and Whall recipe: "12 to 14 lb. dry paint requires 6 pts. raw oil, 1 pt. boiled, and 1 pt. turps." Gives you an idea of how much wet to dry. When I mix any new paint from dry ingredients, I make the planned mistake of getting it way too thick, then thin it as works best.

How about this one: "Good blacking for rigging: $1/2$ barrel tar, 6 gills spirit, 4 lb. lamp black, 2 buckets of boiling brine." I used to know an old skipper who put salt in his pine tar to make the rigging shine, and a spoonful of pine tar in a gallon of white lead paint to make it whiter, so he said. His rigging did shine, and his white was better than most.

I think some barn paint has red oxide as a base, which I think is simply a glorified rust, and therefore durable. Ever try to get rid of a rust stain? I was told by a Deer Isle skipper that in his young days there they used red ochre and tallow, put on hot, for bottom paint. There were no worms in Deer Isle in the old days, and the boats kept pretty clean. White lead and tallow put on hot was once used on the bottoms of iron steamers. I suppose, even without the modern poisons, this scaled off some, keeping things more or less clean. The Arabs use a mess of goat grease and lime, or something very like it.

So start mixing, and let me know how it goes.

THE MALLETS CRIED, HOLLERED, BELLOWED, AND CHIRPED

Something should be said about caulking, an art that seems to be much misunderstood now, or so it seems. I think a professional caulker should be the one to write about it, but none seems to come forward. Many think there is a great mystery about it, which, like so many things, is not so; you simply have to understand what it's about, and then put in plenty of practice, at least to be reasonably fast at it and be able to do it properly.

My credentials for writing on this subject are certainly not as good as a real caulking pro, for it is, at least for craft of some size, a trade in itself. However, having caulked various modest-size craft off and on for years, as many boatbuilders do, being much exposed to professionals at it, and making the seams they were to fill, I have a fair working knowledge of the art.

Some years back at a yard where I was employed, there was a caulkers' strike—everyone walked off for a couple of months. All that was left was the boss caulker, a wizened expert at his trade. Word went out for a couple of guys to volunteer, if they thought they could caulk. Myself and another stepped forward with what tools for it we had; these were immediately swept aside by the boss, and he

provided the very best of Drew mallets and irons, which were in those days, the *only* caulking tools. Nearly 300 other men did not step forward; they were wise, maybe, or we were foolish.

The Boss gave a few mild pointers and said, "Boys, I'm going to beat your arms off," and he pretty near did the first couple of weeks. The norm, which he set, was six seams a day each—thread of cotton (choker) and thread of oakum. The seams were nearly 120 feet long; the garboard was double thread. We were watched closely at first, but the Boss seemed satisfied, except for speed at first. In a few weeks we were quite hot, being constantly pushed by this expert. Drew mallets of black mesquite, with tempered rings, are wonderful tools; we were at it for a couple of months, and "buttoned up" several hulls. The mallets cried, hollered, bellowed, and chirped; it was grand. I've not been right in the arm, head, or ears since, and long ago reverted to what real caulkers call "just chinking around" on lighter craft.

The first *Mariner's Catalog* has some excellent illustrations of caulking irons, so there is little point in describing them, except to mention certain ones for certain uses. Mallets have not been as well covered. The caulker's mallet, to the uninitiated, looks like a most awkward tool; just remember, it's had hundreds of years of development on untold miles of seams. Anyone who thinks he can do a proper job with some hammer or carpenter's mallet should try to visualize, say, a six-masted coal schooner, the thickness of her plank, the many threads of oakum required, and the labor that went into caulking such a craft. These mallets are as nearly "right" as any of Man's other tools.

In use, the mallet requires mostly wrist motion, not like a sledge, or the hawsing beetle. The slots in it are to give it rebound and make it lively, so it's not a dead and leaden tool. The more it yells, the better, for it's got plenty of life, thus helping the caulker's arm. The best mallets have tempered steel rings; cheaper ones have plain steel. The wood, which is the very most important, varies—live oak,

black mesquite, "redwood from South America." Just what this latter wood is, I don't know, but it's much sought after—I have one myself. Having gotten interested in mallets, and made a few, and experimented, I've learned a few things. Fine ebony and locust are "dead"; the above mentioned good ones are the ones that have it. In the 1940s, a black mesquite Drew cost about $25.00; today, I don't know where you could buy a new one for any price.

What caulking is about, besides keeping water from running through the seams, is that it tightens and stiffens the vessel, for by no skill of man can a big craft be perfectly joined. What a craft needs is proper caulking to set up the whole structure. Large vessels had their ceiling and 'tween decks caulked besides the outside planking and decks, and if their sawn frames were filled solid, or "packed," often in the ends and bottom, these were caulked and

A caulking mallet and iron with cotton caulking for the garboard seam, which would be the only seam caulked in this photo.

pitched, too, before planking and ceiling, in an effort to further stiffen the hull. Though before my time, this method was common in very big craft before the introduction of steel strapping.

Oakum was always used, in my day at least, for all heavy work, for cotton cannot be set up nearly as hard as oakum, which, when properly set up, turns into something very like a piece of leather strap, biting manfully into the plank edges as the wood swells, so the ship will not "spew it." A cotton choker was used first, then the required number of strands of oakum on that, and well set down, payed with pitch, plain paint, or red lead, depending on the time, place, and contract requirements, and later usually filled; with what, depending on above or below water, and the cost of the vessel. There is much more to doing a big vessel than this, but I think now most are much more concerned with smaller craft.

Much of the above still applies to lighter craft, say from 50 feet down, though things change somewhat, and a lighter hand and tools are used. Plank 2" down to about $1\frac{1}{2}$", if of reasonably hard wood—say fir, yellow pine, or oak—can use a choker of cotton followed by oakum. You can set the oakum properly—too much setting and you can bust out the back of a plank. Lighter planking, and soft wood—say cedar and pine—use cotton only. Cotton alone is used in most wood decks. The lighter the plank, the less heavy handed you must be, though the same principle applies always: you stiffen the craft as well as seal the seams.

Very light small boats are often caulked with a "wheel," that is, a small tapered wheel on a handle is used to roll the cotton into the seams; sometimes, if this is not quite sufficient, the cotton is set back with a very narrow iron and light mallet, taking care not to "bust out."

Irons must be dry, clean, and bright, with no rough edges, seams clean, bare wood, or you find out quickly that cotton sticks to the iron, and it's impossible to tuck it properly. It often happens that some pitch from the plank, paint that has run through from some job going on inside, or other sticky stuff gets in the seam; clean it out the best you can, and dip the iron in light oil to prevent it from picking up goo and causing the cotton to stick to the iron. It's good practice to stand irons when not in use in a can of oil with some cotton in the bottom. It's the same when using a putty knife—it should be clean and bright; if rusty or dirty, stuff sticks to it. Bright tools of any kind do work better.

Any caulking, cotton or oakum, should be painted thoroughly before it gets wet; never let unpainted seams go overnight, even indoors. Use a narrow brush, preferably a seam brush made for this purpose (still available), and make sure you do a thorough job—go over it twice if necessary—then there is no rush to fill the seam with whatever you intend to use. The often mentioned practice, yes, even in some books on boatbuilding, of soaking cotton in paint then tucking it in the seams, is *NEVER* done; that it has been in print only points out that those suggesting this have never done any real caulking.

About materials: oakum comes in bales for big jobs, and must be picked and spun out on the caulker's knee to work it into condition to use; even this takes a bit of practice to get even and of the right size for the job. Cotton comes in hanks or bundles, usually with brown paper glued around it. Open the package up and spread out the cotton carefully. You will find that there is a pattern to the way it's put up. Through the years it has seemed to vary as to just how many strands it's bundled in. The strands can be separated to the proper size for the job, and single strands can be split for small seams. I never use cotton wicking; this is for other uses and is not good for seams, though it is sometimes used in light work.

In the past there were special paints made for seams; personally I like red lead the best, and many pros do too, though in a pinch, any good oil paint seems to work. What you are doing is preventing dampness reaching the cotton, until the plank have a chance to swell, or "make up" as it's often said, and lock the caulking in place. What seam filling or putty you use depends on size and use of the craft. In large vessels it was once common not to fill any above-water seams for a couple of years, or until the plank had set itself. The seams were simply painted each time the craft was painted; this was common on painted decks of workboats, too. Even on smaller craft, especially if the plank are not totally seasoned, I think this is still good practice.

Every seam compound I know of plays out in time. Honest to gosh real white lead putty, not the 5 percent lead stuff you used to buy, is most durable in a solidly built craft that is thick enough not to come and go much. Pine tar and whiting make a durable filler for bottom seams, as well as asphalt shingle stickum. Some very large wooden craft of the past were pitched under water, and I've seen some that were cemented—the idea is to keep worm and other growth out of the big seams in big craft. I think for light craft, common today, possibly the store-bought things work quite well, once you find one you like. I use International #31, which is white, seems to last well, is flexible enough for small craft that "work" some, and it's easy to apply. However, I can get along quite well without it, simply using some of the older ways. I like the seams rodded back in any new craft, regardless of size.

Knowing few will become professional caulkers on large craft, and if they do, they will train on the job, and some leathery Boss will beat their arms off, I say no more on this, though it is a mighty interesting subject. Rather, some nutshell suggestions for lesser craft. First, remember caulking is to stiffen the hull, as well as seal the seams. Those who in recent years have come up with some seam filler touted "to do away with caulking," may make good stickum, but they don't know the first principles of buttoning up

a boat. Next you learn about the size of cotton threads required for certain size seams and planking; there are no real set rules here. It depends on the seams as well as the stoutness, or lack of it, of the planking. The seams must be caulked solidly, evenly and tightly, but don't overdo it and bust out the back of the plank. It's understood that a caulking seam must be a wedge, tight on the inside and open the proper amount outside. Even a seam that is dried out and quite wide will caulk; you learn about gathering the cotton to make it choke off. A hollow seam, that is, with more open inside than out, cannot be properly caulked, for it won't choke off—you think you have it, then the cotton falls through inside; this is known as "losing it." What to do? Sometimes you must remove the plank, or a Dutchman can be set in to make a proper seam. How you do this is the carpenter's job, not the caulker's. Caulking a garboard or other seam with rabbet and solid back, you can set up fairly hard, even in a small craft. In large vessels they gave this what for; takes two men, one with a hawsing iron, the other with a beetle.

Most often, in craft where the building is protracted, and the planking not too dry, there will be a considerable variation in the width of many seams. No matter, this is where an experienced man can even things up. He starts by looking her over and muttering, and, if addicted to a chew, bites one off. He will make some cryptic marks in chalk, caulk the butts first, leaving tails of cotton out, so when running the seams these get locked in. Then he will do the narrow seams next, usually in part, as narrowness does not always run the length of the seam. The planks will crawl a bit, closing up the wider seams. When the caulker is happy with this patchwork, he will start running the strakes along, often several at a time, shifting from one to another, and shifting sides on the craft if alone, to bring her along evenly. With a crew, on a big craft, men will be working on both sides with the Boss checking on things as the job goes along. One thing for sure, the seams will be painted before quitting time, usually the apprentice's job, if there is one.

There are other little things you learn about caulking by doing; just how much you take off the little tucking bights of cotton to suit the width of the seam; you get a feel for just how much is enough of any of it. You learn by instinct just what iron is required for a given bit of work. There are very many different irons, a number not needed for modest-to-small craft—the dumb or reaming iron for tight seams, often in two sizes, spike irons for tight and close places, in straight, bent, and half-bent shapes, caulking irons, making irons, thin and thick, crease, and double crease, which is for large craft, the various bents and half bents, and the fore-and-aft bent, which is rare. A few others, which are in the usual caulker's kit, include the caulking wheel, rake, which is worked out of an old file oftentimes, and the reefing iron for cleaning out old

Tools for caulking in Pete's shop. Pictured are three mallets, various irons, and a wheel for small, delicate work.

317

seams. Other tools are a can with oakum or cotton in it to stow the irons in, a small stool that usually rocks, a dirty tar-stained bit of canvas for your knee, if you roll oakum, and, of course, the caulker's pride, the mallet. The more voice it has the better.

I can't really tell you how it's done; you pick it up by observation, trial, and, better yet, the real way, under an expert eye, which is not easily available. Next best is to go ahead and do it; no amount of reading will give you the skill, but just pointers on it. Though I no longer like to crawl under some weeping hulk to try and mend her seams, getting my tools wet and sandy, I still very much enjoy buttoning up new work, even though it's now small stuff. Old "redwood from South America" begins her talk, and it brings back memories. Though in a closed shop, her words carry and they often bring in total strangers to see what it's about; even the totally uninitiated are charmed by what she says.

NATURAL KNEES

Since I use natural knees in the small boats I build, I'm always asked, "Where do you get knees?" The stupid answer to what may not be such a stupid questions is, "From trees." The mystery seems to be just how I go about it, mostly because few ever have considered the subject. Nothing does quite as well and looks as good in a traditional craft, large or small, as a wooden knee. Cast metal knees are troublesome and expensive to make and fit. Fabricated bronze is for those equipped to do such work. Besides, metal knees are not good looking and are heavy; wood often rots out under them quicker than wooden ones. Laminated knees are very time consuming to make right, and never look good varnished.

Here is now I acquire knees: Some I get from trimming on my own property, which amounts to only a big town lot, though with more growth than most. I watch where tree cutting is going on, and get there before things are ruined by cutting right at the elbows, which is the way tree removers always do it. I pass the word around that I collect knees; some friends thus informed often drop off a knee or two from their cutting for the wood pile. Surprising how your stock grows, simply by watching for knees.

If you fell a tree, or simply cut up the parts, the sketches show about how I cut for knees. Apple, pear, gnarled hardwoods, such as wild cherry, and other hardwoods that are weather racked give the most crook. Elm, pitch pine, and others that tend to be straighter still furnish a lot of stock. Breasthooks are easily available from crotches. The waste goes on the wood pile.

Once the knees are on hand, there is the matter of rough sawing them out to help them dry and getting most of the bark off (bark often harbors worms). Small knees can well be cut as shown, on the bandsaw, though this takes some skill and practice, and there is some risk. Here, a power plane, or hatchet, to get a couple of reasonable flats, makes the rest easy.

For bigger stuff I rough out the stock with a gas saw; mine is the blade type, which is quite suited to the work, though a chain saw does it too. Knees of any size take quite a lot of sawing, as, even though green, much of this wood is hard, some very hard. I usually cut to a chalk line put on with a batten. You won't find this work easy; my saw is big, heavy, extremely noisy, has a stinking breath (so I always plan to be to weather of it), has an unlimited taste

Natural crooks and their use and placement in a classic Culler boat. These are breasthooks at the stem, knees at the mast partners, and knees bracing the thwarts and sides. The stem itself is also a natural crook, as is the stern knee (not shown).

for fuel, and the cuts are long, so it's quite unrelenting to machine and operator. The only respite is stopping to shift the piece, which is often hard to secure. Breasthooks are especially unhandy. I use wedges, stay pieces jammed in the buck, and an occasional C-clamp; watch that the clamp does not come loose and fall in the saw blade, since there is much vibration. Also, you often get a pinch and have to wedge the cut open, for knees seem to grow under considerable tension. You will have to start a cut at the other end, trying to meet up with the first cut half way through. Once slabbed, a big knee can be split to get a pair; this is not so bad, as flats are easier to hold, but it's a heavy cut in the thickest part.

This roughed out stuff is dead green, so store it to dry slowly; my favorite storage spot is a dark woodshed with a dirt floor. I rack the knees up on sleepers a little above ground and out of the wind. If you have to use green knees, soak them with oil and kerosene and place them in a steam box. This will help things a lot. Green knees tend to twist and check; steam seems to stop much of it. On the other hand, putting in a totally dry knee, with some of the stock I get, is about like working bone, but it stays put.

Some things I've learned the hard way: I've contacted several landscape firms about saving knees for me, showing just what I want and offering coin of the realm. They are avid for the extra buck (so they say), yet up to now none has ever shown up—may you have better luck. Knees are trade goods to other builders if you become overstocked. Bandsaws again: be sure you know what you are doing; you

(continued on page 323)

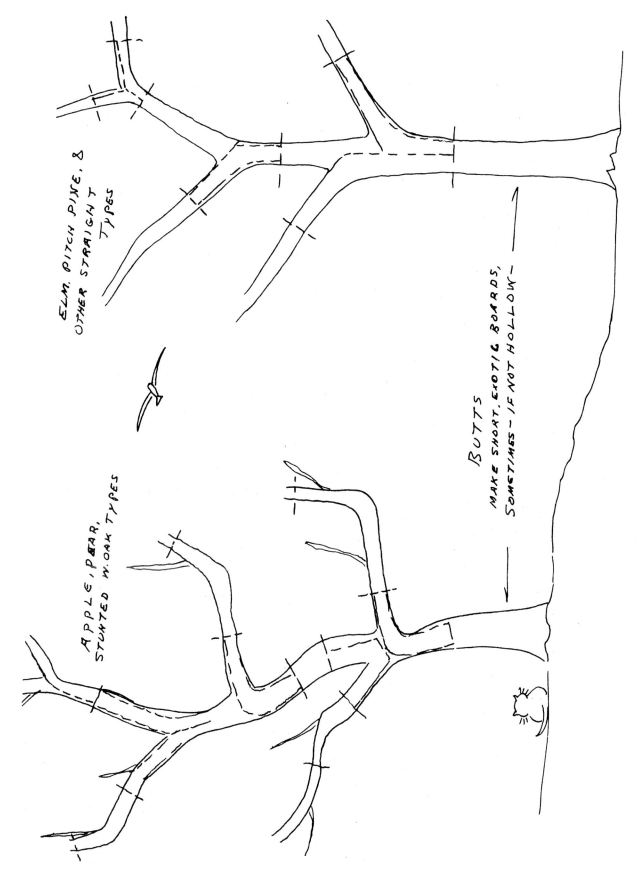

ELM, PITCH PINE, & OTHER STRAIGHT TYPES

APPLE, PEAR, STUNTED W. OAK TYPES

BUTTS

MAKE SHORT, EXOTIC BOARDS, SOMETIMES — IF NOT HOLLOW —

A drawing by Pete Culler showing the likely locations for knee stock in different tree types.

321

SLABBING OFF

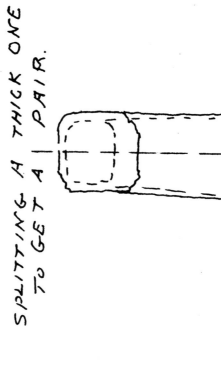

SPLITTING A THICK ONE
TO GET A PAIR.

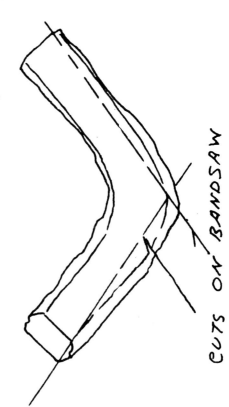

AFTER SLABBING.

CUTS ON BANDSAW

Slabbing off two sides of the crook must be done with care as the log in this early stage is round and irregular. Make certain that the work is held securely when using power saws and cutting equipment. Once you have two sides flat, remove any remaining bark, as this is where boring bugs live.

322

(continued from page 320)

will hang up once in a while, jam her, blow a fuse, or break a blade. Take care. *Never* try cutting knees on a table saw, any cut, even on an about-finished knee. Though the hatchet and hand plane will do it, the power plane is just fine in working flats true. By its nature, a knee has constant changing grain; take

care in surfacing. It may well pay to paint seasoning knees with hot wax to prevent checking, but I must admit that I don't do it. If you have a pond handy, soaking for a while might help—I don't do that either. I simply leave them plenty big and rough, so most of the checks are cut out in finishing.

MOTORBOATS FOR THE MASSES

No doubt, to be quick and dirty in the true sense, a boat should be propelled by pole, paddle, oars, and in some cases sticks and a scrap of canvas, with a piece of board for a leeboard, hung by a lanyard from a tholepin. This is keeping it fundamental, as it should be.

However, for some uses, the advantages of a motor can be very necessary. This also ties in with discussions of air-cooled industrial motors in recent *Mariner's Catalogs*. I show some quick and dirty motorboats I have known. The little 8-footer was built and powered in a hurry simply to get her owner to and from work, which she did for a long time with great success. The installation was rudimentary, which was all that was needed. She had no hand throttle, but simply used the governor on the little $^3/_4$-hp engine. Being so short and rockered, she had a built-in clutch—you simply raised the wheel out with your weight when you wanted to (the engine did not race with the governor). The "steering gear" was simply a paddle chopped out of a handy board. Say what you will, the whole thing worked perfectly.

The 13-foot mullet skiff had a lot of charm. She was built by a fisherman-boatbuilder out of what

he could get, for times were hard. She was of excellent model and well joined, though the stock in her was scrap of all kinds, including much use of mangrove roots, which were free. She even had a tiny fish well, for she was a great part of her owner's living. The engine was a $1^1/_2$-hp Briggs—I own one of these of the same vintage now, and it's most reliable. The installation was very fundamental. Due to a changing scene, this little craft made a hundred-mile trip to a place of better employment as a matter of course. She made many a dollar from fish, for her owner was skilled with the throw net and wise in the ways of 'gators and such.

The Bahama boat was a buxom thing, worked daily as shown, and with the big iron Briggs, with an iron crank, was quite a workhorse. Though simple in installation, she had one failing—an outside stuffing box; being deep, and with little range of tide in the area, this was neglected and was no doubt worn, so it was customary to proceed by constant bailing, said bailers nearly all having pin holes in the bottom. She was always so crowded that she carried two "engineers"; one could reach the crank and nothing else, the other could get at the panic buttons.

These craft all had the same thing in common; they were cheap to build or acquire. The Bahama was a conversion but was picked up for peanuts. Though each installation was slightly different, based on what the owners could cobble up, simplicity was the thing. The fisherman was quite proud of his and kept her well; she had a little open-sided box over the mill. The others ran naked; sometimes, when someone thought to do it, an old coat might be thrown over them. Exhaust pipes were ignored; they simply blatted out through the little squash-shaped mufflers that came with them. However, the big engine had long ago lost whatever she had and simply bellowed into the night. This racket was part of the river scene, and early risers set their watches by it.

Lifejackets and other required equipment were nonexistent. Now, this might not seem safe and sane boating—I say it was, for those doing it knew what they were doing. The Law was busy elsewhere, and these men were doing a job; that's all that mattered.

If these lashups meet the law now, I really don't know; my feeling is, being all in the open, I don't see why not. The same engines power all sorts of things both ashore and afloat. Filling out some state motorboat registration might be interesting— "model, year number, and make of hull." Perhaps I-X (for experimental)-77 JOE might do.

I show a DIRTY with my notions of about how to go about it. You acquire or build a hull of some sort, guessing about how much hull to engine. How you get the engine—its size, make, and condition— is your business. You may have to buy a shaft unless you have friends in the business; this may be the big expense after the engine. It must run true. All I had experience with had bronze shafts; no doubt the present-day noncorrosive white metal shafts will do okay. In fresh water, you might get away with plain steel for quite a while. In the above boats the shaft size was the same as the engine shaft size for good reason (see coupling). Some props were scrounged,

others made about as shown out of brass and bronze. Don't ask me prop size for each hp, I don't know, Observe and experiment. If it's too big, cut it down. All the rigs I was familiar with were pretty heavily loaded with prop, and the engines seemed to take it.

The propeller boss was usually a piece of big prop shaft bored out by some machinist friend; slots for blades were cut by putting two, or sometimes three blades in a backsaw frame, depending on the thickness of the prop blades. The blades were brass, or bronze plate if you could scrounge it, about $1/8$" thick, and cut and shaped by aping some store-bought prop. Some of the boys got some interesting experimental shapes that worked fine. The blades were brazed in the slots, usually by some garage, or slipped to the welder at his place of work. I think with good fits, silver solder will work quite well here. Silver solder likes good fits.

Note the drive pin in the shaft; it's also a shear pin, so carry some spares. Note the slots in the forward end of the boss; these are a cap chisel job. The nuts and cotter are standard. In the gone and much lamented (here anyhow) magazine called *Steamboats and Modern Steam Launches*, there is some excellent stuff on designing and making your own props, by guess who?—Westy Farmer, of course. So I need say no more about propellers—except check your rotation. All these little engines I've had to do with are left handed.

The stern bearing (I warned you about an outside stuffing box) is simply swirly-grained hardwood. Mount and adjust it for square just like a bought bearing; there should be a gasket behind it. Don't laugh, this is a water-lubricated hardwood bearing like our finest steamships have had. It works. Some groove the bottom of the shaft hole with a keyhole saw, saying it gives water passage and a place for sand to work out; I don't really know if that is true.

(continued on page 329)

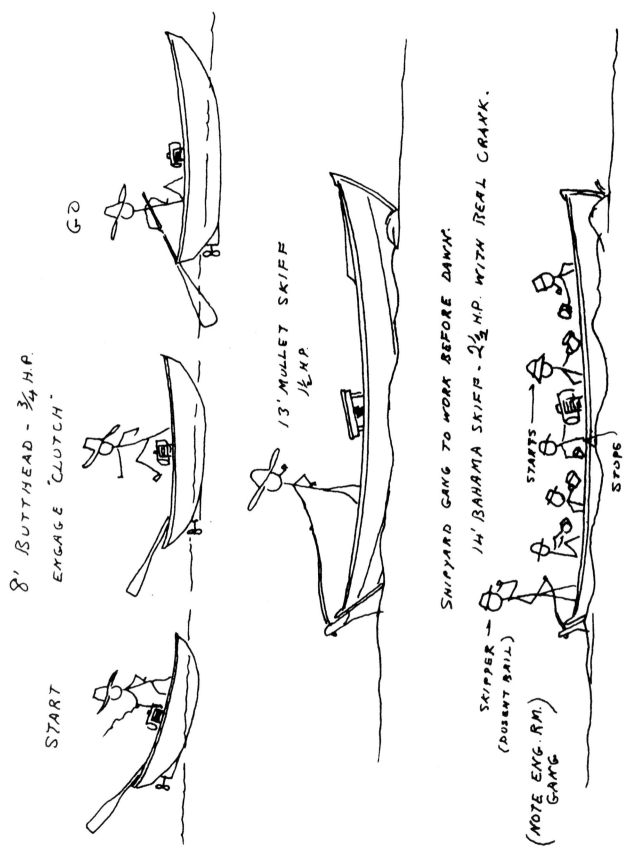

8' BUTTHEAD - ¾ H.P.

START

ENGAGE "CLUTCH"

GO

13' MULLET SKIFF 1½ H.P.

SHIPYARD GANG TO WORK BEFORE DAWN.

14' BAHAMA SKIFF - 2½ H.P. WITH REAL CRANK.

SKIPPER → (DOSENT BAIL)

STARTS →

STOPS

(NOTE ENG. RM.) GANG

This discussion on Quick and Dirty Boats was an ongoing dialogue within the Mariner's Catalog regarding the genre of watercraft that "make do." Naturally, this was a topic near and dear to Pete's heart, and the text and drawings show some of his experiences with the type and the cast of characters that often infused these boats with human interest.

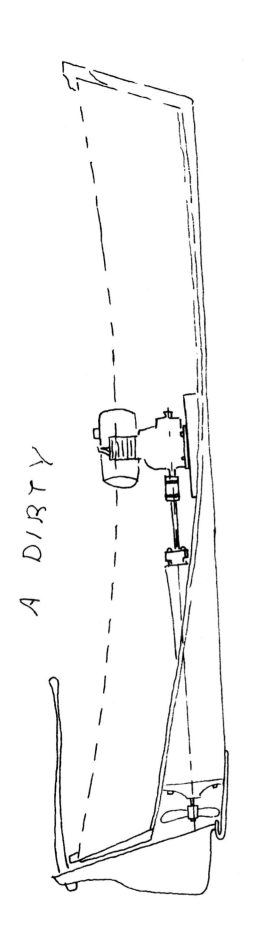

A DIRTY

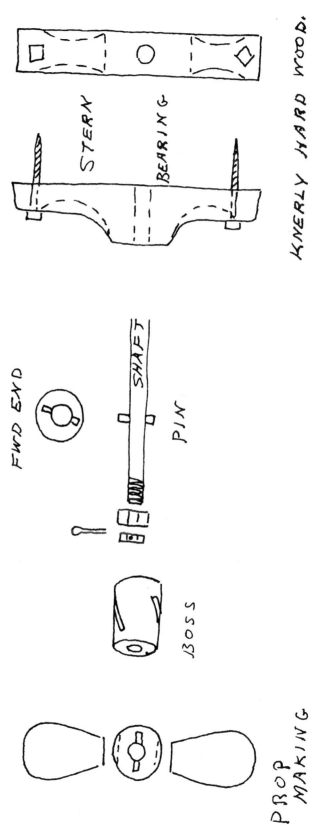

KNERLY HARD WOOD.

STERN

BEARING

FWD END

SHAFT

PIN

BOSS

PROP MAKING

Details of the drivetrain on a Quick and Dirty powerboat.

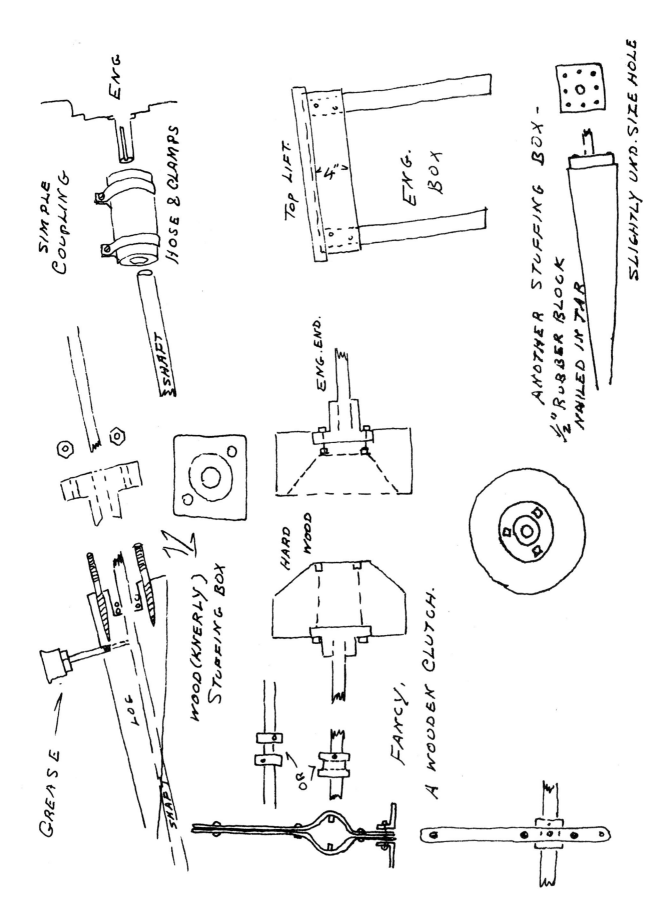

Engineering adaptations when you "make do" with what you have. Scarcity, in all its many forms, is a given with this boat type.

(continued from page 325)

The wedge-shaped shaft log has been standard in flat-bottomed boats for years, well bedded and bolted, 'nuf said. The grease cup in it is very good, dirty build or not, and much helps the life of the packing and box, which you note is of wood. Yes, it works. You can make your own hanger bolts by cutting heads off lag screws; a bit of grinding, for the shanks may be a bit oversize, and threading. If this is all too involved, use the alternate rubber block as shown—in shallow boats there is small pressure on the stuffing box. The coupling is simply a stout suction hose and clamps. It's assumed you know, or are willing to learn, how to line up an engine, even with hose. This drive was once common for marine engine water pumps of good size. This is the point of having prop shaft and engine shaft the same size—if you are real hot, you can bush to different sizes.

Engine box should be totally open; these beasts get hot. Make it big enough so you don't have to take it off to start, work throttle, and stop, only remove the lid. An over-riding throttle lever can be rigged right on the engine, just like many lawn mowers, so it overcomes the governor. Some of these little engines run dead slow remarkably well, especially the older, slower models.

The snazzy clutch is for those who just must have one, or are mad tinkerers like myself. These things, in principle, used to be manufactured out of metal, but I doubt if they still are. Acquire, by devious means or otherwise, two couplings that fit the shafts; saw out as round as you can two oak discs fairly thick; lay out with care the location of the couplings and let in by chisel work as shown—you can rough out the female end to make bolting easier. These won't be true. Bolt down the little beast somewhere solid, put on the coupling with disc, making sure it's tight, rig a tool rest, and turn in place so it's true, true as you can get wood, anyhow. This done, do the other, trying to get a fair match

to the cones. Set collars, or even a grooved set collar, are not hard to come by; the shift lever I think explains itself—scrap iron, rivets, pins—it should be a slack fit on the collar, plenty of play and grease, as there is no pressure on it once engaged. I can picture some hotshot here friction-loading the thing end, so once engaged, a slight pull-back will have the pins out of contact with the collars—no wear. The very sophisticated may still not see how this works. The prop thrust keeps the thing engaged; simply throttle down, shift in, and give her the gas, the reverse in going to neutral. The unnecessary bit of gear is really a way-out, highly "engineered" contraption, for it is self-taking-up for wear, more or less self-aligning, and tends to true up the wood, which always warps somewhat.

Some observations—I've not tinkered with the recent rather higher speed models that have replaced the older engines. As Briggs says, load 'em; if it's too much, whittle down the prop. You put up with the noise. Don't box 'em in; give 'em air. Don't expect other than modest speed. Those I've played with seemed to go best at very modest wave making, a speed-length ratio of about .90 or 1. The boats and engines were small, and thus the waterline length also. The gas "mileage" was fantastic; a gallon in 8 hours with the little old model $1\frac{1}{2}$s.

I've often wondered about the once-common radial-thrust bearing common on the old make and breaks. None I knew used any on the little Briggs, and the engines seemed to take it. It might be a good idea to use one—cut the hose coupling square and put the radial between it and the motor housing, maybe using some big washers, too; same if you use the clutch and coupling.

While somewhat off the subject of true quick and dirty boats, and knowing the great God of speed still rules most people, fuel consumption be damned. I think I could design a fairly fast, though limited-use boat for these air-cooled engines. Right away you consider a fairly big one, a long, lean, flat-run boat of very good but light construction—with speed you have to start thinking light right off—a hull that could "get away from her wheel." Small diameter, large pitch, interesting prop design; careful lineup; and I doubt if you could drive her through a piece of hose. Now we are getting complicated, expensive, and wasteful, so let's take it slow and be happy.

Note that I've given no fixed dimensions for the boat and motor; you fit what you have to work with into something that operates. Proportion, both for strength and looks, is part of mechanics, even though this is the baling-wire sort. There is no reason why a quick and dirty boat has to be totally horrible to look at, and it must do the job intended for it, or there is no point at all in doing it.

Someone gets the urge to turn out 1-X-77, let us know how she works.

TARRED RIGGING AND STROPPED BLOCKS

Mention of tarred rigging today brings forth mental pictures of *Old Ironsides,* clipper ships, and *Two Years Before the Mast,* which book, by the way, gives a good account of tarring down—how it was done, not so much why, as that part of it was accepted in those days.

To consider tarred rigging now might be taken to be reactionary in the extreme, yet with the high cost of boating gear, more and more do-it-yourself building and rigging, it makes good sense—it always did, but like so many things, good sense often goes to leeward. I have noticed many times, in most any harbor, that otherwise-well-kept craft have had standing rigging in deplorable condition, for no other reason than that the owners of them have no knowledge of rigging upkeep, or that properly maintained rigging can last as long as the vessel.

For classic craft, a return to tarred rigging makes sense, especially since pine tar is still available— we're lucky; some commission or do-good outfit has yet to declare it unfit for Man's endeavors!

Stainless steel wire and Dacron line are fine, just the thing for a racer. Though wonderful, they don't last forever. Both take well to tar, yet plain galvanized steel rigging, properly put up to begin with and kept tarred, will last every bit as long. Plain black iron will, too, if you coat and tend it properly, as pine tar is one of the most waterproof of coatings. Tar, by the way, was part of the makeup of the first Atlantic cable.

Rigging already made up and in use on a boat will benefit by being tarred, even if it has been totally exposed without protection. But for first class results, a new gang of rigging is made up with pine tar so that—and note this—with proper retarring, its life, as far as these things go, will be as long as anyone wants it around. Tarring is not for those who still think that new-notion boats don't require maintenance. Whether built by wood butchers, tin knockers, chemists, or masons, any craft to remain seaworthy must have maintenance, and taking care of the rigging is only a small part of it. Those preaching the no-maintenance boat cannot really have gone to sea; real seakeeping is most wearing on any craft.

I will not go into how to make up a gang of rigging for, say, a classic schooner; it's all available in many ancient works on rigging. There are still some riggers who know how to do it, and, with the printed matter available, it's no great feat for the self-taught person with desire to master it. Rather, I will describe the use of pine tar in making up a gang of rigging. It matters not if it's for a small sloop or a large schooner; the principle is the same.

My own system, though it may vary slightly from other practicing riggers in detail, is, or was, the standard of the past. Assuming you have quite a number of splices and servings to do, first you must get some marline of quality and suitable size, which is not an easy thing to do at the moment. Marline is quite expensive now, so you want it to last once it is put on. You will need parcelling—light stuff like drill or strong sheeting. Stout muslin also will do, or, if the rigging is large, light canvas can be used. I've seen friction tape used for parcelling more than once; my advice is, don't. Some riggers cut and roll their parcelling in bandage form, about 2" wide, tying the roll with a bit of twine, then putting many rolls to soak in a can of linseed oil. When they are to be used, some are taken out and stood on end in a tilted pie pan to drain, and the parceling is put on soaking wet. This is good practice. In the past, for big wire, we used to strip up sacking, which manila line came in at one time. This sacking was said "to hold the tar" in the big meshes. Having stripped much old rigging put up this way, I have no doubts but what it made a very waterproof covering.

I like to tar the bare wire or splice before parcelling, whether the cloth is soaked in oil or not. Very big wire may need tarring, then worming and parcelling, tarring again, then serving with well-tallowed marline. This is a most delightfully messy operation, and it's soon apparent, even to the novice, that the great pressure of the serving, using a mallet or board, has forced the concoction to the very core of the wire, and that it is totally sealed, with even the air pushed out. No other method that I know of, put on by hand, in a barn, under a tree, or aboard a vessel, or wherever is handy, can so

secure a splice from moisture and air. Once this treated rigging has set up somewhat (it's always a little flexible), surface maintenance, with tar, is required, and the rigging will outlast you. Can anyone ask more of a simple hand operation?

The bare-wire parts that usually are not served take to tar just fine; the point is, tar it all—servings, bare wire, ratlines, and seizings, if any. The whole works, not forgetting the turnbuckles, or deadeyes if you use them. Turnbuckles and any other threaded fittings, opened up and the threads tarred, will always be workable later on. This applies to both bronze and iron threads—a mooring shackle with threads treated with pine tar will open up easily years later. This same system is great for any kind of threads exposed to weather, salt, road goo, and all the other crud much machinery is exposed to. Just why the use of this stuff on threads is little known is hard to fathom. Sometimes I think Modern Technology outruns common sense, at least where the ordinary boatman is concerned.

Naturally, all sorts of other gear can and should be tarred, as it was in the past—rope strops if you use them, certainly deadeyes and lanyards, for part of the trouble a novice has keeping these tight, or setting them up, is caused by a lack of lubrication and tar, plus a scant knowhow with tackles and seizings. Those who may want to make their own sails may well have to make their own tarred boltrope, now that real tarred hemp is about unavailable; they might also have to tar synthetic small stuff in place of hard-to-come-by real marline. Just how you do this is quite simple, messy, and wonderful smelling. Most people like the smell of pine tar, though some females profess to hate it.

Here are some pointers on the use and thinning of tar for various gear. In mild or warm weather, for making up a gang of rigging, pine tar can often be used as is, though some batches are thicker than others. Cold weather requires thinning in any case. I find several thinners work, but turpentine is best of all, for it's really a by-product of making tar (or maybe tar is the by-product of making turpentine). For making boltrope or lanyards out of new stuff, I make my tar "thin as water"; that is, so it sounds watery running off a stirring stick. Too thin is better than too thick. Often I mix it about like the old-time licorice water kids had as a treat in the distant past. I then simply pass the line through the bucket or can of watery tar and hang it in bights from a spike over the bucket till it has drained, then put it out in the air to dry. If anyone thinks he can dry this stuff in a closed building in the winter, forget it. Put the line out in the air; an open shed is good, though in good summer weather, just outdoors is fine, and it will set well before dew or rain falls. Thus treated it can be used for lanyards. The

line is cut to lengths, the stopper knots are made, the line is well greased and stretched, then it is rove off and set up. Being new, the line may have to be set up a couple of times; then when things seem set, it's tarred all over. The soaking in the thin stuff first insures full penetration.

If the line is to be used as a boltrope, and it seems a bit stiff after the dipping and drying (remember that cold makes it so), I often soak it again, this time in kerosene with some tallow dissolved in it, then hung and dried again. This limbers it up for sewing on as sail roping. I've had quite some success with using Dacron, or a cheap form of synthetic pot warp for tarred roping, as none of this stuff has any stretch. I'm often asked why I tar Dacron, as weather does not affect it and it does not stretch and

The last boat that Pete built was the lovely Swampscott dory Svärmisk *for Chris Wentz, in 1977. (She now lives at Mystic Seaport.) According to Chris, she was fast!* "*While I can't say she planed, she would surge and accelerate and surf on the smallest wave. A very lively boat. We sailed her like a Laser with our toes hooked under her thwarts, hiking for all we were worth.*" (Chris Wentz)

shrink like natural fibers. Not quite so—sun and salt do affect it. Untreated Dacron behaves just the opposite of natural fibers, stretching some when wet, and taking up when dry. Treat it right and it will last as long as you care for it. Manila line can be tarred the same way, and, if it's good stuff to begin with (much of it now seems poor), it works as well as any.

Well-tarred line, though it will chafe, is less subject to chafing than untreated line. Chafe is one of the big pains of maintenance in real open-water sailing. Working up a gang of rigging with pine tar, linseed oil, and tallow is hard on the hands in some ways, yet you will not have the dry and cracking skin some people get when working outside in cold weather—the stuff is good medicine in many ways.

Once a new vessel is rigged and in use, she will require several tarrings the first year, until there is considerable buildup, then she only requires tar each fall at layup or an occasional touch when something gets chafed in use. If you think you can tar, even in hot weather, and then go sailing the next day, forget it. Properly planned, in the North at least, once a coating is built up, putting on tar at layup time poses no problem.

If by chance you hate maintenance work of any kind, and must have instant dry, instant results, and don't care for marlinspike seamanship, forget all this and run your gear till it rots, then replace it frequently. Let's hope it does not let you down in a tight spot.

When I first started in with boats, some working knowledge of marlinspike seamanship was not uncommon among most boatmen; some were highly skilled at it, beyond the everyday needs of their profession, as it is an interesting and satisfying skill to acquire. I was fortunate to have Biddlecomb's *Art of Rigging* as a textbook at an early age, but best of all was learning from the many real seamen then around. I think for the finer details, a person can't go wrong now using

The Ashley Book of Knots. This volume tends to floor some people on first glance. It's really quite easy to use. The section on applied marlinspike seamanship is the most important.

I mentioned such things as tarring block strops and smaller gear, all of which benefit by the tar. Who uses stropped blocks now? You can, especially if you make your own. There have been some recent articles in boating magazines on making blocks, most showing the now-customary internal metal stropping; this is fine if you want to do it that way. I've made many blocks of all sizes, both for boats and tackles for lifting and hauling, and have never made an internal metal-stropped block for my own craft. I only do it on order for boats I am building for others. I've found the rope-stropped block much more satisfactory than metal-stropped and easier and cheaper to make. I'm always asked by those who never have used them if they are strong. I've never had a failure, other than getting one fouled in the undercarriage of a truck, and even it was quite repairable. If such blocks could control the rig in a three-deck warship, or do for heaving-down tackles in careening, I for one need no assurance of their ability.

The various stroppings possible to suit different uses (see *Ashley*), the ready adjustability, the tendency to take a fair lead, and that lack of "fittings" that so much boat gear is cluttered with now, plus the simple and economical building, have made these blocks my choice for many years over the usual standard block. More than once on various craft, when I could not get a standard block to set properly, I've robbed its sheave and pin, junked the shell and metal, then made a rope-stropped shell, tailored and fitted to the job, always with good results.

I find, too, that there is now a rather limited choice in types of store-bought blocks. By making your own you can have all sorts of fine specials that just suit a certain place. I've made non-toppling blocks for boat falls, blocks that can't be fouled, and all the other types, with strops to suit the many purposes. A properly made and stropped block, kept tarred, is a tough bit of chandlery.

I am often asked what wood I use for blocks, and bullseyes, lizards, parrels, and deadeyes for that matter. The answer is: wood that is cheap and available. Most people think in terms of lignum vitae, which is expensive and unnecessary, or teak, which now seems to be the rage for block shells. In over 50 years of exposure to boats, I never heard of using teak for block shells until recently. Most teak splits too easily to make good block shells. If this last remark casts doubt on the knowledge of some modern block-makers, that's fully what I intend.

We are considering here the economical, the available, and the durable, and their workability in backyard shops, or on the deck of a vessel. One of the most available and toughest woods in New England is the common American elm, the one the beetles raise hell with. It's not a handsome wood, but it's quite available off wood piles and fellings. Its resistance to splitting needs no elaboration—anyone who has split elm or attempted to, for stove wood, will get the message. In the South, live oak takes its place. Ash, hickory, maple, and beech are often on a wood pile; all have been used for blocks in the past, as was locust, of course. There is hornbeam and an occasional old walnut railroad tie. In other words, there is more block-making wood just hanging around than a large fleet could ever use.

I've used other types of wood for blocks: white oak, apple, and some I don't know what, except they're hard and tough. And then there's greenheart. Federal dock building, or other very high-class piling work, often calls for greenheart fender piles. The trimmed-off tops of these can often be cadged from dock builders, much battered and split by driving, but you might find some usable stuff for blocks, though there will be much waste due to the splits. This stuff won't float, so if you get hold of a big chunk, be prepared for a heavy lift. A lump of greenheart is just not the thing you toss lightly into the trunk of a mini-car.

I'm sure there are other easily acquired block-making woods, but since there is so much of the above available, I've not looked very far. If ruggedness is the main thing, probably elm is the choice; if varnished looks are the main thing, I prefer ash or locust, both being quite strong enough.

Once a block shell is made, regardless of the type of wood, it is put to soak for two weeks (a month is better) in linseed oil. Once the oil has oxidized, weather will have no effect on the wood. After about six months and some use, wood blocks can be cleaned up, varnished, or painted. If it is done too soon, the oil will lift the finish. This is planning ahead, something that seems to have gone out of style.

A bit of sea lore here: In the days of hemp lanyards for the deadeyes, a properly planned craft had her new lanyard stuff put on the stretch when her keel was laid, a strain being on it in the rigging loft while the hull was being built. There was little or no stretch left in her line when she fitted out; and lanyards were not set up for the final time in cold weather if it could possibly be avoided. Often there was more setting up required after the vessel had sailed some, but this was more because of the settling of the rigging eyes aloft and the splices, than it was because of stretch in the lanyards. And yes, the additional setting up was possibly because of the slight raising of the sides of the vessel as she found herself.

I often make wooden sheaves for blocks, and this works quite well. Such sheaves were commonplace in days long past. If I were to make blocks for a cruising boat, or a day boat of some size, I think it would be well worth buying roller sheaves of the proper size for the various blocks, at least for halyards and sheets. Downhaul blocks, lift blocks, and many others that don't have long, heavy hauls, do just as well with a plain sheave of wood, or metal, if you have a lathe. Scrap shafting of about

Svärmisk made good use of the spritsail ketch rig, of which Pete was particularly fond. (Chris Wentz)

the right size makes fine metal sheaves; for wooden ones I like elm or locust. Bronze pins are worth it, especially if the rollers are bronze, and I like them for wood sheaves. If the rollers are steel, use steel pins. In all cases, keep them greased, pack 'em with it. One exception: if you use blocks for hauling up on a sand beach, run them dry. Grease picks up sand, making a grinding compound.

I make my blocks differently than some recent articles show, not that those ways are not good.

Since I have unlimited firewood, for all practical purposes, to work from, as much as possible I get my blocks out of solid pieces of wood—even doubles and an occasional triple. Simply mill out to thickness, width, and often in longish lengths; mark off and bore most of the mortice in the squared-up state, which is easy to hold. Though the job can be done freehand using a half-baked jig, a drill press is best, using the power paddle bits; I find these best for this sort of thing. When all is bored, I clean out the mortices with a chisel and a rasp, then whack up the blocks in the lengths and shapes that meet my fancy on a bandsaw and sanding disc.

Just what shape I fancy is often guided by the kind of block and its use. I also make it a point not to leave much wood on in places where it does no good; some of the old shapes of the past are quite attractive. In the unfinished square state, it's best to bore for the pins, too, for obvious reasons. Scores for the strap are about the last thing to be cut. Shells can be riveted across as in modern blocks, or you can use a threaded rod if you have a tap long enough to reach through the block—this method was employed by a well-known yacht block maker years ago. He is now out of business, of course. Often small blocks I make out of good, tough stock skip the use of cross fastenings and seem to give no trouble. On the other hand, on very big blocks, for heavy lifts, I've not only cross-riveted, but also have fore-and-aft riveted across the sides of the shell, above and below the pin, and, in some cases, for certain uses, double-stropped them besides.

I've made blocks that range from less than 2" long to 10" long, and one old soaker of a snatch block maybe 14" or 15" long for use as a lead block when pulling with a truck.

That this sort of thing is worthwhile now, in these days of everything off the shelf, is a matter of individual choice. I think it well worth it for many reasons. You can have blocks to suit your type of craft exactly, from both artistic and mechanical standpoints. You can do it economically. If you like to make things, there is a lot of satisfaction in that alone. You avoid a lot of metal fittings; all that is really needed are sheaves, sometimes, and an occasional shackle or hook.

I must have six or eight block and tackles around, some all home built, others partly so, often using rebuilt manufactured blocks that have been salvaged. These rigs vary from quite small to large and are most handy around the shop, house, and in the truck. Things one is apt to bull around the hard way can, with a bit of imagination, be moved simply and safely with a block and tackle.

What sometimes passes for a block now—stainless straps, plastic shells, and composition sheaves—are simply not in the class of the old timers I take great pleasure in making and using. Each to his own.

Deadeyes, hearts, lizards, bullseyes, and all sorts of special wooden fairleads can be made the same way, out of solid stuff, from the previously mentioned woods. Much of this stuff is most suited to turning on a wood lathe; some, however, may not be needed in a true round shape, so it's worked up more or less like in block making. For those who have or can borrow the use of a wood lathe, much of the round stuff can be made quite rapidly. I will not discourse on the use of the wood lathe; it's assumed that if you use one, you will know how, or soon learn how, to hold various work.

DESIGN
COMMENTARIES

RACE POINT
SURFBOAT *COSKATA*

Everyone interested in the sea seems to be familiar with Coast Guard life and surfboats. Such boats, especially those worked off the beach, are fast passing from the scene as stations are closed and air, electronic, and other improvements in rescue methods make them obsolete. This obsolescence probably started with the passing of the sailing ship.

The record and exploits of Coast Guard beach stations are so impressive, many feel this history should be enshrined. Cape Cod National Seashore has done this well, and so have other places, notably Nantucket, where there is a long history of surf rescue work.

Robert Caldwell heads the Nantucket Lifeboat Museum, which is devoted to Coast Guard rescue work in the days of sail. An accurate presentation of just how this type of rescue work was done is displayed for those interested. Obviously, much thought, research, money, and hard work went into setting up this fine museum. I'm proud to have had a small hand in it.

Caldwell thought it would be nice to have a lifeboat to use in the harbor in good weather. Museum property, however, is holy and therefore untouchable.

Besides, a full-size lifeboat requires a crew, and is designed for bringing heavy loads in through the surf. This was not exactly the thing for a pleasant afternoon row, so the problem was turned over to me.

The boat desired was to live ashore on a cart in a miniature Coast Guard boathouse when not in use. Actually, the shed amounted to a two-car garage with a ramp to the water.

The boat designed looks like a lifeboat, and was built like one. The design concessions were that she's sharper for ease of moving, and though there are end decks, the bulkheads were left out for more stowage. The knees are grown apple (naturally), and she has a true keelson for stiffness. Aside from this, she's just about the same as such boats always have been, including sponsons. Because she is a light boat, the two pairs of oars are spruce, 9 feet long. In addition, there is an 11-foot steering sweep. The oars and sweep are of my own make.

Building such a craft is fun. Posts and keel are oak, as are the frames, with sprung "floating floors." That is, the floorboards go in the bays between the frames and fasten separately, keelson over all, with the thwarts bowed and stanchioned on top of the keelson—a rugged but lightweight construction.

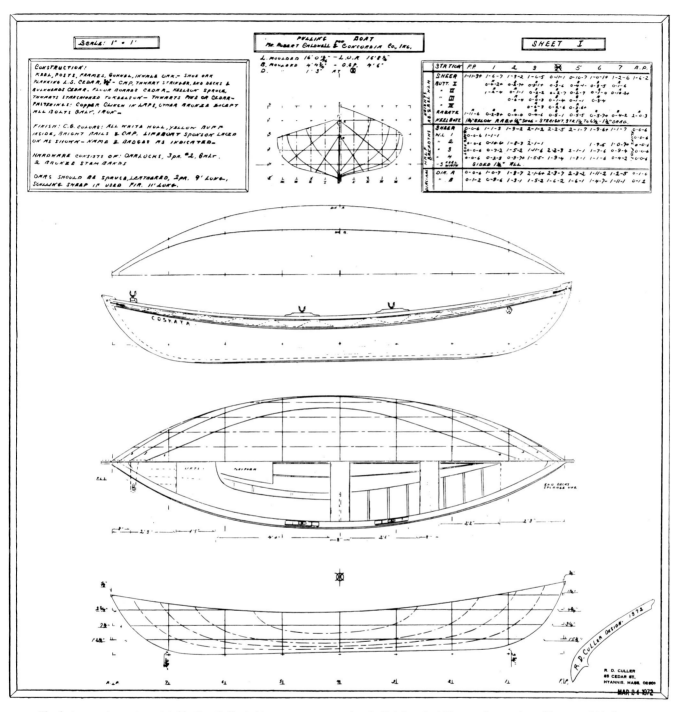

The design requirements as stated by Pete Culler in his commentary were that the little boat look like a surfboat and row like one and I believe he hit the mark. (© Mystic Seaport, Ships Plans Collection, Mystic, CT)

The Race Point surfboat Coskata *is a good example of Pete Culler's talent for taking what worked in the past and adapting it for today's pleasure use.*

Planking is ³/₈-inch cedar; thwart stringer, floor-boards, and end decks also are cedar. The thwarts are Eastern pine, as are the sternsheets, which are in the traditional oval in the interests of pleasure

boating. Rails are oak as tradition requires, and she may have just a bit more brightwork than full-size lifeboats had.

The craft is named *Coskata,* after a well-known Nantucket station. She carries badges on her bows, using the old surfmen's insignia of life ring with crossed oars.

She's 17 feet long, with a 4-foot 6-inch beam and very little draft when stark light. She weighs 263 pounds, a good weight for hauling out. This weight verifies that lapstrake planking is by far the lightest wooden boat construction method. Her colors are traditional: brightwork, buff inside, and all white outside.

I want to add a few remarks on her construction—which is traditional. She is bronze and copper fastened; I guesstimate that there are over 3,000 fastenings in her. I find that a round-bilge double-ender of this approximate shape is slightly easier to loft and set up than a transom-stern boat. And although slightly more trouble to plank, she is easier to frame aft.

She was set up on posts, upright, braced to a timber overhead in the Norse fashion, and was "on the stocks" almost to final finishing. This is a very rugged setup, with little chance for the hull to go out of shape. I think that on a boat of this size or bigger of this construction, that the time spent on one's knees, or more often on a small stool, in the early stages, is more than made up for by not having to reset and true again. This is a great advantage when working alone.

I realize that my views may be slanted, but I think she's sort of attractive.

WHERRY YAWL
FOR A SCHOONER

In these days of small cruising craft, able to accommodate a small dink shaped like a bathtub, or at worst a rubber doughnut of some sort, it's not often that I get to build a proper ship's yawl—one intended to be used as such.

The design was originally made for the schooner *Fiddler's Green,* a vessel quite capable of carrying a good yawl. However, the owners of the wooden ketch *Stormsvalla* also liked the design, and commissioned me, through the Concordia Company, to build her.

Because she is a proper ship's yawl, her construction is in keeping. It is strong, but not overly heavy. The design closely follows that of working yawls of the distant past. Several people, observing her during construction, said, "She looks right out of Chapman *[Architectura Navalis].*" Thus, a backboard was fitted and inscribed to the English-Swedish naval architect of the 1700s. I must say that I find his designs most fascinating.

Few may know today what was required of ship's yawls in the days of sail. They had to carry, be very able for their size, row well, and often sail considerable distances. Such boats had to carry stores and/or water barrels, and sometimes even tow them. They had to run out lines and anchors — once in a while a bower anchor, which took considerable skill. They fished for fun, or necessity. Often they were launched and hauled out in great haste. They often spent long periods of time hoisted up, and, of course, many went to war.

Obviously, requirements are not as stringent now, especially for pleasure use, yet the general design was so sound, nothing new can do any better.

This little craft was designed in the old way, to the inside of plank and perpendiculars of rabbets. By this method she's $10\frac{1}{2}$ feet overall, with a beam of 4 feet 6 inches. Having built a similar working yawl for use on Nashawena Island, I had a good idea of what the weight would be. This one, having a sailing rig with centerboard, stout rudder pintles, mast partners and so on, could weigh more—perhaps too much. Thus, care was taken in the choice of stock—though one could not skimp on strength. In spite of the extra gear she weighs 178 pounds, slightly less than the previous yawl.

To accomplish this, I've made her a monument to all the woods it's said you can't get, all of them durable and rather light. The stem is a natural crook of sassafras. The sternpost is chestnut, as are the

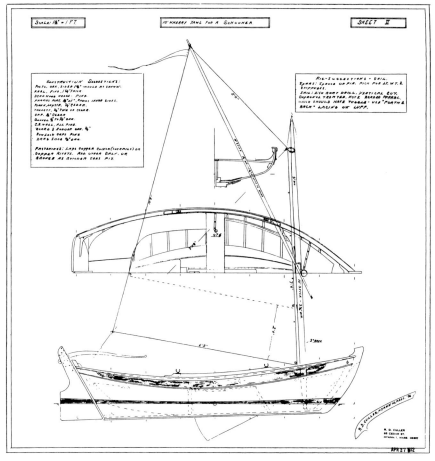

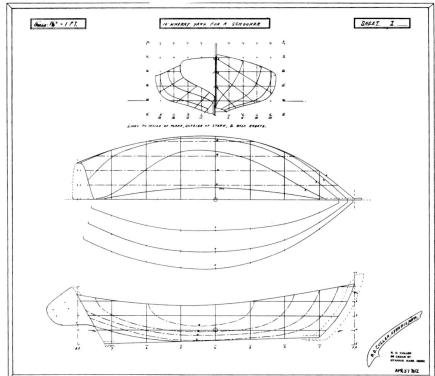

Although short and beamy, this boat has remarkably well-shaped sections. Pete explained why: "Wineglass sections throughout the hull will give slack diagonals in a chunky boat. Now everyone thinks just the opposite (never having planked one), but the Norsemen knew a thing or two! Although not an easy boat to plank, those slack diagonals will help." (© Mystic Seaport, Ships Plans Collection, Mystic, CT)

The owner of the 10'6" wherry yawlboat, designed and built by Pete Culler, takes her for a sail at the Mystic Seaport Small Craft Workshop. Pete comments: "The design follows closely the ships' yawls of small size. The boat is burdensome, yet a good sailer using the traditional sprit rig with good area and there is a reef. These little boats are powerful for their size. The wherry keel was used to provide a good landing for the centerboard well and to allow the boat to sit upright on the beach." (Bart Hauthaway)

stanchions under the thwarts. The keel is Sitka spruce, a wood that is both light and stiff. Post knees are hackmatack, and oak is used for wear shoe, frames, and gunwale trim. Maine cedar is used for the planking. I selected Eastern pine for the thwarts, kneed with apple and pear, and locust for the cleats. The thumb cleats aft are apple, and for the hell of it, it's butternut for the centerboard well cap! Spars and oars are of Sitka spruce. Finally, the stern is Philippine wood, used because it was just right, very red and dense. The fastenings are copper and bronze.

Present thinking might consider this a hodge-podge of lumber, yet each wood was chosen for specific reasons—durability in its function, strength, and keeping weight within bounds. Many

ask where I get such exotic stuff. It's around, under-foot; you stumble over it at times. It's just a matter of keeping one's eyes open. Small craft don't require much stock, so a little goes a long way. Though the hours putting them together always seem to mount up, there is great satisfaction in the work.

The design follows very closely the old yawls of very small size. The boat is burdensome, yet a good sailer using a traditional sprit rig of good area, with a reef. These little craft are extremely powerful for their size. They can sail in quite blowy conditions under short sail—this was one of the old-time requirements. The plank, sometimes called the wherry, keel was used to provide a good landing for the centerboard well, and also to allow the boat to sit upright on a beach. She uses wedge deadwood construction aft, and it is considerably shaped. I very much like to see a thin forefoot and heel in any craft—this is a matter of lofting and allowing enough deadwood to work with. So many boats now have stubby stems and sternposts. In this day and age it's difficult to understand why.

The little craft is finished with a green bottom, white topsides, black wale with varnished bead, bright thwarts and cap, and French gray inside. Her floorboards are oiled, and the bilge is red leaded. To suit present-day boating requirements, she has the usual dinghy fender, but I can't say that it helps her looks. It took as long, with leather ends, and so on, to put this fender on as it took to both frame her out and put in the floor timbers. And the material was far more expensive than oak. Somehow, you always pay more for yacht standards.

YAWLBOAT FOR
INTEGRITY

This design has proved to be a good carrier, is very able for her size, sails well, and rows far more easily than one would think, considering her bulk. She was originally designed to be a schooner's yawlboat. In terms of both design and construction, she is quite heavy. This seems to enhance her ability rather than detract from it. This type of craft is not suited to lightweight construction.

Considering the number built, very few of this general type, for sail, power, or rowing, ever got down on paper as formal plans. In fact, it's a hard type to present formally, though not extremely difficult to build, once one understands the many aspects not present in the usual hull. While now mostly forgotten, and never very well understood in some areas, these craft are, to some extent, connected to the log canoe, which they eventually replaced. That is, much is based on hewing and chopping, and fairing in by eye. Though having built and designed many cross-planked craft, I am still unable to present fully the methods on paper. Chapelle's *Boatbuilding* does it better than any, and should be referred to.

To begin with, these boats are 80 percent art, some skill with tools, and very little science, and this last of a crude, barnyard sort. What this seems to produce is a superior craft compared to the more modern type of V-bottomed boat—long lasting, economical, and often handsome. Just why just this is so is hard to say. Possibly it is because the original developers of the type had a past of much experience. They just plain knew what they were doing.

Materials are not critical. It is possible to build these craft right out of a local lumberyard, plus a bit of poking around in the woods. In case one thinks there are no more woods left, assure him there are, with the same bullbriars, bugs, snakes, and all, along with some stuff very suited to natural knees.

Except for the lapped sides, which are copper fastened—I prefer lapped sides in a small craft, though carvel will do—galvanized iron fastenings are used throughout in craft of my build, unless others are requested. These last quite well and are very stiff. With the amount of wood in these craft, they can be readily refastened in their old age, if the wood is sound. My system is: "Nail where you can, screw where you must, and bolt where you have to."

One now hears nothing but stainless, Monel, and bronze as *the* fastenings. The economics of these

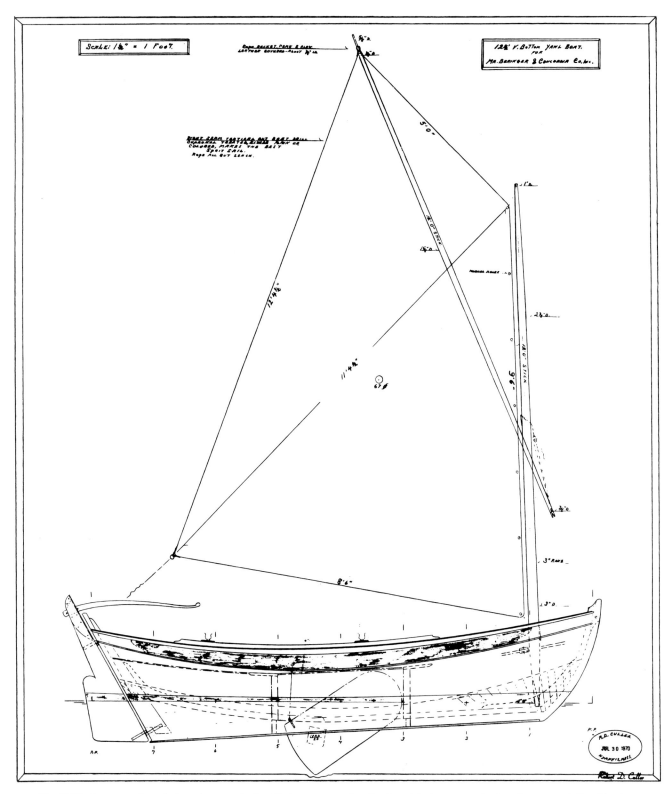

The 12'6" v-bottom yawlboat for Integrity *proved quite able for purposes other than its original one as tender for a larger vessel. Consider that this design, the wherry yawl (page 343) and the "sheep boat" (page 47) are all very similar in model, being based on the small ships' yawls of the past, and these ships' yawls had many requirements. They had to be burdensome: the ability to carry cargo, human or otherwise, between ship and shore or ship-to-ship was a high priority. Another that came up frequently was the ability to work on and off a beach and to navigate shoal water. Also, they needed to sail. All of these attributes would suit the modern small boat sailor, too.* (© Mystic Seaport, Ships Plans Collection, Mystic, CT)

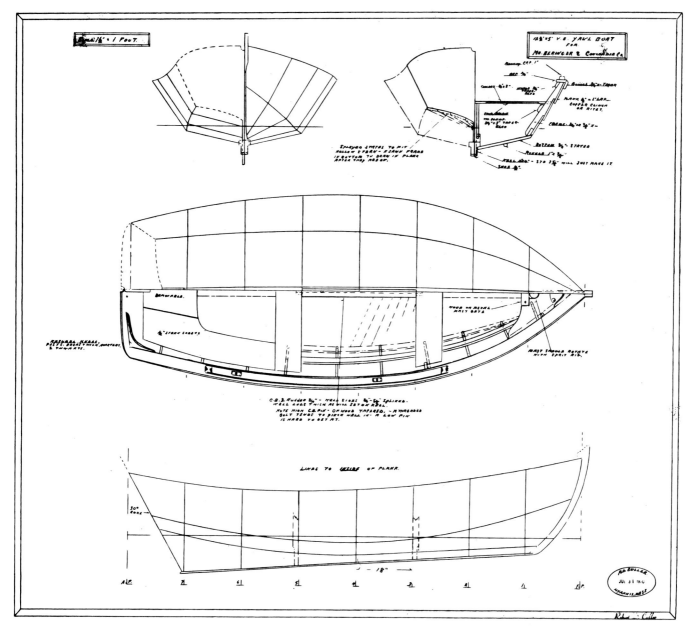

is unsound in the type of craft being discussed. It's my experience that fastening troubles compound in direct proportion to the amount of electric gear on a boat. These small, open deadrises have at most a flashlight, and thus no other problems. Building a lightweight clipper pulling boat is another matter. Stock is very light, scantlings small, and fastenings small and many, a large part of which are not buried and thus subject to sandpaper abrasion. These craft

are at best difficult to repair in their old age. Here nonferrous fastenings make good sense.

Here are some hints learned the hard way. It always does pay to lay down full size. Personally, I use only four molds in boats this size and fullness—midship, two forward, and aft—but more do no harm, and may be better. Staving of the bottom should start forward, never aft, as one loses the wedging effect. It's hard to say just when to change

The v-bottom yawlboat for Integrity *slides out of the second story Hyannis shop. For the first three years after the schooner's launch the 15'9"*
v-bottom beach boat Java *was tender to* Integrity. *Both of these boats were designed and built by Pete Culler for Waldo Howland.*

from butt to lap at chine with the bottom staves. It depends on the model and how one starts and manages the staves—usually somewhere around mold 2. These staves forward, and often aft with a hollow stern, must be shaped out of thick stuff. These staves can be laid tight, or with a caulked seam. *Integrity*'s boat is tight seam. Fitting staves takes time, for there is much shaping, beveling, and final smoothing up. To some modern builders the procedure makes no sense; they think they know a better way. However, the right and traditional way makes a good boat.

These types require no steaming, though a little kerosene soaked into a plank limbers it wonderfully. One must be prepared to shape all plank, chines, thwart clamps, and so on. Spile and shape, then bend. The modern notion of edge setting makes these craft, or most any other type for that matter, extremely difficult.

Again I say, do not edge set. Shape, and it will wrap right in place.

The stem rabbet is picked up from the floor keel rabbet until it dies out and becomes a bevel, and chine bevels are arrived at in fairing down the bottom. It is doubtful whether such things can be projected on paper with any degree of accuracy, which no doubt is why they never were.

Fairing down for bottom planking, doing bow staving, and in this particular case, a little of the bottom aft, are the most time-consuming parts of the whole building job.

If possible, get chines out of a matched pair of boards, or in some cases alongside each other in a wide board. There seems to be less fight to get them to lay alike than if they are out of widely different stock. This applies to a great extent throughout the boat—any boat, for that matter. Things go easy with matched stock—a point now more or less forgotten and not helped by mass-produced stock.

It will be noted that lines are to inside of plank and to back rabbet. There are no offsets shown, as the lines are simple and the scale is large, so they can be lifted directly from the plan. The more usual method was to lift directly from a half model. There will be some errors, which is what laying down full size is about, to get things fair. One must remember that some art and judgment are needed—small-craft building of this nature has yet to become a cut-and-dried science. Even in building several craft alike over the same mold, variations do creep in, for one is building with wood. This is just a part of boatbuilding.

A further word on bow staving. The more the builder keeps the staving upright after starting, and for a while going aft, the more hollow the forefoot he will have—a sought-after condition. The cross section here in the finished craft will not exactly follow a drafted section. The sooner and more the staves are raked aft right forward, the more bulbous the forefoot will be. This seems to be a disadvantage in sailing and rowing models. Getting a reasonably hollow forefoot takes some care.

TWO STEAM
LAUNCHES

We hear much these days about how all boats are becoming production craft—no more individual ideas, no more one-of-a-kind, no more wood. Instead, it's all high speed, both through the water and in r.p.m.

To a great extent this is so. The new and inexperienced boatman has little else to choose from. If he stays with boating, however, this gentleman often seeks better things later on. At least, from the perspective of my shop, it appears that many come looking for classic craft. They want something that will do real work, a vessel that will go to sea in comfort and be a home afloat.

Often one of these seekers—a person with a love of small craft, a modest pocketbook, and the realization that just "messing about in boats" is what really counts—is exposed to a really good pulling boat, and says, "This is the way it should be." The same thing happens with powerboats and sailing vessels, too, for that mater. In *National Fisherman* one time, Bill Durham had an article on the joys of nice, easy-moving displacement launches using modest power. This naturally brought forth some further discussion. The exchanges soon got around to the old steam-launch hulls. Richard B. Hovey of

Prides Crossing, Massachusetts—owner of a small steamer and avid steam fan—liked what he read.

As result, he commissioned me to see what we could do in the say of designing a larger steamer. Well, we submitted the usual proposal drawing, which looked practical. The boiler and engine we had not really nailed down but there were several under consideration. You don't just rush out and buy an engine and boiler, like some machine made in Detroit. You have to know steam, and where this and that can be had, traded, swapped for, and even made. Good steam equipment—or even every poor stuff, for that matter—is not in junkyards today.

Anyhow, the project proceeded. It was decided that a bit more length would be better, so the design ended at 34 feet between the rabbets. It was a foregone conclusion that the boat would be traditional in model and build. As in all steamers, provision was to be made for a really large (by current standards) wheel.

Few today know that many small steamers of the past turned a screw with a pitch $1\frac{1}{2}$ times or more greater than the diameter. Such wheels have real bite. The principle of their operation has little to do with the high-speed internal combustion engine.

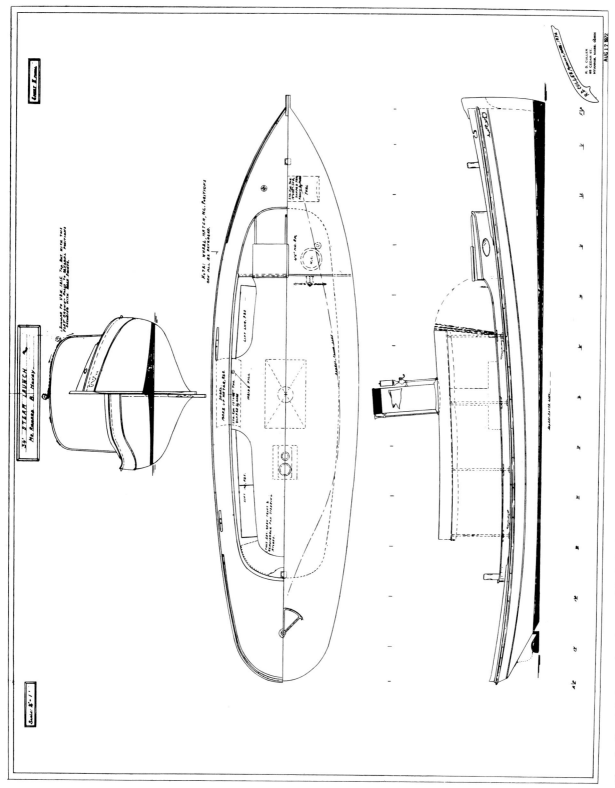

Plans for the original steam launch proposal for Richard Hovey. It was decided that more length and molded depth was required. (© Mystic Seaport, Ships Plans Collection. Mystic, CT)

Being a bit of a passive steam fan myself, having grown up when engine speeds of 300 r.p.m. were common, and also liking older hulls easily driven at modest speeds, I used the best small steamers of the past as a guide. I even referred to those of the U.S. Navy and other navies when naval small craft were steam-powered.

Naval craft were specialized, so many of their requirements were not needed in a pleasure and fishing steamer. Some sort of canvas shelter was wanted, however. This very much follows U.S. Navy practice, although I hope it will be a better fit than some shown in Navy photos!

Bill Durham's book *Standard Boats of the U.S. Navy* has been a big help for details, including tables of construction, weights, and gear. Naval craft, then as now, were loaded down and very heavy. Such weight and displacement are not needed here, but you must keep in mind that a steam plant is very heavy—not so much the engine, for by present standards it seems way too small for

the job. Horsepower rating has no relation to modern internal combustion practice. The boiler, its fuel, makeup water, hotwell, piping, and a host of other things in a steam engine are both bulky and heavy.

The cuddy is mostly to house a toilet, for at times ladies will be aboard, and also for use on the occasional overnight trip. This would be roughing it by some standards, but pretty good shelter, I say, in a snug cove after a day's fishing, with a portable stove and a simmering boiler for company (and to dry things out), and a pipe in the gloaming. There will always be plenty of hot water. Your can even steam-clean the dishes if you wish.

Naturally, many will ask, "Why bother with a steamboat, with all that work, no speed, and no styling?" Such people are afraid of 'em! They often rush to their all-week-buttoned-up cruiser and hit the starter without even checking the engine space. Sometimes they take off faster than intended—straight up.

The 34' Hovey steamers' fantail stern perfectly executed at the Rich Bros. Yard, Bass Harbor, Maine. It takes an artist to design and build this type of stern. Judging from the photo both Pete and the boatbuilders at the Rich Bros. Yard were just that.

There are many very good reasons for owning a steamer. Just as with a lobster, you try one and like as not you are hooked. I can picture this craft all spic-and-span, blowing three long, melodious, somewhat haunting blasts on her chime whistle—say, for the Annisquam Bridge—for she has serious work with the fish off Plum Island. The bridge-tender will do a double-take, and I bet he opens it some fast! He will gawk, unabashed, along with many others, and no doubt forget to lower the bridge until reminded to do it by some irate auto driver.

The craft drips with style, and there is a faint smell of steam oil. She is so quiet, you might even hear the slight beat of the screw. She's doing close to 7 knots, with a couple of knots of tide under her.

Soon she's out of sight around the bend, leaving hardly any disturbance in the water.

Like people dedicated to guns, some are addicted to steam. Good guns are a lot of trouble. So is steam, but that's part of it, working with it. You don't learn it in a few minutes. It's not totally automatic and programmed for you. Fire and water are The Boss, and you learn to handle them, which makes you your own boss, in a way.

Real steam men usually do all their own machinery installation, or supervise it in detail. They then know their rig inside and out, which is more than can be said for many internal combustion engine operators! Outlandish, you say, if not outrageous in these modern times? I don't think so. The owner of this steam craft knows the difference.

FAST OUTBOARD LAUNCH

Designed for Commodore Percy Chubb and Concordia Company. Built by Concordia in 1968.

CONSTRUCTION

1. Keel: 8 × 8 fir.
2. Stem: white oak sided 4 inches.
3. Stern: double (inside vertical oak, outside horizontal cedar).
4. Planking, topsides: $3/_4$-inch cedar, lapstrake, riveted laps.
5. Planking, bottom: $1^1/_4$-inch cedar, cross-planked and caulked, screw-fastened.
6. Shoe: $3/_4$ × $3^3/_4$ yellow pine.
7. Coamings and house sides: Philippine mahogany.
8. Decks and house tops: marine plywood, canvas covered.
9. Deck and house beams: spruce; seats, floorboards, etc.: pine.
10. Fastenings: bronze and copper; hardware: brass, bronze, or wood.
11. Windows: lower house and trunk Plexiglas, upper house safety glass.

This little day cruiser may be of more than passing interest. As outboards go, she is a little larger than most. She operates very efficiently with what, in these days of great power, is a very modest set of machinery.

The design evolved over the years from small workboats used for alongshore shellfishing and other similar uses. These craft have been built in many smaller sizes—15, 16, 18, and 24 feet. All are very handy and able boats with a good turn of speed on modest power. The first question always asked is, "How fast are they?" The answers are that the little ones do 15 to 16 knots with 18 h.p.; the 24-footer, 20 knots with two 18s; and the 30-footer, $23^1/_2$ knots with two 55 h.p. Bearcat outboards. To some, these speeds may not be impressive, but they are service speeds, in hulls built strong enough for working under modest power. A working craft must be able to carry and handle well at low speeds. These craft do this extremely well. The great flare forward and the shape of the bottom make them take very kindly to running as displacement hulls when the need arises.

There is no breakthrough of any kind in the design of these hulls. What you see is a matter of proper flare, deadrise, and chine run, all of which have been proven in use. These features vary slightly, depending on the size of the craft. The result is a boat that handles and banks extremely well, and has sufficient speed for most working purposes. As fast boats go, this is a type of hull that rides rather softly.

(continued on page 359)

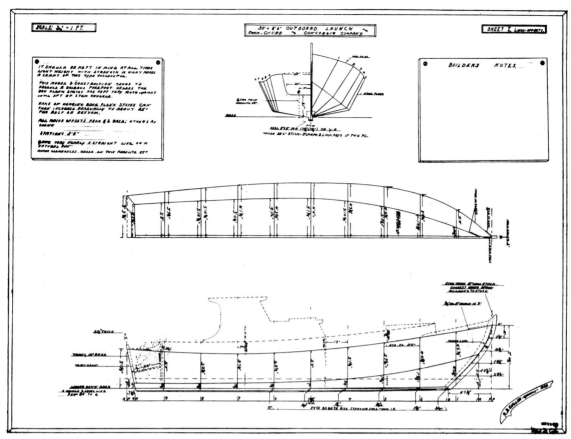

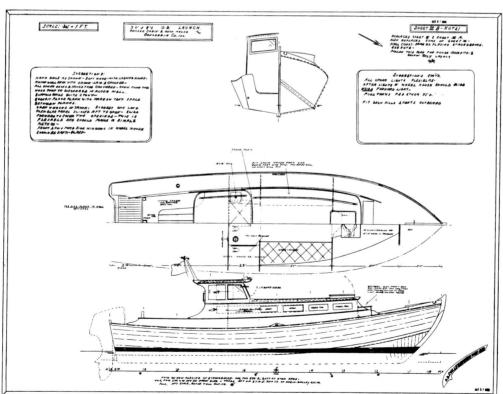

The Chesapeake file or v-bottom is an evolution from the log canoe, which it supplanted. That is, there is a lot of hewing, chopping, and fairing in by eye. With these v-bottom outboards, light weight must be kept in mind along with the other principles Pete Culler discusses in the design commentary. Do this and a fast and sea-kindly boat will result. (© Mystic Seaport, Ships Plans Collection, Mystic, CT)

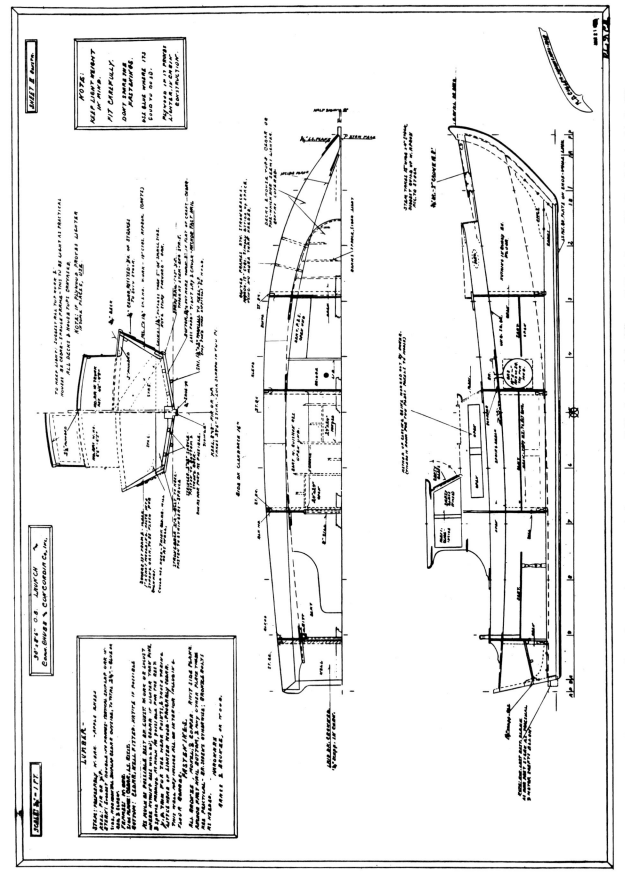

Commodore Chubb opted for the arrangement shown; however, there are several other versions available should needs be different. (© Mystic Seaport, Ships Plans Collection, Mystic, CT)

The 30' outboard kicking up her heels during sea trials. Pete designed and Concordia Co. built this v-bottomed outboard for Commodore Percy Chubb for use on Peter Island, BVI.

(*continued from page 356*)

There's nothing new in construction either, though several methods are combined, for they seem to give the required strength without too much weight. Weight is always the major stumbling block with planing hulls. The topsides are always lapstrake. Bottoms are old bay-style cross-planked herringbone. We are often questioned on this, and doubted too, but it works structurally, and in some other ways not readily apparent. The larger the craft, the more use is make of fore-and-aft stringers and strongbacks. The upper works are more or less standard practice with stress on light weight and durability. Keeping the design simple helps in this respect.

Commodore Percy Chubb's requirements were for a simple but smart boat. He was quite willing to keep accommodations sparse rather than complicate or overload the boat. The result, using Concordia's methods and usual stock, is a nice-handling, long-lived boat, one that is easy to maintain and repair if damaged. She is a good seaboat, and we think quite nice looking.

We take considerable pains to turn out craft with a lot of style—ageless styles that fit the sea.

The next question is, how large an outboard can be used? I don't know. Greater outboard power is available. Fuel consumption, however, might become excessive. In addition, on hulls longer than 30 feet, there are engine shaft length problems. My feeling is that an inboard-outboard might work. This hull design is not suited to conventional inboard power.

CONCORDIA TOWBOAT *GRACIE III*

All boatyards these days seem to have some sort of workboat. Often it is just an outboard skiff, anything that is handy. Sometimes, however, one is built just for the work. Such craft are more rugged than the usual run, and better suited to the work. Such a boat may be called "the towboat." It will often serve quite well, depending on the amount and type of work the yard does, and very much on location and layout.

Concordia Company of South Dartmouth, Massachusetts, has a layout different from many. It is a large yacht harbor filled with moorings and boats, protected by a stone breakwater. Some heave sets in with certain winds, notably from the south and southeast. There is a drawbridge to the north, with a narrow passage. Occasionally strong currents run there. Next door there is a yacht club that is congested at times. A long stone dock, inherited from ancient schooner days, is on the other side. This forms the basin; it is, for the most part, well protected. Here there are floats, electric boxes, water taps, and all the gear we need for modern yachting. Larger craft moor here for service, and the bigger ones berth in winter, afloat. The craft moor all fours, stern in, and to buoys out ahead, as in harbors in

Europe. Spar sheds and a crane are at the end of the dock. The railway and rigging loft are at the head of the basin—a nice but not very common setup in the United States.

Naturally, with this basin, the surrounding harbor, and other obstructions, a workboat was much used. For many years *Gracie I* was the boat of all work, along with a couple of tired but stubborn skiffs. The Towboat was a flat-bottomed thing of undetermined origin with a one-lung Falcon. Though underpowered, for years she did great work, mostly due to skillful handling. Like all things, she wore out, and a similar, slightly larger one was built, this time with a one-jug diesel in her. This is *Gracie II*. She's still working, though becoming outclassed. A trip down the harbor in her is an experience. The vibration points of the engine and hull totally agree, so anyone aboard sees everything double, and your jowls jiggle for a week thereafter.

Times change, and new men and boats appear. Boats with tall rigs, cutaway ends, light displacement, stocky houseboats, multihulls, and hordes of small stuff come along, most ailing at one time or another. A real towboat was needed, and it had to

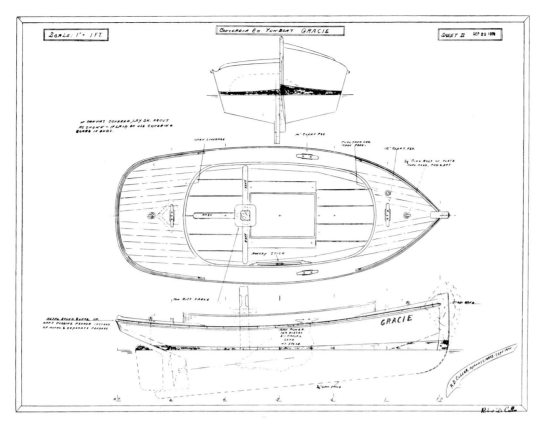

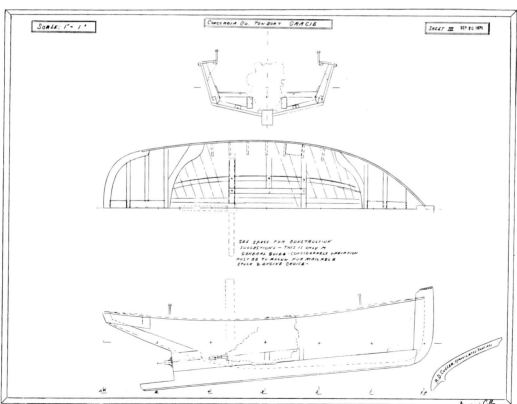

Looking over these plans you are immediately aware of the stoutness of the vessel's construction. Stem, keel, and backbone as well as deck members could be sized for a vessel two and even three times the dimension of this little tug. In building vessels using the v-bottom, Pete Culler has stated, you'll spend the most time on two stages: 1) fairing the bottom for bottom planking; and 2) fitting and fairing the bottom staves forward and in some cases aft as well. (© Mystic Seaport, Ships Plans Collection, Mystic, CT)

be in miniature for the crowded basin. I was asked to design one because I knew so much about conditions at the yard and in the basin and harbor.

There were some limitations: the craft could not be much over 15 feet in length, or have much over 5 feet beam; she had to be able to get into tight places; and she had to be able to *pull*. Having had experience with harbor towboats in the distant past, I felt I knew what makes a good tug, even if it had to be midget size. A tug is grossly overpowered by ordinary standards. She must turn a very large screw. This, along with great displacement, is more important than mere horsepower. Such a boat must be frightfully stout of build, not only to take the pounding of an outsize engine, but also to take the hard knocks of her work. A tug can, and often does, get pinched by her charge: In other words, she often acts as an outsize fender; it's part of her work.

Besides having great displacement, the hull should squat to pull well, and handle in the extreme. In fact, a good tug's handling under an able skipper verges on the acrobatic. The towing bitt and controls must be arranged with understanding. The principles involved in towboating have not changed since the beginning of this art. Those who have violated these principles have turned out tugs "that couldn't pull, and wouldn't handle." Experienced towboatmen think such craft should be done away with, though their words for it are much more vulgar!

The engine having been decided on—a Westerbeke 107—the design and building went ahead. Fantail stern (so she could squat) with no corners to catch up. Cross-planked deadrise because it's durable, and easy to get big displacement in a short hull. Not at all for ease of building, for the craft has the scantlings of many a 40-footer. She is hard to

A testament to heavy construction, the 12'6" towboat Gracie III *incorporates large amounts of material for her size.*

A highly instructive photo showing the manner of staving the bow strakes on a file or v-bottom hull. In this case it is the 12'6" towboat Gracie III. *Pete Culler called this style of construction "undifficult." He also said that describing how it is done is not easy, but that Howard Chappelle did it best in his book* Boatbuilding.

build, with many curves. For taking a beating and standing up to the oversize engine, there is a fine snubbing bitt. She can take pinching to the point of turning up on her side and going down. I don't recall what the draft is; it was decided by the screw and shoe. The keel drag is great for handling. In addition, things were planned so there is little to hang up in working among mooring lines.

Naturally, good fenders were a must; the great hairy Buffalo Nose does just fine. Being an ex-towboatman, I was assigned to make this item. After 30 years away from it, I found I had not forgotten how, only just how hard it was on the fingers! These noses just don't look right until there is an old grapefruit rind jammed in them! I say again that such a short, dumpy, full-lined, and heavy craft is not easy to build, no matter how you do it. Once at

work, however, she has a lot of charm, for she is real, can do her work without effort, and with dispatch—a towboatman's towboat!

This is *Gracie III*. How well does she work? Just like a towboat, working most of the time at nearly closed throttle, with a touch of the gun now and then to start a tow turning or to snub her up. When you pour it on just a little, you get action right away. She can wheel right around and face her charge in an instant, and as mentioned, acts as an excellent snubbing post. She is not dragged along, screaming and protesting, by a tow that has taken charge—something often seen with light craft not built for the work. Like old-time schooner seamen who were "built to the decks," she's built to the water and can hang on to it. Her massive backbone and skeg are backed by a very thick rudder, with the traditional

Gracie III *showing her ability to maneuver larger craft in tight quarters.*

deep groove down the after side to give it bite. There is no rudder stalling while backing; she goes either way with dispatch. In this type of towing there is no time for the tug to back and fill, and then arrange herself for the next move. She must assume the position at once, usually hampered by lack of space.

When watching a good tug at work, I'm always struck by the similarity to certain very stout people on the dance floor. In spite of, or because of, in the tug's case, the apparent hampering bulk, they get around with ease and grace.

For those who might be considering a yard tug in the future, I point out again the most important aspects of designing one. Very great displacement, an upright stem, a fantail stern, and a large flat-pitch screw. Very great horsepower is not the main thing—an engine that will turn a large, slow-turning wheel is. And the engine must turn the screw at once, from a standstill. Occasional heavy but short belts of power are what do most of the work, along with a skilled operator. Brutally strong construction is needed; here I think there are only two suitable materials for tug building—wood for the smaller ones and steel for the larger ones.

Low freeboard is needed to keep the pull on the towing bitt low—many a tug has been rolled over by her charge. A layout that has a minimum of projections that might foul lines, and of course proper fenders, which should be of a material that gets soggy and stays put, are a must. A skilled operator too is needed; this comes with practice. In other words, do it just about the opposite from other power craft. Once you feel a good and responsive tug under you, and develop the skill to use her, it's a fine life—this is towboating! A proper tug, even of banty rooster size, is not cheap or easy to build.

BALTIMORE CLIPPER SCHOONER
LIZARD KING

The rig on this vessel is not excessive by some old standards, yet it will provide enough canvas for general use. It looks as if she will be quite handy under the foresail; I would think she would work very well under it alone.

I don't know just what the spar stock will be, but if there is much choice, use something reasonably light in weight. The dimensions for spars as given are about right for the rig, and would be fine in a light-grade fir, spruce, or, here in the East, white pine—at least for the masts. With a bit of common sense, there should be no problems with this rig. The details shown are in keeping with the type, yet the rig uses some modern-day materials. The rope gammoning you can suit yourself on, through I see nothing wrong with it when properly done. The stem should be well through-bolted fore and aft in that area.

You are no doubt struck by the height of the houses—this is a weakness of the type. These craft are shoal and fine, so there is little actual hull depth. Increasing the freeboard is not the way out, though it's often tried. It just puts all the deck weight high up and increases windage, besides spoiling the looks. The great crown to the houses is not good

either, as it adds cost and makes them difficult to work on, stow gear on, or sit on. I find 3 inches of crown, the width of the house, is about right.

There is the matter of room for ballast also, Depending on the weight of construction materials, she might require 10,000 to 15,000 pounds of ballast. Naturally, tanks, engine, and other heavy gear make this a variable. I have made an arbitrary floor line, using WL 8 amidships, and 6 inches above that in the middle of the house aft, figuring the house heights from that. One could set lower and still have good floor width, but that crowds the ballast space. One must also consider that the frames will mold about 6 inches plus ceiling, which takes up more room.

Here's an idea I use in building any boats under my supervision, regardless of how much data I may have on the weights to go in her. (You will soon know about what stock, engine, and tankage you will use.) When the vessel is along to the point of starting the houses, mock up a floor, having due regard for ballast room, and see just what you can gain here and there. Mock up a house section, too. I rarely increase house crown, for it's miserable with too much. If I do, it's very little. I usually find I can cut down height a few inches. This headroom

(continued on page 369)

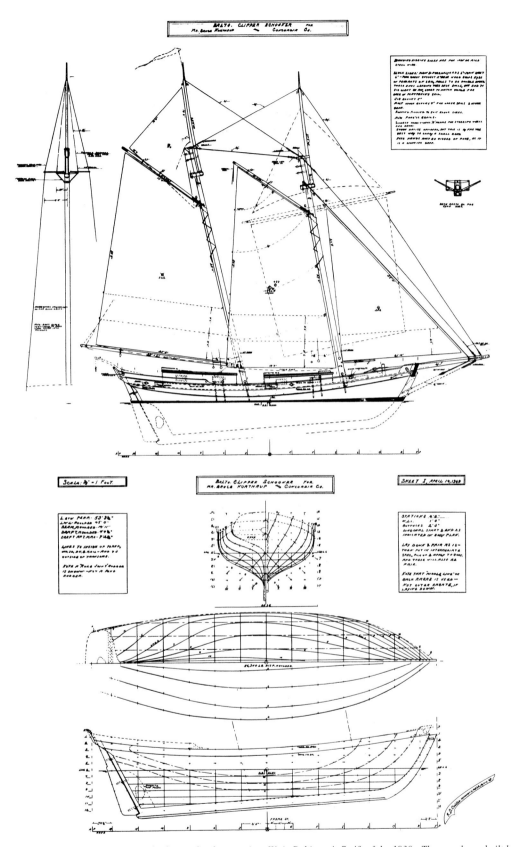

The 53'9" Baltimore clipper Lizard King *was the first such schooner since W. A. Robinson's* Swift *of the 1930s. The vessel was built by Bruce Northrup of Corvallis, Oregon, the same builder of the dogbody shown on pages 95 and following. When the vessel was completed the owner took the vessel on a successful voyage to the Marquesas. The reports were that the schooner handled and sailed very well.* (© Mystic Seaport, Ships Plans Collection, Mystic, CT)

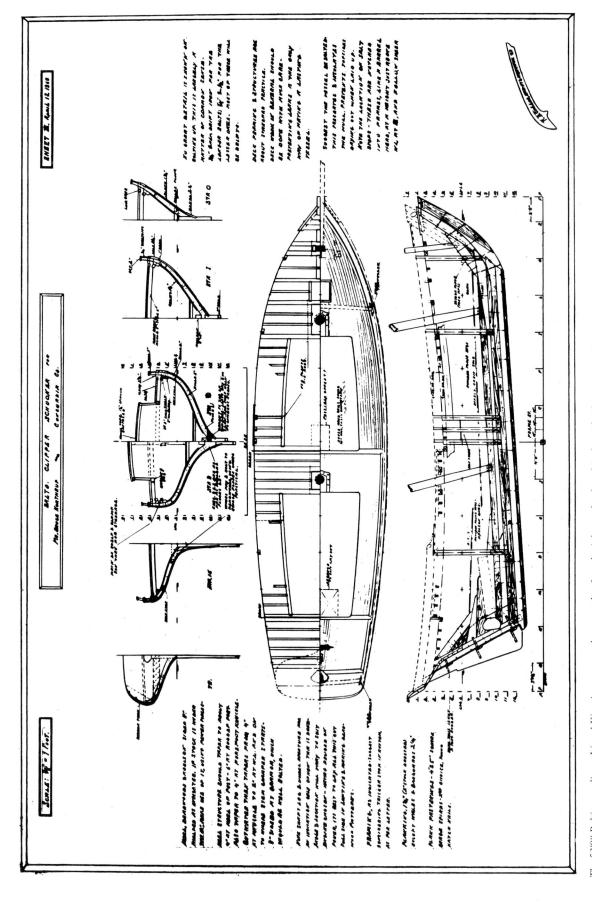

The 53'9" Baltimore clipper Lizard King is a present-day example of a colonial type developed in the mid-Atlantic region for its fast sailing qualities. Some say the hull originated in Bermuda. The model was used by those for whom speed was the dominant requirement, such as smugglers, slave traders, and, of course, pirates. (© Mystic Seaport, Ships Plans Collection, Mystic, CT)

(continued from page 366)

business is a source of great bother, for most yachtsmen are headroom-happy. Thus, it's difficult to get them interested in shoal, fast hulls.

The hull seems quite easy and should sail well. A waterline of 45 feet was needed to get the required room; these craft by nature are not very roomy, as they are shoal in hull and fine ended. I feel she will steer and handle very well. Also, she should be an easy seaboat.

I kept her slightly full forward to bear the square yard. She will, however, do quite well as a main-topmaster with no fore topmast or yard.

Note that the stations are such that frames of 16-inch centers can be used—doubled, out of 3-inch or even 4-inch stuff. I think 3 inches is a bit light in fir, though it would be practical if the craft were well planked and ceiled. One could of course use heavy stuff in the lower parts of frames, with lighter stuff above, and in the ends. This was often done in clipper craft.

This design stacks up very well to the *Swift* and other craft of similar size and sharpness. Compared with Waldo Howland's *Integrity,* this vessel is about a foot longer all around, a bit more beamy, with less molded depth, though of greater heel draft, less tonnage, and slightly more sail area. Also, she is generally much sharper.

I feel she should be a smart sailer, and do well on all points of sailing. Quality sails should make her handy by the wind.

I feel one must always build a vessel well, and plenty stout, but in this design much consideration must be given to keeping down the weight of the upper works. Do this by the proper choice of stock, rather than by too-light construction, which could be weak and hard to keep tight.

The Baltimore clipper Lizard King *gaining an offing. The vessel proved to be able and seaworthy in use.* (Bruce Northrup)

I did not spend much time on the calculations of various ratios used in the comparison, to keep the hours down, but what I did shows very well against other craft of the same size and general type. The quarter beam is very long and flat for such a small vessel—14:1 ratio, if I remember correctly. This should, along with other factors, produce a vessel that is able to keep speed well under passage conditions.

While this sort of thing is helpful in comparing, I feel a lot of it is the effect rather than the cause of a well-balanced hull. There have been too many paradoxes in the past to say a certain set of standards always makes a good or a poor boat.

I'm often struck by this when sailing my open Swampscott dory, which is a tiddly craft with a big rig for her power. Naturally, she is smart in light going. However, in blowing weather, under very short sail, she is a match or better for decked craft 10 to 15 times her weight! Just why, I still don't know, though I've given it much study. Possibly, it's not that she's so good, but that the others are poor.

I think this vessel will be a very nice seaboat, steering easily and laying-to well. Properly trimmed and ballasted, she should have an easy motion.

Assuming sawn fir frames, the more I think of the idea of graduating the siding, the more sense it makes. Consider it like this: Mold 6 inches tapering to 3 at the top timbers, which is about standard for this craft anyhow. In the middle three-fifths of the vessel, up to about the waterline, use 4-inch stock. This will, doubled, give 8-inch siding. From the waterline up, use 3-inch doubled, for a total of 6 inches. This will show steps in the frame sides, but no matter, since it planks and ceils over. The end fifths at bow and stern can be 3-inch stuff. This will keep the weight low, somewhat out of the ends, and put more wood in the bottom where ballast works.

Lizard King sits in frame. The plastic wrap on the sternpost is to prevent checking prior to planking. (Bruce Northrup)

Also, it will provide a stout bottom for iron ballast. This should not complicate lofting or framing at all, except in handling and paying for the heavier stock. As to lofting, layout, and molding, also bevels, one works from the center, so thickness does not mater. It's just more labor for man and saw. It's a thing to consider.

A construction plan is never complete enough—one can only do so much on a small scale. This is about as much as I supply for building at Concordia. *Integrity* had much less, though in that case, I was the boss shipwright.

In these days of poor imagination, and often a background that never makes one cope for oneself, I always have trouble getting any plan complete enough. What really seems to be wanted is every item and part to a very large scale, even full size, with the position of every bolt, nail, and screw shown. If by chance one fastener is shown in the way of another, there's always a beef. Naturally, plans so detailed for a vessel this size are economically impractical—they would cost as much as the vessel itself.

I think that what is here, namely, much more than proposed vessels of this type and period ever had, should be sufficient to build and rig her. As shown, the construction is pretty much as it has always been done, and still is done. The scantlings are sufficient, with some margin, for any of the usual shipbuilding woods.

Plenty of bolt iron, clinch rings, and galvanized ship spikes is all she needs—it always pays off to fasten well and closely. The sizes of everything are about standard for the tonnage.

The planking is thick enough to use a choker thread of cotton, then one of oakum. After all is made, and set back (except the garboard, which should be caulked but not made back till last), it can then be hawsed in. This really sets things up.

I would suggest that what few screw bolts are used, mostly odd length, should be made up out of standard bolt iron, using stock nuts, and clinch rings for heads. All ironwork can be galvanized, except for the rudder straps. It's worthwhile to make these out of bronze.

I think the main problem in building this vessel will be handling some of the timber. Yet, a couple of men who know what they are doing, along with some occasional just plain laborers, can make out. After all, a couple of us built *Integrity's* stern in place, for there was no way of lifting it as a unit. It must have weighed 15,000 pounds, being all white oak, and large anyhow for such a craft. Framing we did with a poor bandsaw, but three of us turned out two a day, from molding to bolting up.

The problem is always the same—how to get the required room in a vessel of a given type. Some additional tonnage, and more often, length, seems to be the only answer.

BOAT PLANS
BY R.D. CULLER

The following boat plans by R.D. "Pete" Culler are available at the Daniel S. Gregory Ships Plans Library, Mystic Seaport. This is George Kelley's list of Culler's plans. All editorial comments are George's. Please inquire for current prices and a list of specific sheets of plans within each design.

Daniel S. Gregory Ships Plans Library

Mystic Seaport Museum, Inc.

75 Greenmanville Ave.

Mystic, CT 06355

860-572-5360

860-572-5371 (fax)

collections@mysticseaport.org

CATALOG #	DESCRIPTION	# OF SHEET SETS
	VEE and FLAT BOTTOM OPEN BOATS	
128.1	10'2" Concordia yard butthead. A utilitarian, square ended work punt.	2
128.2	11' sailing sampan *Jade Arrow*. A very good tender. Rows and tows well.	3
128.3	11'6" vee bottom pod for Paul Glaser. Very small one man tender. Similar to 15' 9" beachboat. No offsets.	1
128.4	12'6" vee bottom yawlboat for *Integrity*. Powerful, able carrier. Rows and sails well.	2
128.5	13'6" original Good Little Skiff. Popular boat. Sails, rows and tows well.	2
128.6	14'6" rowing skiff for Dr. James Wallace. Rows well.	1
128.7	14'6' wheelbarrow skiff for Dr. James Wallace. Centerboard is a wheel.	1
128.8	14'9" vee bottom day boat similar to 17' 7" daysailer, more vee. Also for Dr. Roche.	1
128.9	15'8" flat bottom sailing skiff. The mid-sized of the three Good Little Skiffs. Uses construction plan for the 13'6" version.	2
128.10	15'9" vee bottom, double ended beachboat *Java* and *Cruz del Sur*. No offsets.	1
128.11	16'8" vee bottom catboat for W. H. Hagan, Jr.	3
128.12	17'4" clipper pulling bateau *Otter* built for Pete's own use. 92 lbs.	1
128.13	17' flat bottomed skiff for Maynard Bray. No skeg for backing on beach.	2
128.14	17'9" flat bottomed skiff for Anne Bray. No skeg for backing on beach.	2
128.15	17'7" vee bottom daysailer for Dr. Roche. Shallow draft, Bahama rig.	3
128.16	18'6" flat bottom sailing skiff *Dixie Bell* for Waldo Howland. Biggest of the Good Little Skiffs.	2
128.17	18'8" Swampscott dory for Charles Sayle. Fast, able, and handsome.	3
128.18	20' fast pulling bateau for Dr. James Eldredge. Flat bottom, no rig, one to three people. A big Otter.	1
128.19	20' sharpie proposal for John Parkinson. One sail or two. Lack of lines requires guessing.	2
128.20	24' Sharptown barge. Centerboard, flat bottomed, fast.	2
	ROUND-BILGED OPEN BOATS for SAIL and OAR	
128.21	9' Concordia Baeteka pram, lines only, no rig shown, no construction drawings. [Also inquire about Ships Plans catalog #130.1 for additional plans and specifications.]	1
128.22	10'6" wherry yawl for Ned Ackerman's schooner *Fiddler's Green*. Plank keel with rig.	3

CATALOG #	DESCRIPTION	# OF SHEET SETS
128.23	10'6" New England yawlboat for Stephen Forbes. Known as the "sheep boat." No rig.	1
128.24	13' canoe. Pete's own *Butternut*. Double paddle and lapstrake, one man.	1
128.25	16'4" yawlboat for yacht *America II*. Similar to a Whitehall.	3
128.26	16'7" Staten Island skiff for Richard Hovey. Split rig, handsome, able, and powerful.	2
128.27	16'8" Race Point surfboat *Coskata* for Robert Caldwell. Lapstrake.	1
128.28	16'11" clipper wherry *Seaman's Friend* designed for Nicholas Freydberg.	3
128.29	17' canoe. Dr. Roche's *Cymba*. Double paddle and lapstrake, two man.	2
128.30	17' two sail, double paddle canoe for William Pinney.	2
128.31	17'8" Concordia sloopboat. Minimal construction drawings.	5
128.32	17'8" Kingston lobsterboat. A "reverted" Concordia sloop with shallop rig.	3
128.33	18'8" Buzzards Bay sloop *Beaver*. Based on Concordia sloop but more powerful, able. Lapstrake.	5
128.34	18' fast Cornish pilot gig for Nicholas Freydberg. No rig shown. High performance, light (151 lbs), a really way-out craft. Needs spoon oars.	1
128.35	18'6" clipper pulling boat *Punch*. Fast, three rowing positions, not a sailboat.	1
128.36	19'6" shallop for George Putz. Lute sterned.	4
128.37	20' fast Cornish yawl for Clayton Lewis. Small rig, no centerboard, high performance.	2

INBOARD and OUTBOARD POWER BOATS

128.38	15'6" shipyard work boat/tow boat *Gracie III*. Vee bottom, powerful and heavy.	4
128.39	15' motor yawlboat for schooner *John F. Leavitt*. Very stout.	3
128.40	18' and 16' vee bottomed outboards. Similar to 24' outboard for Chubb. A set.	2
128.41	21'9" outboard fishing/work boat *Long John* with small sprit rig. Motorwell and rudder.	2
128.42	24' fast outboard work boat or pleasure boat with variations in layout for Percy Chubb.	5
128.43	24' fantail motor launch with pilot house for Peter Burling.	3
128.44	25' light motor skiff proposal for Mr. Hankinwell.	1
128.45	25' heavy motor skiff proposal for Mr. Hankinwell.	1
128.46	28'9" round bottomed launch proposal for Commodore Percy Chubb.	1
128.47	27' vee bottomed tug for Mark Marting. Complete, an enlarged "GRACIE III."	3
128.48	30' fast vee bottomed outboard launch. Needs at least 120 h.p.–two 85s or better with one 150.	5
128.49	32' vee bottomed fantail steamer.	3
128.50	32'8" original proposal for Hovey's steam launch.	1
128.51	34' fantail steam launch for Richard Hovey. Really handsome.	4
128.52	35'10" power boat *Susan A*.	2
128.53	39'8" Concordia Nova Scotia motor cruiser. Light and easy moving.	5
128.54	55' fast express cruiser proposal for Drayton Cochran. 1925 style, modern power.	2
128.55	70' motor vessel proposal for Mrs. Brooks. A study only.	2

CUTTERS, SLOOPS, YAWLS, and SHALLOPS

128.56	20' proposal for light daysailer catboat. No lines.	1
128.57	20' proposal for heavy cruising catboat. No lines.	1
128.58	20' Newport Point boat for Dr. John Roche. Deep centerboard, single cat-rigged sail, lapstrake.	4
128.59	21' dogbody for Philip Volker. Two sails, offset mainmast and centerboard. An overnighter.	3
128.60	22' Friendship sloop for Knight Sturges.	5
128.61	25' Friendship sloop *Pemaquid*, mostly redrawn from Chapelle. Complete, a much copied design.	4
128.62	25'10" sloop proposal for Bruce Northrup. No lines.	2
128.63	27' Roanoke/Croatan boat proposal for Mr. Rogers. No lines.	1
128.64	28' cutter for Lars Lindblom. Sleeps four very well, built in Finland.	8
128.65	30' Friendship sloop proposal. No lines.	2
128.66	35' Friendship sloop proposal. No lines.	2
128.67	35'10" British cutter for Bruce Northrup. Two versions: conventional cabin and "stern window" cabin.	5

CATALOG #	DESCRIPTION	# OF SHEET SETS
128.68	36'9" replica of Slocum's *Spray*. Detailed construction drawings with layout slightly altered for Hugh Bigelow.	7
128.69	46'5" cutter for Wayland Purmont. A powerful fisherman with 7-ton hold.	5

KETCHES

128.70	25'10" French dory proposal for Richard Tatlock. A bit of imagination required to use this plan.	1
128.71	26'6" cowhorn dory.	1
128.72	33' ketch for Robin Laggeman. Trunk cabin, shoal keel, nice hull.	3
128.73	34' live-aboard ketch *Plover* for Fred Stanton. Main topmast. Raised deck makes nice, comfortable one-person boat.	8
128.74	36' vee bottomed sharpie *Old Glory* for Franklin Parker.	4
128.75	36' multichine steel sharpie for Dr. Robert Baxter.	2
128.76	37'7" Presto-type sharpie for Admiral Schmidt.	4
128.77	37'7" Presto-type sharpie *Dawn Treader* with slight variations in rig and cabin plan for Stefan Galazzi.	4
128.78	38'6" seagoing, short gaffed ketch for Ted Harper.	4
128.79	40'6" Wabun-type round bilge sharpie for Gordon Mott. Very attractive, shoal draft.	7
128.80	40' ketch proposal for John Kendall. Lines and sail plan only.	2
128.81	45' marconi ketch *Swan V* for William Wood. Handsome, able, and successful.	6
128.82	43'10" ketch for Taylor. Sail plan only.	1
128.83	44'6" unfinished ketch proposal. Could be good. Handsome.	1
128.84	48' marconi rigged motorsailer *Transition* for Addison Taylor.	9
128.85	55'5" albacore troller for Wes Wickham. A sail-assisted fishing vessel with ketch rig.	5

SCHOONERS

128.86	28' schooner for Thomas Doyle. A real toy boat.	5
128.87	32' schooner with loose footed foresail for Malcolm Kirkbride.	5
128.88	32' Periauger scow. A very sketchy idea Pete had for his own boat, which he never completed.	3
128.89	38' Tancook whaler proposal for Thomas Hooper.	4
128.90	40' main topmast schooner *Gallant* for Richard Tilghman. Fast and handsome with flying jibboom.	15
128.91	42' schooner yacht *Prudence* for David Forbes. Somewhat tender.	5
128.92	45' she pungy (Chesapeake) schooner for Eddie Crosby. Fast and rakish.	5
128.93	45' vee bottomed scow schooner *R. D. Culler* for Robert Servais.	5
128.94	47' schooner *Joseph W. Russell* for Buzz Garrahan. Fast and able.	5
128.95	47'6" schooner *Fiddler's Green* for Ned Ackerman. Nearly identical to *Joseph W. Russell*.	7
128.96	46' main topmast pinky with fish-hold for Warren Lemaster.	4
128.97	52' schooner *Integrity* for Waldo Howland. A powerful vessel considered to be Pete's masterpiece.	8
128.98	53'10" Baltimore clipper *Lizard King* for Bruce Northrup. Fast, handsome, but no offsets.	3
128.99	60'2" deep-draft offshore West Coast sealer *Gallant Lady* for Roy Grizzle.	10
128.100	82'6" main topmast clipper for Henry Sears. Based on fast fruit runner.	3
128.101	96' three mast topsail schooner, proposal only for Mr. Currier.	3
128.102	91' coasting schooner *John F. Leavitt* for Ned Ackerman. Another fast carrier.	5
	Scantlings for the *Leavitt* would do for *Kathy Brown* so the construction plan would be the guide for both.	
128.103	125' three mast centerboard coasting schooner *Kathy Brown* for Ned Ackerman. A fast, handsome vessel.	3

INDEX